HUMAI

Beliefs and

This life is all we have –
make it good to be alive

Donated by Chiltern Humanists

 Humanists UK

www.humanism.org.uk

June 2019

The Sussex Library of Religious Beliefs and Practices

This series is intended for students of religion, social sciences and history, and for the interested layperson. It is concerned with the beliefs and practices of religions in their social, cultural and historical setting. These books will be of particular interest to Religious Studies teachers and students at universities, colleges, and high schools. Inspection copies available upon request.

<u>Published</u>

The Ancient Egyptians   Rosalie David

Buddhism   Merv Fowler

Gnosticism   John Glyndwr Harris

Hinduism   Jeaneane Fowler

Humanism   Jeaneane Fowler

Islam   David Norcliffe

The Jews   Alan Unterman

Sikhism   W. Owen Cole and Piara Singh Sambhi

Zoroastrianism   Peter Clark

<u>In preparation</u>
The Diversity of Christianity Today   Diane Watkins
The Doctrine of the Trinity: God in Three Persons   Martin Downes
Death and Afterlife: An Introduction to Christian Eschatology Tony Gray
You Reap What You Sow: Causality in the Religions of the World Jeaneane Fowler
Christian Theology: The Spiritual Tradition   John Glyndwr Harris
Jainism   Lynn Foulston
Taoism   Jeaneane Fowler

<u>Forthcoming</u>   *Bhagavad Gita (a student commentary)*
Confucianism   The Protestant Reformation: Tradition and Practice
Zen

Humanism

Beliefs and Practices

Jeaneane Fowler

sussex
ACADEMIC
PRESS

BRIGHTON • PORTLAND

2 4 6 8 10 9 7 5 3 1

Published 1999 in Great Britain by
SUSSEX ACADEMIC PRESS
Box 2950
Brighton BN2 5SP

and in the United States of America by
SUSSEX ACADEMIC PRESS
5804 N.E. Hassalo St.
Portland, Oregon 97213–3644

British Library Cataloguing in Publication Data
A CIP catalogue record for this book is available from the British Library.

Library of Congress Cataloging-in-Publication Data

Fowler, Jeaneane D.
Humanism : beliefs and practices / Jeaneane Fowler.
p. cm. — (The Sussex library of religious beliefs and practices)
Includes bibliographical references and index.
ISBN 1–898723–70–2 (pbk. : alk. paper)
1. Humanism.   I. Title.   II. Series.
BL2747.6.F68   1999
211′.6—dc21   99–27410
CIP

Printed by Biddles Ltd, Guildford and King's Lynn
This book is printed on acid-free paper

Contents

Foreword by Sir Hermann Bondi

It is a pleasure to recommend this book to the reader. Humanism is important in our day but has lacked a recent thorough and scholarly, yet readable text describing it and entering into its spirit. There has been a long gap in the literature and we have greatly needed a new book from which the subject can be presented and to which one can refer. Jeaneane Fowler has met this requirement very well indeed. Describing modern Humanism is actually a difficult task, for Humanists are individualists through and through. So the word means something slightly different to each one of us. We have no "creed" and no document, adherence to which is obligatory. Yet there is a powerful common strand of thinking, a strong common awareness of ethical issues, an overriding belief in human responsibility, an unwillingness to accept alleged religious "truths".

The author has thoroughly studied and expresses in clear language the breadth and evolution of Humanist thinking and the development of Humanist organizations in both Great Britain and in the United States. The parallel developments in continental Europe and in India still await an author of like gifts of study and of expression. The contrasts could be most intriguing and show how national laws and customs mould attitudes. For example, while to the British and American Humanist the ideal plainly is a common school for all children, irrespective of the religion of their parents, yet our Dutch Humanist friends are proud of their separate Humanist schools.

The contrast between Humanist and Christian attitudes is described thoroughly and with great sympathy to both. This forms a most welcome addition to the modern literature on the topic. The arguments about the existence of god are particularly well presented. Perhaps I may mention here my own individualistic Humanist attitude to religion: The decisive point is not the existence of god (since an undefined god is so amorphous a concept that it can be neither affirmed nor denied), but belief in a revelation as the ultimate and unshakeable truth. It is my disbelief in any such revelation (of any religion, theistic or not) that is basic to my Humanism.

The centre piece of Humanism is its commitment to a humane all-encompassing ethic with its stress on social living and personal responsibility for one's actions. This is well described and discussed in this book, with some excellent quotations from Humanist authors.

I trust the widespread use of this book in schools and in institutions of Higher Education will serve to advance my dearest wish in this field: It is not to argue religious believers out of their faith, but to make the numerous people who now say apologetically "I am afraid I have no religious belief" say in future proudly "I am a Humanist". That this is not happening more is, to a considerable extent, due to ignorance of our outlook, our ethics, indeed our very existence. This volume should be a material help in putting us on the map.

Sir Hermann Bondi, FRS, President, British Humanist Association
Churchill College, Cambridge
March 1999

Foreword by Paul Kurtz

As we begin the new millennium, humanism has emerged as a positive alternative to the regnant religiosity and spirituality in the world. With the decline of Marxism, the resurgence of fundamentalism, the New Age cults of unreason, and the appearance of postmodernism, secular humanism offers a viable cosmic outlook that is based on science and moral virtues that are rooted in reason, yet have wide appeal. Secular humanism seeks to transcend the intolerant rivalries of multicultural ethnic differences by providing common ground for shared values.

Unfortunately, the meaning of the term *humanism* has often puzzled friend and critics alike: Is humanism a religion? Is it simply equivalent to humanitarianism? Is it so inclusive that it applies to everyone?

Dr Jeaneane Fowler has attempted to answer these questions, and she has done so with objectivity and sensitivity, skill and virtuosity. Indeed, in my judgement, she has written the best source book on humanism that is currently available. Reviewing humanism from its inception in classical Greece and Rome, through the Renaissance and the Enlightenment, down to the present day, Dr Fowler has shown how contemporary humanism has arrived at its present perspective: Humanism today is basically *secular* and *naturalistic*. It is not religious. It can find no compelling evidence for the existence of God. In this sense, secular humanism shares its scepticism of theistic claims with atheism and the freethought tradition; and its emphasis on reason and science makes it the heir to the rationalist tradition. Yet its defining principles are basically *ethical*. For humanism, the focus is on the preciousness and dignity of each individual, the capacity for autonomous reflective choice, and the responsibility for shaping his or her own destiny.

This form of optimistic humanism is in sharp contrast to the pessimism and nihilism that is rampant today, and it provides a much-needed antidote to theologies of salvation and otherworldly doctrines of immortality. Humanists maintain that life can be worthwhile, and that we need to realize the highest potentialities of which we are capable. Humanists are stalwart defenders of the open society and they wish to develop a democratic world community which makes this possible. For the humanist, ethics is grounded in human interests and needs and is tested by human experience; it thus presents the best opportunities for individuals to choose meaningful eupraxsophies.

Humanism: Beliefs and Practices is especially valuable because Dr Fowler not only deals with the theory of humanism, but its practical applications. She demonstrates how humanists deal with moral questions – such as equality of the sexes, education, abortion, euthanasia, genetics, etc. She also points out that humanists celebrate the rites of passage – all contributing to shared experiences within communities. For all of these reasons, I am glad to recommend this unique and comprehensive work.

> *Paul Kurtz is Chairman of the Council for Secular Humanism, Editor-in-Chief of* Free Inquiry *magazine and former Co-President of the International Humanist and Ethical Union. He is Professor Emeritus of Philosophy at the State University of New York at Buffalo.*

Preface and Acknowledgements

Well over a decade ago, when I found myself head of Philosophy and Religious Studies in an institute of higher education, I had *carte blanche* to plan an entire curriculum for my subject. As an individual passionately interested in the ways in which human beings in other cultures live their lives – indeed, in the way any human being responds to life – I was able to indulge such interest in the study of cultures near and far. I found myself co-exploring with my students the religious, philosophical, historical, ethical and social aspects of many cultures. Thus it was that I came to explore, not just the immediate religious cultures of my former student years and specialisms, but also such far-flung ones as Taoism and far-eastern Buddhism. In those days, as now, I believed wholeheartedly that the study of religion is an academic pursuit, and that it is a discipline that is as subject to critical analysis as any other. Moreover, for my undergraduates to become specialist graduates in the discipline of Religious Studies, I felt it was necessary for them to have a sound understanding of the wider *dimension* of religion. But in planning a balanced curriculum in this specific area, it was always clear to me that atheistic and non-theistic challenges to religion were essential in the creation of such an understanding. It was for this reason, that I included in my curriculum the study of Humanism.

The shift in emphasis in the study of religion from Christianity to other religions is now half a century under way, though there are some that still see the latter as an inferior line of inquiry. But, if we are to examine the life-stance of the Christian, Jew, Hindu, Muslim, Buddhist and Sikh, then the life-stance of the Humanist must take its place alongside. And in my experience of the teaching of Humanism over the years, it has proved to be the best area for breaking down barriers of intolerance and conditioned prejudices in students. In short, it opens the minds of students; it clears the canvas of the brain a little, so that rational academic inquiry into all life-stances can take place with more reasoned brush strokes. This book has arisen from these experiences in curriculum planning and quality assessment. For Humanism has always remained one of the most popular courses with my students. This is for two reasons: first because it *does* open students' minds, and it therefore changes their attitudes as human beings by broadening their perspectives of life, and, second, because it is an ideal area for critical debate and reasoned argument. This latter reason facilitates lively group discussions and the exploration of, and challenges to, personal beliefs.

From a purely practical point of view, this book has come into being to fulfil the needs of students. There was space for a comprehensive, but academic, view of Humanism in one volume – a view that dealt not only with the varied *beliefs* of Humanism, but also with some of the underpinning philosophical issues that provide its depth. There was also a need to bring into such a book, some of the issues with which Humanists identify, as well as the *practices* that inform a Humanist life-stance in the way of celebratory life-cycle rites. Some of the topics included – such as morality, abortion and euthanasia, for example – may be of particular value to both in-service, and prospective, teachers. But while this book arose primarily out of an academic context, it is also aimed at a wider general audience, for it has many messages about individual existence. Indeed, Humanism is a stance for *life*, for a positive and affirmative life, and the general reader will glean much from its agenda. But, from the outset, it must be emphasized that there is no *one* Humanist viewpoint, and the reader is likely to find very different expressions as to what Humanism is or isn't, worldwide. The reason why this obtains will be made apparent in the text.

I owe, once again, my considerable thanks to the team at Sussex Academic Press, in particular, to Tony Grahame, who has the art of making every author feel valued, and who does not inhibit creativity by pressurized time-scales. It is a privilege to work with such a person. I am also indebted to my husband for proof reading the script during his Christmas break, and for his constant support.

My thanks are conveyed here, also, to Lesley May, Deputy Head of Library and Learning Resources at the University of Wales College, Newport. Without her help with resources during the vacation period this volume would have been completed with difficulty and over a much longer timescale.

I am indebted to Sir Hermann Bondi and Professor Paul Kurtz for agreeing to write forewords to this book. Their perceptions on the wider issues and placement of Humanism in society today add a much needed, and appreciated, perspective to the text.

I would also like to thank the Executive Director of the British Humanist Association, Robert Ashby, for his critical comments on the text, and his assistance and advice throughout the project. Julia Beard and Ann Furedi of the British Pregnancy Advisory Service kindly examined and commented on some of the material on abortion in chapter 8, and I am grateful for their time and advice. I have tried to eliminate any errors in the text, but any that remain, are my own.

The author and publisher gratefully acknowledge the following for permission to reproduce copyright material:

Anonymous, "Native American Indian Marriage Ceremony"; The British Humanist Society for permission to use material from Jane Wynne Willson's *Funerals without God*, *Sharing the Future*, and *New Arrivals*; Samuel Butler, "I fall asleep in the full and certain hope" from *Thoughts on Death*; Canon Scott Holland, Canon of St Paul's Cathedral, "Death is nothing at all . . . ", from *Facts of Faith*; Ewan MacColl, "Take me to some high place" from *The Manchester Hiker's Song* (© Harmony Music, London); Frank Yerby, "You are part of me" from *American Negro Poetry*, ed. Arna Bontemps (New York: Hill and Wang, 1974); Visva Bharati, for poems from *The Collected Poems and Plays of Rabindranath Tagore*.

The author and publisher apologize for any errors or omissions in the above list and would be grateful to be notified of any corrections that should be incorporated in the next edition or reprint of this book.

Jeaneane Fowler
UWCN, March 1999

To my sisters
Cherie and Nancie.
To their families, Alan, David, Claire
and especially Alison.
And to those who helped me to find them.

Introduction

There are times in life when the more reflective of humankind ask themselves the searching question *"Who* am I?"*. The question is posed to elicit, not the kind of information that would be appropriate on a driving licence, a passport or a *carte d'identité* but, rather, the more profound question of "Who am I in the deepest elements of my being?" Few of us ordinary mortals have been able to answer such a searching question satisfactorily. So a less complex question might be *"What* am I?"*, and here we are on safer ground. I, for example, am female, I am white, I am a writer, and in the more abstract sense I might add some aspects of my personality. Others might say they are Asian, a Muslim, an idealist, a pessimist, a Christian, a politician, a teacher, a homosexual, a shopkeeper – a myriad such responses to what one is. This book asks of the individual both of these questions: "Who am I?" "What am I?"

In posing the first of the questions, *"Who* am I?" the reader is asked to think about his or her beliefs and theories about life. More particularly, the text that follows brings to the fore the means through which people may be able to respond positively to that question. In posing the second of the questions, *"What* am I?" the chapters that follow are designed to present an articulated response from one who might claim identity as a Humanist. And it may well be that, after reading this book, some readers may want to say "Yes! I am a Humanist", and identify with the kinds of philosophical, societal and practical issues with which Humanists in general are concerned. On the other hand, there are those individuals who do not like to "belong" to any particular religion, political party, social group, or the like. And yet, they will find that they are intimately bound to humanism as a life principle. It is in this last sense that the two questions "Who am I?" and "What am I?" converge, for, while many of us may never be officially Humanists, we are all, nevertheless, humanists – in the general sense of the term – at heart. Essentially, we are all fundamentally involved with the hopes, aspirations, sadness, complexities and vicissitudes of what it is to be human. We are humanists when we care for others, when we cry in joy or in grief, when we share the experiences of others, when we want to help people, when we feel sorry for people, and even when we identify with heroes and heroines in novel, film or drama, or even in the secret world of our own fantasies. To be truly human we *have* to be humanist. So the word *humanism* is already well known to us. In this work, then, I shall differentiate between *H*umanism and *h*umanism, though there are many official *h*umanists who do not like the former.

I am not writing this book as a Humanist but as a teacher of Humanism. It is therefore written primarily with the aim of introducing students to the Humanist stance for life. I have tried not to write *my* view of Humanism but to present Humanism objectively. Inevitably some subjective evaluation and personal views will emerge, but I do not think this violates the Humanist values in the pages that follow. Indeed, each Humanist views Humanism differently: I have but attempted to be fair to its general principles. And in order to write a comprehensive analysis of Humanism, I have not diverged too much in order to present the views of its critics. The aim here is to avoid an over-convoluted text. Similarly I have used mainly Humanist sources in the preparation of this text, and these are indicated widely in order to introduce the reader to some of the main writers in the Humanist field, both past and present. There is a considerable output of perennial past writings in Britain from giants in the field of Humanism such as Harold Blackham, Hector Hawton and A. J. Ayer. But there is a need for something new from the British scene that will reach out to the student as much as the informed general reader, and that deals with the broad spectrum of Humanism as it is today at the beginning of the third millennium. *Humanism: Beliefs and practices* aims at filling this gap. I have tried to write a text that does justice to the aim of *introducing* students to Humanism; previous knowledge of Humanism, past or present, is not assumed.

While I have tried to be objectively true to general Humanist principles, I have always been a fierce individualist – and this element is one thesis that pervades the text throughout. But since Humanism, too, is such a fierce defender of individual potential, status, dignity and uniqueness, I do not feel I have indulged too much in subjective statement without academic justification. Indeed, there are three elements running through this work which inform its thesis of the primary importance of individuality and fulfilled individual potential in life. They are: a firm anti-reductionism; a profound belief in the freedom of individual life – albeit with some qualifications; and an equally profound belief that, through the exercise of choice, human beings can shape their own destiny in unique ways that can run counter to genetic and social conditioning. Inevitably, then, I shall seek to demonstrate that it is individuals who are the key to societal improvement, and not *vice versa*.

Is Humanism a life-stance? I think it is, though I must say that many Humanists would not agree. Their objection stems from the point that Humanism does not have set creeds, doctrines, beliefs, or the like, by which it can be readily identified. But unless it is a life-stance it is difficult to see how it can have sufficient *identity* to count in the educational field for one and in collective societal life for another. Indeed, what impact can something that has no "stance" at all have? There are sufficient general principles that inform Humanism in order for it to emerge distinctively, albeit without formal agreement on general principles.

Typical of the lively debate that so characterizes Humanist thought is the support and antipathy for the term "life-stance". The Humanist Harry Stopes-Roe writes – and I thoroughly agree – that the "recognition of Humanism as a life stance represents a threat to those who are religious in the supernatural sense, for it threatens their dominance in ethics, moral education and life".[1] Contrast these words with those of Nicolas Walter: "I don't think that the phrase *life stance*, taking the words in their normal senses, means what its proponents want it to mean; humanism isn't necessarily a stance, and it isn't necessarily about life."[2] I take it *h*umanism, rather than *H*umanism, is exigent to Walter's statement. Be that as it may, I think Humanism today is *very much* about life! If not, then there is no purpose to it, no goal for it, no hope for it! Harry Stopes-Roe defines the term well when he writes, "a life stance is an understanding of the world and of what is ultimately important in the world; fully developed, it is life lived under this understanding".[3] He is critical of Walter's over-sensitivity to the term "life-stance" as one normally used for religious belief and practice.

Despite such controversy, I am happy to retain the use of the term "life-stance" throughout this book to refer to the position any Humanist might wish to take in the way in which he or she approaches life. It is a useful term, and students are well aware in the study of the Jewish life-stance, or the Hindu or Christian life stance, that there is not *one* life-stance for the Jew or the Hindu, but a multiplicity of stances within each religion. The general reader will easily understand the Humanist life-stance in the same way as multi-expressional, but as presenting an alternative to religious stances for life. The term is clear, apt, and indicative of a stance against religion. I defend it here as not at all offensive to the expression of *H*umanism. And while I shall retain the expression "life-stance" throughout this book, I shall also refer to this contemporary life-stance as *H*umanism, though the reader needs to bear in mind that there are many Humanist organizations and individuals that would object. In 1994, the American Humanist, Paul Kurtz, coined the term *eupraxsophy*, "good, practical wisdom", to define the Humanist non-theistic life-stance. Derived from Greek *eu* "good" or "well", *praxis* "action" or "practice" and *sophos* "wise", *eupraxsophy* is indicative of living life well, actively and wisely. It is a term coined to epitomize the Humanist life-stance – its rational inquiry in a cosmic world view, and the wisdom that informs a sound ethical approach to life. Kurtz is unequivocal that eupraxsophy, or Humanism, is certainly a life-stance.

The chapter content has been selected as representative of Humanist beliefs and practices. Chapter 1 gives a brief outline of humanistic trends in the past to provide a historical basis for an examination of Humanism in the contemporary world. This is followed by a discussion of what might be said to be the focus of this book – the nature and potential of the human being. The Humanist case against religion has informed so much of its thinking past and present that there has been much to write on this topic both philo-sophically – the tone of chapter 3 – and practically – the tone of chapter 4. The individual in society is the subject of chapter 5, and the distinctive Humanist stance that morality can obtain independently of religion concerns chapter 6. Since Humanism bases its claims on rational and reasoned analysis of empirical knowledge, this is the subject matter for chapter 7. In relation to Humanist practices, no book on Humanism could be complete without addressing the many issues in which Humanists have been involved both in the past and in contemporary society. But since these are legion, I have focused on three main issues, genetics, abortion and euthanasia in chapter 8. These three areas are of particular interest to students though there are many other Humanist issues that might have been selected. Finally, in chapter 9, I have dealt with Humanist ceremonies for the celebration of life, marriage and death – the practices that can be engaged in collectively.

1

What is Humanism?

To some extent everyone is a humanist, for in its broadest sense the word *humanism* suggests that it is concerned with what it is to be human, and that the word is *human-being* centred. Indeed, it is practically impossible to claim "I am not a humanist" in any serious vein, unless, perhaps, one is a staunch fundamentalist whose individuality has become lost in the grip of the inflexible tenets of a movement, sect or régime. Everyone is a humanist in so far as he or she has some concern or interest in what it is to be human. On the one hand, then, humanism is a general term but, on the other, it can refer to more particular, organized movements. The main concern of this book will be to examine Humanism in the latter sense, as a response to life which is in contrast (and often open opposition) to the religious stance for life, but it is important at the outset to examine also other ways in which the term is used. I shall begin with some analysis of the term *humanism*, followed by a historical outline of the rise of Humanism in Renaissance Italy, its expression in the period of the Enlightenment, and the modern Humanist movements. But, in fact, the word *humanism* was not actually coined until the nineteenth century, and this needs to be borne in mind when the term is used, somewhat anachronistically, in relation to the waves of humanistic philosophy, literature, art and so on, which pervaded Europe in the years following the Dark Ages.

Whether or not you are a Humanist in the narrower sense of the term will depend mainly on just *how* you view humankind. You may, for example, have some kind of belief in a supernatural divine being, in which case your view of each human being is as the specific creation of God, and perhaps as subject to his omnipotence and omniscience. In this case the importance of the human being is somewhat lessened through a desire to place God at the centre of things. On the other hand, you may view the human being as part of the natural order, part of Nature, like other species and organisms on our planet. This is a more scientific view of the human being. Or you may view the human being as the most important evolutionary phenomenon to date, and as having within his or her make-up the potential for mastery of all kinds of knowledge, and the potential for unconstrained self-development. All these views reflect some degree of humanism, and many of us would have viewpoints that reflect aspects of one, two or all three of them, but only the last two characterize some of the most important tenets of modern-day Humanism.

It is the degree of emphasis on *human-being-ness* and on the exploration of the nature of human beings and their innate and developed potential which characterizes true Humanism, and this really necessitates a human-being centred rather than a God-centred perspective. This kind of interest in the human being was particularly evident in classical Greece, a period which we shall need to explore when we look at the historical development of Humanism. It was at this time that, as Alan Bullock very aptly comments: "The constant demand of the humanists was for philosophy to become a school of human life, addressing itself to the common problems of humanity."[1] Here, the emphasis on humanity was not so much on the nature of the human being in relationship to the divine and the metaphysical implications of such, but on the more existential view of the nature of the human being related to life itself. And this necessitated receptivity to different and challenging ideas – a hallmark of Humanism in the present day.

From the outset, then, I shall be exploring what it is to be a human being in the complexities of today's society. This is the context in which individuals can, and should, develop their fullest potential, contributing at the same time to the active development of societal and global prosperity and happiness. Essentially, such a goal begins with the individual, and throughout this book I shall take up the challenge of individualism as a means to a better life for each human being, as well as its related corollary of an improved society, through the fulfilment of individual potential.

The complexities of the term "Humanism"

So far, I have only indicated generally that there are differences between the words *humanism* and *Humanism*. But these terms themselves have their own particular complexities which make definition elusive; indeed, it is often because there are so many facets of what it is to be human that there must necessarily be a multiplicity of humanist theories. Since everyone must to some extent be a humanist, then the more general term *humanism* is a factor of life. There are those like Jesus of Nazareth, Guru Nanak, the Buddha, Karl Marx, Confucius and so on, who have contributed more powerfully to a humanist ideal, and present-day cultures owe much to their humanist attitudes. Similarly, religious groups such as the Society of Friends (Quakers) who have campaigned so much for social reform and equal rights for all, have been thoroughly humanistic in their approach to humanity. Such examples illustrate the broad nature of the term *humanism*. But in the case of Humanism also, to quote one Humanist, "there seem to be as many different varieties of Humanism as there are grades of wine and cheese",[2] and breadth of interpretation is no less evident. Since Humanism is involved with life, it is necessarily wide in dimension. And this is an important issue, for it contrasts sharply with more narrowly defined belief systems. Those who criticize Humanism for its general lack of a central core of beliefs – even if these obtain in some individual organizations – serve only to damn it with praise, for its particular dynamism *makes* it indefinable, fluid, constantly changing and non-rigidified, in line with the characteristics of life itself, and distinctly out of line with dogmatic definitions. It is a flexible term but fundamentally connoting ideas of the humanity and equality of all human beings. Lack of definition can be a distinct advantage! And those who look for clear definitions in the *Oxford English Dictionary* will hardly be the wiser, as Tony Davies warns:

> The seven distinct sub-definitions of humanism rather conservatively offered by the *Oxford English Dictionary* in truth represent only a fraction of the senses and contexts in which the word has been used, and a drastic simplification of those. It is one of those words, like "realism" or "socialism", whose range of possible uses runs from the pedantically exact to the cosmically vague.[3]

Necessarily, then, Humanists will be very different in their beliefs and may even disagree with each other over what may seem fundamental issues. Those who stress the importance of individuality and *human-being-ness* could hardly wish for it to be any different: the vagueness of the term, far from being a disadvantage, is an asset. In his preface to his book *Humanism: What's in the Word?*,[4] Nicolas Walter notes that "*Humanism* has often been used in a Pickwickian sense, to mean just what ever the user chooses it to mean". This is

very much true of Humanism today, even if there are basic statements of what Humanist organizations consider as essential in
defining their position. In a way, then, there is not so much a phenomenon as Humanism, there are only the Humanists who compose it:
Humanism is what all these Humanists believe and, again, it is the
living individuals who express the collectivity of the concept.

Then, again, the term Humanism is vague because, as Nicolas
Walter points out, there were humanists in the past who didn't call
themselves humanists, and there were many who did call themselves
humanists who would not, by today's expectations, be Humanists at
all.[5] Humanism is, therefore, something of a generic term, necessarily
vague, and allowing each Humanist to contribute his or her own
perspective. This is a brave characteristic in a world that seeks to be
reductionist, seeks to define and compartmentalize in an orderly
manner. Those who criticize Humanism for its lack of collective belief
fail to see the point of its lack of restriction on individuality – and this
is necessary if it is to remain *human-being centred*. And while, negatively, there are those who classify any Humanist as an "unbeliever",
the more open-minded prefer to concentrate on its essential message
of *human-being-ness*, what it is to be fully human. Alan Bullock,
though concentrating more on historical humanistic perspectives,
defines the way in which he wished to use the term *humanism* in his
detailed historical study:

> I have taken humanism to be, not a school of thought or a philosoph-
> ical doctrine, but a broad tendency, a dimension of thought and belief,
> a continuing debate within which at any one time there will be found
> very different – at times opposed – views, held together not by a
> unified structure but by certain shared assumptions and a preoccupa-
> tion with certain characteristic problems and topics, which change
> from one period to the next.[6]

This dynamism, fluidity and flexibility of Humanism is no less
evident today and, given basic assumptions concerning the essential
value of the human being and his or her contribution to society and
the world at large, they are characteristics that allow Humanism to
stand in sharp contrast to restrictive codes of beliefs so characteristic
of many belief systems. However, while Bullock's words are suited
to their historical context, the more organized expressions of
Humanism today have lifted it from a "broad tendency" to a clearer
status.

A working definition

Despite the vagueness of the term *Humanism* it is necessary to have some kind of working definition. Primarily, in using the term *Humanism* there must be a concentration on what it is to be human. Indeed, the fundamental meanings of all the words related to Humanism have this connotation – *humus* "ground, earth", *humanus*, "human", "earthy", *homo* "earth-being" etc. And such a focus on the human contrasts, and often directly opposes, concentration on the divine. This suggests that Humanism is concerned with the secular, rather than the religious; with this life, as opposed to projections of life beyond death when the *human* no longer exists; and with the immediacy of the temporality of human existence rather than any suggestions of the eternal nature of the human. These will be issues to be explored later. It is around such ideas that organized Humanism of today is built, and it is the modern Humanism of today, not its antecedent roots in the past, which will be the main focus of this book.

The emphasis on the human and not the divine serves to dislodge Humanism from overly religious perspectives and, therefore, though it has much to say against religious belief, Humanism encompasses atheist, rationalist, naturalist, ethicist and secular viewpoints. But while there are extant a number of general statements of belief which serve to define it as a movement, Humanism, I feel, does not have *a* system of belief which rigidifies it to a more static movement. Yet, while Humanists are very unlikely to agree on *a* definition of Humanism, those definitions that exist are likely to emphasize the necessity for the self-preservation, self-realization, happiness and creative energies of humankind without recourse to divine super-naturalism.

Since Humanists come from many walks of life, their own disciplines will tend to modify their Humanist perspectives. This lack of a *specific* belief *system*, other than an explicit concern for humanity which cuts across differences in belief and culture, does not enable the Humanist to be be so readily defined as the Jew, Muslim, Christian, Buddhist, and so on (though it is debatable whether, even in these more clearly recognized belief systems, the beliefs *per se* can be easily defined). For Humanism, free expression – so necessary for the full dimension of the word *human* – as well as morality which is secularly decided and not religiously dictated, will bring about differences in opinion, but differences which do not depart from the basic tenet of the fulfilment of individuals and societies everywhere in a peaceful, happy existence.

Given this broad definition, it is easy to see why the label "Humanist" might be a debatable one, but we might include in its spectrum such well-known names as Pierre and Marie Curie, Albert Einstein, Sigmund Freud, Julian Huxley, Jean-Paul Sartre, A. J. Ayer, John Stuart Mill and Bertrand Russell, the last named being dismissed from Cambridge University and imprisoned for six months because of his Humanistic pacifist views during the First World War. What Humanists have in common – and therefore what can be said of Humanism as a whole – is the vision of the *dignity* of the human being and the acceptance of the capabilities of the human being for rational reflection and choice. This is a vision of a human being who is unrestrained and free from the constraints which society, culture, religion, state oppression have so often imposed – a gospel for the individual. While it could not be claimed that Shakespeare was a Humanist – and it would be anachronistic to do so – there is so much existential focus on the human being in all his and her variety, tragedy, humour and vicissitudes of life in his works. One fraction of a passage from *Act II* Scene 2 of *Hamlet* is quoted by many writers on Humanism because of its wonderfully congratulatory expression of the sheer marvel of a human being:

> What a piece of work is a man! how noble in reason! how infinite in faculty! in form and moving how express and admirable! in action how like an angel! in apprehension how like a god! the beauty of the world! the paragon of animals!

Such words epitomize Humanism's belief in the full potential of the human being. Humanism stresses human responsibility in existence: indeed, as H. J. Blackham put it: "This notion of human responsibility is the nuclear idea in the definition of Humanism."[7] It is the individuals who make up humankind who are responsible for shaping life, not something beyond them. And it is those individuals who are responsible for shaping their own existence and for creating a society that will allow each individual to fulfil his or her potential, at the same time maintaining a responsible attitude to the rest of society. Humanism thus views each individual optimistically, and has a profound belief that free will and liberty are prerequisites for a "whole" life for each individual.

In view of these Humanist conceptions of the great potential of the human being which is independent of external sources, it is easy to see why religion is rejected by modern-day Humanists, though it is not exclusively so and has not always been so. Indeed, it is also easy to see why any concept of a God who bestows grace, favour, rewards, punishment, an extraneous code of behaviour, and the like, *diminishes* the ultimate responsibility of the individual as well as the innate potential for full personal evolution. Full attention to this rejection of religion will be given in a separate chapter.

In 1996 a finalized *Minimum Statement* was formulated by the International Humanist and Ethical Union (IHEU), and has become, according to Walter, "the official basic definition of *Humanism*":[8]

> Humanism is a democratic and ethical life stance which affirms that human beings have the right and responsibility to give meaning and shape to their own lives. It stands for the building of a more humane society through an ethics based on human and other natural values in a spirit of reason and free inquiry through human capabilities. It is not theistic, and it does not accept supernatural views of reality.

Important to note here is the expression *minimum* statement, a factor which allows for the dynamism of expression which Humanism has built in to it, and also for free thought and rational, reflective choice of individuals in coming to their own views of Humanism. Were it to be otherwise, it would be no better than legalistic religion. The IHEU agreed the above definition for member organizations to use if they so wished. However, the British Humanist Association voted against it, regarding it as deeply flawed. This is indicative of the problems involved in creating a definition. The BHA prefers a simpler definition of Humanism as "an approach to life based on reason and our common humanity, recognizing that moral values are properly founded on human nature and experience alone."[9] The human being is on his or her own and has one life in which to develop his or her potential and to leave behind an improved world. Of necessity, Humanism is an ongoing process not a static system; it cannot be defined in any way which would lessen its dynamic nature and it has to leave space for individualism to be true to its ideals. Humanism is what Humanists believe – ideas formulated by human minds out of the existential conditions of life and experience. It is, to use Bullock's words "a continuing debate in which very different views have been and still are presented".[10] Essentially, Humanism leaves room for an individual to interpret it in the particular perspective of his or her own distinct humanity.

The history of the humanist tradition

Before embarking on a more detailed analysis of Humanist beliefs and practices in the world of today, a brief summary of the roots of humanist thought in the past is pertinent here. Since the word *humanism* was coined only in the early nineteenth century it is, of course, anachronistic to apply it to earlier periods of time. But it is useful to do so, nevertheless, in order to gain some kind of chronological perspective. And the roots of humanistic thought lie far back in classical Greece, to the time of the great Greek philosophers such as Plato and Socrates. Classical Greece was a period which saw the beginning of education as we know it, the beginning of the study of history, philosophy, drama, grammar, rhetoric, logic, mathematics and astronomy. It was a period that strove for excellence and perfection, for absolutes of knowledge, for the truths in knowledge and "made one of the great assumptions of western civilization – that it is possible to mould the development of the human personality by education".[11]

Here is seen the emphasis on the potential of the human being and the interaction of individual and society that contributes to its achievement. In the Greek view, the more educated a person the more human that person was. This conception and kind of education as the means to individual fulfilment has influenced much of our educational provision in the western world, and it is only in the last decade or so that vocationalism has ousted the classical view of education for its own intrinsic value. I shall have more to say on this last issue when I examine the concept in more detail in chapter 5. What is important about the ancient Greeks is their perspective of the human being. Indeed, the two later periods of history which feature humanism as a particular ethos – the Renaissance, and the age of the Enlightenment – looked back to classical Greece as an exemplar for humanistic thought and expression.

With the influence of Greek thought and culture on so many areas outside Greece, it could be said, therefore, that it is in the arena of Greek ideas that humanism really begins. Classical Rome was to take up the Greek emphasis on education in the liberal arts, *enkyklia paedia*, and to translate it into Latin as *humanitas*, but it was more of an elitist principle in Roman thought, reserved only for the Romans themselves as opposed to the uncivilized and barbaric non-Roman world. The word *humanitas* was to remain as a legacy of the classical world that referred to knowledge of the arts in relation to the world of the human being. This contrasted with the term *divinitas*, which was concerned with the study of theology.

The Renaissance

The Renaissance of the fourteenth and fifteenth-century[12] that began in Italy looked back with admiration to the ideals of the ancient world of classical Greece and Rome and to the greatness to which the human being could aspire. But those who sought to mirror the depth of study and pursuit of knowledge exemplified by the classical world and to create a *renaissance*, or rebirth, of its ethos, were confined, in Renaissance Italy, to intellectual circles, though not necessarily scholastic ones. In some ways there was something escapist about the focus on what seemed like an ideal past, but, on the other hand, there was a creative energy which widened the mind and provided a foundation for the future. Essentially, focusing on the classical world was a focus on the secular rather than the religious, on humanity rather than divinity. Yet in its characteristic broadness, humanism in the period of the Renaissance was as much Christian as secular.

Still, however, the word *humanism* did not obtain, though of the different university faculties of teachers there were *umanisti* – "humanists" – who were engaged in the teaching of the study of humanities, *studia humanitatis*, in particular, the teaching of grammar, classical languages, philology and rhetoric. As only one element in university education, their role should not be seen in any systematized sense, for there was nothing of a humanistic "movement" in Renaissance Italy, only a general ethos of inquiry into classical education and ideas and an opening up of the emphasis on human capacities. The interest in the human being informed so many aspects of the Renaissance that the words of Hamlet above would have suited the period well. If we think, for example, of the way in which Michelangelo and Leonardo da Vinci strove to perfect their understanding of the anatomy of the human being, and how this was reflected in art and sculpture, or of the emphasis on the power and potential of the mind in philosophical debate and analysis, we can see how *humanistic* the period was.

In focusing on the classical past Renaissance humanism engendered a certain air of self-confidence, exploration and discovery in the present, and opened up the dimensions of the human self to future possibilities. But the focus was mainly on antiquity. Nicolas

Walter is critical of these so-called early "humanists" as being far too rooted in the past, in that they were disposed to oppose such modernity as printing or the use of vernacular languages, preferring hand-transmitted manuscripts and the remote languages of Greek and Latin.[13] While, then, there was an emphasis on human potential, there was not such a concentrated focus on what has been called "a radical inflation of the power of the human will",[14] as some critics believe. Another valid criticism of Renaissance "humanism" was its elitism, its roots in the intellectual and aristocratic world that were far removed from the rest of humanity. It was not a *general* age of humanism in the sense that it reached out to the ordinary person. Eloquence in Renaissance Italy was of the essence, just as it had been essential to debate and oratory in classical Greece, and modern vernacular languages of Italy were seen as unelegant and commonplace: the elitism is obvious. But if some in Renaissance Italy hankered back to the classical age, in other respects commercial enterprise and expansion saw a widening of horizons and the development of Italian cities which, Bullock notes "produced a class of educated laymen with a self-confidence hardly known elsewhere in Europe".[15] There was a clear message in Renaissance Italy, that the non-indolent individuals could use their creative powers to progress in public life. There was an avid interest in the self, in self-assertion, and in self-portrayal in art and literature, with a desire to reproduce things with greater artistic reality. The potential of the individual was realized through education, in which, while the general ethos was the classical past, the corollaries for the future are evidenced in the innovative discoveries of Galileo and the anatomical studies of Alberti, Leonardo da Vinci and Michelangelo. Such Renaissance giants in their field may not have been "humanists" but they were able to express what was a new emphasis on individuality.

The Italian Renaissance had much to offer the future, for it influenced so many areas of European thought. What helped the spread of such humanistic ideas was the fact that this was the time when printing developed sufficiently to spread scholarly works of literature and poetry, Greek texts, and those in Hebrew and Latin. Elements of humanism were to be found in the study of theology and history as much as literature and art, and Greek, alongside scripture, became the standard subjects taught to children in school for many centuries.[16] Humanistic ideas could be spread more freely through the printed text, which was a welcomed break from the traditional religious monopoly of the monks, who had copied texts by hand. The literature of the Italian "humanists" is known to have reached many of the other university libraries, as well as private collections in Europe.[17] But, despite the rise of the new universities, such as those at Wittenberg in Germany, and new colleges at Oxford in England and Vienna in Austria which broke with traditional university education,[18] many universities in Europe retained the more traditional teaching which was divinity centred, and some were certainly hostile to the more "humanistic" ideas of the age. The fact that more human-centred rather than God-centred studies were evident at a wider level should still not lead us to see humanistic studies as a conscious "movement". Many of those who embraced the new learning were great travellers, but their ideas were not formulated into a consistent system; they simply spread their varied ideas through discourse in the intellectual circles of Europe.

An important feature of the Renaissance idealism was its ability to become dislodged from any association with religion. The very fact that classical Greece and Rome pre-dated the Christian era made it possible to place more emphasis on human potential rather than divine providence, and on secular progression rather than theological determinism. Instead of being so overtly involved with metaphysical speculation – though the Greeks had certainly concentrated inquiry in this direction – the temporal world became of more importance than the divine one, and human beings were felt to be able to command something of their own fates rather than have them divinely mapped out for them. And instead of the usual emphasis on humility and the innate sinfulness of human beings in their miserable existence, there were expressions of the dignified heights to which humans could aspire, their excellence, and their ability to shape their own existences. This is not to say that religion was eschewed; it was, rather, set aside in the same way that many people can categorize their lives into religious and secular in modern-day existence. And even when religion organized itself to stem the tide in intellectual secularism, the message of the dignity of the human being was not entirely obliterated. Others, however, were able to blend the rebirth of classical ideas with biblical study. Such a person was Erasmus (1466–1536) who can be highlighted as creating what might be called the roots of Christian humanism.

It was the Reformation that began in Europe with the polemics of Luther that, theoretically, ended the period of the Renaissance. B while there were certainly tensions between the reform mover that Luther began and the humanistic elements of Renai

Europe, the influence of the latter had been sufficient for many of the ideas it promulgated to have been widely taken on board. And there were many "tools, skills and perspectives", as Matheson terms them,[19] which were incorporated into the Lutheran Reformation, and even the Catholic Counter-Reformation. If we consider Luther's emphasis on education, on the importance of understanding scripture in the home, and of speaking out against the injustices of vague religion and elaborate religiosity, it is easy to see elements of humanism in his ideas, even though he retained the centrality of God and reduced the human being to the pawn of the divine. Many note the debt Luther owed to the tools which the humanists supplied for textual analysis, particularly the impressive way in which he wrote and spoke, gleaned partially from skills in rhetoric which the Greeks had so loved.[20] But the decline of humanistic tendencies in sixteenth century Europe also occurred because the optimism of the time could hardly be maintained in the face of the perpetual vicissitudes of the everyday life of European humanity. The existential fact of life was not a rosy one, and it is difficult to maintain optimism in the light of perpetual misery: humanistic expression fell from favour. And since it was never an organized phenomenon, in the face of more systematized Reformation and Counter-Reformation movements, it could not last.

The Enlightenment

It was not until the so-called Age of Enlightenment that humanistic ideas emerged again with any kind of full expression. Like the term *Renaissance*, that of *Enlightenment* is used retrospectively and anachronistically to refer to an age of optimism which characterized eighteenth and nineteenth century Europe. The grip of religious dogma in the Reformation and Counter-Reformation era had resulted in a certain pessimistic view of humanity. But this was replaced by a growing spirit of optimism in human nature, not one based on the ideas of classical antiquity, but a more scientific optimism that saw the likes of Isaac Newton (1642–1727), and philosophers such as Immanuel Kant (1724–1804). It was Kant, indeed, who probably coined the description of the age as the *Enlightenment*.[21] This period of time saw a more definite break with religious thought and a more conscious effort to express distaste at many of its superstitious facets. It was an age of Reason, and an age that was responsible for the separating off of the different scientific areas. So physics and biology, psychology, and history and economics, emerged as independent disciplines. Instead of the religious base for knowledge, and the divine answer for the way things are in the universe, human beings were expected to find rational and intellectual answers for the many aspects of human existence. And these were answers that were believed to lie in the scope of the human mind itself. The dignity of the human being was reinstalled and the stance against religion brought freedom from the guilt of sin, so profoundly instilled by religious doctrine of the past. It was a freedom welcomed by the more reflective after the grip of religious dogma. While critical of humanism in general, John Carroll succinctly comments: "What Luther had not foreseen was that reason and free-will in practice would produce the steam-engine and penicillin, and that material abundance and the conquest of disease would weigh the scales for a very long time against the darkness of faith."[22] This was the case until the French Revolution when the image of the guillotine again put the fear of God into people, by showing where "Enlightenment" could lead.

While the Renaissance confined humanistic expression to the intellectual elite, the Enlightenment was also concerned with other aspects of humanity – toleration, criminal justice, anti-slavery – humanistic issues which particularly came to full fruition in the nineteenth century. Yet the extension of humanistic benevolence to the masses was limited; the new ideas were, in the main, intellectually orientated. It was science, and technological and industrial advances which were the real hallmarks of the Enlightenment, like James Watt's (1736–1819) steam engine. It was a new era of faith in individual expertise and knowledge that left behind the humility of humankind before God which religion had so long taught. Aside from science, the study of the *Humanities* – classical and other languages, philosophy, literature and history, and the arts in general – became one aspect of university education, the term *Humanities* being retained to the present day as the non-scientific and non-technical branch of knowledge.

Much of the intellectual discourse of the Enlightenment was centred in Paris and promulgated by a small but influential group of *philosophes*, the great thinkers of the eighteenth century like Voltaire, Montesquieu, Diderot and Rousseau. And even though they were joined in thought by thinkers from elsewhere like David Hume, Adam Smith, Immanuel Kant, Jeremy Bentham and the like, the language of discourse was French, and the tone of the discourse was distinctly secular and not religious. Importantly, Reason, rational criticism and free inquiry informed prolific debate, but not the elevation of Reason which reduced the human being to an emotional void, it was the kind of Reason which could venture to question orthodoxy and be critical of established dogma and opinion. For many thinkers this involved an outright rejection of religion, if not overtly, then by paying lip service only to it. And here we have the spirit of atheism arising from Enlightenment ideas, freeing the individual from the shackles of the guilt of sin in this life and from fear of the next. The critical mind, once applied to the religion of Christianity, found it wanting in scriptural validity and was sceptical of its ritualistic practices. While some did not go as far as rejecting the concept of God entirely, and accepted a Supreme Being who was responsible for the natural world, others became totally anti-religious, accepting a more scientific basis for rational views of life than the old theological ones shrouded in myth and mysticism. This contrasted considerably with Renaissance "humanism" where, while there was some rejection of religious belief in favour of a view of the dignity of the educated, in general, the humanistic ideas did not mutually exclude Christian belief; the work of Michelangelo epitomizes this kind of complementarity very well.

It was a period which championed the science of humanity as opposed to the omnipotence of the divine, the Cartesian "I think, therefore I am" providing a kind of fundamental assertion of the independent identity of the human being in existence. The "science of man" became the occupation of the intellectual. And coupled with this emphasis on the human being came a utilitarian emphasis on the greatest happiness of the greatest number. It was the first time that individuals and their effect on society became intimately linked, and political and social reform was viewed from the point of view of its outcome for society at large. This kind of thought culminated in John Stuart Mill's *Utilitarianism* in the mid-nineteenth century.

Although such ideas involving the elevation of the human being, along with the theory of the improvement and general happiness of society, were humanistic, it was not until the beginning of the nineteenth century that the term *Humanismus* – "Humanism" – first occurred in German. But this was not to depict the humanistic emphasis on individual and societal fulfilment, the term was used as referring to an aspect of the German educational system based on the "humanities" – Greek, Latin, and classical history, culture and literature. Indeed, the impetus of the Enlightenment was somewhat halted by the lengths to which it seemed to have been taken in the French Revolution. Fear of the kind of uncontrollable events which characterized the French Revolution, exacerbated by the wave of revolutions and uprisings in Europe at the end of the first half of the nineteenth century, were sufficient to bring about the demise of the Enlightenment, and a certain *laissez-faire* attitude to life in the hope that if the *status quo* were to be maintained, the horrors of the French Revolution would be avoided.

Humanism today

I have dealt with the classical, Renaissance and Enlightenment periods in some detail, for they are the periods in history which, retrospectively, reflect some of the characteristics of modern-day Humanist views. Yet this last, like the earlier periods, has the same looseness of identity and expression, the same non-systematization but, in many ways, the same kind of reshifting of the perspective of life to place the human being in a more dignified view. However, while there are complementary parallels in ideas from past and present-day Humanism, a neat chronological development of ideas, roots forming great trees, is not evident. There are similarities between past and present but there are sharp contrasts too. The very fact that there was no word *Humanism* as such before the nineteenth century should be a warning against too close an identification of present and past. Yet the past always influences the future ahead of it, and it is more the influences in ideology that travelled through the years which are to be compared with those of Humanism today. The average Humanist today, however, probably has little knowledge of classical antiquity or of the humanism which expressed itself in Renaissance and Enlightenment Europe. This suggests that there is a radical difference in ethos, as much as there are similarities in focus on the human.

Those approaching Humanism today would be justified in finding the various designations conjoined with the term humanism somewhat confusing – scientific humanism, political humanism, naturalistic humanism, romantic humanism, liberal humanism, and even Christian humanism. The three most common are secular humanism, religious humanism and, formerly, evolutionary humanism. The word *h*umanism is important here, for these designations tend to stress the importance of the initial term – "scientific" or "Christian", and append a general humanistic outlook as a secondary aspect. But *H*umanism is somewhat different, and has come to refer to a distinct movement, even if Humanists themselves do not always agree on just *how* they should be designated. This is healthy for Humanism in the twenty-first century, healthy for on-going inquiry, freethought and critical debate, but it will be helpful to examine some of the other terms in order to dispel confusion. In its general sense today, humanism stresses the importance of human beings in many aspects of life, and is against anything that deper-sonalizes an individual. And that may be the family, society, nation, religious denomination, educational institution, and it may occur worldwide or between two individuals. It is for this reason that humanism can be characteristic of any group or ideology, and why we can speak of Christian humanism, ethical humanism, Greek humanism and so on. However variously humanism has been expressed in the history of humankind, it has not, in the past, neces-sarily rejected religion. Today, however, Humanism – standing as a word on its own – could be said to reject religion and its concomitant doctrines. It is in this sense that the word will be used in this book.

I am not, then, concerned with religious humanism which retains its religious identity – perhaps in Christianity, or Judaism – but at the same time incorporates a humanistic theology or practice. The Society of Friends, the Quakers, for example, is one of the most humanistic religious groups within the Christian fold. "Religious humanism" might describe the Friends very well (though they do not use the term). And a giant of personality such as Albert Schweitzer might be well described as a religious humanist. Then, too, secular Humanism has sometimes been referred to as religious humanism, not in the sense of humanistic religion, but in the sense of being "reli-giously" devoted to Humanism's ideals. Religious humanism is thus a dedication to Humanist values, and faith in those values. But the basis of *religious belief* of any group serves only to qualify a particular *type* of humanism, not to epitomize *the word itself*. For "Humanism" leans heavily towards atheism, and this is a useful asset, since it often prevents the misuse of the term in theistic senses by religious groups. In fact Christian humanism concentrates more on religion than human beings. This is really a contradiction since humanism is, or should be, primarily human-being focused. So whereas in the past religious belief and Humanism were compatible bedfellows, today they tend to be in separate rooms and, in most cases totally divorced.

But there are other kinds of qualifications of the term humanism such as political humanism and liberal humanism. The former would embrace both Marxism and Communism for example, both being non-religious ideologies. But while both were human-being centred in theory, in practice, they were systems that would not allow sufficient freedom of ideas, speech, inquiry, political dissent, to be truly humanist in practice. The latter, liberal humanism, refers to nineteenth-century bourgeois belief in science, individuality and progress. So both political and liberal humanism have aspects of humanism but are not Humanism *per se*. We come closer to what humanism today really means when we speak of scientific humanism and naturalistic humanism. Scientific humanism is also atheistic, placing science and technology as the means to the understanding of our universe in opposition to biblical or other mythology. And it promotes the power of humanity to unfurl the secrets of the universe, to stride forward in the pursuit of knowledge, to take control of its own existence and to promote the well-being of the species. These are certainly humanistic ideas but have belonged to the scientific (and often socialist) world.[23]

Naturalistic humanism comes much closer to the centre core of the word Humanism. It was a designation given by the American philosopher Corliss Lamont who saw Humanism as a philosophy of life which rejected supernatural beliefs of any kind, in favour of Nature as the only reality in which the human being can operate. Science alone can provide the necessary facts of existence and the human being is the result of evolutionary development through the products of Nature, just the same as any other aspect of Nature. It is the human being alone who has the potential of free choice, of solving the problems of life, of basing ethical and moral decisions on existential grounds alone, and who can work for the promotion of the happiness and common good of all people, in every aspect of life. These are all aspects that have been embraced by many Humanists today and are ones which will need to be taken up in more detail in the chapters that follow.

Possibly the best qualifying term to use is that of *secular humanism* and this, indeed, is what this book is about. The term immediately defines humanism as firmly rooted in existence itself, and as in contradistinction to religious belief. And this is the way in which most people would view humanism today – an atheistic stance to life which stresses the fulfillment of the potentialities of each human being in a happy, just, democratic and peaceful world. It has come to be associated with a non-religious ideology and philosophy which stresses one life for each person, and total annihilation at death. Because of this rejection of religion, the term *secular* humanism is a good one, for we are immediately aware of the non-religious (and occasionally definitely anti-religious) nature of humanism, the secular as opposed to the religious, the emphasis on this life as opposed to some ideological afterlife. *Naturalistic* humanism, however, has similar viewpoints. This highly non-religious character has been a feature of British secular humanism in particular, American secular humanism being slower to reject all religious aspects entirely.[24] Despite these qualifying terms that prefix Humanism, it is the term *Humanism* itself that remains the essential word. And since this single word refers to particular movements of the twentieth and twenty-first centuries – movements that have developed significant and clear profiles and agendas – it needs the initial letter in the upper case – *Humanism*. This is how I shall use the term in the remainder of this book. When it is unqualified it, itself, connotes the emphasis on human life in its fullest dimensions and potential. The word contains nothing religious, nothing supernatural to the human, placing all emphasis on *human-being-ness*, in contradistinction to *God-ness*.

The emphasis on the human being is, of course, not without its critics. David Ehrenfeld, for one, entitled a book of his *The Arrogance of Humanism*,[25] and the arrogance of western humanity in its destructive manipulation of the planet is a particular problem that the modern-day Humanist has to turn to face. This, too, is an issue to which I shall need to return in a later chapter. The existential condition of humanity does not always will the greatest good, and the twentieth century has witnessed human beings at their very worst – in an age of scientific and technological advance. The pessimists on this planet see the *deterioration* of humanity, not its improvement of societies and the world at large. The optimists, on the other hand, see humanity as the means by which the challenges which face this planet can be faced with courage, and conviction that it lies within the scope of human potential to solve them. What cannot solve them is some kind of supernatural being, some kind of God.

Humanism, then, does not deny the existential condition of humanity, for much of its philosophy is itself existential. However, it does not accept the same kind of existentialism that talks of the "dilemma of man" or "man's predicament" as a state of suffering and misery. Humanism remains optimistic about humankind. But it *is* existential in its stress on the importance of existence, of humankind, and the interdependence of humankind and the world in which it is placed. The world is seen as complete in itself and human beings alone have the capacity to understand it. They have the ability *themselves* to make it a better place, to improve existence, to bring humankind to maturity and prosperity, equity and happiness, and to create an open society where mutual respect, democratic freedom at all levels, and general welfare, are important. So it is a *forward moving* existentialism, optimistic, creative and positive. Corliss Lamont expresses this optimism very well in the following words:

> The philosophy of Humanism constitutes a profound and passionate affirmation of the joys and beauties, the braveries and idealisms, of existence upon this earth. It heartily welcomes all life-enhancing and healthy pleasures, from the vigorous enjoyments of youth to the contemplative delights of mellowed age, from the simple gratifications of food and drink, sunshine and sports, to the more complex appreciation of art and literature, friendship and social communion. Humanism believes in the beauty of love and the love of beauty. It exults in the pure magnificence of external nature.[26]

This was written over thirty years ago, and today we have to reckon with over-use of additives in food and drink and the danger of skin cancer from over exposure to sunshine. But Humanists will face such problems with optimism, all the time maintaining that it is human beings alone who can provide the answers to their own existential problems. Far from arrogance, this seems common sense.

Another criticism of Humanism is that it is intolerant and over-critical itself of belief systems – particularly religious ones. And if it becomes overly concerned with opposition to attitudes and alternatives of cultures and ideologies outside its own self, it can be in danger of no longer being the champion of the very individualism which it so strongly defends. In the main, however, it is the *dehumanizing* effect of other ideologies which Humanists are quick to criticize, those which place the answers to life in the afterlife basket, or those encouraging providential views of life which inhibit individual fulfilment by engendering acceptance of one's lot in life. Or it is critical of those political movements which stifle the improvement of society and prevent the lack of individual freedom.

An interesting criticism of Humanism is that it lacks a base culture. John Carroll is one who supports this view.[27] Standing in opposition to established Catholic and Protestant religion, it could be said that Humanism has no roots of its own, whether in history, in societal and cultural evolution, or in religious belief. But if true, this could be said to be an advantage in that Humanism is free from the intricate conditionings which longstanding cultures impose on almost every aspect of society. Indeed, this is an area dear to Humanism, for, if it *does* find itself over critical and intolerant of religious culture, it is especially so in those areas which have conditioned people into passive acceptance of the *status quo*. So when Carroll writes of the humanism of the Enlightenment and its culmination, as some critics would see it, in the Reign of Terror of the French Revolution – "We are back to the fact that humanism on its own is not a culture, and the attempt to make of it more than it was opened the way for demonic forces that only real cultures can check"[28] – today's Humanists could well point to the *laissez-faire* attitudes which the so-called "real cultures" subsequently imposed. And these were attitudes which could allow exploitation of small children in factories and mines, the apathy to the potato famines in Ireland, and the like, and *fear*, fear to change, and tread in social reform where people – and not angels – had not hitherto been.

For those who need something beyond themselves on which to rely, Humanism will not fill such a vacuum. Ehrenfeld has criticized Humanism in that he believes it fails to supply families and communities with "something better, or even with something that functions at all".[29] But this suggests an inherent weakness of individuals. Can human beings exist only if they have something beyond themselves on which to rely? Or is it that they have been so conditioned through the centuries *to* rely on something beyond themselves that they cannot stand alone? Humanism affirms that people must stand firm in their own natural identity, and couples this with an optimism that such a life-stance can be realized.

There are those who have written of the failure of humanism of the past and of Humanism in the present: Ehrenfeld because the tenets of it have not been tested,[30] and Bullock because so frequently in this century, evil has arisen out of good.[31] As Bullock points out, the natural goodness of humanity is not so readily evident, or optimistically possible. But Humanists probably would feel that there is, on the contrary, much to point to that endorses the good that people can do – longer life, medical advances, education, better living and working conditions. And those who suggest humanism fails in the world might also suggest that religion, with its more clearly identified roots which stretch to antiquity, has been no less successful in promoting peace, and no less to blame for the perpetration of evil.

Religion failed as much as governments, or Humanist Rationalism and Reason, to provide an explanation for the Holocaust.

Today we live in a humanistic age in which religion, for many, has taken a back seat, and most people – certainly in Britain – would rather do the garden or clean the car on Sundays than visit a place of worship. It is an age of increasing technology, an age in which we can test our assumptions empirically or, for most of us, have them tested for us by advertisements which tell us of the latest products of the technical age. There are just as many challenges to humanity in this kind of complex age, perhaps more than hitherto. If society has moved away from the pre-set norms of established religion, then it has moved into a human being orientated world and this will bring its own specific challenges. To fully mature, humanity has to learn to live by its own rationalized norms. Humanism has the difficult task of inculcating new values and optimism for the future.

The modern Humanist movement

At the dawn of the third millennium it could be said that Humanism has become an established "movement". But the process by which this has come about is a somewhat complex one, and I can deal with it only briefly here.[32] This movement today has emerged from various groups of people in the past, such as the Freethought movement, the Ethical Societies, and the Rationalist movements of the late nineteenth and twentieth centuries, some of whom retained a non-theistic religious ethos until very recent times, some members retaining such views to this day. However, nineteenth century humanism became more and more secular and atheist in character, particularly in the latter half of the century. To begin with the term "Humanism" was not widely used and not in any specific sense – hence the need to qualify the term very frequently – but today it has a much more recognized character.

Freethinkers

The late nineteenth century, in particular, was a time when progressive thinkers amongst the middle classes emphasized the importance of free thought, and since social injustices provided a good deal of their agenda, there were many in the working classes who were

attracted to their meetings and by their literature. Free thought – and
this really meant freedom from the kinds of restraints imposed on
society by religion – emphasized social morality and responsibility
informed by individual choice and rational reflection. Education was
seen as one important medium for promoting such aims. In the early
1880s an international federation of freethinkers was established fed
by groups from many countries.

In Britain the freethinking movement was, in some cases, more
overtly linked with secularism. The Secular Society was founded in
1852 by George Jacob Holyoake, a man who, a decade earlier, had
been imprisoned because he was an atheist. He was known as the
Father of the Cooperative Movement, and fought for such issues as
education, freedom of the press, political reform, and the enfran-
chisement of women.[33] He was editor of a publication called the
Reasoner as early as 1846. It was Holyoake who was mainly responsible for the term *secular* which is so readily associated with
Humanism today. Thus, in 1849 he coined the name "Secularist" for
the freethinking movement. This resulted in what Tribe calls "spontaneous outgrowths of secularism".[34] In 1866 the Secular Society
became the National Secular Society, and was joined by a number of
separate groups. Charles Bradlaugh became its president. It
produced a journal called the *National Reformer*, later, in 1881, to
become *The Freethinker*,[35] a journal that has remained in currency to
this day. In its early years the tone of *The Freethinker* was distinctly
opposed to religion and set out, mainly, to attack Christian belief and
scripture aggressively. Its first editor, G. W. Foote, was quickly
imprisoned for blasphemy, an event that may have influenced his
more moderate later material, which was characterized by a prudent
shift in emphasis to content dealing with morality. The kinds of issues
which have informed the content of the journal are education, secular
marriage, changes in divorce laws, contraception, illegitimacy, abortion, euthanasia, homosexuality, Sunday restrictions – in short, those
areas of life which, often as a result of religious dogma, serve to
restrict common sense and individual freedom. Today, the NSS is a
militant campaigner for all kinds of civil liberties, for ethics based on
rationalism, and for freethought.

Ethical societies

Similar to the freethought groups were the *Ethical Societies* that emerged after the mid-nineteenth century. Like the freethinkers, members of the Ethical Societies were opposed to the kind of dogmatic religious assumptions that characterized so much of the religion of the time. But they were especially concerned with the issue of morality – in short, they challenged the claim that only religious people can be moral. This is another important dimension of Humanism to which I shall need to return below in chapter 6. In the United States, Felix Adler founded the Ethical Culture Movement in 1876, which became the American Ethical Union in 1889. This was concerned with broad social issues – education, nursery provision, training colleges, educational summer camps, housing, nursing, schools on Sunday. It exists to this day with a keen role in promoting the freedom of individuals' rights, in campaigning against racial prejudice and capital punishment, and in promoting the care of the mentally sick, for example.

In Britain, too, Ethical Societies existed in many cities, the first being in London in the late 1880s. Ideas had reached Britain from America, mainly through the Chicago Ethical Society and one of Adler's disciples, Stanton Coit. Of these Ethical Societies, the South Place Ethical Society is pre-eminent. It had its roots as far back as 1793 with a group of non-conformist Christians who met in a chapel in East London. It was to become an important Unitarian Chapel under one of its ministers, William Fox. In 1824 it moved to South Place in Finsbury. Coit became the minister of the South Place Chapel from 1887–91, renaming the chapel the South Place Ethical Society, which still exists today. When he resigned in 1891 he founded the West London Ethical Society which amalgamated with other groups in 1896 to become the Union of Ethical Societies. This became the *Ethical Union* from 1920 on. But the tone in the early days under Coit was somewhat religious rather than being wholly secular. Harold Blackham, a prolific Humanist writer, was one of the Ethical Union's most powerful figures in the post-Second World War years, and he was responsible for steering the Ethical Union on a more distinctly secular course. He also expanded the Union to include numerous affiliated societies. An International Ethical Union was founded as early as 1896. The extant South Place Ethical Society has now moved from Finsbury to Conway Hall, where it has been since 1929. It is a centre for study and discussion and has long abandoned its theistic prayer and belief, and even its ministers who, since 1899, have been replaced by a panel of appointed lecturers.

The British and American Humanist associations

Today's British Humanist Association, the BHA, has its roots in a number of like-minded associations. In 1950, under the initiative of Hector Hawton, the Humanist Council was formed. It was to link the Rationalist Press Association (RPA), the Ethical Union (EU) and the South Place Ethical Society, the English Positivist Committee and the National Secular Society. But the EU and the RPA were the more closely allied, and in 1957 formed an interim Humanist Association. This became the BHA in 1963. Subsequently, however, in view of difficulties concerning charity status, the EU and RPA – though always remaining closely aligned – nevertheless became separate bodies, the EU retaining the BHA title. It is the BHA that is the main official representative of Humanism in the United Kingdom. As a registered charity since 1982 it has over fifty affiliated local groups. It has charity status because of its aims for the mental and moral improvement of humanity and for the advancement of education through the medium of Humanism.

The major Humanist associations in the United States are the American Humanist Association (AHA) and the Council for Secular Humanism (CSH) at Amherst, New York. The CSH is housed at the Center for Inquiry, which is an international centre of secular humanism and free thought. Its libraries and conference and seminar facilities are used by secularists worldwide. The CSH has recently helped to set up the *Campus Freethought Alliance*, encouraging secular, freethought organizations on a large number of university campuses. Essentially, CHS is a non-profit making and tax-exempt educational organization that seeks to promote democracy and secular humanism. It is committed to free inquiry throughout society. The CSH produces a journal entitled *Free Inquiry*. Amherst is also home to the major publisher of books on Humanism and humanistic philosophy, Prometheus Books. In a lengthy "statement of purpose" in the winter issue of *Free Inquiry* in 1997, the basic tenets of today's Humanism are epitomized well in the opening sentences:

> The aim of Free Inquiry is to promote and nurture the good life – life guided by reason and science, freed from dogmas of God and state, inspired by compassion for fellow humans and driven by the ideals of human freedom, happiness and understanding. Free Inquiry is dedicated to seeing that one day all members of the human family thrive by embracing basic Humanist principles.[36]

In the United States Humanism has been, in the main, a non-political movement which, nevertheless, aims at social and cultural reform. Clearly, however, religious influence infiltrates powerfully into the many facets of government, and this has gained ground through the mass media. Today in the United States, there are noticeably overt moves to project Humanism into a more active political role, in order to counteract this religious influence – an influence that is often antithetical to Humanist stances on human freedom. There are also overt signs to suggest that Humanism in the United States is beginning to think in terms of more cohesive statements of its stance for life, though this is, as yet, embryonic.

Literature

The literature associated with the various groups has been, and is, extensive, and it is prudent to mention here only the most well-known, present-day, sources. The British Rationalist Press Association, the RPA,[37] began in 1899 with a group of freethinkers under the leadership of Charles Watts, and published prolifically by the early years of the twentieth century. These publications emphasized the importance of education, and the necessity of basing knowledge on rational, scientific facts rather than religious dogma. During its foundational years the RPA was particularly concerned with the dissemination of low-price, secular writings to working-class people, despite censorship. The role that this association has provided in the informal education of so many people, is considerable.

As the twentieth century proceeded, the RPA was instrumental in developing Humanism through many conferences, publications and meetings. Its modern journal is the *New Humanist*. This is committed to rationalism, which it defines as "the mental attitude which accepts the supremacy of reason and aims at establishing a system of philosophy and ethics verifiable by experience and independent of all arbitrary authority".[38] The *New Humanist* began life as the *Literary Guide* in 1885, changing its name to the *Humanist* in 1956, its present title having been adopted in 1972. The RPA has been a major publishing outlet of the Humanist movements in the United Kingdom, but the BHA now has an extensive publishing output for schools, and for the general public. The BHAs journal has recently had its name changed from *Humanist News* to *Humanity*. Under its old name of the Ethical Union, its regular newspaper was called *News and Notes*.

Humanist organizations

So in the late nineteenth and twentieth centuries leading up to the First World War, Humanism, in a variety of forms, was expressed by organizations and societies throughout Europe, the United States, Australia and New Zealand. Such groups referred to themselves by various names – Rationalists, Secularists, Ethicists/Ethicalists, for example. Some retained religious, if non-theistic, identity, particularly groups such as the Unitarians, but others eschewed all religion and supernaturalism. The term *Humanism* was slow to emerge as the generic name for such diverse groups, some being enamoured of the term and others not. The move towards more recognizable *Humanist* organizations, and to Humanism as a movement, has been a post-war phenomenon. The British Humanist Association in Britain, the American Humanist Association of the United States and similar associations in other countries, represented significant expressions of this more formalized organization. In 1952, at a conference in Amsterdam with Julian Huxley as its president, the International Humanist and Ethical Union was established, the IHEU. It depicted modern, ethical Humanism as fivefold – democratic, characterized by creative not destructive use of science, ethical, characterized by personal liberty combined with social responsibility, and as a way of life.[39] Individuals such as Julian Huxley, Harold Blackham and Hector Hawton in Britain and Corliss Lamont in the US were key figures who accepted and promoted Humanism – in theory and name – as a specific movement. In Europe the major Humanist Association is the European Humanist Federation, and there are major organizations in Holland and Norway. India also has a large and active Humanist movement.

While not defining Humanism as such, there were sound and successful attempts to crystallize some of its basic concepts. Thus, the American Corliss Lamont formulated a set of five basic principles of Humanism in 1942, extending these to ten in the final sixth edition of his work *The Philosophy of Humanism* in 1982. The ten principles are particularly clearly formulated, representing Humanism as a movement rather well, and were to influence the growth of the movement considerably. An earlier *Humanist Manifesto* of 1933, which clearly did not abandon religious overtones even if it abandoned overt theism, was replaced in 1973 by the *Humanist Manifesto II* with seventeen principles of Humanism drafted by American Paul Kurtz. Again, this did not seek to define Humanism, but moved more clearly away from the religious overtones of its predecessor.

Is Humanism a religion?

From what has been said so far, the question "Is Humanism a religion?" might seem to be a superfluous one. While it could easily be claimed that humanism as a facet of life could as well incorporate religious elements as much as socialist, literary or artistic characteristics, Humanism as a distinct movement has journeyed far from religious belief to a position of categorical unbelief. I cannot see why, in the third millennium, Humanism has to have any connection with religion at all, even if in the past, it was slow to shake off certain religious dimensions. And as to calling it a "quasi-religion"[40] because it has a vision for the future,[41] or because it can sometimes be concerned with the same aspects of human life as some religions,[42] or because it elevates Science and Reason,[43] these are insufficient reasons to place Humanism alongside other religions of the world. Since, as a movement, it offers an alternative to religious stances for life, it is an injustice to Humanism to see it as a reform movement in the religious fold. It is also an injustice to Humanism to suggest that it has "ultimate allegiances", to quote John Smith's description.[44] Any principles suggested for Humanism have been formulated with care to avoid over definition of the term, and with similar care to avoid the kind of dogmatism of language so pervasive in religious creeds. Most statements of what Humanism is, amount simply to common sense about the world, and articulate rather well what many people in today's more secular world are inclined to accept. Moreover, from what has been said so far, the sheer diversity of expression and beliefs of those who call themselves Humanists militates against any towing of a specific general party line. John Smith, then, might be criticized for overstating the case when he wrote:

> even if there is no counterpart for worship in the widely illustrated religious sense – involving awe, devotion, gratitude – Humanism nevertheless, has its *ultimate allegiances*. These take the form of reason and science, free inquiry, democracy, a naturalistic outlook, opposition to the supernatural, to name but a few, all of which, if we take seriously

what Humanists say, demand from them an *unconditioned loyalty*.[45]

It is the word "unconditioned" here which is particularly offensive
to Humanism, for it is a word that does not belong with individualism, with reflective and critical inquiry, with forward thinking and
vision, and with personal, societal and global evolution. Humanism
may well emphasize the importance of science and technology in
assisting empirical inquiry and rational belief but, in today's world,
it hardly does so blindly and in fundamentalist fashion – which is
what the term *unconditional* implies. Yes, Humanism has a vision, but
it is of human beings that are unconstrained in so far as communal
living will allow. They are human beings who can explore the full
dimensions of what it is to be human, but that exploration will make
each person different, each person's perspective of life different.
Definitive statements as to what an individual *must* believe as a
Humanist, do not obtain, and are alien to Humanism as a life-stance.

The separation of Humanism from religious belief has been a long
process. Renaissance humanists saw no problem in compartmental-
izing their classical focus with their traditional Christian belief,
though there were many who paid lip-service only to the latter. Much
the same kind of dual allegiance characterized the time of the so-
called Enlightenment. Here there was a considerable criticism of the
wealth and materialism of the Church, and many were only nomi-
nally Christians. But, for the masses of ordinary people, superstition,
fear, habit and tradition, kept them neatly in the fold of the Church.
In the late nineteenth and twentieth centuries it was the Freethought
movement which tended to eschew religion quite forcibly, with individuals such as Foote, as we have seen, aggressively attacking the
Bible and, with it, the Christians who slavishly accepted its myths
and discrepancies. The Ethical Societies were less hostile to religion,
and tended to support a more balanced religious outlook than
orthodox religion. They opposed the supernatural and superstitious,
ritual and the mystical, and they sought to release ethics from its religious context. But religion was not entirely abandoned and there
were those who spoke of a "religion of humanity", a "humanist
religion", or "the Religion of Humanism".

It was mainly the Unitarians who, though embracing Humanism,
retained the notion of themselves as a religious group. They rejected
the Trinity for a unity of the divine but, for those who rejected theism,
it was a short step to naturalistic as opposed to supernaturalistic
belief – in short, to Humanism. There are many still in the Unitarian

fold, particularly in the United States, who would consider their type of Humanism to be religious Humanism, but there are also many who are keen to say that Humanism is distinctly a non-religious approach to life. There are those who see Humanism as analogous to religions in that it provides a comparable, if dissimilar, stance for life. There are those who have called Humanism "a commitment, a faith", and those like Julian Huxley who believed the word *religion* could be extended to include non-theistic systems of belief – his "evolutionary and humanist religion". But we should remember that Humanism is itself a dynamic and evolutionary movement; it incorporates a multiplicity of ideas, and caters for individual belief and reflection. It is still evolving, and the shifts it has made in recent decades suggest a definitely non-religious stance for the third millennium: many of those who once used the word "religion" in association with Humanism are inclined today to omit it.

Thus, while there are differences of view, Humanism has emerged as atheistic and naturalistic – the former characterizing it as devoid of belief in deities, the latter as devoid of belief in anything supernatural. At the same time it is in the main secular, that is to say that it places all its emphasis on this world, this life and the functioning and interaction of humanity within it. It is a world in which science, technology, rational reflection and reasoning can assist humanity, and one that denies that there are divine entities to afford such assistance. These are the kinds of issues that will need to be raised in later chapters.

Humanism has no creed but many convictions. These convictions are about personal and societal life and the ways in which the evolution of each individual in one lifetime can create a better existence for one and all. It is an alternative to religion and represents what van Praag describes as "a process of mental emancipation".[46] It will inevitably have different expressions and different meanings but its diversity and expansive meaning reflect rather well, the unconfined mind, potential and diversity of *human-being-ness*.

2

The Human Being

The preciousness and dignity of the individual person is a central humanist value. Individuals should be encouraged to realize their own creative talents and desires. We reject all religious, ideological or moral codes that denigrate the individual, suppress freedom, dull intellect, dehumanize personality. We believe in maximum individual autonomy consonant with social responsibility. Although science can account for the causes of behaviour, the possibilities of individual *freedom of choice* exist in human life and should be increased.[1]

How far you yourself are a Humanist will depend partly on just how you view yourself. Do you, for example, believe that you are a result of the genetic inheritance acquired from your parents and your ancestors, emerging through the combining of sperm and ovum to become the unique person you are today? And do you think that without your brain to *be* the person you are that you would not be anything? Do you think that you, as a distinct individual have unique *self-value*, and that your personality is of value to your family and friends, and to society itself? If you answered affirmatively to these questions, then you hold some of the basic beliefs of Humanism about human beings. You might be less sure about the questions to which most Humanists would respond negatively, like "Do you think God made you?" "Do you think you will be reborn?" "Do you think that you will live for ever after your death?" You could, in fact, test yourself by writing down some of the reasons for your own answers to these last three questions just to see how much evidence you think you have for your answers. I suspect that many people would find it difficult to state their reasons for giving a firm "Yes" to these more difficult questions, and many would fall into the "I don't know" category of responses. Humanism has a way of making you face a good many questions about the nature of your own self, about your particular beliefs about life and about your own potential. Human beings are immensely resourceful and resilient, and are full of hidden resources that Humanism asks to be brought forth. The purpose of this chapter is to examine the nature of the human being and to elicit some kind of Humanist assessment of what it is to be a person.

The Christian view of the human being

There is much to be said in favour of the permissive society, for there is a lot to be said for the kind of permissiveness that has gained people the freedom to act independently within the contexts of their own self-assessment of the ways in which they wish to exist. The taboos about sex, homosexuality, pre-marital sex, abortion, voluntary euthanasia, and many such aspects of life, are much more openly debated, out in the open and acceptable today than they were even a quarter of a century ago. And even the most conservative of parents often have to accept the "partner", in other words, the person with whom their son or daughter is cohabiting. And where such cohabitation exists, the neighbours are no longer sniggering critically behind the curtains of their windows. At least a secular society has moved to a less critical view of our fellow humans and to a "live and let live" attitude to others, even if there is further to journey in terms of tolerance in a number of areas. The difference between today's world and the not-so-long-ago, is that now if we make mistakes in life, we have to live with them or sort them out. But we don't have to experience the deep-rooted *guilt* or even *sinfulness*, in a more secular world, in the same way as in the past.

Those Humanists who are opposed to religion in any form are quick to see it as partly responsible for guilt-ridden consciences in people past and present. Indeed, there has been a long tradition of prudery and subjection to religious morality. Morals became codified according to the particular religious denomination or culture. Indeed, the Protestant Reformation headed by Luther sought to thwart any kind of humanistic endeavour. John Carroll graphically depicts the very worst kind of subjection of the human being in his description of Lutheran determinism:

> With his "faith alone" and "no free-will" he sets about forming the new Christian and subjecting him to fate. His message is that I shall so bury you under your own guilt, your own pitiable weakness, your total dependency on the Lord God that I shall have you living on your knees in prayer. You are nothing. You are nobody. I shall fling you back into

the spiritual dungeon where your thinking faculty has no chance of
creating the illusion in you that you have some control over your own
destiny. It is down there in the dark, where the light of neither reason
nor law shines, where only God can help you, that you may find grace.
It is all determined. Your fate is set. Subjugated as you are to this over-
bearing condition I shall give you gravity and depth. Without them
you will not be able to stick it. I shall give you the openness to faith, to
becoming a rock.[2]

These are strong words, but they were the legacy to Christian thought
which, while far from the minds of most western thought today, have
not failed entirely to have their effect on the human subconscious in
the passage of time. Religious principles become part of the psyche
of a culture, part of the instilled inheritance. With the concept of a
suffering God, Christianity can hardly expect to nurture a happy
humanity. Indeed, suffering has been a major part of the Christian
ethos throughout history. Religious life has always been a preparation for what follows beyond life, and what is suffered in this one is
rewarded in the next. And if you think the words above about
Lutheran concepts of humanity are outdated and inapplicable,
consider, then, the more recent words of C. S. Lewis, the author of the
timeless Narnia chronicles:

Whenever we find that our religious life is making us feel that we are
good – above all, that we are better than someone else – I think we may
be sure that we are being acted on, not by God, but by the devil. The
real test of being in presence of God is, that you either forget about
yourself altogether or see yourself as a small, dirty object.[3]

The denial of the self is not, then, just an old Lutheran concept, but is
applicable to some aspects of modern Christianity too. We cannot
really escape the fact that religion has conditioned people in the past
to feel that *self*-assertion and *self*-affirmation are sins about which we
should feel a considerable amount of guilt. And the effects of such
conditioning have not been altogether radically eschewed in
contemporary life.

Christianity has also instilled into human values an idea of
striving for perfection, not perfection at one's job, or at school, or as
a mother, or as chairperson of a local something or other, but perfection in suffering, in *denial* of the self, in humility, meekness, in loving
enemies and in serving the poor. In other words, the human being is
to be a saint: *Be perfect!* is the command. And we all know that we
cannot be perfect, not in any sense at all. And in the existential life-

conditions in which we find ourselves the goal of perfection is as realizable as reaching the stars. If we set ourselves such a goal we *must* fail, for it is not in our natures to be perfect. The problem with this kind of unrealizable goal is that it engenders a sense of unworthiness as well as a sense of futility that we can ever be any different. Of course, not all Christians would see their role in life as pessimistically as this, and the younger generation, which is developing in a more secular age, might be partially free of the cultural overtones of self-sacrifice which generations past have found embedded in their collective subconscious.

The value of life

All this is alien to Humanist thinking. To begin with, Humanism does not accept that there *is* a life after death, and therefore one has to reassess life in relation to the present. Death is final, and that makes life more precious. To have lived and lived well, experiencing the beauty of nature, love, hopes matured and hopes lost, the myriad opportunities which life offers, the complexities of interrelationships with other human beings, success, failure, the vicissitudes and joys of life – all these are valuable to the Humanist as part of human self-development and experience. Harold Blackham once referred to the "privilege of human existence",[4] and if human life is a privilege, it is important how we live it, and it is important that *all* human beings enjoy such a privilege. But Blackham did not mean that because life is a privilege we should therefore take what it allocates us; he meant that we have the privilege to *shape* our own lives, to work at them in every possible way. And we should also work to ensure that others can shape their lives to bring quality and value into them. In a much earlier work Blackham wrote: "The person is invited to make of his own life, and therewith of himself, a work of art."[5] He likens living to the artist who can abandon all the contemporary traditions and create something new, one who "is out on his own having to take full responsibility for what he does without reference to justifying precedents".[6] The important corollary of this kind of view of life is that we have *choice*: we can choose to change our lives, we can choose what we wish to believe, we can have opinions about ourselves, others and issues with which we identify. And we can reject what we find is not worthy in life, and that may well include old traditions and expectations that we find are no longer relevant to the way in which we want to shape our lives. To quote Blackham again: "The humanist begins his choice of life by choosing to live"[7] and this is tantamount to saying that a good deal of self-assertion *is* necessary in life, *contra* any residue of Lutheran subjection of the self that we may have inherited, or any religion which might accept the degrading picture of the human being posed by C. S. Lewis.

Death

Death is the end of life and Humanists contend that there is nothing beyond it; immortality is a myth. Is it the fear of death that makes people cling to religious belief? There are many who will consider that they have formulated some kind of rationale for religious belief, and will have their answers to this question. But many others will only think about religion *per se* perhaps at weddings and funerals (if they really do *think* about it at such times). The terrible thing about death is that we miss people, but it usually helps to know that those who have died have led a full and fruitful life – important dimensions of Humanism. If there were no such thing as death and we could live for ever, would we need to believe in God? And is Carroll right when he says that: "Without God, without a transcendental law, there is only death"?[8] Humanists would not agree with this in any way. If fear of death and belief in God serve to make an individual put all his or her eggs into the afterlife basket instead of into *this* life, then that individual is only living a half of a life.

There are those such as David Ehrenfeld who suggest that Humanism ignores death too much, even to the point of denying its existence.[9] Ehrenfeld claims that by ignoring death, the will to survive is sacrificed, and there is a certain denial of life. This is absurd. In fact, Humanists face death rather well; indeed, it is somewhat easier to face death if there is no "long dark tunnel", no rebirth, no assessment and punishment of sins, just, instead, non-threatening nothingness. When he presented his final documentary on death, Professor Robert Winston, in the British Broadcasting Corporation's television series *The Human Body*, reminded his viewers that the atoms of which we are composed exist in combinations only for the brief span of life that we have. When we die, those atoms are recycled for use in another form, and then in countless other forms in the evolutionary process.[10] We are, temporarily, of the stuff of the universe. And anyone who has been to a Humanist funeral would be able to witness that death is not denied, it is simply put into perspective, and life is hailed as precious. Humanists believe that we do not need something outside ourselves to make sense of death. Death is a common denominator for all humanity, it cannot be ignored. But the best way to put it in perspective is to ensure that the life which precedes it is full, fruitful, dynamic, self-evolving and self-assertive in ways that not only enhance an individual life, but which also serve to enhance the society within which one is placed.

The existential life-condition

Existentialism is concerned with existence, with the life-conditions in which human beings find themselves. While some religious philosophy and theology is existential, that is to say focused on the human life-condition, secular Humanism is wholly so. But while Humanism, with its emphasis on the human being and society could hardly fail to be existentialist, not all existentialists could be said to be humanist or to espouse Humanist ideals. However, in using the term "existential" it is intended, here, in its broadest sense, though at the same time incorporating something of the negative condition of humanity which existentialism often takes on board.

There are few that would make the claim that life is particularly easy. As human beings we find ourselves faced with the many good things in life, but also with its vicissitudes. Some of us regard the difficulties of life as interesting challenges, others find such difficulties burdensome and stressful. While we may now feel that Rousseau's celebrated words that man is "born free, but is everywhere in chains" are inapplicable to ourselves, there are those in contemporary society who might agree. Human beings *do* suffer, and life is *not* easy. But the answers to the problems of life cannot be solved by passive acceptance and hope for reward in the hereafter. Life is epitomized by struggle, but Humanists believe that it is important to move forward in life and to have the courage to do so. There is much that is tragic and unfulfilled in life, but there is also much that is brave, good, and forward moving. It is against the nature of human beings to be *absolutely* perfect, and to strive for this kind of perfection in any area of life is to strive for the impossible and to place an unnecessary stress on oneself. No one has perfect health, perfect mental stability, perfect interpersonal relationships, and few would be able to claim that they are totally in control of their own lives. Most of us get anxious, have too much to do, have difficult spells in life and encounter problems in the home, at school, at work or with our friends. This is the existential life-condition in which human beings find themselves. No one has a monopoly on problems – they come to us all – but they are balanced by the more positive elements of life and, most importantly, we have to learn to accept the negative aspects of life and *still* develop the kind of self-assertion that enables us to develop as individuals and to evolve personally in this lifetime. Any idea that what one suffers in this life will be balanced out in the next one, is anathema to the Humanist. Humanism asks one to stand firmly on one's own two feet and face the present and the future with confidence and courage.

One of the most well known existentialists was Jean-Paul Sartre (1905–80), whose particular existentialism was humanistic. As an existentialist he held a certain anthropocentric view of the human being; that is to say, he placed the human being at the centre of reality. He was also an atheist, so God was completely removed from the centre stage of life. He wrote:

> Atheistic existentialism, of which I am a representative, declares with greater consistency that if God does not exist there is at least one being which exists before it can be defined by any conception of it. That being is man or, as Heidegger has it, the human reality. We mean that man first of all exists, encounters himself, surges up in the world – and defines himself afterwards.[11]

Such an existentialist atheism (delivered at a lecture in Paris in 1945) sees individuals as making of their own selves what they will. And individuals are capable of projecting their purposeful wills towards future goals, towards future perspectives, in other words *into* life. Goals may not be finally achieved, but the fact that they can be idealized and that they are the responsibility of individuals means that each human being can take control of his or her existential life-condition. Sartre referred to this as *subjectivism* – the freedom of the individual subject, with an essential impossibility of transcending such human subjectivity.[12]

This view of individual subjectivity is, however, not a view that isolates human beings in any way. Sartre believed that, as each person makes choices for his or her own self, these are choices he or she would wish to apply to all humanity. Existential coming-to-be of the human being is, then, as much involved with humanity as with individuality. Sartre wrote: "I am thus responsible for myself and for all men, and I am creating a certain image of man as I would have him to be. In fashioning myself I fashion man."[13] Of course, this suggests that the individual *ought to* make the right choices; men such as Hitler clearly didn't. But what is important here is the kind of anthropocentrism that removes God from the arena of human choices. The human being becomes – at least theoretically – autonomous, and can will what he or she wishes to be, as well as what he or she would wish humanity to be. This is a positive affirmation of life, even though we know that there are many who make the wrong kinds of choices. The Cartesian statement "I think, therefore I am" is taken on board by Sartre to emphasize the centrality of human existence as the foundation of epistemological reality – our knowledge of the world. But it is taken further in a very humanist sense in that Sartre believed that it is impossible to be a subjective self in isolation from others and, therefore, it is "inter-subjectivity"[14] which is central to his humanistic existentialism.

Humanity

Sartre's view of the human being was, thus, somewhat anthropocentric. The Judeo-Christian view of the creation of humanity is also anthropocentric in that, if we take the first account of creation in *Genesis* 1, human beings were the very apex of creation, were made in the image of God, and were superior to all other aspects of existence. There are many Humanists who also have an anthropocentric view of humankind, but there are other Humanists[15] who suggest that we should beware of placing humanity on a false pedestal of superiority. Human beings are highly evolved creatures, but they were not specially created ones, and are only a phase of evolutionary development. The cosmos is vast and the universe does not revolve around humanity. Humanity is not a super power and though human life is the most evolved type of life that we know about it is unlikely to be the *only* form of life in the universe. We can only succeed in part in achieving a better individual, family, societal or global life. Perfection is impossible, but humanity has the ability to choose high aims that are conducive to its progress.

Humanism itself has often been criticized for deifying the human being through an explicit anthropocentrism, and for placing the human being in the idealist position of being able to know all, do all, achieve all. I think Humanism has had some elements of this but I think, too, that it has a much more common-sense view of humanity. It does not say that perfection can be achieved, only that sound and rational aims might achieve good results. Bullock is one critic who accuses Humanism of belief in the natural goodness of man (*sic*) and his perfectibility.[16] And he states that anyone who has witnessed the atrocities of the twentieth century can hardly lay claim to such idealism. But Humanism as a movement today hardly accepts the *perfectibility* of human life; indeed it is generally critical of the "Be perfect" teachings of the Christian faith. Let us say that it is optimistic about humanity, and that it accepts that humanity will make mistakes but can learn from, and move forward from, those mistakes.

Humanity is a complex phenomenon and each personality that composes it equally so. The more we try to understand humanity or personality, the more they are capable of surprising us. Of course, anthropologists, sociologists, psychologists and molecular biologists will have their own view of what people are, but there is something, yet, that transcends each of these disciplines and all of them together. And, as Albert Cantril aptly notes: "Each observer in his own way sees that something has been added in the latest chapter of the long evolutionary story."[17] The diversity and changing nature of societies and humanity cannot really suggest reductionist definitions of what humanity is. To a great extent our view of humanity is coloured by our own particular personality and self-consciousness. The pessimistic person is likely to have an equally pessimistic view of humankind and it is our own life-condition and life experiences that are projected into wider contexts of our impressions of our fellow human beings. But it is also a changing perception, because our life-conditions and those of society and the world at large are constantly changing, and because we cannot control all the choices with which we, as individuals, are presented in life.

The Humanist view of humankind is diverse, but, nevertheless, it is generally positive. Sometimes it is an *over* positive, and it has to be said, *idealist* view. Corliss Lamont, for example, expressed his hope that before the close of the twentieth century "the human race will emerge onto the lofty plateau of a world-wide Humanist civilization". His belief "that human beings, using their own intelligence and cooperating liberally with one another, can build an enduring citadel of peace and beauty upon this earth"[18] is far too idealist, but should not however, be eschewed as an aim. Our aims are rarely achieved, but they help us set relative objectives that *can* be realized. Harold Blackham, too, once gave a long list of the very best desirable traits of humankind, in a somewhat idealistic sixties view,[19] though he admits it is a too flattering picture. He even suggests that studies of

Humanists in the sixties indicate that Humanists as members of Humanist organizations are "better educated, more often male, doing a more responsible job, and therefore in a higher social ranking" than non-Humanists, and "An ill-educated woman doing menial work is not the typical humanist".[20] I think there must be few Humanists now who would wish to identify with this kind of statement. And his description of the Humanist woman that follows[21] would be no less unflattering to the progressive woman of today! This kind of idealist impression of humanity and Humanists (and in this case rather an elitist one) is now tempered by more common-sense views I feel, and yet the vision for a better future – both for individuals and for society – is never compromised. "All human values are human creations", says Nicolas Walter,[22] and this suggests that humankind can make of itself what it wills. It makes sense, then, to have the very best of aims in mind for humanity.

Human beings have considerable innate abilities both collectively and individually. Humanism believes very profoundly in the development of such abilities to enrich the life of each person and the wider context of family, society and the world. And, what is more, human beings have the ability to see *quality* in their experiences and achievements. This is something which Cantril terms "value attributes" which, he says, are experienced "in the humble, ordinary activities of life: in saying "hello" to a neighbor, in cleaning your house, in taking a bath after a hard day's work. You sense the value attributes of disappointment, disturbance, or sorrow when things go wrong".[23] It is this "value attribute" as a dimension of human life which individuals search out, recapture, develop, in the rich variety of experiences which life offers. Cantril believes that it is the *enhancement* of the value attributes of experience that is the most generalized goal of humankind, the "top standard of human experience".[24] This is an important ingredient of humankind for it is this kind of intangible, non-empirical aspect of life that is often behind the progress any individual makes in life. And the fact that "value attributes" are impossible to assess in human beings rather militates against the reductionist view of them – the idea that they can be reduced to their psychological, behavioural, genetic, biological and chemical components, and nothing else.

The fact that we have terms like *humankind* and *humanity* suggests a certain intimate linking of human beings globally. The simple, basic linking factor of humanity is that it comprises a species that is a part of the natural world. On the one hand, humanity is intimately linked with the natural world on which it is dependent for its existence, but on the other hand, it is sufficiently distinct from it to be able to make conscious changes in the natural environment. Moreover, each individual cannot really become *human* unless there is some interaction socially with other human beings – unless an individual is *part* of humanity. "Society", indeed, is a nebulous term that cannot exist independently of individuals. It is the actions, transactions and interactions of individuals that make society – and humanity – what it is. And if this is so, then we can make of society and humanity what we wish, providing our aims and objectives have some degree of commonality. In fact, we create the environments in which we exist in the present, and we are, then, certainly capable of changing them for the better in the future. To form a secure and positive society we have to act, react, interact and transact with care, sensitivity, informed knowledge, and skill, eschewing greed, insensitivity, ignorance and destructiveness. We can make of society what we will.

Human potential

How many times have you heard someone say "I'd love to have done x", or, "If I had my time again I would have . . . "? As individuals we have so much potential and to be really Humanist is to strive to realize, in one lifetime, as much of that potential as we can. If there is only one life to live then, when the end is reached, it should have been fulfilled in whatever dimensions are right for any individual, and for society as a whole. There should be few regrets, and assurance that, while there may be some potential unfulfilled, the best possible efforts were made to develop as a human being. Perhaps the most well-known statement associated with Humanism comes from Protagoras, the fifth century BCE Greek teacher and philosopher, who said "Man is the measure of all things". It is a statement that, to Humanists, is indicative of the human being as an independent agent, one not dependent in any way on a divine agent for existence, for the way in which life is lived, or for the means to a future existence beyond death. Since there is only one life, and no God responsible for the way it is lived, human beings have the potential to stand on their own feet and view existence and their role in it *now*, in the present.

But even if each individual has the potential to become what he or she wills, it is common sense to suggest that we don't always have the freedom to make this possible. This point raises three issues that will need to be examined in more detail in later chapters – the issues of freedom, equality and the nature of society. Our dreams may not be fulfilled because of constraints in our own mental and physical beings, but also because of certain restraints that are placed on us by aspects of society. But not *all* our dreams fall into this category, and each person usually possesses some dormant or little developed potential which, with some effort, can evolve. And I do not think that this is just "imagination", "fancy" and "fantasy", to use some of the terms which John Carroll adopts in his criticism of the tenet that one can become what one wills.[25] It is more a question of fostering the right kinds of experiences to promote the "value attributes", to go back to Cantril's term, which help an individual to progress in chosen areas of life. As a tutor in Higher Education I have seen, so many times, the development of the potential in students in abilities they didn't know they had. Typical are the mature women who begin undergraduate courses so fearfully but who obtain the degree that at one time was not even a seed in their minds. And I am sure that, given the opportunities for the development of potential, many, many individuals *will* achieve beyond even their wildest dreams in all sorts of contexts. This is not "fancy", this is the positivity of humanistic emphasis in life which is integral to the principles of any kind of Humanism. The important thing is to *strive* to realize one's goals in life, not to retain them as unexpressed dreams. Again this is an anti-reductionist dimension of the human being. Human beings strive to bring quality into their lives, even if their striving is sometimes in misguided directions. It is this striving for quality of all kinds in life, which reveals the potential of a human being, and it is this aspect of the individual which has so much to fulfil, to develop, to offer society at large.

The nature of the self

The West has inherited from ancient times a theory of mind–body dualism that originated in Greek thought. The legacy that the western world owes to the Greeks is a colossal one. In 334 BCE Alexander the Great had succeeded in conquering large areas of the Near East and, although he died at an early age, his successors, the Seleucids, held his empire together politically. During his career Alexander had a vision, not only of a political empire, but of a cultural one too. And although the Hellenistic era never witnessed the same might and influence as the Roman empire in the political sense, culturally, the Greek world was to leave its mark on civilization throughout the centuries to the present day. The great philosophers of the classical period of Greek history – Pythagoras, Socrates, Plato, Aristotle, to name but a few – are still household names, and the influence of such men on the subsequent thought of most later philosophers is immeasurable. It has been said that Plato occurs in the footnotes of more books than any other author! Plato was born in 428 BCE and died in 347 BCE, his life marking a time that witnessed the height of classical Greek philosophy, mathematics and culture. It is small wonder, then, that Plato's highly developed views of the self were so influential in the millennia that followed.

Plato was a dualist, both in terms of his metaphysical view of a world of Forms or Ideas that totally transcended and was separate from the world of matter, and in his division of the self between body and soul.[26] The rational part of the soul, he believed, belonged to the divine realm, but the body, as matter, to the world below. What would ensue was a battle within the self to realize the pure, rational and divine soul at the expense of the gross body – a recurrent theme taken up by subsequent Christianity. Paul, for example, in the *New Testament* reflects this idea of the body being the prison house of the soul. It led to the belief that bodily needs had to be denied and suppressed in order to allow the soul to be free – an anti-holistic approach to the self which has been a major influence on Christian thought, and even popular belief, right up to the present day. In Plato's thought it was important not to be trapped by the gross, appetitive part of the self which sought bodily pleasures. Thus, while it was not necessarily wrong to drink wine, it *was* wrong to enjoy it! This kind of thinking was to affect Christianity considerably; the past (and sometimes present) Christian attitude to sex is one example. The fundamental aim of a philosopher according to Plato should be to dissever the soul from communion with the body for the body is a hindrance to knowledge. And if we change the word "knowledge" here to "salvation", the message could have been a Christian one – one that has been echoed in some form or other in the centuries of theology to the present day. Today, then, many people tend to accept that when you die, the "soul" departs to some divine realm, or is reincarnated, and the body disappears. It is a theory entrenched by the French philosopher René Descartes (1596–1650), often called the founder of modern philosophy, and although Descartes was to link the mind and soul together, which he separated from the body entirely, belief in the dualism of the self was firmly in place. We sometimes refer to this as *Platonic-Cartesian dualism*.

Humanists reject this theory of the composite and dual nature of the body and soul or mind, claiming that body and mind are one, and both disintegrate at death. This is a *monistic* theory as opposed to a dualistic one. The idea of one-ness as opposed to a dual nature of body and mind is essential to Humanism, for the monistic theory precludes any possibility of a supernatural life in any form beyond death: immortality is an impossibility. To the Humanist, then, man and woman consist of body, mind and personality in an indissoluble unity. Mind and personality, indeed, are felt to be products of the conditioning environment, the end products of genetic inheritance and interaction with the stimuli in the physical and social environment, and the result of responses to the countless choices that are made in life's varied tapestries. The self is thus an interfunctioning of mental, physical and emotional qualities that form the unity of the individual.

As to a "soul" which is somehow connected with mind or the brain, the Humanist view is that it doesn't exist. Neither, for that matter, is the "mind" something separate from what goes on in the brain. Indeed, Arthur Atkinson considers the word "mind" to be a "misconception"[27] and claims that we could do away with it altogether with all sorts of synonyms. "At best", he says, "the mind is hard to find and difficult to identify when people think they have caught up with it. But we confidently go further and claim that it is in fact a conceptual error."[28] While I do not think that we need to go to the lengths of ridding the English dictionary of the word, particularly since it has some pertinent uses in English phraseology, the separation of mind from the functioning of the brain is, I agree, a tenuous proposition.

If we analyse what constitutes the human being, then, it is difficult to see what he or she is apart from chemico-physical components and a mind/personality, the latter being wholly dependable on the senses. Suppose we take away all senses from a person so that he or she has no experience of sight, taste, smell, touch, hearing. What thoughts could this "person" have? What thoughts can *you* have independently of the senses that enable you to experience things? Can the "mind" exist without the thoughts that the brain permits? Thinking is a function of the brain in the same way as seeing is a function of eyes or hearing of ears, and "mind" is purely the sum total of the thoughts and experiences, knowledge and impulses stored by the brain. I think we have to have "mind" to represent this kind of accumulated storage of brain data, and to suggest that there is a good deal of difference between what is in one mind from that of another. But to suggest that the mind is separate from the senses is illogical. So there is nothing beyond the natural body – certainly no supernatural soul which transcends it at death. The human being is, within the bounds of genetic constraints, what he or she makes of his or her self, and this will be the sum total of reactions to sense stimuli, environmental conditioning and the kinds of choices made in life. The individual is "nothing else but what his life is", as Sartre put it.[29]

The essential element of the human being is *ego*, that ingredient of the human being that is all "I" centred. Like "mind", it is different for each person, but for Humanists it is not something to be denied in order to reach some kind of ultimate knowledge and state of equilibrium that transcends the world, as in much eastern thought. Nor is it something that has to be subjected to divine will as in much western religious thought. The ego is self-assertive, self-identifying and is something to be given value and respect in the human psyche. It is ego that makes us respond to the world and to the multiple stimuli that the environment presents us. It is ego that makes us choose this as opposed to that, and that causes us to respond to life in ways which are particular to ourselves and not to any other person. Humanism sees nothing wrong in the encouragement of egoistic drives and self-assertion for this is what makes individuals progress, what makes life go forward instead of stagnating. All our drives are bound in ego, but they are the drives that are essential for personal and societal existence. Ehrenfeld, for one, is critical of the increase of personal ego in the world today which, he says, "has left us with no alternative but to love ourselves best of all".[30] But it could be argued that without love and respect of the self, how can the human being extend love and respect to others? Self-denial and self-humility are not the ingredients of a balanced person in the eyes of many Humanists. Human consciousness is of necessity egoistic identity, and to operate in life without ego is impossible. It is ego that is bound up in *feelings* and *emotions* of individuals and these are essential ingredients of humanity, not disposable ones. As Saumur comments, "it is not enough to say that a human being *has* passions, but it is more exact to say that he *is* his passions, which he cannot choose not to be unless he literally chooses to become someone other than himself".[31]

In today's world genetics is now known to affect not only the way we are physically and our propensities to certain illnesses, but the way we live our lives, our likes and dislikes and our emotions. This reduces the self to an extent, and it would be possible to say that, given the specific genetic constitution of a particular human being, he or she would be *likely* to develop this or that, to be more of one thing than another in terms of personality, and so on. But, while there are certainly some genetic factors that have predetermined results, for much genetic propensity, we can only claim *likelihood*. The human being can always surprise: and I dare say there have been many characters similar to Hitler's genetic constitution, but there are invariable factors in life which made Hitler Hitler, and invariable factors in human consciousness and personality which operate against genetic background. This is why people stemming from working-class backgrounds can often outstrip their middle-class contemporaries, sometimes in the very face of genetic propensity. While his language is tinged with reductionism, Paul Kurtz points out the obvious fact that: "The human organism is able to respond to stimuli not only by conditioned behaviour but by expressing creative impulses and demonstrating cognitive awareness."[32]

Asserting egoistic identity and self-assertion places human beings on the centre stage of life, leaving no room for God. Denial of the self, in one way or another, has always been important to most religious belief, but this kind of thinking is alien to Humanism, otherwise it denies the very *human-being-ness* which is essential to the term *Humanism*. And such is the ego that conceptions of the divine are usually projections of the collective ego of a culture, which is probably why depictions of Jesus in Christianity are so thoroughly physically Aryan. Feuerbach (1804–72) believed that human beings project onto God the kinds of characteristics that they themselves, in fact, are thoroughly capable of.

To a degree these ideas are anthropocentric, and there are, as noted above, many who accept this kind of vision of the self; though there are others who temper the centrality of the human being somewhat. But Humanism, by its very nature, stresses the concept of *human* beings, and emphasizes their power, dignity and value. It holds that individuals should be encouraged to respect their own dignity and to fulfil their own potential. There is an emphasis on the *self* – self-responsibility, self-direction, self-worth, self-dignity, self-respect, self-assertion, self-control – but, at the same time, a philosophy of "do to others as you would have them do to you". Humanism, whilst recognizing people's limitations, has faith and confidence in humankind and respects its infinite possibilities. It never suggests that human beings should subject themselves to a superior authority, whether that is God, an institution, the government, tradition, and so on. Humanists should not feel inferior in any way, or should have imposed on them doctrines or practices that lessen their individuality. But it is sensible to work for common legal and social frameworks in which individuals can interactively exist.

Thus the human self is a noble one, and if it is not composite, but a holistic unit with no part of it surviving death, then each individual self becomes far more important, for there is only one life in which it can find fulfilment. And this one life becomes crucial in the development of the self. Humanists are well aware that such human potential and fulfilment cannot be achieved without a supportive environment, without the altruistic goals of others to provide the physical, intellectual and emotional soil on which the self can develop. So Humanism affirms the value of the self, but also the value of others in the process of self-assertion in life. As will be seen in a chapter 5, there is considerable emphasis on what is termed the social good.

Spirituality

In removing God and religion from the human dimension it might be argued that the *spirituality* that many people claim to experience, and which indicates to them the presence of the divine in the world, is either ignored or denied by the Humanist. This is not strictly true for, while some Humanists might claim that spirituality does not exist, it might also be possible to interpret it in a more secular sense. There is no doubt that the word is connected with religion according to its usage in centuries past. The *Oxford English Dictionary* links the word with ecclesiastical persons, revenue or property, but also to that old dualism of spirit and matter suggesting that it is concerned with the things of the spirit as opposed to material or worldly interests. In this latter sense the word can be used of immaterial or incorporeal "spirits" or "essences". This suggests that the word *spirituality* has to be rejected by Humanists on two counts: first because of its religious connotations, and, second, because it opposes the monistic nature of the human being.

In getting rid of this word, however, I think Humanists need something in its place, or need to redefine it in a secular sense. It would be difficult to deny that there are times in life when the material world slips into insignificance for a moment or two, and the self experiences something of the depth of life, the *quality* of experience. This is usually the result of some kind of stimuli in the environment – beautiful music, magnificent scenery, the view from the top of a mountain, a sunset, snow, sex, a particular painting, holding your newly-born baby – indeed, there is no end to the stimuli that can promote a "transcendent" feeling, a feeling as if the material world is, even if for just one moment, utterly transcended. This has much to do with the depth of life and experience of the self in its more subtle modes. But I do not think it is a part of the self that can be denied.

In a sensitively written and searching article, Robert Ashby, Executive Director of the British Humanist Association, attempts to define "spirituality" in Humanist terms. In writing of "that strange light of the shore at night, the shifting glimmer of the swell . . . the peaceful sound and rhythm", he clearly knows what spirituality is all about. But I would take issue with his over-analytical approach to it. In fact, he admits that "the re-assertion of language destroys that spiritual experience, or at least makes it a memory".[33] Such experience may well be an *emotional* one – and I think Ashby is correct here – but I would argue that it is a *suspension* of ordinary perception and language that facilitates "spiritual" experience, along with a natural enhancement of sensitivity without the interference of articulated conscious thought. This certainly makes it a mode of more *intense* experience of a moment or moments of life without the encumbrance of our usual modes of thinking and being. Ashby clearly feels this:

> the spiritual experience is a particular focus of *this* life, not some new sort of sense, hitherto undiscovered by scientists. This is quite simply because, as I have said, the experience is one of greater contact with one's real life, that moment of being, away from all the distraction of the world around. It is a concentration on life and the self. It is quite at odds with the bombardment of images around us, which suggest that life and self are about work, clothes, money, lifestyle and so on – all of which are concepts that have arisen extremely late in the process of evolution of the human brain.[34]

In the final analysis he emerges with the definition of spirituality as: "Moments of being composed of emotion, imagination and memory – which somehow link up to take us beyond everyday awareness to an enhanced sense of reality."[35] Why not, I ask, "moments of being" *sans* analysis?

So Humanism can stress the importance of the awareness of

beauty and the appreciation of Nature as part of the necessary experience of the self. Indeed, without this kind of experience there is a certain void or gap within each human being, and such "transcendent" experiences could be said to fill certain gaps in individual selfhood, and serve to add quality to the living experience. Moreover, this is one dimension of the human being that humanistic psychology suggests flies in the face of reductionist theories of the nature of the self. And in answer to Antony Flew's perplexity as to what HMI[36] has in mind when inspectors talk of the "spiritual dimensions of a school's life",[37] they probably have in mind the secular aesthetic awareness of beauty; the care of others; the care of animals and the environment; the appreciation of moving poetry; the ability to share emotion through story and poetry; the ability to enjoy good music and the opportunity to express these areas in their own ways; a sense of awe and wonder at Nature which are often the catalyst for later inquiry – in short, much that would please Humanists!

Bernard Farr's interesting article "Becoming Spiritual: Learning from marijuana users"[38] equates the process by which a marijuana user becomes a marijuana user and the way in which a Charismatic Christian becomes charismatic. Farr proposes that one must *learn* to be either. But I do not think "transcendent" experience (if I may use this term as a synonym for "spiritual" for the present) is a learned experience, "a kind of human performance."[39] I propose that it is a *natural* experience that we don't learn to *be*, (and that is why it doesn't even make sense grammatically), but which we spontaneously experience as a result of some stimulus or other. In fact, we can't *become* spiritual, though we can *become* a Charismatic, or a Humanist for that matter. To say that we can become spiritual is like saying we can become beautiful or intellectual, through a learning process. Against Farr, I do not think that "spirituality", "transcendence" or, a term which is shortly to be explored, "peak experience" is an "activity",[40] but a state of being, an emotion, a feeling. And we do not normally bother to learn how to express emotions at will unless there is something psychologically wrong with us or we are particularly good at acting. Moreover, when we experience some sort of "transcendence" or "spirituality" or "peak experience" we are often alone, so the acquisition of "techniques" in spirituality is not to be obtained from group experience, as in marijuana use or charismatic meetings.

So if Humanists want to argue against spirituality *per se*, suggesting that it doesn't exist, I think they are on difficult ground. What is more attractive is a redefining of the term to posit a more secular experience. In this context the term "peak experiences" used by the humanistic psychologist Abraham Maslow seems to me a very adequate one to reflect the dimension of the human being which is capable of transcending the here and now, and of experiencing heightened consciousness. As a humanistic psychologist Maslow allows for a more flexible, creative and personal role of the individual in shaping his or her existence. This means that personal experience of something that expands consciousness, however profane the context, has become a valid part of humanistic psychological inquiry.

Helen Graham has demonstrated remarkably well that individuals, particularly the youth in society, are characterized by an ability to search for the kind of personal fulfilment that transcends the norms of social patterns, and therefore the norms of reductionist psychological study.[41] The sixties era of psychedelic drugs and flower-power, the modern era of creative sex and the drug Ecstacy, for example, show that people look for something meaningful beyond the traditional patterns of society. Are they, then, looking for the transcendent experience? Are they looking for the experiences that will transform them from the mundanities of existence to new heights of consciousness? And are such experiences a search for the spiritual or are they confined to the profane in life? Most young people would suggest the latter.

It was Abraham Maslow who did extensive research into, and coined the term, "peak experiences", and presented considerable evidence to suggest that such experiences are part of the natural expressions of human life. They can occur in any context – music, sex, being in love, gazing at the stars – and have many similarities to the kinds of "spiritual" experiences people claim to have had in the religious context. Maslow suggested that such "peak experiences" involved special perception, something he called B-cognition, and this involved the sort of holistic experience of things in life as opposed to D-cognition that is really basic knowledge about life. When a "peak experience" occurs, the stimulus, as Maslow says, "is seen as if it were all there was in the universe, as if it were all of Being, synonymous with the universe".[42] And there is much about such experiences which is similar to religious claims of spiritual experience – heightened awareness, egolessness, unity and absorption in the object, suspension of time and space, unity of all things, the feeling of wonder and awe, the indescribable nature of the experience and, overriding all, the sense of *value* in the experience, something of Cantril's "value attributes" noted earlier. And according to Maslow it is the more evolved person who is prone to such "peak experiences". He terms such people "self-actualizing" and claims that they are more integrated and less egocentric personalities:

> We may define it [self-actualisation] as an episode, or a spurt in which the powers of the person come together in a particularly efficient and intensely enjoyable way, and in which he is more integrated and less split, more open for experience, more idiosyncratic, more perfectly expressive and spontaneous, or fully functioning, more creative, more humorous, more ego-transcending, more independent of his lower needs, etc. He becomes in these episodes more truly himself, more perfectly actualizing his potentialities, closer to the core of his Being, more fully human.[43]

Thus Maslow sees a certain outcome of peak experiences in terms of the way in which life is lived so that there is a degree of ethical awareness, of self-autonomy, of realization of potential.

The point here is that any Humanist denial of spirituality, suggesting that human beings *imagine* some kind of false religiosity that does not exist, is somewhat wide of the mark. Transcendent experiences *do* exist, they just do not have to be associated with religion, and if the word "spirituality" can only relate to religion, then it is the wrong term to describe many transcendent or peak experiences which are wholly secular. In fact, religiously-minded people are likely to describe such experiences as spiritual, while the non-religious person would use other terms.

In many instances the type of experience is probably the same. Following a lengthy analysis of transcendence in *The Farther Reaches of Human Nature*,[44] Maslow concludes with the following condensed statement:

> Transcendence refers to the very highest and most inclusive of holistic levels of human consciousness, behaving and relating, as ends rather than means, to oneself, to significant others, to human beings in general, to other species, to nature, and to the cosmos.[45]

In short, peak or transcendent experiences are a dimension of the human self which serve to give it quality, and it is not the "religious" person who has a monopoly on such experience. All human beings probably have an innate potential for such experiences and these experiences are natural and not supernatural, secular and not religious. Maslow stated:

> We must take the word *"religious"* out of its narrow context of the supernatural, churches, rituals, dogmas, professional clergymen etc.,

and distribute it in principle throughout the whole of life. Religion becomes then not one social institution among others, but rather a state of mind achievable in almost any activity of life, if this activity is raised to a suitable level of perfection.[46]

This is a choice between the religionizing of the secular and the secularization of the religious. Those Humanists who are prepared to accept transcendent experience as a facet of the human self will clearly accept the latter of the two propositions. Theravada Buddhism has the same kind of approach to transcendent experience. It does not deny that it exists, it simply secularizes it. The transcendent experience of *samadhi* in meditation is not experience of a supernatural divine part of the self, it is just the transcending for a while of the subject-object differentiation associated with normal life. All human beings, then, are capable of peak or transcendent experiences, it is only the religious person who might translate these to suggest "spiritual" experience.

Individuality

In the past humanism has often given the impression that it is so utilitarian that individuality is sacrificed for the common good. In fact, I think both individuality and the common good are almost two sides of one coin, for we do not learn to be autonomous individuals outside the common good and the common good can only be reinforced by the projection of the quality of individual lives into the social sphere. Because Humanism is a fierce defender of human potential, it has to begin with the individual. And the fact that it is so much associated at an organizational level with the defence of human rights reiterates its concern for individuality alongside its concern for society and global issues.

Each person has his or her own distinct individuality and character. We may be similar to others in some ways but are never identical. Some people are like plants, they follow the sun, turning only where life lists. They imitate others rather than developing their own innate potentials and personalities. Others are highly dynamic and live life to the utmost, striving forward in many directions. Some overdo life, and some hardly get going. People are highly complex, and while some will explore the latent and innate abilities of their own selves, others need the catalyst from outside themselves, they need the opportunities presented to them, and encouragement on the way at almost every turn. But given the differences in each individual there *are* latent and innate potentials in all of us. And life is not lived to the full unless at least some of these potentialities are explored – not necessarily fulfilled entirely, but at least developed from the *status quo*. Harold Blackham once wrote that:

> The vessel has to be filled before it overflows. One has to be friends with oneself before one is fit to be a friend. Nobody else is responsible for taking care of one's interests, satisfying one's needs and desires, fulfilling one's chosen possibilities, making a job of one's life. Doing the best for oneself can be the best one can do for others.[47]

But if one is to do the best for oneself it follows that individual life needs to be active and dynamic in order to reach its full or even part potential. This means being alert to the challenges of life and being capable of living life with positive courage and worthwhile, creative action. Hector Hawton used the term (if sexist!) "the whole man"[48] and this is a powerful term, for it suggests that a human being can be whole in this one life, in mortal existence. "Wholeness" is not something dependent on a life after death or on immortality, for if we are not immortal then fulfilment has to come from this one life and each individual is responsible for achieving this for his or her own self, but also for facilitating the achievements of others.

All this reads as very idealist and we know that the existential life-condition of so many human beings is anything but perfect, and the necessary conditions to develop the "whole" man or woman are simply not there. Humanists would answer this challenge in two ways. One would be philosophical, in that there would be an attempt to understand why individuals themselves and society at large are not capable of such a goal. Another would be active, in that action needs to be taken to ensure that the right kind of conditions obtain in society and the world at large in order to promote the development of "whole" men and women. What, then, is a "whole" man or woman? This is a person with mental and material well-being, one capable of rational choices, an ethical person, one who in some measure realizes his or her potentialities both intellectually and phys-ically. Importantly, the "whole" man or woman is a questioning one, one who submits beliefs to constant examination and who, therefore, will not accept blindly the dictates of others. This is a happy person who can face the vicissitudes of life with courage and optimism. Paul Kurtz, who has dealt at length with this concept of the "whole" being,[49] sums up his analysis with the very apt statement: "The ultimate courage is to be and to *become* in spite of existential reality, and to overcome adversity and exult in our ability to do so." Essential to such "wholeness" is reflective self-awareness of the type that enables analysis of one's own values and beliefs. Ronald Fletcher makes this point when he says:

> Each person, though in deliberation with others, must work out his own standpoint in accordance with his own lights. To accept without question the pronouncements of others is never to have moved towards, let alone achieved, self-direction, powers of judgment, maturity, and fulfilment in one's own nature.[50]

Human personality is constantly changing and never becomes a finished product: it is always in a state of becoming, but it is this fact which, to a Humanist, is so exciting. Individuals *can* shape their own destinies, they *can* be optimistic about the future, and they *can* take charge of the world and steer it to a better future. Individuals normally do strive forward providing that their inner security is not over-compromised. We are all in what Robert Fisher has described as "a process of ongoing creation"[51] realizing one potential before we go on to the next. And, he rightly says: "The process of becoming a person is never complete and never finished."[52] What is essential is to be open to the opportunities for the development of one's own individuality and personhood – to travel with an open mind. Ronald Fletcher reiterates this same point of a process of self-creativity:

> The making of character, the seeking of excellence in qualities of character, is thus a creative activity, both personal and social, of the utmost worth to the Humanist. Here . . . the quest for truth and value is not only a matter of *knowing* but a matter of *becoming*, a matter of self creation.[53]

The fully mature individual is an autonomous person. *Autonomy* is a word which suggests self-government and personal freedom, so an autonomous person is one who is in a position to make reflective and informed choices about life and one who is critically reflective about the outcomes of those choices. No one is ever completely free and it is rare that a person is able to make choices without taking into account restrictions that affect such choices. The truly autonomous person knows this but accepts that, given a variety of pathways, he or she is free to make choices as a result of his or her own personal experiences. People who simply obey rules or who follow a prescribed code are a long way from developing any kind of autonomy. The autonomous person makes intelligent, rational decisions before acting, understands what he or she is doing, and has valid reasons for doing it. This kind of autonomous person is the highest outcome of education and society: it is the aim of Humanists for all individuals. But this does not compromise the distinct individuality of a person – indeed, it enhances it. As Blackham has said: "An autonomous person with well-founded self-confidence is the model human being, but his personal identity is particular, and unique."[54] While "model human beings" probably do not exist, for Blackham, autonomy means the achievement of "full identity".[55] What this suggests is that one needs to be a fulfilled individual first and foremost, not in the sense of having completed that fulfilment, but in the sense of knowing that one is travelling in the right directions. Only then, when the individual has value in his or her self, can that person make a valuable contribution to society.

From all that has been said about the human being, I think that we can take the reductionists to task. The human individual is something more than his or her biological, physical, behavioural and psychological components and even transcends genetic and environmental backgrounds. In the normal human need to interact with others, to love and be loved, to be valued and respected, there are a myriad ways of living our lives, and the inter-complexities of the world in which we live extend us beyond our mere selves in all sorts of dimensions. Of course we have basic genetic make-ups, but this does not reduce us to conglomerated automata that will always behave in a certain way in a certain situation. There are so many individuals who have risen beyond the confines of environmental and conditioned behavioural backgrounds. And the interaction of environment and genetic make-up, open the door to the transcending of the genetic self in many directions. In fact, the problem with reductionism is that, even if the human being can be isolated psychologically or genetically or behaviourally or physically, it is the *interaction* of all these factors along with so many others that contributes to any individual make-up, even to behaviour in, and response to, one particular situation in life. There is no reason why an individual experiences what he or she does; and it is these experiences which form individual character and personality. Even collectivism is ultimately transcended by individual identity for, as history has shown, after long years of collectivist régimes, individualism emerges like subterranean streams long suppressed. Generally, human beings are not contented with things as they are, and in the striving forward –

whether materialistically, socially, educationally or in any way – the variables which affect the individual far transcend reductionist theory. Characteristics of any individual may be chromosomatically dictated, but not the life-experiences that contribute to the formation of character. It is perhaps because the many variables that contribute to the make-up of an individual cannot be so easily subjected to empirical research that reductionism has been so much accepted. We change as we live, and mostly we do so beyond the bounds of reductionist theory. Any Humanist, in fact, who accepts reductionist theories of human beings, or anti-personalism, can wave goodbye to the aim of fulfilment of human potential, for some human beings, according to reductionist theory, would have little or none to fulfil. I think Robert Fisher is right when he says studying persons means accepting "unresolved mysteries, tensions, paradoxes, and even contradictions; the study of persons demands the continual questionableness of what is said about them, and the perpetual need to revise, rethink, and restate what we imagine to lie at the heart of personhood".[56]

Humanism is, then, generally anti-reductionist, though some Humanists accept partial reductionism, leaving immense scope for maximizing of human potential. I would, therefore, take issue with Kate Soper's criticisms of representatives of the British Humanist Association as being so scientifically orientated as to reduce human beings to mere scientific objects. She writes of the BHA:

> Despite the claim of A. J. Ayer, one of the Association's presidents, that the British Humanists are not committed to any set of doctrines and have nothing in common except their atheism, a shared philosophical orientation is clearly detectable: in their concern to avoid the irrationality of religion, they have embraced a positivist conception of the rationality of science. Since they approach human beings as objects of scientific inquiry essentially no different from those in the non-human world, such humanists assume them to be amenable to very similar forms of investigation. They therefore come to identify a "scientific" knowledge of humanity with what emerges from studies which attempt to abstract from values and systems of belief.[57]

This is a highly reductionist view of Humanism and is offensive to its view of each individual as of unique value. I agree that a "shared philosophical orientation" *is* discernible – fulfilment of individual potential and happiness, a sound societal life in which the "Good Life" is available to all, morality that is humanity based and not divinely ordained, and so on. However, Soper's views here are clearly out of touch with modern Humanism. She is also wide of the mark in her claim that for Humanism "happiness is to be achieved not through any alteration of values or of the 'needs' they breed and endorse, but by organizing the environment in such a way that it corresponds more closely to the demands that our behaviour reveals we possess".[58] But it is precisely human values and human needs that Humanism *primarily* addresses, and with the hope that by changing individual values and aspirations, society will become a better place for all. But the starting point is the individual, *not* the environment.

Emerging from this study of the human being is, I hope, an impression of the actual and potential dignity of all human beings. Indeed, if we cannot hold this maxim in life then we ourselves could hardly lay claim to the word human in all but its biological sense. It is a positive view of humanity even if, at times, it is idealist. You are what you make of yourselves. Aim high, aim for the stars, and you may yet clear the rooftops. You will need courage, tenacity, motivation and a good sense of humour on the route. Quality of character, happiness, fulfilment of potential and of human needs can be improved through changed values, through redirection of individual life, by a process of personal change, and personal evolution.

3

The Case against Religion: The Rejection of God

Humanism believes in a naturalistic cosmology or metaphysics or attitude towards the universe that rules out all forms of the supernatural and that regards Nature as the totality of being and as a constantly changing system of events which exists independently of any mind or consciousness.[1]

While, historically, humanism in its broadest sense is not specifically anti-religious, modern secular Humanism is much more overtly so. In particular, it stands opposed to the tenets and practices of the Christian faith, and to the supernaturalism of religious belief and practice which militates against the full development of each human being. With its dream of individual and social fulfilment and its optimism, positivity, and firm foothold in the present, Humanism tends to view religion as the opposite – pessimistic about life, negative, and rooted in the traditions of the past. This chapter, then, will be concerned with the kinds of reasons secular Humanists might have for the rejection of religion, in particular, reasons for the rejection of belief in, or the existence of, God.

It is not improbable that religion originated as a response to empirical existence. Early human beings sought to explain anomalies in their natural environment by reference to some hidden force or forces, some supernatural element or elements that would make sense of those aspects in life that were inexplicable. But such early forms of religion arose, fundamentally, from empirical life and need, from the natural and not the supernatural. And the need to explain floods, thunder, earthquakes, the rains at the wrong time, the rainbow, lightning, the sun rising each day, birth and death of all things, and experiences of awe and wonder, was both individual and collective. From such human need came the simple or elaborate myths of the supernatural to provide reason for the inexplicable. Today, of course, we know why it thunders (though the archetypal fear of it remains for many), and inexplicable areas of life are fewer. Those remaining are pushed beyond the physical environment that science has so competently explained, to the more metaphysical and intangible aspects of the cosmos that still elude us. It is here that the individual looks for his or her supernatural answers. But the principle of inquiry is the same as that of early humanity; it is simply subtler. While religion stems from the needs of human nature, it has a tendency to focus on the supernatural to the extent that it transcends the human world in an elaboration that often serves to obscure thoroughly its original, natural, purpose. And in the elaborate development of the supernatural perspective, dogmatic rigidity sets in, and tradition and custom begin to dictate religious belief. The ability to analyse *why* religion is accepted becomes difficult; it becomes a way of life, something people accept on *faith*.

In the world of today, secular Humanism asks for such an analysis of religion. It asks – in the same way that it would for any other aspects of life – what are the *rational grounds* for religious belief? And if such grounds are not convincing, then any areas of secular existence that are influenced by religious reasoning are influenced unjustly and irrationally. Thus, if there are no rational grounds for religious belief, then there are no rational grounds for accepting the intervention of religion in such spheres as medical ethics, the judicial system and education, for example. Neither are there rational grounds against the right of any individual to make personal, informed choices on issues such as homosexuality, abortion, contraception, and so on. It is the *collective effect* of religion on human beings that is at issue here, a collective effect that prevents personal direction and fulfilment.

It is important, however, not to define religion – as we know the term in today's world – too narrowly. Indeed, any analysis of the concept of God (to which I shall return below) immediately illustrates that there is no single, general phenomenon of *religion*. Neither is it possible to refer to the Christian *religion*, or the Buddhist *religion* or any other *religion*. In fact, there are only Christians, Buddhists, Hindus, Jews, Muslims, etc. and enormous varieties of each in terms of belief, scriptural interpretation and religious affiliation. We must be careful, too, of claiming categorically that religion deals with the supernatural whereas secular Humanism does not, for there are aspects of both the religions of Buddhism and Hinduism that also reject such supernaturalism. While contemporary Humanism is beginning to address itself to major world religions, nevertheless, secular Humanism as a western phenomenon confronts the revealed religions of Judaism, Christianity and Islam more readily – three religions that have such strong elements of supernaturalism. These are the religions that are within the existential experience of secular Humanism, and it is to Christianity, especially, that it addresses the request for rational grounds for religious belief. Important to note, also, is that, as was seen in chapter 1, humanism has not always eschewed religion entirely, and there would be humanists today who may be inclined to accept a deistic view – a view to which I shall return below. However, secular Humanism is today characterized by an atheistic or agnostic stance, though the converse – that atheists embrace a Humanist life-stance – is certainly not the case.

In today's world the committed secular Humanist, while having still the task of criticizing the vestiges of religious control of what should be purely secular matters, has less of a problem in convincing the average human being of Protestant heritage that his or her religious viewpoint needs rational analysis. The established churches are all but empty, and most people spend little or no time of the day in thought of a remote God, even at times that are special in the religious calendar. Certainly in Britain a religious day like Easter Monday will find the car parks surrounding DIY superstores packed with very secularly minded people. The scene in the United States, however, is somewhat different. Having some religious affiliation is much less expected in Britain than in the US. In fact, Paul Kurtz, for one, is concerned about the subtle conformity to religion that pervades the American psyche. He writes:

> Apparently, belonging to a religion, whatever it is, is considered a mark of moral character and patriotism. Those who do not profess a religion are considered pariahs. No politician will admit to being an unbeliever. Similarly for leaders in business, industry, the media, and academia. . . . The paradigm shift toward religiosity now occurring in America is both subtle and widespread.[2]

Clearly, the American public displays a greater and more overt trust in God than its British counterpart. The fact that the President of the United States abjectly apologized for his "sins" to the American nation, in the light of the Starr Report, suggests that he and his advisors made a prudent assessment of the American nation as fundamentally "religious" – at least outwardly. Although most people in Britain seem to retain belief in God, few participate actively in religious services. Belief in God, and affiliation to a religious denomination, have been declining amongst the British populace for some time.[3]

We live in an age of rapid technological and scientific advance in which the boundaries of our perspectives of the universe are constantly changing. Old biblical ideas of creation are long out of mode, except for the fundamentalist few. Secular Humanism rejects the concept of a creator God, and that there has to be a beginning in time imposed by a supernatural deity. Considering the vastness of the cosmos, it seems inconceivable and illogical that there can be such a being as an anthropomorphic "God" who is responsible for the creation, salvation and punishment of a select number of people calling themselves Christians, on a planet that is but a speck of dust in the cosmos. The divide between science and religion often remains a deep one. George Smith makes the relevant point that science is concerned with explanation of coherent reality, whereas theology is concerned with the postulation of a "reality" that is ultimate, incoherent, and mainly unknowable.[4] Where such an unknowable, theological "reality" is said to be knowable, it is claimed to be only through the supernatural "presence" of an alleged manifestation of that reality in the form of deity. It is this kind of supernaturalism that secular Humanism rejects.

Given the rejection of any reality that is not "natural", Corliss Lamont, in the opening quotation above, uses the term *Nature* to refer to the exclusive medium by which human beings are able to build any epistemology, or theory of knowledge. Nothing can be known outside of Nature, because we would have no certain and irrefutable evidence on which to base such knowledge. This is *Naturalism*, the theory that Nature provides us with a *real* and *material* world in which to operate, in which to formulate our knowledge, and in which to develop our ideas and concepts as a result of such knowledge. To suggest that we have to go *beyond* Nature for some of our answers – to a supernatural sphere – is rejected by secular Humanism. Only the knowledge gained through the medium of Nature is empirical, even if it is later adapted in view of new evidence – indeed, there is enough to be known in all Nature, all life and the whole of the cosmos! All supernatural knowledge is incapable of being subjected to logical and empirical investigation. It can, at best, be nothing more than a subjective perspective of life held by different individuals who cannot substantiate their knowledge by anything beyond subjective experience.

With the rejection of any form of supernaturalism and an epistemology that is rooted in the reality of Nature, secular Humanism necessarily rejects religious belief. The efficacy of the teachings of established religion, and the institutions of Church or Churches that promote them, are rejected. And with the rejection of supernaturalism there is a denial of the dualistic theories so important to religious belief – the dualism of body and soul; the dualism of an earthly world and a divine world; the dualism of heaven and hell and their concomitant dualism of rewards and punishments in an afterlife; the dualism of a material and spiritual world, and of worldly and spiritual morality. Such a rejection turns us back to the intrinsic value and potential of each human being. The human being is no longer *denaturalised* and split between body and soul, aiming for fictitious rewards in a fictitious heaven, but is an *integrated* human being capable of fulfilment of his or her own, true and natural nature in this, present, existence. Most people today are sufficiently secularly minded to give body - soul dualism hardly a second thought, or God for that matter. But the vestiges of religious belief remain – participation in Christian life-cycle rites; the sending of children to attend Sunday school; harbouring of feelings of guilt from so-called "sins"; acceptance of religious control of some aspects of life. Secular Humanism challenges such apathy.

The world that the secular Humanist sees, then, is a universe without beginning and without end, a diverse world of a plurality of forms, and a real world, in which all exists independently of our perception of it. It is in this universe that the human being operates, and it is all that is needed in order to operate. It is an exciting and challenging universe in which to live, a world in which much has been discovered, much is to be discovered, terrible mistakes have been made, and wonderful things have been achieved. It is a dynamic world in which we live and in which we need dynamic response, co-exploration, and well-reasoned aims and objectives at individual, family, societal and global levels. Where men and women remain unfulfilled in any dimension of their personalities as a result of religious belief, and where society is in any way constrained by religion, secular Humanism is outspoken in its criticism. But it is not so naïve as to deny that there are those in many religions who lead exemplary lives for the good of others and for the fulfilment of themselves as individuals. But then, there are many non-believers whose lives are equally exemplary. One does not have to be religious to be "good" or "moral" – a point to be taken up in chapter 6.

Atheism

The secular Humanist is generally *atheist*, that is to say, he or she has no belief in God. The term *atheism* is worthy of some examination here, since it should not be confused with that of *non-theism*, which is rather different in meaning. *Atheism* is the belief that God does not exist (cf. Greek *atheos* "without God"). The term stands in contradistinction to *theism* which, in its widest sense, means belief in a personal god, goddess, gods and/or goddesses. The term *atheist* is normally used to express *belief* that God does not exist, whereas it doesn't necessarily work the other way round. Someone might claim that he or she does not believe that God exists, or might say "I don't believe in anything" but would nevertheless not use the term *atheist* to describe his or her stance. The term *atheist*, therefore, tends to suggest a certain ownership of belief, an adopted stance in life, an assertion of something, and secular Humanists are often thus characterized.[5] Nevertheless, atheism is not a belief *system* with clearly articulated criteria, as in other belief systems like monotheism, pantheism and so on.

To define atheism as not having theistic belief[6] is misleading. This is because it is possible for a person to reject theism but retain belief in some kind of transcendent Absolute. Aspects of Hinduism, classical Taoism, mystical Islam, some Buddhism, and even some aspects of Christianity, fall into this category. These aspects are *non-theistic*; they reject the idea of a personal god/goddess/gods/goddesses, and even the term "god", but retain belief in transcendent divinity. *Atheism* and *non-theism*, therefore, are distinct terms, the former suggesting no belief in God *of any kind*. The problem with such definitions occurs because western philosophers and theologians confine definitions to western religion, in which case the terms are inapplicable in the wider context of other cultures. But since secular Humanists reject the supernatural they are clearly atheist and not simply non-theist

I think we have to be clear, then, that an atheist is one who rejects belief in God and the existence of God. And it will not do to label "someone who positively asserts the non-existence of God" as a "positive atheist", and "someone who is simply not a theist" as a "negative atheist".[7] Indeed, someone with a profound belief in a transcendent divinity might – and with some justification – take exception to being called an atheist of any sort. Atheism is clearly naturalism versus supernaturalism, and belief in a transcendent

Absolute, since it pertains to the latter, is excluded from the term atheism but not from non-theism.

Aside from the rejection of the supernatural, atheists are opposed to the subjection of the self to a deity beyond. While the average human being is beyond such submissiveness in today's modern world, there is still a strong element of religious ingraining that emerges in psychological "cross bearing", and in the submitting of the self to subjection in different areas of life, relationally, politically and socially, because of old religious mores that die hard in the subconscious. And for the more overtly religious, such submission of the self may be more harmful to self-worth. Religious submissiveness as part of the individual psyche is often behind the perpetual receptivity to social, economic and political abuse. The class and caste systems of India are a typical example here, where, even in a theoretically casteless religion such as Sikhism, caste continues to operate at the practical levels of life, even outside India. Atheists rely on logical and empirical evaluation to support their belief that there are no supernatural forces. Those in the religious field, however, have to appeal outside empirical evidence – to the supernatural itself – for evidence of their claims. Secular Humanism, which is overtly associated with atheism, requires of religion rational ideology for its beliefs, in the absence of which, it rests its case. The atheistic position is put succinctly by Kai Nielsen: "given the very peculiarity and obscurity of the concept of God we are not justified in believing in God if no good evidence can be given for believing that God exists".[8]

But atheism is not an alternative to religion. It has no set criteria, no stance for life, no ethical, societal, or global aims and objectives. It is more a characteristic than an independent system. Secular Humanism is thus characterized by it, but does have more clearly articulated goals, more systematized philosophies. Yet, as I pointed out in earlier chapters, Humanism is a broad phenomenon under whose umbrella a multiplicity of individuality is both encouraged and evident. Importantly, then, while atheism is a ubiquitous characteristic of secular Humanism, the most that can be said of an atheist is that he or she does not have belief in any kind of deity; the majority of atheists have no connection with Humanism at all.

Undoubtedly, atheism has had a bad press in the history of humanity, and the "godless" have suffered imprisonment, alleged eternal damnation in hell, and the social stigma of concomitance with evil. Perhaps this is why people are reluctant to come out with the word even in today's more secular world, and would rather disguise their belief or lack of it in more euphemistic and innocuous language. On the other hand it seems that once the cat is out of the bag and the word is said a number of times, courage causes the identified atheist to succumb to irrational statement in an all-out attack on religion. Biased atheists abound as much as biased religionists and biased Humanists! While we might not want to be wholesale sceptics, applying doubt to all areas of knowledge,[9] it is important in life to maintain clear analysis and logical evaluation of criteria, and to travel with a certain open-mindedness. The atheist, Humanist, theist – whatever – is as capable of closed fundamentalist views as any other person, but the discerning mind sorts out the chaff from the wheat.

Agnosticism

The term *agnostic* was coined in the mid-nineteenth century by the British biologist Thomas Huxley. As a man who was uncertain in which direction his religious beliefs lay, if in any direction at all, he found no appropriate *–ism* to fit a person like himself who had none of the supernatural beliefs held by fellow religionists. Thus, he wrote,

> I took thought, and invented what I conceived to be the appropriate title of "agnostic". It came into my head as suggestively antithetic to the "gnostic" of Church history, who professed to know so much about the very things of which I was ignorant. . . . To my great satisfaction the term took.[10]

Today the word has various connotations and can express both uncertainty about belief in God, as well as a more epistemic denial of the possibility of ever having, or being able to have, knowledge of a God that is beyond the material world. It is this latter meaning that runs closely to atheism but, either way, agnosticism conveys the idea that there is an absence of knowledge that makes any veridicality possible in propositions about the existence of God: we do not know and cannot know whether God exists. In terms of value judgments, agnosticism is a more innocuous word than atheism, and is frequently used by those who, reluctant to be labelled as atheists, prefer to be labelled as "don't knowers". But, like atheism, it is not a system of belief but merely a characteristic of non-belief.

Pascal's Wager

Western society is not characterized by an overtly religious culture and for most people religion is divorced from daily existence. Unlike most eastern religions, the average westerner thinks not a jot about God while he or she is munching his or her wheaty-bangs in the morning, or during the working day: most do not even consider saying their prayers at night to thank, request of, or praise, God. Yet many of these people are reluctant to abandon God entirely, reluctant to take an atheistic or even agnostic stance. This reluctance is probably a form of what is known as *Pascal's Wager*. Blaise Pascal (1623–62) was a French mathematical physicist and philosopher. While giving his name to the *Wager* he was not its inventor[11] but, rather, the main articulator of the idea. His *Wager* is thus, that given the unsatisfactory end of death to which we must all succumb, and which must surely be on or in the minds of all mortals, should we take refuge in the idea that God exists or that he doesn't exist? We cannot know that there is a God because if he does exist he is beyond the comprehension of humanity. At an epistemic distance from humanity no reason can establish his existence. Therefore we have to gamble. Should we believe that he does exist and so, if he does, we shall have eternal life as a reward after death? Or, should we wager that he does not exist and that death brings annihilation? In which case, if he *does* exist, we shall be eternally damned. Of course, the *safe* bet is to go for the former, the belief that God exists, *just in case*, because that is the only way in which we can't lose. It is perhaps this kind of inherent threat that hangs over in the human psyche, a threat that makes it difficult for a human being to eschew the very last vestiges of religious belief by denying overtly belief in the existence of God. Today, of course, there are far more options for an individual than the limited belief or non-belief options that Pascal offers, but retaining belief in God as a safe bet – even if it is in the recesses of the mind – obtains widely, for the old conditioning and bribery of the mind dies hard.

Theism and Deism

The term *theism* comes from the Greek *theos* "god", which merely has –*ism* added to it to make it a type of belief. It is a word that can incorporate a number of meanings; however, its basic one is belief in a deity or deities, as opposed to its opposite of *a*theism, which has no such belief at all. It is a term originally used in western philosophy of religion in relation to the Christian view of the divine as one God expressed in a Trinity. And since Christianity is a monotheistic religion, then we sometimes find the word theism being used to refer to monotheistic Christianity, as opposed to other religions that are pantheistic or polytheistic. Another more restrictive sense of the word theism is also found in western philosophy to depict belief in a God who has *revealed* himself to his people, a God who thus has some kind of *personal* involvement with humanity. This view incorporates the notion of a God as a creator and also sustainer of the world in a very real way, a God who reveals himself to humanity in many ways and with whom human beings have a personal relationship. This *personal* relationship is an important characteristic of all theism, but is particularly important to Judeo-Christian theism.

Definitions of theism can be very diverse because of different conceptions of divinity ranging from transcendent perspectives of the divine as that which transcends human understanding, to more describable aspects of divinity to which humanity can more readily relate. Despite this diversity of theistic belief, however, it is always essentially *dualistic* in its perspective of the divine. That is to say, God and the world, and God and human beings are dualistically related to each other. This dualism is essential to theism because without it, God could not be worshipped, prayed to and experienced, could not have discourse with humanity, intervene in history, send his prophets, save his people, incarnate, and so on: he could not be a God of revelation, a revealed God. Dualism is also essential to western theism in that it maintains a firm differentiation between creator and created and is antagonistic to any theory or belief system that might seek to conjoin the two too closely. For this reason creation is *ex nihilo*, "out of nothing".

Today, theism is extended beyond its western context to other religious cultures, like eastern religions. It is a term now used to characterize belief in a deity, deities (god, goddess, gods and/or goddesses) with whom human beings have a dual and personal relationship. The meaning of theism can be further qualified by the prefixes *mono*- meaning belief in only one deity, *poly*- belief in many deities, *pan*- belief that divinity is the totality of existence[12] and *panen*- the belief that God is within the totality of all existence but ultimately transcends it.

All religious belief systems have their particularly problematic philosophical areas, but theism lays itself open to some insurmount-able ones, and it is in these areas that secular Humanists and atheists find the arguments considerably lacking in defence of theism. Some of the major issues that invalidate theism will be taken up below in the context of discussion about God, but it is important to note that Humanists may not, in fact, entirely eschew all notions of God, though secular Humanism mainly does so. It is particularly theistic, dualistic, revelatory supernaturalism that is so far-fetched and beyond the bounds of reason. Some Humanists, therefore, retain belief in a creator God but reject any involvement of that God in the realm of human affairs. This is rather like a watchmaker who makes a watch, winds it up or puts a silicon chip in it, and then leaves it to work on its own. Those who hold this kind of view are *deists*. They do not accept that God reveals himself to humanity in any way at all. But even here, deists might be accused of accepting some supernat-uralism of a first cause that is beyond the naturalism of the universe and, since science is showing that the origins of our universe are more explicable in natural than supernatural terms, deism is thus some-what outmoded. Nevertheless, Humanists are not incapable of experiencing the mysterious interconnectedness of the universe; they are not mortals incapable of appreciation of the profound "depth" of life, to use Paul Tillich's term for those finer moments of experience,[13] but they would not accept any connection of such experience with theistic divinity.

Theism at its most dualistically intimate – and its most philo-sophically and theologically problematic – occurs where divinity is incarnate. This is evident in the Christian acceptance of the Trinity, where one God is at the same time incarnate on earth and manifest in heaven, and also is the Holy Spirit, a kind of emanating, immanent force in the world. Hinduism has much the same idea with its concept of *avatars*, the "descents" of the deity Visnu. However, whereas Hinduism with its more cosmic perspective would not exclude the possibility of incarnations in other parts of the cosmos, those Christians that accept the Trinity – and not all do – regard the partic-ular incarnation of Jesus as unique. Thus we have a God who is pertinent to a particular group of people on a particular planet who incarnates for just a few decades in the history of humanity but who, it seems, does not incarnate elsewhere. Theism is at its weakest where incarnation theories are accepted. And one particular problem of resultant Trinitarian ideas is the unequal status and nature of its three divine aspects: God is considerably demoted! Thus, while the exis-

tence and nature of God may be debated philosophically and theologically, the emphasis of Christianity is far from *theo*logical, but is
overtly *Christ*ological. The Christian centres not on God but on Jesus
whom he or she regards as the Christ. How far this Christocentric
emphasis is evident is easily portrayed. Why, for example, am I able
to say to an acquaintance "For God's sake, close the door", without
too much offence (other than the bluntness of the request), but if I
happened to say "For Christ's sake shut the door", the statement
becomes offensive! This is surely a one-sided Trinity!

Trinitarian views, or, more pertinently, the Christocentric and not
theocentric emphasis of Christianity, are what differentiate it theologically from Judaism. While sharing the beliefs of the *Old Testament*
section of the Bible with both the Jews and the Muslims, the *New
Testament* provides the more important Christocentric emphasis for
Christians, just as the *Qur'an* supplies a different emphasis for
Muslims. All three are held as independent monotheistic faiths, but
Christianity, once it divides divinity (especially unequally) must
logically be accepted as polytheistic. After all, the Hindus, whom
westerners persistently consider to be polytheists, have a concept of
one ultimate reality that they call Brahman, and Brahman becomes
manifest in not three, but a multiplicity of forms, and whether three
or three thousand and three, the principle is the same.[14] There is not
the space here to trace the development of the Trinity (for developed
it was), the weaknesses of the concept or its western and eastern
Orthodox differences. Suffice it to say that it is not a doctrine held
with the same force today as hitherto, and while some trained,
Protestant clergy may refrain from passing their doubts to their
congregations, many have rejected its tenets. Roman Catholicism and
Eastern Orthodoxy both retain it as a fundamental, though differently articulated, doctrine. And while both Judaism and Islam reject
the concept of the Christian Trinity, the three religions have very
different conceptions of what, theoretically, is supposed to be the
same God.

It is against theism, then, that secular Humanism is outspoken.
The idea of an omnipotent, omniscient, omnipresent and
omnibenevolent *Being* who bestows his grace on humanity, or punishes its sins, are expressions of basic theism that have no basis in
rational thought. But secular Humanists go beyond rejection of theism to the rejection of any supernatural forces outside natural
existence. There is no God, no heaven, no hell, no life beyond death,
no angels, no miracles. Human happiness is the result of what indi-

viduals do, or have done to them, *in life*, it cannot be the result of the "grace" of some being that intervenes in the life of individuals. Indeed, Marvin Zimmerman appropriately points out that: "There is more than enough wretchedness in the world to justify overwhelmingly the tenet that if there were a deity, he would be either a devil or insane."[15] The destiny of each human being belongs in his or her present existence, not in some paradisal, supernatural afterlife. Western theism has conditioned people into belief in a God that is so often accepted without rational thought. Secular Humanism requests that the individual challenges his or her own beliefs with rational inquiry as to their validity.

The Bible

The source of knowledge for the Judeo-Christian God is the Bible, still the world's bestseller, and a book that has had a remarkable impact on individual and societal life. Modern scholarship has demonstrated well the complexities of its compilation, much of the *Old Testament* being the result of basic sources and traditions emerging from different religious circles, and being blended together by redactors, editors who tried (but failed) to formulate a coherent account. The *New Testament*, too, is the result of a variety of sources that attempt to portray events that needed to be written down for the growing new community of Christians. Those books that are included in the Bible are those selected from many texts, though with as much integrity as possible, and reflect the prevailing religious temperament and needs of the time of the Early Church. But no serious scholar of the biblical material could accept its material on face value, the anomalies of its text in terms of style, content, history and theological teaching being too consistently obvious for anyone but the staunchest fundamentalist to claim that its words are absolutely true. One thing is clear, and that is that the biblical material is profoundly *theistic*. While many philosophers and some theologians may want to de-anthropomorphize the Christian God, they would have to fly in the face of the biblical material to do so. The biblical God is distinctly male, intervenes in history, such as at the exodus of the Hebrews from Egypt, and has dialogue with kings, priests, prophets and ordinary mortals. Supernatural events abound, and in the *New Testament*, we have a gradual shift to the utmost supernatural anthropomorphism in the alleged incarnation of God.

Given that it is illogical to regard the biblical text as absolutely and literally true, is there anything that can be salvaged? Most would say a good deal. Apart from technical reasons, such as the fact that it provides us with our main source of classical Hebrew, and a good deal of history, some particularly good story, and some wonderful poetry, it also has, in parts, some sound advice and much deeply reflective material. But it is not the only book of this kind. Nothing can beat stories like the Hindu *Ramayana* or *Mahabharata* for exciting narrative interspersed with some sound guidance for life, or the terse but profound Chinese *Tao Te Ching* for poetic imagery and soothing simplicity. Each culture has such literature to offer, but it is literature that has to be seen in the perspective of the time in which it was written. We glean something from all the books we read, but there is something about the term "Bible" that causes it to be read with the suspension of reason, and that is not good.

Much emphasis today has been placed on the *symbolic* truth of the Bible, but this doesn't say much for the God whom Christians believe inspired it, for symbolism is variable, hence Roman Catholicism's insistence that only the Roman Church should be its interpreter. But since within Christianity there are so many different denominations and sects, interpretation of the symbolic truths of the Bible are very different indeed. And where does the symbolism end? Carl Lofmark made the very pertinent point that: "If the literal sense is wrong and modern theologians are right, then it has taken Christians an inordinately long time to find out what their own holy book really meant."[16] Claims of symbolic truth are thus fraught with difficulties. So can we say that the Bible is *partly* true? The obvious problem here, however, is that if it is partly true then it is also partly false, and how do we determine which is which? And why would God, who is supposed to have inspired the Bible, deliberately have distorted the truth in such a way?

The combined acceptance of symbolism and part truth allows each Christian, as well as the theologian, to pick and choose his or her way through the biblical text. A classic example of this, is in *Genesis* 1, where we have the creation of world. The "firmament" of verse six is a solid dome, a *rāqiya'*, separating heaven from earth, on which, in verse fourteen, the stars, the sun and the moon as "light", are stuck. No one in their right mind would accept such an idea in today's world, but when – and scarcely later in the same creation account – in verses 26–27, God makes humankind *in his own image*, this bit of useful theology remains essential teaching to the present day, despite the limitations it would place on God and the naivety of the statement! But if symbolism and truth are problematic, so is the moral truth that has merit in some places and is shocking in others. Clearly, if God inspired all the Bible, then his knowledge of physics left much to be desired, his authorship and inspiration were unclear, and he permitted, and did, some pretty terrible things.

It is the idea that we should not subject the biblical material to any kind of rational query that might *devalue* it that is at issue here. For as soon as the Bible is found to be in error in any area, shifts in interpretative emphasis occur in order to recreate its value, and so we find it "demythologized", or its symbolism or underlying truths are stressed: incorrect content is rarely entirely eschewed. Thus, as a book about God, the Bible does not favour rational inquiry and the search for knowledge. Rather, total faith in God is still expected, regardless of the anomalies in the concept of him in the biblical text. So poor old Eve does the wrong thing in stretching out her hand for knowledge (*Genesis* 3), and the teachings of Jesus are deliberately concealed from the wise and to those outside the circle of Jesus' disciples (*Matthew* 11:25 and *Mark* 4:11–12. Indeed, the "wisdom of the wise" is to be destroyed, and the "cleverness of the clever" thwarted (*1 Corinthians* 1:19). But it is impossible for human nature to turn away from knowledge. Most Christians today, though not all, accept the evolutionary development of the world rather than the biblical account of creation in six days. Yet, in an attempt to rescue biblical accounts of creation and reconcile the theological and scientific perspectives, theological "truths" are searched for in the narrative. Others like to claim that the Hebrew word for "day", *yom*, in the creation narrative of *Genesis* 1, can indicate a long period of time – enough to bring the biblical creation account in line with evolutionary theory. But this is simply wrong, for *yom* can only indicate a lifetime, or harvest time, or a long time span within one's life. Thousands of years are not encompassed in its meaning, let alone the whole evolutionary scale.[17] In any case, the biblical text makes it clear that a specific day is meant by the use of the motif: "And there was evening and there was morning, one day".[18] An evolutionary creation was beyond ancient linear thought, and cannot be supported by the biblical text in any way. Our knowledge here, as in many cases, has far outstripped biblical myth.

Christian theologians, and others, who make serious study of the biblical text, are well aware of its many anomalies, but it often takes an atheist or an objective analyst to see what the eye accustomed to the biblical text cannot. The anomalies in the biblical text are widely cited, but Carl Lofmark has presented a very humorous account of many of these anomalies and the reader is directed to his work on the nature and composition of the Bible.[19] He cites the description of a hare as an animal that chews the cud (*Leviticus* 11:6) and the class of four-footed birds and four-footed beetles! (*Leviticus* 11:20–23). Amusingly, he writes:

> It is somewhat startling to read that God himself was unable to drive off an enemy tribe "because they had chariots of iron" (Judges 1,19), or that the people of Edom rebelled (2 Kings 8,22) after Joab had killed every male of their race (1 Kings 11,16). Similarly, every male of the Midianites is slain and every female is captured (Numbers 31,7–18), yet the Midianites later manage to defeat the children of Israel (Judges 6,1–5). The Amalekites are "utterly destroyed" by Saul (1 Samuel 15,7–20), but they rise against David, who defeats them and "left neither man nor woman alive" (1 Samuel 27,9) after which they attack him again (1 Samuel 30,1–17).[20]

Then, again, Solomon makes a circular bowl for the temple with a diameter of ten cubits and a circumference of thirty cubits (*1 Kings* 7:23 and *2 Chronicles* 4:2), from which, points out Lofmark "it follows that $pi = 3$"![21] And if maths were a problem for the *Old Testament* mind, physics was also, for God created the sun three days after light! Biblical scholars have long regarded there to be two accounts of creation in the first two chapters of *Genesis*. Differences in style, in the use of the divine name, in the order of creation, and in the creation of the plurality of humanity in the first account and a single male in the second, typify well the inclusion of different traditions of belief about the origins of the world and of human beings in particular. Why the Adam and Eve account, the second of the two in *Genesis* 2:4b-24,[22] has always been the more popularly accepted one, is difficult to say, but probably Sunday schools have a lot to answer for in finding this account easier to transmit to young minds than the more transcendent ideas of *Genesis* 1–2:4a.

The anomalies found in the *New Testament* are well-documented by biblical scholars themselves as much as by those who are critical of theistic belief, and I do not propose to list the textual problems here. The classic example of a highly significant anomaly is the impregnation of Mary by the Holy Spirit, a factor that should give Jesus lineage only through his mother and not his father. But, as everyone knows from the singing of Christmas carols, Jesus came from the house of David, the lineage of the ancient King, David, a royal lineage, and this, which Matthew (1:1–17) and Luke (3:23–28) clearly tell us, is the lineage of Joseph and not Mary.[23] As another example, of an impossibility of physics, and a misguided (literally) supernaturalism, Lofmark provides us with the following, equally humorous, account:

> After the birth of Jesus wise men from the east come to bring him gifts. They follow a star. The star leads them to Jerusalem, which is the wrong place. There King Herod's priests and scribes tell them the child is to be born at Bethlehem. The star now leads them again, this time from Jerusalem to Bethlehem, where it comes to stop (Matthew 2, 2–9). To accept this we have to believe that a star was observed to move first westwards to Jerusalem, then another six miles in a south-westerly direction, at the speed of a camel, in broad daylight, until it finally came to rest over a particular stable.[24]

One difficulty that is paramount for the Christian theist is the urgency with which the gospel message was given, an urgency that was promoted by the expectancy of the arrival of a long-awaited *Kingdom of God*. This was a time when the normal order (in particular, Roman rule) would be overthrown and God's divine Kingdom and rule ushered in. It is impossible to read the *New Testament* without gaining the impression that this is what it is mainly about. But the Kingdom of God never came! Jesus was clearly wrong here. However much biblicists might want to argue that the Kingdom of God had arrived with Jesus (*realized* eschatology), or was to come in the future (*futurist* eschatology) or that it had come with Jesus but would come to fruition in the future (*inaugurated* eschatology), it clearly hasn't come yet! Equally clearly, according to the Markan account, Jesus expected the coming of the Kingdom of God in his own lifetime (*Mark* 9:1; cf. 1:15, 13:30; *Luke* 9:27, 21:32; *Matthew* 10:7, 10:23; 16:28, 23:36). Indeed, without this central teaching of Jesus, it is difficult to see that there could be a gospel.

But apart from the anomalies of the Bible there are some extremely horrific and sometimes obscene aspects of it. The genocide demanded of the early Hebrews by God in the more violent sides to the conquest of Canaan, and in which *innocent* old and young, pregnant women, babes and children are recounted as having been slaughtered without any mercy, is appalling.[25] I think it must be granted that these are ancient war tales portraying the conquest of a country that was sometimes peaceably managed and at other times violently perpetrated. But episodes such as these have no place in the context of a book that is supposed to be inspired by a benevolent God.

The picture portrayed of God here is one of vengeance, one according to *Leviticus* (26:14–39) that causes massive poverty, devastation, plagues, population decimation, cannibalism, that will cause people to eat their own offspring (*Deuteronomy* 28:53) – all because people "walk contrary" to God. There are many Christians who gloss over these dreadful passages of the *Old Testament* while some face them head on. But most would claim that it is the *New Testament* concept of God, revealed through the medium of Jesus, that is the more meaningful one to the Christian, and that the old warlike God of the earlier biblical books is a misguided ancient conception of what God is. This of course, is to state rather plainly that any nasty bits of the *Old Testament* are simply not true, while any good bits are! And yet, what we have in the *New Testament* is the sacrificial crucifixion of a being – whether human or divine – at the will of God (*Acts* 2:23), and eternal hell as the fate of the majority of human beings.

And what of miracles? If we really want to eschew all rational thought, acceptance of biblical miracles as true, certainly requires the suspension of common sense. Most scriptures contain miraculous events; they are associated with the hagiographic portrayal of the founders of religion and normally seek to illustrate the special nature of that founder or person. If the virgin birth of Christianity is difficult to swallow, the Buddha was born out of his mother's side! Common sense tells us that certain things are impossible, and just as we are likely to raise our eyebrows in disbelief that one of the heroes of the Hindu epic the *Ramayana* had a body like a monkey, and could expand himself large enough to leap from the southern tip of India to the island of Lanka (*sic*), just so, we should be equally justified in regarding Jonah's survival in the belly of a whale to be something of a tall story. There must have been many miracles in ancient times because there were so many inexplicable events that people had no natural knowledge to explain. Is this why miracles are fewer today, because there is less to assign to the supernatural when there are more readily available the possibilities of rational explanation?

Those who are not prepared to accept the partial historic truths of the Bible or to reject its anomalies and illogicalities are far fewer in today's world. But the Roman Catholic faith demands of its adherents the acceptance of the phenomenon of miracles in both their historic and modern contexts, the virgin birth of Mary, the mother of Jesus being essential teaching. Outside the Roman Catholic faith there is more fluidity and license in belief. But there are still those who adopt a fundamentalist view of the Bible, taking its contents literally or semi-literally, and there are those who, conditioned by the more rigid type of Religious Education of the past, still retain outmoded beliefs.

What is true of the Bible, the sacred writings of the Judeo-Christian tradition, is true also of other cultures. The *Qur'an* is a good example. It teaches nothing exceptional in its ethics; indeed, Islam was extremely eclectic in its scriptural foundation, mixing pre-Arab, Christian and Jewish cultures, and the *Qur'an* even includes words foreign to Arabic. There are contradictions, inconsistencies and problems with the text of the *Qur'an* as there are with the Bible. But because *reciting* the *Qur'an* is so important, *examining* it is less so. Contradictions in the *Qur'an* are explained by the need God felt to abrogate a command by a later revised one (even though some revisions are earlier than the abrogated commands!). Why would an omnipotent God need to revise his words – words putatively reproduced from those in heaven?[26]

God

There are two fundamental ways of viewing the concept of God: either God is so all-encompassing and absolute in the sense of lacking nothing, that conceptions of him can be multiple, or he is so absolute that nothing at all can be said of him. The former view necessitates the acceptance that all views of God have some validity but none can be absolutely right. The latter excludes any ordinary reality or definition (including the third person masculine singular and even the term "God") so, in this case, nothing said of God can be true either. The most popular conceptions of God are multiple ones: few Christians have identical perceptions of God even where they belong to the same denomination or sect, and the variation in the human psyche rarely allows for identical perceptions of the mundane, let alone for the metaphysical. If all believed in an "IT" about which nothing could be said, history would have been entirely different. But the fact that it is *theistic* perceptions of the divine that have informed western religion in particular, has had a massive impact on the development of human beings as individuals and societal creatures. Peter Kreeft did not exaggerate when he wrote:

> The idea of God has guided or deluded more lives, changed more history, inspired more music and poetry and philosophy than anything else, real or imagined. It has made more of a difference to

human life on this planet, both individually and collectively, than anything else ever has.[27]

To accomplish thus, it would have to be admitted that whatever God is, whatever he is not, and whether he is at all, is radically different to different people. And whether one or a plurality of divine beings are evident, divinity is that posited to make sense of the things in life that the human cannot, so there have been a great variety of divine beings and other attendant, supernatural forces throughout the long journey of humankind's existence on this planet. Supernatural forces have been worshipped and propitiated for everything from their creation of the cosmos to the control of the weather, divinity acquiring greater sophistication as human progress and knowledge expanded. The early God of the *Old Testament* is one that some might want to describe as a "despotic and capricious sadist", a God who is "brutal, partial and murderous", who is "passionately partisan" and "has little compassion for anyone but his own favourites".[28] However, God does not change his people as much as people change their concept of God as they begin to develop and expand their own individual and social minds.

Theistic belief is fluid and varied. It posits something supernatural that is beyond the natural world and outside natural laws, capable of powers that are outside the normal cause and effect processes of our physical world, and something able to be approached by human beings to exercise those supernatural powers in favour of the human world. It is a very naïve concept, and a contradictory one, for it accepts a supernatural divinity outside natural law on the one hand, but within natural law for the purpose of personal approach to, and expectation of. The interaction of God with humanity is the hallmark of the Christian Bible, and anyone who reads it through from beginning to end, as they would any other book, cannot refrain from the impression that this God, although depicted in very transcendent terms in so many passages is, nevertheless, a God who is believed to intervene in the natural world. The *overall* picture is not of a remote God, but a theistic God, a *personal* deity of a people. One has to go outside Christianity to find the truly inexpressible concepts of deity (if, indeed, the term deity can be used at all), to the Brahman of Hinduism, the *Dharmakaya* of Buddhism or the Tao of Taoism, for example. In fact, concepts of God range from the *totally* inexpressible, non-conceptions, to the most highly anthropomorphic theism. The Judeo-Christian conceptions of God lie somewhere between these two extremes, with the Christian concept of the incarnation of God being highly anthropomorphic.

To suggest that divinity is unknowable, beyond the conception of the human mind, is to say that God is beyond all phenomena, ideas, designations, differentiation and dualities by which we make sense of the world around us. Hindus have a term for this as *neti neti*, "not this, not this", and the Chinese *Tao Te Ching* states: "The Tao that can be expressed is not the eternal Tao." In other words, the moment you ascribe anything to divinity, you have limited it. All that can be said of it, in those religions that accept such a totally transcendent Absolute, is that it is in some way evident as the subtle essence of all things. It may even be the *absence* of essence in all things, the *sunyata* or "emptiness" of Buddhism. The only way in which anyone could "know" of such is to experience "sameness" with it, when there is loss of the phenomenality of the world for a few moments, in deepest sleep, or in experience of the emptiness of all things. Many people have some kind of "feeling" that if there is a God it must be of this kind of non-thing, something bordering on deistic ideas that informs the universe in some way, but does not interfere in its processes. It cannot be verified, may not be impossible, but leaves the question agnostically open. Of course the criticism often made of such nega-tive theology is that there is really little to differentiate between *no-thing* and nothing at all.

Western religion has rarely ventured down such non-definition of divinity, for its biblical basis grounds it in theism. God *is* predicatable and knowable according to the Christian theist. Sometimes the theist wants to have it both ways, claiming that God is unknowable and yet making a multitude of statements about him, always assuming that he exists, that he is omniscient, omnipotent, infinitely good, and so on. And even by using the term "God", there is the limitation of male-ness.[29] Theistic unknowability is a contradiction; the theist cannot have a personal God that is unknowable. And even where God is given non-anthropomorphic attributes such as omnipresence, there is still a defining of God here, a *thinking* about God in concrete terms, and an *acting* out of life according to such belief. Any definition of divinity restricts it, and theistic conceptions of the divine, therefore, invalidate divinity. Christians might respond by saying that they know *something* about God but that he(!) is *ultimately* unknowable; again, this is giving God extensive predicates but trying to maintain his incomprehensibility; it is having it both ways.

At the other end of the scale from the totally transcendent

Absolute that cannot in any way be described, is the anthropomorphism that is so characteristic of most religion. And while philosophers may debate about the nature or existence of God, the average conception of God is theistically anthropomorphic. Even the term "God", with its inherent maleness, is an anthropomorphic term. Christian theism has to be highly anthropomorphic because it has a belief in an incarnating God. This makes God knowable, so the theist believes, in a radically anthropomorphic and personal way. Indeed, theism at its most expressive emerges when the divine is believed to have come to earth, as in the whole Christology of the Christian belief in Christ or in Hindu *bhakti* with the *avatar* Krsna. But anthropomorphism is theism at its weakest, which is why strict western philosophical theism has a tendency to avoid it. Consider the following statement made by the theist and philosopher J. P. Moreland in his eloquent debate against atheism with Kai Nielsen:

> As a university student in 1968, I met Jesus Christ personally and He changed my life. I have had close to two decades of walking with Him and fellowshiping with Him and falling more and more in love with Him daily. He has given me a power for life that I did not know before, and I have had personal experiences of Him.[30]

Whatever the arguments for or against the existence of God, these words of Moreland clearly demonstrate how the Christian theist translates any concept of the divine into the anthropomorphic. Now I know that Moreland is speaking metaphorically, but all the same, the language of the theist is the language of anthropomorphism. It is also a language that many find distasteful, and I can see that many would agree with Anthony Flew in finding such words "absolutely grotesque".[31]

But my point here is that, although theists might want to see God as inscrutable and incomprehensible, they readily limit the concept of divinity by outright anthropomorphism that defies all logic. And even predicates of love, mercy, goodness, grace, justice and the like are anthropomorphic attributes of divinity even if they are prefaced with the words "infinite" or "divine" to make them more extraordinary. These are humanly originating terms launched into anthropomorphic supernaturalism. Actually, there is a tendency to slot God neatly into the inscrutable, and Christ into the anthropomorphic, enhancing the theocentric and christocentric divide, with the distinct emphasis on the latter. Perhaps this is what took place in Moreland's defence of Christian theism when he allowed a discussion of belief in God to lapse into the personal, anthropomorphic and distinctly christocentric.

From what I have said so far, it should be clear that the term "God" has either no meaning at all or a multiplicity of meanings. In either case it is a nebulous concept. It is a concept fraught with anomalies, particularly once it is defined in theism. To claim *rational* belief in God in the light of such anomalies is impossible and, many would claim, it is downright *irrational* to accept on faith something for which evidence cannot be assembled. God is made in the image of man (*sic*) and is physically culture bound. It is surprising how many western adults are shocked to think that Jesus was a Jew. He was also dark-skinned, and probably not very tall. Yet western conceptions of him are pictorially and psychologically of an Aryanized tall, blonde, blue-eyed, aquiline-nosed, handsome man. He probably had none of these characteristics, but such is the power of anthropomorphism: people give shape to divinity to suit their psyches. The concept of deity is moulded only by present knowledge; God can never really outstrip his worshippers' conceptions of him. So as humanity develops, its metaphysical conceptions of the divine develop also, mirroring the progress it makes in conceptual thought. But God is never too far ahead of what theism can make him.

Some religions such as Hinduism have always held a more cosmic view of reality and posited a non-conceptualized *Brahman* that is either monistically identifiable with the totality of existence or, is pantheistically identified with it but somehow transcends it. Western religious conceptions have been much less cosmically orien-tated, and the result is a theistic God who is somewhat tied to an exclusive number of people on a tiny planet, in one among billions of galaxies. What possible purpose can this vast cosmos serve if there is just one real God for a fraction of humanity on this tiny planet? This, surely would be a remarkably limited concept of God – so limited that the word "God" would be conceptually diminished to the level of a managerial chairman of a localized human group. And even though scientists are suggesting that for life to emerge anywhere in the cosmos an exceptional "fine-tuning" is necessitated – a "fine-tuning" that is so unimaginably fine as to be virtually impossible – one wonders why billions of galaxies are necessary, if only one tiny planet in one minor galaxy has life on it. What was God about in such creative vastness if he only created life on one minuscule planet when there was brilliant scope for a myriad of different life forms else-where? And if the odds against life occurring elsewhere in the universe are practically nil, why did God make such a mess of the only creation in cosmic existence? He could have done better!

God is sometimes referred to as a "God of the gaps". That is to say, as human knowledge progresses and natural explanations are possible for aspects of existence that were once inexplicable and supernaturally explained, so the role of God diminished or changed radically. Theists have always run a great risk in assigning to God those aspects that are inexplicable to modern science: as Smith pointedly notes, "gaps of knowledge eventually close, leaving god without a home".[32] In making too many statements about God theists find their conceptions of God subject to what is called *Occam's razor*. William Occam was a fourteenth-century English philosopher who is credited with articulating the principle that in any explanation of something the fewest possible assertions should be made. The more assertions you make the greater the possibility of their subsequent error. This is the case with theistic statements about God; many assertions about God have been made to fill gaps in our knowledge, but the gaps are continually being eradicated, including the assertion of the existence of God himself.

Theodicy

Put simply, theodicy (Greek *theos* "God", and *dike* "justice") is the problem of the existence of evil and suffering in a world said by Christians to be created by a good and loving God, as well as responses to that problem. It is a problem that has defied solution in the Christian faith, for all responses to it remain, at best, tenuous and fragile in argumentation. The poet Browning pertinently asked:

> Wherefore should any evil hap to man –
> From ache of flesh to agony of soul –
> Since God's All-mercy mates All-potency?

This neatly poses the question with which theodicy is concerned. If God is omniscient then he must know of the evil in the world. If he is infinitely good then he must want to do something about it, and if he is omnipotent, then he is *able* to do something about it. But (and let us have in the front of our minds the real and graphic pictures of the atrocities of the twentieth-century Holocaust when the following point is raised), evil exists, and God, apparently, does nothing about even the very worst of evils. If he doesn't prevent them although he could, then he cannot be all good. But if he cannot prevent them, then he cannot be omnipotent. Either way we end up with a limited God. If his goodness is jeopardized then we would have to say that a God not all good is partly evil – and who would want to devote himself or herself to such a God? Or, we have a God who is limited in power, who cannot intervene in existence to prevent evil. Clearly, "there is little doubt that the problem of evil is *the* most serious intellectual difficulty for theism".[33]

In Christianity, evil and suffering are not considered to be part of the original created order. They are believed to have been introduced into God's perfect world when the first human beings sinned against God. The story of Adam and Eve's transgression in disobeying God by eating the forbidden fruit is taken in Christianity to indicate the reason for all the suffering in the world. As a result of this original sin, pain, toil, drudgery and death are introduced. Even those many Christians who regard the story of Adam and Eve as mythological often claim, and believe in, an underlying theological teaching here that suffering is the result of sin or evil, and that both originate with humankind, not God. The narrative of *Genesis* suggests that the first people, having failed a divinely appointed test, bring into the previous harmony of creation the first sin, the first evil.

Stated thus simply the doctrine of sin and evil seems clear, but beneath its surface there are grave anomalies. How could these human beings sin if they were created as perfect beings? Does the idea of perfection exclude the propensity for evil, or could they still be perfect with it? Did God create the *potential* for sin and evil? Christianity seeks to absolve God from sin and evil by placing the responsibility for it squarely on the shoulders of humanity. But this will not do, because if God is not responsible for evil in creation, from whence does it come? Did it arise *ex nihilo*, "out of nothing", in which case God's power is limited and not absolute? And is it possible for evil to arise *ex nihilo* in a *perfect* world? But if God is the creator of evil, is he really good? And why would he create creatures with a potential for evil that, given his omnipotence, he must have known would at some point be realized?

Even if he gives them free choice (which in fact he doesn't do at all in the narrative of *Genesis*) whether they sin or not, he must have created the potential for sin. And what of the evil serpent? At least his evil pre-dates that of the first humans. Was the serpent a fallen angel as later medieval views supposed? But if he were, then we would have to raise the same questions about pre-creation – evil must have come about *ex nihilo* in the divine world of God and angels.

The theologian and philosopher John Hick, for one, makes the point that no educated person today would accept the myth of the "fall"[34] but does not for one moment suggest that the narratives have no underlying theological truths and purpose. He sees the creation and "fall" narratives as symbolic of the separation between God and humanity and turns the whole biblical soteriology around so that we are evolving *towards* the perfection of paradise, rather than having begun with it. This is a very liberal theology which leaves us in an even worse position, for by it God would deliberately create a pretty rough world and an interminable amount of evil and suffering through which humanity has to evolve before it reaches the goal of perfect unity with its maker. This cannot be a good God that puts humanity through misery as part of what Hick calls a "soul-making" process, and there is something inherently sinister and sadistic about "an existential involvement in the long, slow, difficult, painful process of 'soul-making'", suggested by Hick.[35] And if the sufferings of the Holocaust victims, the children of Dunblane or recurring famines are part of the divine plan for such "soul-making", then God is thoroughly evil. It is equally evil and trite to claim "Ah, but the rewards are in heaven" as Hick does in the following:

> As regards the millions of men, women, and children who perished in the extermination programme, it gives the assurance that God's good purpose for each individual has not been defeated by the efforts of wicked men. In the realms beyond our world they are alive and will have their place in the final fulfilment of God's creation.[36]

The subject of this incredible statement is the "Christian awareness of the universal divine purpose and activity". It is a purpose that cannot rationally be accepted; no one in their right mind would suggest that means justify an end. There are levels of suffering that are too deeply scarring to credit reward in a remote Kingdom of God. The solution of other theists is equally difficult to swallow. John Roth can write: "If God raised Jesus from the dead, he had the might to thwart the Holocaust long before it ended." His putative solution is a "theology of protest", yes, you can protest that God doesn't *do* anything about evil, but you must still believe in him![37]

From a different point of view, if God exists then he must be responsible for evil, otherwise his status as "God" is compromised. We know that moral evil is the result of human machinations – war, rape, murder, torture, ethnic cleansing and genocide, to cite some of the worst examples, are humanity's crimes and no one else's. But what of natural disasters? These predate the advent of *Homo Sapiens* – the meteor that wiped out the dinosaurs (which, by the way, are known to have suffered from arthritis); the climactic changes; storms; earthquakes. Did God build such evils into the planet? And what of the suffering that evil creates, particularly innocent suffering? Christians often explain it as a means of bringing human beings back to God, of helping them to repent of their sins, even though the best of biblical individuals like Job and the prophet Jeremiah, had little to repent of. Again, there are certainly depths of suffering that go well beyond the rationalism of a corrective principle. Any theodicy that bypasses human suffering is no answer to the problem. Smart makes the point that it is not impressive for theists to claim that the presence of evil serves to highlight what is good, for the reality of suffering negates this, as does the premise that evil is finite and good infinite.[38] Neither eliminates God as the means of innocent and sometimes unbearable suffering. And if God truly has omnipotence, why should he need such appalling means as part of his divine purpose?

We return then to the statement that either God has no power to do anything about the evils that exist in the world and never has had the power to do anything about them or, he doesn't wish to do anything about them. Neither way, can this "God" still retain the status of a deity. Of what use is a deity without power? And of what use is a deity that is guilty of evil by default? And if all the answers are to be found in an afterlife, then, as Smith justifiably points out "the claim that God is all-good has no relevance whatsoever to our present life".[39] There is, of course, a good deal of suffering and evil that is obviously caused by humanity, but humanity did not create a world in which one animal preys and feeds on another, or parts of the world prone to natural disasters. Margaret Knight once asked "Can the cancer cell, the tubercle bacillus, the tapeworm . . . be conceivably ascribed to man's misuse of freewill?"[40] We might well be able to say in today's modern, scientific world that carcinogenic matter exists through the machinations of human beings as a result of their interference in the natural processes of nature. But, all the same, if this is an evil that humanity brings into being, why cannot God prevent it, or why does he limit his creative activity in favour of human creativity? Or did he create the cancerous potentials in the first place? God cannot win in theism. In the face of the suffering and evils that have befallen his people the Psalmist poignantly says:

Rouse thyself! Why sleepest thou, O lord?
Awake! Do not cast us off forever!
Why dost thou hide thy face?[41]

Clearly, God was as much absent in the face of suffering in the days of the Psalmist as he is today. And he cannot "awaken" if he is not there!

The biblical text is of some help in this difficult theodicy debate. But it is not in favour of any limitation of the omnipotence of God, and attests widely to God's instigation of evil. The *Old Testament* abounds with massacres of the enemies of the Hebrews as a result of the divine command. Communities are destroyed with plague or famine and sometimes wiped out entirely. The God of the *New Testament* – supposedly a more evolved one – demands the sacrifice of his son, and punishes non-believers in eternal hell. Indeed, the Bible abounds with evidence to suggest that evil occurs through the power of God.[42] God must, then, be the perpetrator of evil and therefore cannot be wholly good, particularly since, as we all know, it is not always the wicked but also the innocent who are at the mercy of evil. If God is *perfect* and *infinitely* good, then we should not find a scrap of evidence to the contrary, but since evil exists and God instigates at least some of it, he can hardly be said to be perfectly good.

In the *New Testament* we have that incomprehensible concept of hell, incomprehensible because how a benevolent God could assign the bulk of humanity to everlasting torture defies logic. No sensible person could accept such a doctrine, though it is still widely held in all areas of the Christian Church especially in Roman Catholicism. There is no way in which such a doctrine can logically be accepted even on an allegorical or metaphorical level. It is a doctrine of injustice, cruelty and sadism, and one of the most illogical outcomes of theistic conceptions of divinity. Even if understood metaphorically as separation from God, this still suggests an eternity of psychological despair that is as cruel as physical torture. Unless salvation is universal in the Christian message, its God is not good, not loving, not just and not merciful. And along with the doctrine of hell we have Satan, the arch foe of God and humankind, and the extraneous cause of evil in the world.

Dualistic belief in an evil force on the one hand and a good one on the other, as well as the concomitant beliefs in a rewarding heaven and retributive hell, are a legacy of the ancient Persian religion of Zoroastrianism to both Judaism and Christianity. Jesus inherited this legacy; he did not institute it. In the *Old Testament* there is neither a concept of Satan nor one of hell until the Persian period and the heyday of Zoroastrianism. Indeed, this little-known religion in the present age – shrunk to small communities mainly in Iran and India – has exercised a colossal influence on both Judaism and Christianity. After Cyrus the Great had conquered Babylon in 539 BCE he was hailed as the awaited messiah by the Jews (*Isaiah* 42:1) because he allowed the Jews who had been taken captive to Babylon half a century earlier to return to the city of Jerusalem and rebuild it. Cyrus embraced the religion of Mazdaism, Zoroastrianism. His tolerance to the Jews opened the floodgates for Zoroastrian influence and it is from this time that Mazdaism infiltrates Jewish theology. The idea of a good God and an evil devil was absorbed into the Jewish religion, and a whole body of apocalyptic literature arose as a result. Though Judaism had its own eschatology, concepts of heaven and hell, resurrection of the body, the Kingdom of God, and a last judgement with life everlasting for the righteous, were clearly absorbed from Zoroastrian belief. Beliefs in a messiah, and in angels and demons, also became highly developed as a result. Notably, at the time of Jesus of Nazareth, Zoroastrianism was a powerful religion in the Near East (the so-called wise men at his birth were Persian, Zoroastrian *magi* or priests). In turn, Christianity, too, came to inherit the beliefs of its parent religion. So any vestiges of belief in heaven, hell, Satan, and resurrection (Jesus did not invent resurrection but inherited the concept), along with developed angelology and demonology, have come from outside the Judeo-Christian heritage. Even the concept of a messiah is to be found in Zoroastrianism. Who knows what Christian theists would have believed today, or would have to defend, had Jewish history taken a different turn? And in relation to theodicy, it is highly unlikely that wicked, fallen angels were around at the time of creation; they came late on the Jewish scene.

Free will

The theist's answer to the issue of theodicy is that God has granted individuals freewill, the freedom to choose between right and wrong, between good and evil. But this limits the omnipotence of God unless he actually has some control over the outcomes of such choices (in which case freewill is partial). Some theists suggest that for God to be *truly* good, he would have to give his creatures unlimited freedom "with all the possible implications for the production of evil that this might imply".[43] Such a limitation of omnipotence would be necessary in order for human beings not to be reduced to mere automata, puppets, and their nature as human beings compromised. But this will not do, for two questions are left unanswered. First, why does God allow so much *innocent* suffering as a result of evil? And why does he permit radical, natural evil on a scale such as the Ethiopian famines, and moral evil on such a scale as the extermination of the Holocaust victims? The second question relates to the *degree* of evil. If God created the world and the potential for choice that would involve some wrong and amoral choices as well as good choices, why didn't he place some kind of limitations on the degree of evil that could result? Or, why didn't he create creatures that had an abundance of choice but could only choose to do what is good? Mackie makes this point when he says:

> If there is no logical impossibility in a man's freely choosing the good on one, or several occasions, there cannot be a logical impossibility in his freely choosing the good on every occasion. God was not, then, faced with making a choice between making innocent automata and making beings who, in acting freely, would sometimes go wrong: there was open to him the obviously better possibility of making beings who would act freely but always do right. Clearly, his failure to avail himself of this possibility is inconsistent with his being both omnipotent and wholly good.[44]

The problem here, is the omnipotence of God, which either has to be abandoned in order to allow freewill, or, if any omnipotence is retained, he cannot be all good.

But there are problems, too, with the omniscience of God in relation to freewill. For if there is an *all-knowing* God, then he must know all things past and present, and all things that are *going* to happen in the future. And if this is the case then how can it be said that human beings *really* have freewill? Moreover, if he knows all things that are going to happen in the future, then they must really be predetermined, and this *really* curtails freewill and makes only a pretence of it. It also suggests that if God exists, then he, too, will have no choice about changing the already known future. If he is able to change it then it is not foreknown and he is not omniscient. And at what price is freewill? Anthony Flew pertinently points out that it is a gift that "seems in fact to be being purchased at an unacceptably high price in all manner of most unjustly distributed consequential evils".[45] Couldn't God have done better?

What, then, are we left with? We are left with a God whose omnipotence and omniscience are seriously in question and whose goodness is equally suspect: these are issues arising out of theistic conceptions of divinity. And there are other problems of this concept of God, for once he can be given personality – and the biblical text clearly does this – then there are all kinds of anthropomorphic conceptions of God that are open to question. God is portrayed as a jealous and egoistic God, one who must be worshipped before all others and who created human beings to praise and worship him. And he is culture bound, the God of *a* people, of *a* culture, that becomes elitist and intolerant: few Christian theists could worship God as black, or as blue (like the Hindu Krsna). He is supposed to be a God of love who created human beings out of love, but he also created the cruelty of nature, whereby humans eat animals and animals eat each other. He created carcinogens, viruses, parasites and destructive aspects of nature – disease, plague, earthquakes, floods, famines, volcanic disasters. In this context, Robert Green Ingersoll once wrote:

> What would we think of a father who should give a farm to his chil-
> dren, and before giving them possession should plant upon it
> thousands of deadly shrubs and vines; should stock it with ferocious
> beasts and poisonous reptiles; should take pains to put a few swamps
> in the neighbourhood to breed malaria; should so arrange matters that
> the ground would occasionally open and swallow a few of his darlings;
> and, besides all this, should establish a few volcanoes in the immediate
> vicinity, that might at any moment overwhelm his children with rivers
> of fire? . . . And yet this is exactly what the orthodox God has done.[46]

The theistic God, in fact, is a projection of the human perceptions of balances of good and evil, love and hate, acceptance and intolerance, grace and vengeance, salvation and punishment, freedom and constraint, and so on, into the divine realm. Theists have created a dualistically characterized deity. And because theism has to person-alise God as a creator, then he has to be involved some way in the flaws of the finite world that he has created.

In whichever way we view theistic conceptions of divinity, limitations are placed on the concept of the divine. If there is a God, how can humanity know that which is beyond its own reality? And if God is brought into the realm of the finite world in any way, or is believed to make himself known to human beings in any way, then God is no longer incomprehensible, unlimited and unknowable; he is no longer ultimate divinity. And in what way could that which is postulated as infinite exist in any way in the finite? What is infinite cannot be temporal, otherwise infinity is subject to the transience and change of temporal existence. If there is a level of ultimate reality then it exceeds dualities, is beyond differentiation and mind limitation, and nothing can be said of it. This is antithetical to theism.

Can it be proved that God exists?

In the history of Christianity there have often been philosophical attempts to prove that God exists; the Roman Catholic Church, in particular, has always condemned *fideism* – the idea that God can only be known through faith. Though still evident to some extent, the old "proofs" of the existence of God have been largely discredited by theologians themselves, and many would argue that the existence of God is something that cannot be subjected to logical philosophical argument. Such proofs fall fairly neatly into three categories, *cosmological*, *teleological* and *ontological*. Generally, newer so-called proofs fall into these categories, though there are some that fall outside. In a way, the old proofs still tend to make sense to the average person. Thus, put very simply, many feel that there must have been a First Cause of all things (cosmological), that the world is characterized by such planning that there must have been a supreme Designer (teleological), and that there must be some kind of being that is greater than anything we can imagine, and this is God (ontological). Of course, with the advance of science there is a kind of see-sawing one way and another, particularly in the light of theories about the beginnings of the universe, but science, and particularly evolutionary theories, dispel many old arguments about the existence of God.

Many of the present arguments against the existence of God are concerned with epistemology, the theory of knowledge, with the difficulty of establishing any particular criteria of knowledge that establishes beyond doubt that God exists. Theists often claim, on the other hand, that knowledge of God is self-authenticated knowledge and does not need to go beyond itself for proof. But whatever is claimed of God cannot amount to any verifiable truth. As Nielsen points out: "We have no idea at all what would or even in principle could, establish or disestablish such claims so that we could have some idea whether the persons attempting to assert or deny a claim were probably or even possibly saying something that is true" and, "if we cannot, even in a stammering manner, say *what* it is we are talking about when we speak of God, our conceptions of God are incoherent".[47] Some critics question whether the term "God" has any *linguistic* validity in philosophical debate about God. After all, "God" as the subject of a predicate is not like any other term; it is itself a subject that cannot be proved to exist. So any premise made about God becomes linguistically, and therefore philosophically, invalid. Indeed, it is arguable whether proof of the existence of God is ever philosophically veridical. Another problem here is that, even were it to be proved that there must be a first cause in the universe or that design is evident in all nature, there is no need to make the further metaphysical leap to the existence of *God* as First Cause or Designer.

In all assertions of the existence of God, there cannot be any direct perception. It might thus be said to be the case that God can only be posited through *inference*. Yet inferential knowledge that is valid is so only because of universal concomitance. Thus, if in all cases of the perception of smoke we can infer that there is fire, valid knowledge is inferred through the universal concomitance of smoke and fire. No such universal concomitance is evident, however, in the case of God and his existence. And neither term, "God" nor "existence", are perceptible; whereas in cases of inference, one of the two aspects that are concomitant would need to be.

It seems, then, that the only validity for belief that God exists can be *testimony*, both scriptural and personal. Scriptural testimony is highly contradictory, and personal testimony is highly varied: this latter aspect is one I shall be taking up in chapter 4. Here, in this context, it needs to be pointed out that personal testimony that suggests the existence of God is purely *psychological* and subjective and, like any psychologically subjective experience, is very different in every individual. Since there is no universality of experience, there can really be no evidence that *one* personal God exists as opposed to a plurality of different deities appropriate to different psychological *feelings*. All that we have in the case of theistic personal testimony are many people who believe that their psychological feelings of a certain kind cause them to believe that there is a personal God. How they can possibly interpret such feeling to incorporate attributes and characteristics of the personal God remains a mystery. Belief that God exists is not the same as *perceiving* that God exists. Smart suggests that those who argue for the existence of God from the point of view of religious experience have feelings "as if" there is some kind of God[48] and, in fact, we all have "as if" feelings of one sort or another. As we saw in chapter 2, some heightened experiences may be seen as secular, for others, religious, but for both, it could be claimed, they are "peak", or "spiritual" in the sense that the deeper parts of the self are affected. This is perhaps what Moreland refers to as "numinous perception".[49] All such experiences are different, it is only the self-designated *religious* experiencers that want to assign their experiences to a common factor, call that factor "God", and then claim that God exists. However much an "as if" factor is adopted, and however much the effects of the "as if" beliefs are pragmatic in life itself, those effects cannot really suggest that there is one *real* cause, or that this is God.

Cosmological arguments for the existence of God

Cosmological arguments for the existence of God are based on the premise that every effect must have a cause, but to avoid infinite regress there must be a *first cause*, something that started it all. Put in another and more sophisticated way,[50] everything in existence depends on something else for its existence, but it doesn't have reason for its existence contained within it. So the world itself must depend on something else for its existence, a "something else" that must have existence in itself, otherwise that would also have to be caused by something else *ad infinitum*. This "something else" is the only thing that has reason for existence within itself, something that has *necessary* existence, and cannot *not* exist, unlike everything else in the world. Theists maintain that this is God – a notion, Flew suggests, that contends that "a hierarchy must have a summit".[51]

There are many difficulties with such views. To begin with, the original premise that every effect must have a cause isn't true if there is a first cause. There is also absolutely no reason why, if there *is* a first cause, that it should be God. And if there were a first cause, who is to say that it still exists? Why, too, should there be *a* first cause and not numerous first causes? And why shouldn't more recent *antecedent* causes be the causes as opposed to a remote cause? In any case, once a first cause that is itself uncaused is accepted, then there is no reason why there cannot be other uncaused causes. Moreover, given the immensity of the cosmos and a universe that stretches out through vast, irregular distances, infinity is neither improbable nor impossible, making the idea of a first cause unnecessary in an infinite universe that is self-contained.

Once again, the more theistic the conception of a first cause, the more problematic the concept. Theists like to think of God as the First Cause, one that created the cause - effect principle of the universe. But even though present theories accept the "Big-Bang" origins of our universe, there is no reason to posit "God" as orchestrator of it. In any case, if such a God exists, why would such a "being" wish to create such a world? Was he not perfect enough without it? Did he simply want to be a "creator"? And if he did, what *caused* him to do so? And why should any first cause be animate, conscious and intelligent, as theists suggest? There is no need, in fact, for the universe to have any reason for its existence; the fact that it does exist is sufficient. There is no need, in fact, for a theistic supernaturalism to explain the origins of the universe; there may be no real origins to explain. Existence itself is the "first cause" and all subsequent causality arises in it.

Another angle to such cosmological argument is the idea of the first cause being an "Unmoved Mover", that is to say that which does not change, but which causes the transience and change of all other things. The analogy is often given of an engine that pulls the carriages of a train (or a hand moving a stick), each coach being dependent on the one before for its mobility, while the engine is the ultimate mover. But it is not a good analogy because it demonstrates well that the First Cause or Unmoved Mover has to be part of the natural process to have an effect on it and is not able to affect it if transcendent to it, as when the engine is separated from its coaches. While it is true that there is an element of "sameness" and continuity in an existence that is subject to flux and change – an acorn, for example, grows into an oak tree and not into a sycamore tree – there is no reason why there has to be a changeless prime mover to bring about the continuity amidst flux. Indeed, to do so would necessitate change in the mover, again, like the engine that pulls the train. In any case, sub-atomic physics is beginning to show us that all existence is subject to motion but that it is not all neatly cause–effect natured.

The progression from acorn to oak as an analogy is important in another way. Theists accept that a First Cause is superior to the effects that follow it. But in fact, as far as existence is concerned, it is the case that effects are more frequently superior to their causes; life could hardly evolve were it otherwise. So the tiny acorn becomes the mighty oak. In fact, the more remote the cause, the more unrelated it is to an evolutionary end product. Causality is hierarchized in favour of the effects and not the causes, so these effects do *not* have a summit, but are multiple. And a multiplicity of causes normally inform one specific effect, most of them immediately antecedent. It makes no sense to posit a single, remote cause. It is also improbable that creation occurred strictly *ex nihilo*, it is more likely to have been what Paul Davies summarizes as "the conversion of pre-existing energy into material form".[52]

The arguments to design

Arguments for or to[53] design are based on the belief that a supernatural, conscious and intelligent Designer must exist because the universe exhibits such careful planning, its whole design being beyond the possibilities of chance. It is thus an argument that posits design as that which underpins the universe. The idea stems from ancient Greek philosophical thought, from an Aristotelian belief in an abstract, intelligent force or principle that informed all things but which did not affect them. The thought was taken up by Thomas Aquinas, the thirteenth century, Roman Catholic Dominican monk and theologian, whose theological ideas and proofs for the existence of God, were to become the foundation of Roman Catholic theology in the late nineteenth century.

Arguments for a supernatural and supreme Designer are *teleological* in nature, that is to say, they accord *purposeful* design to the universe. Theists claim that this phenomenon of design is so well ordered and seems so carefully planned, that there must be a supreme Designer of it, and that this Designer must be God. The secular argument accepts that there is *order* in the universe, rather than design, but claims that this is purely the result of a fairly ruthless natural selection process. This is a natural selection that takes place naturalistically, within Nature, and not supernaturally in any way. Most theists also accept this process of natural selection, but claim that it is God that controls genetic mutations according to a divine plan. The main problem with this last view is that the "design" evident in the world is often harmful to existence. Yes, there is beauty in the world and wonder in the growth of a tiny seed to a mighty tree, but what of the fact that this orderly world exists because the strong have survived at the expense of the weak? And what about malignant viruses? Robert Green Ingersoll once pointed out the remarkable degree of design and beauty in the cancer cell:

> By what ingenious methods the blood is poisoned so that the cancer shall have food! By what wonderful contrivances the entire system of man is made to pay tribute to this divine and charming cancer! What

beautiful colours it presents! Seen through the microscope it is a miracle of order and beauty. All the ingenuity of man cannot stop its growth. Think of the amount of thought it must have required to invent a way by which the life of one man might be given to produce one cancer. Is it possible to look upon it and doubt that there is a design in the universe, and that the inventor of this wonderful cancer must be infinitely powerful, ingenious and good?[54]

The obvious question here is why would a supposedly good God design such a heinous illness, beautiful to behold, but deadly in its purpose? It is obvious that any "Designer" does not have to be a righteous or a good one. And how would natural disasters fit into this scheme of design? In teleological arguments for the existence of God everything has a specific purpose in life. But was the nose *really* designed to hold a pair of spectacles on it, as Voltaire suggested? And were rabbits specifically designed with white tails so that they could be shot? "I do not know how rabbits would view that application", said Bertrand Russell of such nonsense.[55] Natural selection means *constant* adaptation through the process of evolution. This means a process of ongoing change, not a once and for all design, and chance variations of cause and effect must occur in such an intricate process of adaptation and survival.

From a philosophical point of view there is little justification in making the metaphysical leap from a degree of order in the world to a Designer, and then to the belief that that Designer is the omnipotent, omniscient theistic God. And since much of life is subject to laws of cause and effect, it stands to reason that there will be much observable order in it, without having to postulate something supernatural. Causality necessitates order in life, but it has nothing to do with "design". The universe *is* orderly. Were it not, it would be impossible to function in it, no life could exist. But order is not synonymous with design, and there is no need to posit a God that creates order.

In the late eighteenth century a clergyman by the name of William Paley likened the world to a watch. Just as the watch must have a Designer and Maker, unlike a stone, so the intricately ordered world also must have a Designer/Maker. And if we compare a watch to the intricacies of the human being, or the intricate functioning of parts of the body like the eye, it seems sensible to suggest that they had a Designer, and that that Designer is God. Again, however, there is no reason why a Designer should be a theistic God. And if God is posited, it would have to be claimed that God would need to design *all* things – those inimical to humanity as much as good for it, and the stone as much as the watch. There is a difference, too, between the *natural* aspects of the eye, and the human being, and the humanly engineered product of the watch: Paley does not compare like with like, and the analogy is not a good one. In any case, watches are rarely designed and made by the same person (and in today's world may have had multiple agents involved). Should there, then, be two or more causes? The major problem here, however, is that designers design and that is that, they do not *maintain* and adapt and support their design, and do not have to outlive it, so if this Designer is God, then he does not, now, need to exist.

More modern forms of the teleological design arguments incorporate recent advances in scientific knowledge about the origins of life on this planet. As noted above, it is now believed that the chances of life arising require such impossible "fine-tuning" that it is remarkable that any life at all exists, and unlikely that any obtains elsewhere in the universe. This has led some to believe that a Designer is not such an impossible idea after all.[56] But then, why the waste of a vast cosmos, when only one planet has life? It would be like owning a mansion and furnishing a square foot! Moreover, if we think about life itself, highly improbable things happen every day. The odds against certain things happening in the course of a day – say, an aeroplane landing on the roof of my home, or on me as I walk my dog, are infinitely remote, and yet we know they *could* happen. The improbabilities of some things occurring in life are considerable, but they *do* happen. Some of the new teleology is inclined to make the leap to a "Fine Tuner", because of a perceived necessity for a cause of a universe that has intelligent life in it – intelligent life that is capable of observation and analysis of the rest of its finely-tuned environment. Such a premise is enhanced by the awe in which modern physics views the extraordinary physical laws – at cosmic and sub-atomic levels – that have brought about, and inform, our universe. Nevertheless, an ultimate "Fine Tuner", "Designer", or "First Cause", always remains an unnecessary extension of logic. But the "fine-tuning" concept is interesting in another dimension because it suggests a certain harmony to life, a certain "interconnectedness" of the cause– effect processes of the universe and an interrelated orderliness to the patterns of the cosmos. And it is possible that the human being is sometimes capable of experiencing a fraction of this natural "interconnectedness" – again, the "peak" experience, the direct experience of what *seems* to be the numinous, of what may *seem* to be supernatural. Nature is an impersonal phenomenon and cannot react to us. But if we are in harmony with its impersonal laws, understanding the cause–effect processes that inform so much of it, then we are likely to benefit. But we do not need to have a "Cause" for such impersonal order.

Generally, then, the arguments for a supreme Designer are not sound, and to extend such arguments as far as a theistic personal, omnipotent and omniscient single God is equally unsound. Even if such a theory could be proved there is no reason why a Designer is anything more than a deistic beginner of creation, setting up a system that is allowed to function independently, subject to its own impersonal laws. In fact, since effects are often more complex than their original causes, and existence seems to reflect adaptation to more intricate ends, it would be quite conceivable that the end products of a Designer are more complex than the Designer itself. And if such a Designer were ongoing, creation couldn't possibly be complete. The Designer would be creating over a ridiculous period of time, with some very cruel means, only to reach a stage now at which life still feeds on life, and the most powerful and useful survive at the expense of the weaker and the obsolete. Human life, so important in the theistic scheme of things, would have come about after an interminably long time, and after many species had evolved and devolved. What a long and risky business! This is a long way from the Creator who created the world instantly by divine fiat in the *Genesis* account. The argument for a Designer would be more appropriately termed the argument for an Experimenter.

The whole issue of an argument to or from design is one that begs the question, for it assumes that there *is* design in the universe. There may well be, as we have seen, *order* in the universe, but no one would claim that order necessarily has to have an *orderer*. The processes of cause–effect can ensure the presence of order for purely natural reasons. But *design*, now that certainly demands an agent of design. The premise of such teleological arguments, therefore, falsely starts with an unproved theory – that there is design in the world – and attempts to move from that premise to a conclusion that there must be a Designer. The premise, however, has never been proved. The question, therefore, is begged – "a most gigantic begging of the question" as Flew terms it.[57]

The ontological argument

The ontological argument is the most philosophical of the arguments for the existence of god. It was formulated by the Christian St Anselm (1033–1109) and taken up by the French philosopher Descartes (1596–1650). Its basic assertion is that God is a being greater than which cannot be conceived, a perfect, complete being that lacks no attributes. This is a being that exists in the mind. But a being that exists in reality, is greater than one that exists in the mind, and since God is a being greater than which cannot be conceived, he must exist in reality, therefore he exists. Further, since we are able to conceive of such a being, and cannot have a conception of a non-existent being, then he must exist: lacking no attributes, he is bound to have the attribute of existence.

Immanuel Kant, the eighteenth century philosopher contested this argument claiming that existence is not sufficient as an attribute to make something concrete. I can think of the existence of a fortune in my bank account, but that doesn't mean to say that it is really there! I can combine the attributes of redness and lion to conceive of a red lion, but that doesn't mean one exists. In saying that a lion *exists*, the word *exists* is not an attribute, for it is *lion* that tells us of the nature of the thing that exists that is a lion. Thus, to say that we can think of a perfect being, *therefore it exists* is fallacious. Additionally, to claim that God is perfect because he is not lacking in attributes is suggestive, not only of positive attributes, but of some pretty negative things one can say about God! The ontological argument is a circular one, assuming the premise that it tries to prove is true, and we simply cannot prove that a being, greater than which we cannot conceive, really exists.

Rejection of an afterlife

If there is no sound reason for the acceptance of the existence of God, then there is equally no sound reason for the acceptance of life after death. For the whole point of belief in God is to provide answers for the problems of existence beyond the grave, to provide answers to the problems of innocent suffering and the reasons why the evil in life remains unpunished. Take away belief in an afterlife, and the case for God would collapse. Secular, atheistic Humanism believes in the monism of the human self, that is to say it does not believe in the concept of dualism of soul and body, or mind and body. When the body dies, there is nothing that remains that can survive. This is a belief that prevents any solution to existential vicissitudes being projected to another life. It asks of each human being the courage to face life's problems in the here and now, the courage to supply necessary answers and remedies. Happiness is of one's own making not in any heaven "above the bright blue sky" (to use the words of an old hymn for children). The theist's belief that only God knows the answer to the problems of innocent suffering and that rewards are in heaven for those who tow the party line are seen as an evasion of facing life itself. Putting one's eggs in an afterlife basket evades solutions in this life.

In 1963 the Bishop of Woolich, Dr John Robinson, published a highly controversial book in that it questioned the theistic dualism that is part and parcel of Christian theology. The book was called *Honest to God*.[58] In 1974 a well-known Humanist writer, Margaret Knight, published a book entitled *Honest to Man*[59] in which she powerfully takes religion to task. Concerning the Christian belief in the afterlife, she particularly criticizes the concept of reward *after* death. Two main issues are involved here. First, you can do as much good as you can, give as much love to your fellow human beings as you can, but you will never benefit from this until you die. This makes death optimistic, but it is wholly pessimistic about life. Second, while Christians are told that they ought to be humble, the idea of personal reward in heaven promotes egoistic self-interest and elitism; the good one does is for one's own rewards. This is seen both individually and collectively. Teilhard de Chardin once commented that: "The essential law of cosmic development is not the egalitarian fusion of all beings, but the segregation that allows a chosen elite to emerge, to mature and to stand alone."[60] He described the Christian as "by right the first and most human of men".[61] This kind of exclusive and elitist thought runs the danger of becoming unconcerned about the "sinners" – in whatever way we would want to translate that word in relation to the lives of those in the twenty-first century.

This world is more important than the next one, for if human beings do not know how to find value in life, then death will be feared. In the more secular world of today, there is perhaps less concern with the rewards that may be reaped in heaven and more hope of a national lottery win or paying off the mortgage. But there are many Christians who maintain the elitist view of reward in heaven – whatever that may be – if the vicissitudes in this life can be faced with equanimity and acceptance. After all, Jesus himself, although concerned for the poor, the sinners and the sick, had a tendency to encourage homelessness and poverty amongst his followers. Even when the *Parousia*, the second coming, failed to materialize, the next world, rather than the present one, remained the more important.

Secular humanists reject this kind of negative view of the present existence, and the concept of life in a wonderful existence beyond the grave in some kind of resurrected and reconstituted physical body. The rejection of dualistic conceptions of the self, and the rejection of a theistic, anthropomorphized deity who rewards and punishes those who worship or reject him respectively, makes belief in an afterlife unnecessary. Secular and atheistic Humanism believes that this life is all that we have, and we should therefore be optimistic about what we wish to do in it and what we are able to do in it. It is a positive view of life, with high expectations for individuals within it. Rewards are not in heaven, they are on earth, and they are both necessary for the individual in his or her own realization of personal goals, and for broader, societal and global benefit. What greater reward can a person have in life, than to know that he or she leaves behind at death some contribution to a better world?

4

The Case against Religion: The Rejection of Faith

We human beings must find our destiny and our promised land in the here and now, or not at all. And Humanism is interested in a future life, not in the sense of some fabulous paradise in the skies, but as the on-going enjoyment of earthly existence by generation after generation.[1]

It might surprise some readers to know that there is a considerable gap between the beliefs held by many Christian priests and ministers of religion and the sermons that they deliver. Those who enter the established Church today as a permanent vocation pursue academic study no different from the student of theology elsewhere (who usually has no intention of entering the Church as a profession). Academic rigour in analysis of scriptures, however, produces a dichotomy for the would-be priest. Should the problematic and doubtful areas of scripture be disseminated to congregations or, should these doubtful areas be set aside for the purpose of the Sunday sermon only? Since it is deemed inappropriate to dispute whether or not Paul wrote a certain letter, whether the Last Supper of Jesus was a Passover meal or not, whether Jesus lived at Bethlehem or Nazareth and whether there are distinct anomalies and contradictions related to a specific text, all such difficulties are set aside in order that the "faith" of the flock is not inappropriately harmed. Thus, the theology and christology of the academic is vastly different from the faith of the average believer. The Jesus of history and the Christ of faith have become poles apart, creating what one author has called "a generation of biblical illiterates".[2] I think this raises certain ethical questions about the nature of what is disseminated in the context of the Church: is it morally right to say something to your congregation that you yourself do not believe is true? For while biblical scholarship has progressed in all sorts of ways over the last century or more, the faith and understanding of the lay person has not shifted at all. Biblical facts that are now largely discarded are still maintained by what can only be termed deliberately misguided flocks. How critical this is, is put clearly by Van Harvey:

> The gulf separating the conservative Christian believer and the New Testament scholar can be seen as the conflict between two antithetical ethics of belief. Viewed from the moral standpoint of the scholar, the issue may be put in two ways, both of which are morally offensive to the conservative Christian believer. . . . New Testament scholarship is now so specialized and requires so much preparation and learning that the lay-person has simply been disqualified from having any right to a judgment regarding the truth or falsity of certain historical claims. Insofar as the conservative Christian believer is a layperson who has no knowledge of the New Testament scholarship, he or she is simply not entitled to certain historical beliefs at all.[3]

These are very strong words and are partially true, but not wholly so. I do not believe that the average "conservative Christian believer" is devoid of sufficient sense to conduct some analysis of the biblical text – enough to see that there are problems with the historical account. Indeed, it is not difficult to do this, it simply involves a different method of reading the biblical text, a method sufficient to render the reader both qualified and certainly *entitled* to raise questions – perhaps of his or her local minister! Later in this chapter I shall deal with the biblical account of Jesus and will indicate how a more critical analysis *can* and *should* be undertaken by every reader of the biblical text. The fear of the Christian minister, of course, is that to become sceptical about biblical material is to lessen, or even lose, faith.

This is an issue problematic enough for some clergy to throw their own scepticism into the depths of the subconscious. But even Roman Catholic theologians are today allowed more scope in critical analysis of *New Testament* historical material in the light of growing academic pressure. But Protestant theologians have more than a century of critical work behind them. Many no longer believe in hell, the idea of a devil, or original sin, and some are also sceptical about the basic tenets of Christianity such as the Incarnation, the divine nature of Jesus, and the virgin birth. These are issues that I shall come to below. Indeed, the more progressive and liberal Christians – few as they are – reject much of the supernaturalism of the Christian religion; some, like John Hick and fellow Christians, arguing well that Jesus was *not* God.[4] Even fundamental doctrines like the Resurrection of Jesus – arguably the most important of Christian doctrines – has come under critical scrutiny and has been rejected by some modern Christians. It is easy to see, then, that lay faith is well behind the critical stance taken by the academic Christian. But one question that glares at us from the facts of these sceptical and critical approaches to *New Testament* study is, as George Smith has raised: "It is at this point that we must wonder how the liberal Christian differs from the non-Christian",[5] particularly if even the Resurrection itself is rejected. It is a sound question, and might suggest that many Christians should move to the agnostic side of the fence. Perhaps the average secular person of today's society already has difficulty in accepting the claims of Christianity and has come to reject views of a virgin birth, hell, Satan, and all supernaturalism through a faster route than the theologian. For many today, religion has no meaning, is old-fashioned, is antiquated in its language, and has little relevance to the third millennium. Others still find need for it in old or new ways.

What is religion?

At the beginning of chapter 3 I pointed out that religion arises from the need to explain the inexplicable, such explanation emerging in the supernatural. But what is it that *maintains* religion in the face of scepticism, outmoded beliefs and a technical and scientific age? Why does the human being cling to religion despite what seems to be some shaky evidence for its foundational claims? Before answering these questions, it is necessary to reiterate some points about religion. A rather neat definition of religion is given by Raymond Firth. "Religion", he says, "is a name for some of man's most audacious attempts to give meaning to his world, by giving his constructions a symbolic transcendental referent."[6] Again, this reiterates what I said at the beginning of chapter 3, but I think there is a need to extend the definition here to include religion as that which inherently attempts to make sense of those inexplicable and needful aspects of the personal self, the individual. Such attempts to provide meaning can be a means to both the positive and negative in outcome, positive when they bring out the best in a person or in a culture, and negative when they bring out the worst. Of course, religion is not the only medium by which any such outcomes occur. Much later in his book,

Firth states that "religion represents a vast series of rescue operations and fields for exercise of the human imagination",[7] and it is this point which I should like to take up in more detail below in some analysis of the reason why human beings seem to need religion. Firth believes that religion arises out of the human need for salvation from individual and collective life, and the postulating of some kind of goal for this salvation. But he makes the point that such postulates are ultimately human creations, "a massive output of human enterprise."[8]

John Hick believes that religion is about "the transformation of human existence from self-centredness to reality-centredness".[9] But this is not really different from Firth's view. Religion is a focus on the wishful transformation human beings would like from the existential life-condition of individual and collective existence to a level that transcends it. The human need is the origin of the goal and the need and the goal amount to religious consciousness. The goal that is postulated is a supposed reality beyond the transient and finite world in which we live. It may be an abstract concept like the Brahman of Hinduism, the Tao of Taoism and, as such, devoid of theistic approach to it. Or it may become formalized into a theistic being, one that requires worship and ritual for the salvation it offers. And when it does become formalized, religion conforms to the culture that produces it; it is a social product diversifying and evolving with the expansion of the societies from which it emanates. Such diversification too often brings concomitant divisiveness, not only from culture to culture but actually *within* cultures themselves: Northern Ireland is a case in point. And since society creates its own God, religion is sometimes prone to support its society against its own religious tenets. The Church did not speak out against Hitler, Mussolini or Franco (all Roman Catholics) and, as Lofmark reminds us, Stalin was trained as a priest in the Russian Orthodox Church.[10] The divisiveness and elitism of religion has resulted in the arrogance of proselytizing and converting by, and within, the Christian faith, and the idea of conversion by force in Islam. It is easy to drag up the historical past of either Christianity or Islam to witness the atrocities perpetrated by religion – though here it has to be said that there are many -*isms* apart from religion that are guilty of past sins – but it is the divisive tendency in religion that has caused much of its past and present inhumanity. The chasm between eastern and western Christianity, between Christianity and other world faiths, between Protestantism and Roman Catholicism, the kind of bigotry that causes racism, the twentieth-century holocaust, and South African apartheid, are all examples of the divisive and intolerant views of religions that see their own views alone as right.

Clearly people do not attend church in any great numbers in today's world (athough, as will be seen below, there are increases in the Charismatic movements). But it is likely that this was the case in the nineteenth century as much as the twentieth, despite the "decline" in religion usually cited.[11] Yet most people are reluctant to say that they have no belief in God. Does this mean that they still have the basic *need* of religion but not the *means* to express it? The rise of the Charismatic movements might suggest that this is so. It is possible that just as the academic theologian is radically altering his or her stance on belief, the non-academic lay person is altering his or her *practice* of belief, breaking through normal barriers of stiff ritualistic worship while, at the same time, retaining an anthropomorphic conception of divinity. Again, Charismatic movements seem to suggest this is the case. As was pointed out in the previous chapter, God is a cultural phenomenon that is anthropomorphically portrayed in the mind of the average religious person, however much the academic theologian wishes to de-anthropomorphize and abstract the concept of deity.

Why do humans need religion?

Existentialist theologians have long recognized the gap between the human life-condition and the goals, language and hypotheses of religion. None of us is, at this moment, in perfect health, perfect psychological, physical, emotional and mental condition. Most of us find life pretty hard graft; stress is a factor of the age in which we live and the complexities of living at the dawn of the third millennium are more subtle and more covert than in previous centuries. So if we are searching for "reality-centredness" to transform our world, why do we do this? What are the needs in humanity that we wish to transform and transcend? If we recognize that there *are* needs to be transcended, we have to admit that there are weaknesses in the human – individually and collectively – that are answered by that other "reality". Do we not, then, see that reality as the absence of our own needs? Do we not create a reality in response to the weaknesses of what it is to be human? This, it would seem, is exactly what the theistic, anthropomorphic conceptions of divinity amount to.

So what are the needs that we as humans feel in the depths of our selves? Bearing in mind that most Humanists reject soul–body dualism, I think we all know what we mean by a *yearning or longing of the soul* for that inner something. This may be no more than a deep feeling that we could do with a bit of "peace and quiet", a bit of "space", time to smell the roses, time just to "be". It may also be a yearning for something that is more subliminal or even for oblivion, for total *nothingness*. But the idea of a transcendent reality in which peace and quiet, space, bliss, harmony, and so on, is existent, becomes a projected goal. And there may well be moments when we experience a glimpse of peace, a glimpse of harmony, that reinforce the goal, but that does not make the permanent state of it a reality. There is much of this harmonious goal in the words of the Humanist A. Eustace Haydon, who wrote early in the twentieth century:

> The humanist has a feeling of perfect at-homeness in the universe. He is conscious of himself as an earth child. There is a mystic glow in this sense of belonging. . . . Rooted in millions of years of planetary history, he has a secure feeling of being at home, and a consciousness of pride and dignity as a bearer of the heritage of the ages and a growing creative center of cosmic life.[12]

Beautiful words – and I am sure if Humanism could produce more material like this, one need of the human being would be fulfilled as much by Humanism as it is by religion! One is reminded of the words of the Roman Catholic theologian and scientist Père Pierre Teilhard de Chardin who accepted a unifying principle in the whole cosmos:

> Everything that moves and lives in the universe represents, in one particular aspect, the modifications of one and the same thing; and every monad, if it looks into itself, can find that thing as the initial point at which all things make contact in their inmost essence.[13]

While a modern Humanist writer like Paul Kurtz argues strongly against any underlying, unified reality to existence,[14] the celebrated Humanist Sir Julian Huxley wrote an introduction to Teilhard de Chardin's book *The Phenomenon of Man*. In this he confided that his quest was the same as that of the theologian, Teilhard. For he saw the universe in its entirety as "one gigantic process, a process of becoming, of attaining new levels of existence and organisation, which can properly be called a genesis or an evolution".[15] Huxley identified very much with Teilhard's view of man as increasingly realizing his (the language of the book is sexist) fullest potentials – as any Humanist would. Huxley could not follow Teilhard down the path of supernatural Christianity, and he made this clear,[16] but he could accept an interrelated cosmos – and in that sense a unified one – and the goal of an interrelated humanity in which "evolution was at last becoming conscious of itself".[17] Some fusion of religion and science was seen in the friendship and work of these two great scientists, and in their dream of global unity characterized by variety of expectant and fulfilled potential.

Thus, some Humanists – at least in the past –accepted that there is some kind of unity and interconnectedness within the cosmos, something of which may occasionally be glimpsed at the human level. But they do not project it to the supernatural, and certainly do not make the metaphysical leap to religious deification of the process by which it exists. But, to return to the major point, human need of something that transcends the self, some yearning for something beyond the sufferings and vicissitudes of life, is one of the weaknesses of human existence. And if at times the experience of harmony and "the peace that passes understanding" occur, well, it's a good feeling, one that we want to recreate. The combination of its possibility, along with the stress of life, makes an alteration of consciousness from the mundane to the harmonious desirable. On the mundane level, drugs, stimulants and alcohol fill the gap. What I am talking about here is probably the human search for "spirituality" that we examined in chapter 2. Indeed, Hoffman pertinently wrote in his preface to an inquiry into modern spiritualities: "Pressed for the mysterious something "missing" in everyday life, spirituality is cited as the ingredient that seems to have disappeared from modern society and left it, and us, struggling for a meaning that transcends the ordinary – the humdrum."[18] The word "spirituality" no longer needs to remain the prerogative of a religious consciousness. Using the word in a wider sense, Peggy Morgan suggests, it "seems to allow us to emphasize what is deep, personal, inner, experiential, and authentic in people's lives".[19] It may be that intuition – a word often derided by Humanists – runs close to the subliminal observation of the spiritual.

Another inherent need of the human being is the desire for what one author calls "a deep-felt yearning for *permanence*"[20] in a world that is obviously totally transient and impermanent. Here, again, is one of our deepest weaknesses as human beings, and positing a transcendent, permanent divine being that can grant immortality must surely be one of the oldest concepts of the divine that answers such a weakness. The promise of immortality offered by religion alleviates one of the deepest of human fears. "Man deceives himself about his ultimate destiny so as not to be tormented by the contemplation of it", says Paul Kurtz[21] and, indeed, it would be difficult for many human beings to accept that the finitude of this life is all we have. But what have we to fear from non-existence, from oblivion and nothingness? This seems a far better option than the trauma of a judgement in which we may fare negatively. Death has become a subconscious fear for most people, a fear that has been fostered over the centuries by the thought of punishment at death for all but a few. When the finitude of life cannot be faced with courage, then life is lived with a deep subconscious fear and profound dread of death. Part of the Humanist outlook is the fostering of a healthy attitude to death, and an openness in facing it as the total extinction of a life. The thought is reminiscent of a verse from a poem by Omar Khayyam, the eleventh-century Persian poet and astronomer:

> Oh, threats of Hell and Hopes of Paradise!
> One thing at least is certain – this life flies;
> One thing is certain and the rest is lies;
> The Flower that once has blown forever dies.

The idea that there is a theistic being who will save us from our present finitude develops from our weakness in facing that finitude. And the salvation that is believed to be there is conditional on best behaviour, on faith that a particular deity exists exclusive to any other, and on active veneration of that deity as part of the bargain. But because only the most arrogant of religionists could say that they are always on their best behaviour, we know that we will always fail the test for we are humans, and so the fear of finitude must, ultimately and subconsciously, remain.

Then, too, the human being is faced with more tangible *uncertainties* of life, the uncertainties of daily existence – financial problems, employment loss, ill health, stress. Uncertainty often equates with insecurity. Ian Cotton is one writer who points to the present uncertainty that science can solve the late twentieth-century issues that are passing into the third millennium, threats created by nuclear power, the threat of cancer, of AIDS, and the like.[22] He speaks, too, of the greed of the twentieth-century eighties, beset by the underlying uncertainty that economic doom may not be far behind.[23] A certain anti-materialism often underlies human desire for wealth and materialistic status. Money cannot buy happiness, for it does not remove inner uncertainties, and the subtle levels of insecurity in many individuals remain, despite materialistic fulfilment.

Because human beings exist in a world characterized by constant flux and change, there is a need to posit some kind of *intelligible order* in the whole of the cosmos. In reality order is only one side of the coin, for chaos and disorder are also part of our universe: in a way, all things revert to their chaotic state because they are finite. What order there is in our world, as we saw in chapter 3, can be as negative as it is positive. But the more human beings recognize chaos and disorder, the greater the need of order. Hence, the stretch of mind to an order that can only be *good* and a *good* God to make it so. In this context Raymond Firth's thesis is that religious beliefs occur as a result of human need for coherence in the world.[24] He describes religious beliefs as "active weapons in the process of adjustment by the person who holds them" and explains:

> What I mean by personal adjustment is the continual process of striving for order by the individual in his relations on the one hand with his physical and social universe, and on the other with his own logical system of categories of thought and his own set of impulses, desires and emotions. I think that it will be admitted that there is a continual and real need for such adjustment or adaptation on the part of every individual.[25]

Religious beliefs, then, arise from the need to make sense of things – especially when logically things do not make sense, when chaos and the vicissitudes of life challenge the coherence and order that we want to project into it. Human weakness in facing reality as it is creates the chimera of a concept of deity to ease the reality of life and to make sense of it.

In a different and more externalized dimension, there is a strong human need for *identity* that is answered by religious belief. Religion is largely, though not always, a communal phenomenon. Kurtz calls it a "social support system" in which human beings can huddle together to face adversity on the one hand and participate in joyful celebration on the other.[26] It is this communal aspect of religion that provides identity in terms of ethnicity or sectarianism, but all too often this communal aspect of religion makes it divisive, exclusive and elitist. It is also the communal religion that gives religious and moral identity through enculturation of the young; most children develop into adults without questioning the deeper conditioning of the culture into which they were born. It is this kind of deep and subtle conditioning that on the one hand provides the security of identity with the wider cultural group, but on the other, the insecurity when in, or faced with, anything beyond the pale. In India such enculturation has rigidified into caste-bound practices, and in religions such as orthodox Judaism and Islam, or in the Mormon sect of Christianity, many aspects of daily life are prescribed for male and female. The price of religious identity is too often rigid, but it fulfils needs, providing orderly social and moral norms dictating belief and behaviour – a coherent world.

Religion also fulfils the need for *personal identity* supplying a pre-shaped set of beliefs and conditions that the individual can use as a yardstick for personal development and consciousness. Religion is a ready-made package for life; it takes away the need to upset coherence by private, critical thought; it avoids the harder DIY stance for life. The personal need is also fulfilled through the many rites and ceremonies that religion has to offer, for those rites of passage which human beings so love to celebrate with pomp and "style". The very fact that great expense is lavished on such occasions reveals how important they are to the human psyche. Similarly, colourful festivals provide a time in life when the daily routine of life is transcended. People need to "let go", to "unwind", or "chill out" to use the current expression. Hector Hawton once wrote that in the case of religion: "The mind is playing a strange game with itself which is rich in emotional satisfaction or it would not be so hard to give up."[27] It is as well to remember these words for unless Humanism as an alternative to religion fulfils the emotional needs of the human being it cannot gain ground.

Emotional needs are concerned also with extraneous guidance, with care and security. It was Voltaire who said: "If there were no God, it would be necessary to invent him." It is interesting that the divine is so frequently anthropomorphically portrayed as a father, incorporating the notion that just as one is guided and cared for by an earthly father so there is the concept of a perfect and divine father who can proffer that ultimate kind of care and security. It is those religions that stem from patriarchal, nomadic, tribal origins that conceive of God as male, while those with agricultural and fertility-based origins can conceive of the divine in female form, but with the same concepts of protective care and guidance. In both cases, there is certainly a link between the concepts of an earthly figure and a divine one.

There is another dimension of the human being that religion appeals to, and that is the *imaginative* and *fanciful*. Religious stories, in particular, are full of fanciful myth, legend and colour that have colossal *appeal*. The fact that so many religious stories have found their way to the cinema screen testifies to the quality of the material in terms of satisfying the human need for creative drama. Religions may be projected fantasies but the human psyche *enjoys* fantasies, from those created by others to the ones woven in each individual mind. Fantasies satisfy the emotion and religion is full of them. Imaginative creativity is integral to human nature and religion is replete with the creative genius of many writers whose words have appealed to individuals for many centuries. And apart from the imaginative and fanciful, there is the related *miraculous* and *magical*. Human beings often long for the miraculous and magical in their personal lives, the former to overcome the stresses and vicissitudes of life and the latter to add sparkle to it. Religion abounds with both in its literary dimension particularly. Interest in science fiction, and in the paranormal, provide a modern focus for this dimension of the human psyche.

In summation, then, we have a whole list of reasons why individuals might want to perpetuate supernatural belief, particularly theistic belief. All the reasons cited above – and I am sure there are many more – arise out of *need*, out of weaknesses of humanity: it is human weakness that reinforces religion. Of course it could be claimed that religious belief is verified pragmatically, that is to say, because religiously minded people feel more secure, more fulfilled, more spiritual, and less uncertain about life, that religious belief must be valid. But I am sure that there are many psycho-therapists, many counsellors and many positive individuals who would claim that the same pragmatic positive results could be obtained by other methods. Religious belief may help an individual feel better but this is only if that individual has *faith* that it will. But let's say I visualize a golden light suffusing my body from head to toe, ridding my body of the tiredness. The same positive results may occur as those some would claim for religious belief, but I would know jolly well that there is no such thing as the golden light. What I am really doing is altering my thoughts, re-programming my mind to think differently. Both religious faith and the visualization technique have *functionalist* outcomes, but truth claims are only being made about religious belief. Meaning and direction for the living of life can be gained by many methods, but "the mind is playing a strange game with itself"[28] if it distorts reality to cover its weaknesses.

Do *Homo Sapiens* have a *biogenetic propensity* for religious belief? The question is debatable. The needs that have been outlined are probably certainly biogenetic but I think it is probably the *collective* manifestation of them that gives rise to a need for something beyond empirical existence to answer profound questions about life. God is a projection of human needs, a social fantasy into which is woven the myths, ethics, rites, ceremonies, rituals, worship patterns, dogmas and the whole religious phantasmagoria. In the words of H. L. Mencken:

1. The cosmos is a gigantic flywheel making 10,000 revolutions a minute.
2. Man is a sick fly taking a dizzy ride on it.
3. Religion is the theory that the wheel was designed and set spinning to give him a ride.[29]

If human beings have to rely on a social fantasy to fulfil their needs then they must ultimately remain unfulfilled, like the painkiller that removes the pain but not the cause of it. And of course not all people do rely on religion as a palliative in their emotional make-up. I am sure that the religiously conscious person will note the concept of love, particularly in its expression of compassion, as the hallmark of religious belief. Certainly, religion that motivates to love and compassion is widely attested in all cultures. The need for love and compassion reflects the very deepest human need of all, a need projected on a theistic God. Where love reveals itself, humanity can be transformed, but love and compassion are hallmarks of the non-religiously conscious person as much as the religiously minded. The Buddha is perhaps that one figure for whom compassion was a way of life, but he emphasized that there was no creator God, nothing beyond his manifest life to motivate that compassion. History also bears witness to the fact that the religious consciousness is often devoid of any love and compassion both individually and collectively.

If Humanism is to promote itself as an alternative path to religion, if it is to stand firmly as a dynamic and fluid option for an individual to accept, then it has to know what the needs of individuals are. True happiness is not something that comes from without, it bubbles up from within, but it can only do that when each individual is anchored in his or her own self, is not deluded or caught up in fantasies that inhibit full autonomy and full potential. To be free, is to know the self in every way, is to evaluate and validate one's own beliefs, is to travel through life with an open mind, and is to have the courage to face life fully, and to change it in as many ways as possible for the better.

Adverse effects of religion

From what has been said it could be claimed that there might be some advantage for at least some individuals in the psychological projection of the needs of the self onto a God the belief in whom, whether or not he exists, seems to have some pragmatic outcomes in life. Indeed, such is the power of the human mind that if you convince yourself of something it probably *will* change your life. It may help to pray to that God, to articulate one's feelings, one's problems or joys, and I am sure that this has some psychological benefit in the lives of many religious adherents. However, what of the adverse effects of religion? The very fact that so many people point to the failure of religion must suggest that "faith" in its old-fashioned views is simply not there in the lives of many. I remember a few years ago walking into the Philosophy and Religious Studies lecture room for one of the first sessions of the academic year. I was lecturing to a new intake of students. I was annoyed, and embarrassed, to find slogans (rather poorly presented) decorating the walls of the lecture room. "The wages of sin is death", "Repent and be saved!" was the tenet of the message they conveyed. I am sure many people feel the same revulsion when they pass the churches and chapels that tell us how sinful we are, and that we must repent of our ways! People do not want their souls saved today, they want their jobs to be secure or their mortgages paid, they want a full life and a view of it as positive and not sinful.

To go back to what was said at the beginning of this chapter, some of the outmoded beliefs of the Protestant faith in particular are now rejected by Anglican clerics, and yet the same outdated language and belief is often offered to their congregations. The God who was believed to control the harvests, heal the sick and bring success in battle has been replaced by technology, improved medicine and political success. Scientists are more important than priests because they can answer the natural difficulties that life presents, and religious precepts are often against the modernity of artificial insemination, voluntary euthanasia, genetic engineering, contraception and homosexuality. Religious establishments are accepted without participation in them or with only surface participation in them. As one male Roman Catholic who has undergone a vasectomy recently said to me: "The Pope doesn't have to bring up four children as an unemployed man." The Roman Catholic Church may preach against contraception, but in practice it obtains widely. Hector

Hawton appropriately stated that people "accept the religious establishment as they accept the monarch and the Lord Mayor's Show. It is colourful, they are used to it, and whenever it suits their convenience they will ignore it".[30]

For the vast majority of people, religion in the West is not something that belongs in the hectic working world of today, and many see devout Christians as a "peculiar lot", an anomaly in society. Yet the needs of the human being still reach out to the spiritual, the transcending of the normal pressures of life for something that is different and that answers the deeper parts of the subconscious. At least preaching about hell fire and salvation has begun to take a back seat to more applicable existential themes of life in many Sunday sermons. Today we live in a scientific and highly technical age in which scientists can create life, study the never-ending galaxies of the universe and the Milky Ways in which this Earth is but a grain of sand on a vast seashore. The theistic and anthropomorphic perception of God with a rewarding heaven and a retributive hell does not fit into this scheme of things. Without the crutch of theistic religion the individual has to stand on his or her own two feet, within finite existence, facing the limitations that one lifetime imposes with a positive view of self and societal fulfilment.

Most of us are familiar with Marx's famous assertion that religion is the opium of the masses. It is worthwhile quoting the entire passage in which this statement occurs:

> *Man makes religion*: religion does not make man. Religion is indeed man's self consciousness and self-awareness so long as he has not found himself or has lost himself again. But *man* is not an abstract being, squatting outside the world. Man is *the human world*, state, society. . . . Religion is the sign of the oppressed creature, the sentiment of a heartless world and the soul of soulless conditions. It is the *opium* of the people. The abolition of religion as the *illusory* happiness of men, is a demand for their real happiness. . . . Religion is only the illusory sun about which man revolves so long as he does not revolve about himself.[31]

What Marx referred to here is the individual who is oppressed because his or her self-awareness is not developed, it has not evolved; identity is imposed from without and not experienced from within. And when decisions about life are imposed from without they are not thought out critically and *owned* from within. Rousseau's well-known statement that "Man is born free and everywhere he is in chains" reflects the same point about the conditioned human being that does not take identity from within his or her self, or ownership of his or her own being. Western religion often preaches the humility of the self, eastern religion the loss of the egoistic self. Humanism calls for the *assertion* of the self and the development of its fullest potentials.

The concept that all human beings are sinful is alien to Humanism. It has so often been a tenet hurled from the Christian pulpit, though less from the Anglican ones in this day and age. The idea of *original* sin – that is to say the idea that *all* human beings are inherently wicked and sinful as a result of the original sin of the biblical Adam, a sin passed through all generations through procreation – is a monstrous idea that devalues human life, sex, procreation and the exemplary lives of millions of people who struggle in the tide of life and win. People are not inherently evil, but no one is perfect, and no one can be perfect. Every individual will make mistakes, will make wrong choices, will think, do and say the wrong thing countless times in his or her life. This is not sin, it is what it is to be human. The word "sin" should be deleted from general vocabulary as antiquated. Bertrand Russell in his frank lecture *Why I am not a Christian* stated:

> When you hear people in church debasing themselves and saying that they are miserable sinners and all the rest of it, it seems contemptible and not worthy of self-respecting human beings. We ought to stand up and look the world frankly in the face. We ought to make the best of the world, and if it is not so good as we wish, after all it will still be better than what these others have made of it in all these ages.[32]

The problem with the concept of sin is that it has a concomitant concept of guilt, and both are psychologically harmful to human development. Indeed, there are still people in today's world that view God as a kind of invisible force watching and judging human actions. The Islamic faith, especially, encourages this. And while people may repent, confess their sins and feel that they may be forgiven by God, they often repeat the same so-called sins, either in thought or action, only to build up an even greater level of guilt. Guilt is another word I should like to remove from the English dictionary. As humans we make mistakes, some of them dreadful ones. But to be really human we have to turn and face those mistakes, sort them out, do what we can to remedy them, and then leave them to begin anew. What we don't need to do is carry the burden of all our mistakes with us, though it is useful to carry the experience of them with us, helping us to formulate our choices in the future. In this context, conscience is usually conceived of as a religious concept, and Christians often believe that it is instilled in human beings from creation as a deeply-rooted, divinely orientated, moral guide. Conscience, however, is no more than the moral conditioning supplied by the do's and don'ts of family, educational, and social environment, something that is flexible, changeable, but deeply embedded in the human psyche.

One of the most psychologically damaging effects of the Christian religion in the past has been its attitude to sex. Jesus was unmarried, unlike some of the great leaders of other faiths, such as Guru Nanak of Sikhism. For a Jew to be unmarried was unusual, for Judaism to this day holds family life in high esteem. There is a hint in *Matthew* 19:12 that Jesus favoured a celibate existence, and in *Luke* 20:35 this is stated more explicitly. Generally, however, the texts that have come down to us suggest that Jesus was not particularly interested in this matter, unlike Paul who, even if we could forgive his words because he believed the second coming of Christ was imminent, had a very narrow view of women and a very unbalanced view of sex. These are points I shall return to below.

Over-zealous religious conditioning is not good for the psyche, fulfils few needs of the individual and creates more problems than it solves. Lofmark, though he does not cite his sources, suggests that independent surveys undertaken in Britain and elsewhere point to higher delinquency in Roman Catholic schools than in others (two to three times higher than in the population as a whole). While the criteria for assessment of delinquency would be important here, and Lofmark did not give it, he makes the point that a quarter of the prison population in Britain is composed of Roman Catholics, despite the fact that Roman Catholics amount to only a tenth of the general population.[33] Religious faith may promote some pragmatic solace for the weaknesses of the human psyche, but this is clearly balanced by its adverse affects, fear of death, because of fear of judgement and the unknown; fear of punishment for sins that cannot be helped; repression of natural instincts; and, importantly, fear of facing life itself without the prop of supernatural theism. Ibn Warraq points out that the whole ethical system set down in the *Qur'an* is one based on fear, fear of the wrath of Allah for lack of piety and lack of obedience.[34]

Belief

Most of our beliefs are culture bound and they vary from those that are firmly and tenaciously held to those that are more peripheral and vague. The important thing about belief is that it should be held for sound reason and knowledge, for the right reasons, and with verifiable evidence, and it should always be subject to change in the light of new evaluation and relevant criteria. The truly autonomous person has beliefs that are not certain truths, they are what are held to be right at a particular time. But many of our beliefs are given to us on a very subtle plate. They are imbibed through cultural upbringing, assimilated without thought, and sneak into the subconscious without careful digestion. Religious belief is often of this type, though adolescent years, especially, are those in which cherished ideas are often subjected to challenge. The more mature individuals are, the more they are able to analyse their beliefs to ensure that they are rationally based, and the more they are able to adapt and change belief in the light of new criteria. The result should be beliefs that are both personally, intellectually and socially pragmatic and viable. This is a process of *reason*, a process that leads to claims about things that are verifiable.

Beliefs, then are of two types, those that we can verify and articulate, and those we simply accept without verification and which we more vaguely express. The more of the former we have, the more developed we are as human beings. Religious belief differs from many other kinds of belief because it is incapable of verification by the same standards as other beliefs we have, and it is also difficult to articulate clearly the nature of it and the reasons for it. Claims for religious belief have to be based on premises that cannot be verified, or on internalized, intuitive knowledge that cannot be articulated. Because religious beliefs are mostly culturally inherited they are reinforced by cultural traditions and the many customs and modes of individual and collective life that stem from ages past. When we meet a Jew, a Hindu, an Anglican Christian, a Greek Orthodox Christian, a Spanish Roman Catholic, we recognize both what the individual is at this moment in time, and also the past heritage that makes him and her what they are now. Many of the beliefs such people hold are ingrained and are not receptive to modification. We have to be very astute individuals if we want to have autonomy about what we think and who we are. As an anthropologist and a humanist, Raymond Firth believes that there is at least some truth in every religion in that each one reflects something of the conception of the world of the society that creates it. But he adds:

> It is a human, not a divine truth. In every society the beliefs and practices of religion are modelled on secular beliefs, desires, interests, fears

and actions. These are raised by religion to a higher power, given an alleged external authority and legitimacy, because, in their abstract, figurative, often symbolic form they are ultimately an outcome of the human condition and an attempt to remedy its difficulties.[35]

To reiterate an earlier point, religious faith becomes a psychological projection of the individual and communal identity to a divine, perfect self.

Beliefs are not true because we personally think they are, or because a number of people collectively, but *subjectively* think they are. For something to be true it has to be demonstrably so, and consistently so, with universal concomitance. Religious beliefs, relying so much on "faith", have very varied truth claims, none of which can be demonstrably proved. It might be argued, as some Jewish rabbinical traditions did,[36] that God *is* a subjective experience and therefore each individual will necessarily experience him differently, but only religious pluralists would endorse such an idea; for many of religious faith, there is a feeling that their own perception of religious "truth" is the right one. It is also irrational to have such a multiplicity of varying truth claims about one posited supernatural being. To hold rational beliefs we need to subject them to inquiry, not just accept them "on faith". As Paul Kurtz aptly states: "Faith never proves a point; it only registers our convictions."[37] It is perhaps because the veracity of truth claims about religion is so shaky that there is often a considerable gap between what religious people believe, and what they actually *do* in daily existence. When belief is rational, such a gap is less likely.

Faith

Faith may sometimes be synonymous with belief when the latter has no rational basis for it. If one has faith *in* something, then one has belief in it. But faith is normally a word that suggests belief for which no tangible evidence can be found. It may be based on the testimony of others, or on something that we subjectively believe to seem to work practically. The reasons why a person has faith in something are difficult to validate in empirical terms. So I may have faith in a remedy for colds, or in a particular person, or the weather forecasters, or the religious tenets of a particular denomination, sect or religion, but although we might want to say subjectively *why* faith in such things is justified, it is usually difficult to *prove* such justification.

Normally we have faith in things that we believe are beneficial to us. Faith is thus a highly subjective kind of thought; it is subjective belief. To have religious faith suggests that one has *certain* beliefs. That is to say it would be necessary to believe in God – Christ, Allah, Brahman or Buddhist *bodhisattvas*, for example – concomitant with, or preceding, one's faith. If we could prove that God, Christ, etc., existed in the sense that religions say they do, then there would be no need for faith. I do not have to have faith that two plus two equals four since it is an established, verified and universal belief. Faith is needed where the criteria for belief are suspect. But since faith has no real epistemological basis, because it is knowledge that cannot be proved, it is inferior knowledge, indeed, it could hardly be said that it is knowledge at all. It is, rather, a subjective feeling.

Perhaps the human need for the miraculous and the wonderful makes us susceptible to things that we have to accept on faith, and the testimony of religious scripture to the wonderful and the miraculous perhaps encourages people to accept its validity in the only way possible – through faith. The word "faith" has a tendency to crop up when arguments for the validity of beliefs fail to convince. It is a "fallback" word, one used by those who find themselves unable to defend their religious belief empirically, and so have recourse to the statement: "It all depends on one's faith." When fundamental issues like theodicy are raised to the person of faith, illogical answers like "We cannot fathom the ways of God" are produced. Faith blinds a person to reason. It can also produce false psychological states: if we will something hard enough, we may momentarily, or for a short time, come to believe that what we will has come true. This seems to be the case with much faith healing, though there is no evidence to suggest that momentary "cures" are sustained.[38] It is just that temporary psychological changes in the self create temporary relief.

Faith underpins the radical stance of the conservative evangelical Christian (the modern term for the fundamentalist). Here, faith can be as radical as to accept every word of scripture as absolute truth, despite the inconsistencies of the textual material. Dialogue with such people is almost impossible, for rational thought and critical debate are most usually reduced to the bottom line of faith – a concept alien to reason. Islam, in particular, expects blind faith from its adherents, and dissenters can end up being publicly hanged, expelled from their academic posts, imprisoned and tortured or forced into exile.[39] Most Muslims still believe that the *Qur'an* is the literal word of God and must be obeyed without reason or question.

Faith is normally a word pertaining more to theistic religions, that is to say where there is belief in a deity or deities with whom one has an alleged personal relationship. It is a word less applicable to the more mystical, non-theistic types of religion such as Hindu Advaita Vedanta, classical Taoism and some schools of Buddhism. It has characterized Christianity at times in the past, influenced to some extent by Neoplatonism, and its eastern expressions are attracting present-day westerners who are searching for some means to overcome the stresses of modern existence. Indeed, many medical practitioners advise their patients of the strengths of meditation as a preventive for stress-related illnesses. For some, such meditative approaches to life are part of a search for a transcendent – and therefore supernatural – reality, an "Absolute" that is the ultimate, but indescribable, principle behind the cosmos. In this sense there is a kind of faith in an ultimate reality because it is believed to be experienced in some way in the deepest self, particularly through meditation, when the mind is stilled. Again, Humanists generally reject such claims of an Absolute, though agree that there are times when individuals can feel at one with Nature or with the universe beyond it. So there is no rejection of the claim to such experiences but, rather, a rejection that they are supernatural in any way, or project one into a supernatural level of reality.

Such "mystical" experiences have been described by one Humanist author as "a veritable ecstasy of aesthetic delight".[40] However, the visionary experiences of some mystics are dismissed as mere products of the mind. To begin with the object visualized always has to be known first: someone who knows nothing of the Virgin Mary of Christianity does not have the capacity to mystically visualize her. Humanists always look to the natural world for physiological, psychological and scientific reasons for explanations of the so-called supernatural. Indeed, meditation is known to alter the breathing rate of the body, and therefore levels of oxygen and carbon dioxide. In fact the yogic practice of *pranayama*, breathing exercises, is done to promote meditative experiences. Fasting, excessive solitude, ascetic practices, whirling dancing, and the like, can produce mystical experience because they alter the physiological condition of the body which in turn alters the mental state. Consciousness *is* altered, but naturalistically and not supernaturalistically so. It is clear that in any religion mystical experience does not seem to occur without aids – visual stimuli, deprivation of sleep, of food, of light, or of ordinary sense perception. But in minor ways it is promoted by the beauties of Nature, and by those moments in life that transcend the normal for the sensual.

The Christian faith

Christian faith is built on a number of basic propositions:

- A person called Jesus historically existed.
- Jesus was born of a virgin.
- Jesus taught people that the Kingdom of God was imminent.
- Jesus performed miracles.
- Jesus was crucified and then resurrected after death, appearing to a number of people.
- Jesus was the expected Jewish Messiah.
- Jesus is the Son of God.
- Those accepting Jesus in faith will have eternal salvation.

These are the basic truth claims of the Christian faith. But it is exactly these basic claims that have been the subject of critical analysis by theologians for over a century, and the state-of-the-art conclusions are considerably speculative about the historicity, and even the very theological nature, of such claims. To begin with, the reader may well believe that Jesus was a unique person, with a unique teaching. Well, Randel Helms opened his book *Gospel Fictions* with the following words:

> In the first century of the Common Era, there appeared at the eastern end of the Mediterranean a remarkable religious leader who taught the worship of one true God and declared that religion meant not the sacrifice of beasts but the practice of charity and piety and the shunning of hatred and enmity. He was said to have worked miracles of goodness, casting out demons, healing the sick, raising the dead. His exemplary life led some of his followers to claim he was a son of God, though he called himself the son of a man. Accused of sedition against Rome, he was arrested. After his death, his disciples claimed he had risen from the dead, appeared to them alive, and then ascended to heaven.[41]

I am sure most readers will have concluded already that the subject of these words was Jesus, but in fact, the words refer to one Apollonius of Tyana, who died about 98 CE. The story of Jesus is, then, not unique, and parallels are not hard to find for his life and fate, as well as for individual aspects of the gospel portrayal of his life.

Despite his effect on the centuries that followed him, there is little extra-biblical evidence for the historical Jesus, and certainly not enough to suggest that he had anything but a very minor impact on the people of his time.

The traditions that have come down to us about Jesus – those recounted in the four gospels of the *New Testament* – are only four among a variety of those circulating in the century after his death. And the four that we do have, ascribed to Matthew, Mark, Luke and John, are four very different pictures reflecting four different traditions and coming from four different communities whose needs and aims were equally as different. Each of the gospel writers presents a Jesus that suits his own theological position and this brings about a considerable number of contradictions in the historical account of Jesus from one gospel to another. One writer may even amend the words of another to suit his own theory, or to give prominence to something he considers important.[42] Both Matthew and Luke are found to have altered Mark's earlier account where the material needs to be suited to their own audiences. But it is only by reading the separate incidents parallel to each other that the discrepancies become obvious. Much material is likely to have been legendary, circulating in a particular community, with different legends, or variations of one legend, in other communities. Many of the stories and legends about Jesus in circulation were not eventually included in the canon of the *New Testament*. This is not to say that these stories were less authentic, they simply did not suit the purpose of the Church at the time the canon was formulated.[43] The whole issue of faith, then, is important to the Christian whose knowledge of the scriptures has undermined the basic truth claims contained within them.

The problematic gospels

Since the whole canon of the *New Testament* is only a selection of the considerable amount of literature that was circulating in the early centuries of the first millennium, the order of the books of the *New Testament* might be expected to be historically chronological. But they are not so: *Mark* was written earlier than *Matthew* which precedes it in the canon, and the letters of Paul, the *Epistles*, are earlier than any of the four gospels. Though Mark's gospel was written earlier than the others, he has no material on the birth of Jesus. He seems to know of Jesus only as an adult. No doubt, there is basic material in the four gospels that is factual, but basic facts are undoubtedly overlaid with much legend and fabricated tradition. Attempts to sort out the strict historical facts from the gospels have failed, and the approaches of both form critics and redaction critics have not resulted in any analysis that has finally clarified what we may accept as fact. In her introduction to her commentary on *Mark*, Morna Hooker reiterates the problems that besiege the student of the gospels.[44] When we read any gospel it is difficult to know what is fact, what is recorded tradition, what is the author's own viewpoint, what are the localized community's needs that are imposed on it, and what are later interpolations by a Church that needed to amend and crystallize its theology.

Then, too, some authors point out that modern scholarship is none too sure about the identity of the respective authors of the gospels, and it was not until the second century that the names of the four evangelists were finally added to the title of their respective gospels.[45] However, the tradition that Mark was the interpreter of the apostle Peter still tends to be the mainstream hypothesis, making a date for this early gospel at around 70 CE. And since Peter would have known Jesus well, this might explain some of the touches of an eyewitness account in Mark's gospel. But we should not forget that Peter was an uneducated Galilean fisherman, and Mark's Greek and style of writing is far from polished. The use of *Mark* by the other evangelists as one of their sources is clear, but it is likely that they felt the need to edit that material in the light of the poor quality of Mark's account, as well as the needs of their own respective communities on the one hand, and their own theological position on the other. Sometimes words seem to be superimposed on Jesus in order to provide authenticity for a custom or institution in the growing Church. Jewish women could not divorce their husbands, yet in *Mark* 10:12, Jesus is found discussing the issue of a woman who divorces her husband and remarries. The subject of divorce might well suit a non-Jewish audience, but would have been out of place in the context of Jesus' teaching to an all-Jewish audience.[46] Similarly, many passages from the Jewish scriptures (what Christians patronizingly call the *Old Testament*) were reinterpreted to relate to Jesus in a prophetic way, many passages being taken right out of their contexts to become prophetic pronouncements concerning the future birth, life and death of Jesus. Blatant borrowings from the Jewish scriptures by Matthew and Luke also seem to be evident.[47]

Much gospel material, then, is not so much about Jesus but about people's views of Jesus. Does this, then, make them partly fictional? Randell Helms is one person who thinks as much. While he recognizes that historical works contain some fiction and fiction contains some history, he regards the gospel material as mainly fictional.[48] Indeed, if what we find in the gospels is not what Jesus actually did or said, but what later tradition *thought* or even *wished* he had done or said – admittedly based on traditions about his life – then we do come very close to fictional accounts. When we say "Jesus said" or relate what Jesus did, we really mean to say "What Jesus in the eyes of the author said or did".[49] Then there is the problem of the gospel of *John*. It is a perfect example of interpretation of material to suit the author's own theological perspective. The writer of this gospel was the most theological one, and his theology pervades its chapters. But the discrepancies between John's account of Jesus and those of the other evangelists are striking, not on minor details but in major issues that are basic to the Christian faith.

The Jesus legend

Most people take it as an established fact that Jesus existed historically. It is beyond the scope of this work to enter into the debate concerning the evidence for and against the historicity of Jesus. For my own part, I consider that there was indeed a man, Jesus, of whom, some credible information is available, but whose life and works are bound by obscurity. The reader is directed elsewhere for sound analysis of the question.[50] But the warning of John Hick is, I believe, relevant here, and this is, to suggest that Jesus did not exist at all is an "eccentric" view. Hick makes the pertinent point that "the issue is, to say the least, not at the cutting edge of research concerning Christian origins".[51] But even so, Hick agrees that we have no direct vision of Jesus but have to view him "through thick layers of first-, second-, and third-generation Christian faith".[52] Jesus was certain to have been a product of his age, accepting the ideas of his time and would have been thoroughly familiar with all the facets of his Jewish faith, its dietary rules, festival procedures, fast days, worship and beliefs. He would have accepted current beliefs about heaven, hell, bodily resurrection of the dead, the doctrine of the end of days – the Day of Yahweh. He would have been familiar with the hopes and aspirations of the Jewish people for a messiah – whether an earthly, political one, or a divine one – and would be thoroughly versed in the Jewish scriptures, and the Law, the *Torah*. Yet his message for the Jewish people of his time was clearly concerned with the end of time.

To understand the problems of the gospel material, and to arrive at a critical perception of the narratives they put forward, needs a *thematic* approach. A straightforward reading of the gospels will hardly suffice as a critical method of inquiry for the reader who is not a continuing student of the *New Testament*. However, given that it is the biblical text that is the basis of study for the multitude of theological tomes of the past and present, the biblical text itself is all that is needed to conduct a profound and critical analysis of the gospel material. The best approach is to read different episodes, parables, narratives *across* the gospels. Thus, in examining, for example, the trial of Jesus as a theme across the gospels, a far better perspective of the historical viability of the narrative will emerge.

The birth narratives of Jesus are full of inconsistencies. To begin with if we look for the birth of Jesus in *Mark* it is entirely absent. This important event, the birth of a messiah, the Son of God has no mention at all in this, the earliest, gospel account. Mark's account begins with Jesus as a mature man and with his baptism by John. To be sure, Mark gets straight to the point of his message of the messianic nature of Jesus, implicitly, or secretly, conveyed in the text, but nowhere does he go back to the important issue of parentage and birth. Many people who are familiar with the Christmas nativity narrative will remember that Jesus is said to come from the House of David, that is to say his ancestry goes back to King David, the first real, and idealized, King of Israel. He is also said to have been born of the virgin Mary. Why does Mark not mention this, why does he not mention this important lineage of Jesus? The virgin birth of Jesus is found only in *Matthew* and *Luke* and nowhere else in the *New Testament*. Not even Paul refers to it; in fact, Paul does not mention Jesus' parents at all. Matthew takes the trouble to trace Jesus' lineage through from Abraham to David and to Joseph, and then quite inconsistently gives an account of the virgin birth that renders Joseph of no blood relation to Jesus in any way! Luke also traces Joseph's ancestors back through the Davidic line, but the lineage has different names from those of Matthew!

From Matthew's gospel we learn that Jesus was born in Bethlehem, fulfilling the prophecy of *Micah* 5:2, was then taken to Egypt, and then went to settle at Nazareth in Galilee (*Matthew* 2). It is clear from the events that Matthew describes that Mary and Joseph were not just visiting Bethlehem, but were living there. Luke, on the other hand has Mary and Joseph living in Nazareth, leaving Nazareth for Bethlehem for the purpose of a tax census (despite the colossal problems the Romans would have had with people having to return to their birthplaces all over the land!) and then returning to Nazareth after undertaking the ritual for the firstborn in Jerusalem (*Luke* 2). This is a good example of two differing traditions presented by the respective writers.

The gospels portray Jesus as an extraordinary man who could perform different kinds of miracles with authority over Nature, over those possessed by demons, even over death itself, raising the dead to life. He made the blind see, the deaf hear and the lame walk. Once so important to the Christian tradition, however, the traditions concerning miracles are either now rejected entirely, or placed on the periphery of Christianity, by all but Roman Catholics and conservative evangelicals.[53] The miracles make colourful, and sometimes powerful reading. One of the most graphic miracles is the healing of the leper in *Mark* 1:40–42. It is not the resulting healing that is the miracle, more the atmosphere of the moment portrayed by the writer, and the words "moved with pity, he [Jesus] stretched out his hand and touched him".[54] The writer conveys a powerful scene here, and we can well imagine the astonishment of the leper himself, and of the onlookers, as Jesus reached out to touch the withered hand of a man to whom tactile contact was alien. But the real issue behind miracles is the question of faith. It seems that faith is necessary for a miracle to occur, and Mark tells us that Jesus was not able to perform miracles where faith was absent in his own home area (*Mark* 6:5). While the other evangelists exclude this rather embarrassing piece of information, they likewise illustrate in their treatment of healing miracles that faith is an important corollary. John, however, does not portray this at all, and in his theological approach to the nature of Jesus, sees faith as arising as a result of the miracles, that is to say, as a result of divine authority and presence.

A detailed analysis of the biblical text is beyond the scope of this chapter, but it is not a difficult task for any reader to compare the material in each of the gospels related to the same theme. The same discrepancies can be found in their respective traditions concerning the trial of Jesus, and even the last words of Jesus spoken on the cross. Matthew and Mark preserve the tradition of a very human Jesus in his last moments with "My God, my God, why hast thou forsaken me?" Whoever Jesus was, these words suggest the psychological agony of denial of all that he thought he was, even if they are a reiteration of *Psalm* 22:1. But Luke and John put different words into the mouth of Jesus at his moment of death, totally contradicting the human elements of Mark and Matthew. And when did Jesus die? Was the Last Supper a Passover meal, as Matthew, Mark and Luke recorded? Or did it happen the night before the Passover, so that Jesus died at the same time as the ritual slaughter of the Passover lambs, as John has it?

It might be expected that there is textual agreement on some of the major truth claims of the Christian faith. Because there is not, Liberal Christian theologians no longer feel it necessary to accept the doctrine of the Incarnation, the idea that Jesus *was* God incarnate. Indeed, textually, Jesus – at least outside John's gospel – does not claim *identity* with God, and we never gain the impression that he *is* God in the sense that Krsna as the incarnation of Visnu is in Hinduism. That Jesus was the Messiah, the Christ, is a claim Christianity also sometimes abandons. The term "messiah" means "anointed" and was used to refer to kings, as well as to the expected earthly, political or supernatural figure that would be the instrument of salvation for the Jews. Yet there are many Christians who consider the term "messiah" and the term "son of man" – both terms being used in wider contexts in the Jewish and other traditions – to have been attached to Jesus in the eagerness of the early Christians to give Jesus divine status.

The most important miracle of all in the Christian tradition is that of the Resurrection, and it is this that is the real basis of the Christian faith. And since miracles cannot be proved in any way, Christianity cannot really base itself on a truth claim. It has to base itself on something in which it has faith. In the Resurrection traditions presented by the biblical text there are considerable anomalies. It should be remembered that the epistles of Paul are significantly earlier than the gospel accounts, but Paul clearly has no knowledge of the empty tomb. While the Resurrection is critical to Paul's theology, he gives no account of it. Those to whom Jesus appeared after his death are different in Paul's account than in those of the gospel writers. Indeed, there are discrepancies concerning these highly significant post-death appearances of Jesus across the accounts of the evangelists themselves, and it is not possible to put these different accounts of the Resurrection into something that makes sense. Not only do the people to whom Jesus appeared differ in the accounts, but the places where he appeared also differ. Indeed, contradictions between the Lukan account and *Acts* seem to suggest that Jesus eventually ascends to heaven, but has to come back again for more appearances! Events at the empty tomb are also different in the various traditions. The presence of so many contradictory accounts of one particular miracle really nullifies the basic claim of Christian faith. Anthony Flew pertinently remarks that "absent that resurrection, there remains no sufficient reason for accepting either that the man Jesus is to be incomprehensibly identified with 'God the Father Almighty, Maker of heaven and earth,' or that his actual teachings, whatever they may have been, are thereby revealed to be supremely authoritative".[55]

If the Jesus that we find portrayed in the gospels is one on whom later traditions have been projected, then it is almost impossible to know what he really said and did. The Jesus that is portrayed by the gospels does not really come across to us, on balance, as divine; he might have been an exceptional human being, but he seems human nevertheless. It is odd that Paul's letters say nothing of the teaching, the miracles or the life of Jesus; it is almost as if he knew nothing of these things. Jesus' central teaching on the Kingdom of God, his established way to pray with what is now the "Lord's Prayer", seem to be unknown to Paul. But the closest Paul ever came to Jesus was in the voice he heard on the road to Damascus.

Any analysis of the teaching of Jesus cannot fail to see that the arrival of the Kingdom of God was the central theme, and Jesus clearly felt that he had a message for the Jews of his time concerning this impending doom on the one hand, and salvation on the other. Because it did not occur, some have called Jesus a "deluded apocalyptist" as did Albert Schweitzer, and some of Jesus' contemporaries obviously thought he was deluded, too (*Mark* 3:21). None of the things that Jesus thought would happen did so either in his own lifetime, or in the two thousand years subsequent to it. And there are many modern theologians who recognize the fallibility in the message of Jesus, but at the same time they retain faith in the Christian tradition through the acceptance that somehow Jesus had a special personality that ultimately transcended the inconsistencies of his own teaching. After his death, his expected imminent return also did not materialize, and this must have been a considerable embarrassment to the early Christians.

But aside from the failure of his central teaching, Jesus comes across to us as a rather human individual with views that could hardly be applicable to life in the two thousand years that have followed him. He is a man who wants the destruction of his enemies

(*Luke* 19:27) and who wants people to leave their homes and families, even deserting their children in order to receive a reward in heaven (*Matthew* 19:29). He is reputed to have said that he came to set son against father and daughter against mother, and that one's enemies would be those in one's own home (*Matthew* 10:3–36). He said it was impossible to follow him without hating one's family (*Luke* 14:26). In *Matthew* he is distinctly partisan to Jews and not Gentiles (*Matthew* 10:5–6, 15:22–28, cf. 25:24,26), although the Lukan narrative, contradictorily, sees his message as being one *to* the Gentiles. Jesus clearly favoured the poor and not the rich (*Luke* 51:2–3), and if you were not poor, hungry, perpetually miserable and one of the downtrodden, then God help you in the afterlife according to the Sermon on the Mount in *Matthew* 5. If we lifted such concepts into the modern day, it would be a criticism of anyone who has done well in life. In the words of one writer, "Christ is an impartialist".[56]

Because Jesus believed that the Kingdom of God was imminent, he taught that people should take no heed of what they ate or wore or for any aspect of their life. (*Matthew* 6:25–34). It was advice appropriate perhaps for the end of the world (which shows how deluded he was), but not for an ongoing society. The remarkably human side of Jesus was conveyed in his anger. The Pharisees and Scribes had a really bad press in the criticisms he hurled at them (for example *Matthew* 23:27–28 and 23:33), but the Pharisees did a great deal of good work in the villages and amongst the poor. As a group, they did not really deserve the impression we are given of them in the gospel material, and we should remember that Jesus taught that we should love our enemies and turn the other cheek. He certainly didn't!

The picture of Jesus that is conveyed to us has the hallmarks of human weakness, but it also has the strengths of the human being conveyed clearly in his immense compassion for his fellow human beings. He seems a man for whom knowledge of what it is to be human was experienced deeply, and he had a great empathy for the poor and the sick of his time. He certainly stands out as one who could transcend the religious institutions of his day and the rigidity of the Jewish faith into which he was born. Whatever his shortcomings, whatever the doubt concerning his historicity, and however he is viewed, the perspective of him is not entirely without value. But this is irrespective of reason. It is always necessary to view the biblical material here with common sense, with a rational and critical approach, and assess, in the light of analysis, whether there are fundamental claims that could be said to be true, in Christian faith.

Paul of Tarsus

The Christian faith is as much or more due to the character Paul of Tarsus as Jesus of Nazareth. Indeed, the point is often raised that it was Paul and not Jesus who was the founder of the faith. Paul left his mark not only on Christian theology but also on history, and he was responsible for the founding of a number of centres of Christianity during his travels of something like 6000 miles. There was much in Paul's character to earn him the title "saint", for there was a deep sincerity in him and he was as honest with himself as he was with others. His writings have an urgency and vitality that communicate very passionately held beliefs. C. H. Dodd described his thought as "soaring, strong and adventurous" saying that Paul "had a white hot zeal for the truth of which he was convinced".[57] But there were great dualities in his personality and this is seen in his virulent persecution of the Christians on the one hand, followed by his later ardent passion for the Christian cause on the other. Such dualities abound in his character, and this is revealed in a considerable number of contradictory statements in his letters.

Paul never seems to have done anything by halves, and what is found in one situation may prove to be untrue in another. For example he can write well, but cannot deliver his message well orally (*2 Corinthians* 10:1, 11). In person he often seemed weak, but his letters can display a bullying firmness. He seems a man who needed appreciation and acceptance, but if such were not forthcoming he could be quite petulant (*1 Corinthians* 11:5). While he could show genuine modesty, he was extremely fond of using the word "boast". There is something of an egoistic character about Paul, as the second chapter of *Galatians* suggests, and Michael Grant writes of him: "His character was torn apart by inner conflicts. One of the strongest of them was a clash between genuine modesty and overwhelming self-confidence."[58] This apparent self-confidence may have concealed an inner inferiority. He seemed keen to let everyone know that his experience on the road to Damascus made him just as much an apostle as the twelve who had known Jesus. "Am I not an apostle?" he says, "Have I not seen Jesus our Lord?" (*1 Corinthians* 9:1). In fact, he had never seen Jesus, he had only heard his voice, and he must have felt it keenly that the status of apostle was given only to those who had had personal contact with Jesus both before and after his death. Was he jealous of the apostles? It seems so, for he refers to them caustically as "those who were reputed to be something (what they were makes no difference to me; God shows no partiality)" (*Galatians* 2:6).

Considering that many traditions about Jesus must have been circulating at the time Paul wrote his letters to the various churches, Paul says very little about Jesus – nothing about his birth, his life, his teachings, his authority in miracles – indeed, we might sympathize with Jung's criticism that Paul hardly allows Jesus of Nazareth to get a word in! But perhaps this was because he was unfamiliar with the life of Jesus, or that there was nothing remarkable about Jesus' life. But Paul was certainly egoistic and there are many times when he seems to suggest his own importance rather than the man Jesus whom he follows. "I think I have the Spirit of God", he says (*1 Corinthians* 7:40) and "I urge you, then, be imitators of me" (*1 Corinthians* 4:16; 11:1). Even more obvious is the statement "In my flesh I complete what is lacking in Christ's afflictions" (*Colossians* 1:24). But Paul's view of Jesus is essentially theological; he takes the Crucifixion and Resurrection as the starting point, and not Jesus' life or teaching. He certainly grants Jesus divinity, but the overall message is that God may have been in Christ, but Christ was not God himself (*1 Corinthians* 3:23; 15:28; *2 Corinthians* 5:19). The theocentric and christocentric concepts in Paul are very blurred and at times intimately woven (*1 Corinthians* 15:20–28), but identification of Jesus *as* God does not seem to have been part of Paul's message.

Where Jesus sought out sinners, Paul at times expressed a loathing of them bordering on the fanatic. He had a basic view of sin – particularly the fleshy ones! There is no holistic approach to the self with Paul, and there seems to have been a great conflict in his own self between body and mind. Man (Paul was certainly sexist) was a doomed, guilty, perverted and lustful creature (*Romans* 1:24) living in an evil world. Paul's response to what he saw as the sinful condition of man was to ask the impossible, even if he did believe that the end of the world was imminent: "let those who have wives live as though they have none, and those who mourn as though they were not mourning, and those who rejoice as though they were not rejoicing, and those who buy as though they had no goods, and those who deal with the world as though they had no dealings with it" (*1 Corinthians* 7:29–31).

Paul wrote some well-known words about love: "If I speak in the tongues of men and of angels, but have not love, I am a noisy gong or a clanging symbol." Indeed, the whole pericope of *1 Corinthians* 13:1–7 contains images of great beauty, and there are also some words of great humanistic value in Paul's letters (*Romans* 12:17, 18). Was this softer side that spoke of love the inner or outer personality of Paul? For balanced with this side of Paul are the incredible invectives against those who disagreed with him. Paul simply could not "turn the other cheek" as Jesus had advised, and the Jews that refused to accept Christ he called perverts and homosexuals! (*Romans* 1:26). His vitriolic outburst against them is more like an adolescent tirade than the words of a saint, for he accuses them of "wickedness, evil, covetousness, malice. Full of envy, murder, strife, deceit, malignity, they are gossips, slanderers, haters of God, insolent, haughty, boastful, inventors of evil, disobedient to parents, foolish, faithless, heartless, ruthless" (*Romans* 1:29–31)! Paul did not invent anti-Judaism/anti-Semitism, but he provided a good deal of fertile material to feed it for the future, as such outbursts illustrate. His accusations that the Jews killed Christ must have been particularly offensive to the Jewish Christians and the apostolic Church who emphasized that it was the *Romans* who killed Christ. Reading the Pauline letters carefully suggests a definite rift between Paul and the Jewish Christians. This, together with his massive attack on the Jewish Law, created an irreparable split between the Christian and Jewish faiths for all time. Even today there are those who believe that whatever befalls the Jews is because the Jews killed Jesus, and it is to Paul's words that we owe the origin of such nonsense:

> For you, brethren, became imitators of the churches of God in Christ Jesus which are in Judea; for you suffered the same things from your own countrymen as they did from the Jews, who killed both the Lord Jesus and the prophets, and drove us out, and displease God and oppose all men by hindering us from speaking to the Gentiles that they may be saved – so as always to fill up the measure of their sins. But God's wrath has come upon them at last. (*Thessalonians* 2:14–16)

All in all, a close examination of the personality of Paul from his letters suggests that Paul was a man of opposites and contrasts in his personality, a difficult man, capable of behaving in one way, or saying one thing, only to reveal the opposite characteristic in another context. His view of humanity was thoroughly negative: Grant, for example, considers that Paul was "obsessed by the utter, catastrophic degradation of the world. Even the best men and women, and the best of their accomplishments, seem to him tainted or poisoned at the core".[59] His view of women and sex belong in another context[60] but it is generally not a good view. Why, then, did he have such an impact on Christianity? Of course, he was an intrepid traveller, he must have had massive energy, fervour and passionate belief in his cause, even if he seemed to be formulating his ideas as time went by. This is the Paul that we generally know about, for we are rarely presented with the aggressive and fanatical Paul. We do not see his adverse personality traits unless we examine his letters carefully, forgetting the "saint" part of his title, forgetting what we have been conditioned to think about him. A good psycho-analytical study of Paul reveals a fascinating man, but a man with problems, a fanatic, a man who could probably curse others more than he could love them, a man with a definite problem with guilt, sex, what it is to be human. How this man could have any impact on *present* existence is beyond anything common sense and reason could suggest. I suppose his supporters pick and choose their way through his letters, discarding the sour for the sweet: and for some, his words remain palatable in their entirety.

The charismatic phenomenon

If Paul's personality is something of a problem to the academic, he remains the standard-bearer of Christianity to those who "have faith". And while it may seem to some that Paul's views have some relevance for modern-day Christian theology, but that he has an ethic that belongs in the past, there is one strand of Christianity that has become remarkably popular in recent years, and that has outright fundamentalist views on the alleged truths of the Bible. The regular worshippers in Protestant churches are few and far between, despite an honest attempt of the Church to present more liberal and modern approaches to its teachings, but the rise of congregations in evangelical, charismatic Christianity is quite incredible. This branch of the Christian faith accepts miracles, faith healing, speaking in tongues, uncontrollable possession by the Holy Spirit, and just about every aspect of supernaturalism possible. And as Ian Cotton notes in his research on this phenomenon: "Far from being on the fringe, Evangelicals are currently taking over mainstream."[61] His research, as recent as 1996, suggests that there are 400 million Charismatics across the world, and that they represent a quarter of Christians. One of the reasons for this growth may well be because of the spiritual needs of people, the starchiness of mainstream Christianity being too remote. The ranks of the evangelicals are joined today by Roman Catholics as much as Protestant and Non-Conformist Christians.

The term *charismatic* comes from the Greek *charisma* meaning "gift". Such "gifts" refer back to the time of the first apostles when the Holy Spirit is said to have descended on them giving them the gifts of the ability to speak in different tongues, to heal, to prophesy, and to go out into the world and preach and convert. The original experience of the apostles, whatever it may have been, and whether or not it occurred, is conveyed in *Acts* as something accompanied by great dynamism, powerful collective energy, and ecstatic emotion. Adult baptism is usually required for those who enter this evangelical strand of Christianity, such baptism being characterized by this same emotional ecstacy – something that becomes characteristic of the gathered worshippers where hysterical laughter or tears, falling to the floor, or fainting are usual. Such a phenomenon is not isolated, says Cotton, "this is a truly international movement, a genuine prototype of the global culture envisaged for the twenty-first century, a network linked by computer, jet and fax. . . . The result is global Christianity, a new-look, high-tech spirituality of unprecedented drive and clout".[62] Far from any religious decline, this suggests a considerable religious revival. Indeed, longer established sects like the Jehovah's Witnesses are also finding a considerable increase in interest and numbers in their fold.

There may well be those who would find "going under the power" being "drunk in the Spirit" or being "slain by the Spirit" as thoroughly embarrassing to witness as to participate in, but such is the experience of "going under the power" that charismatic evangelicals have often been nicknamed "holy rollers". Speaking in tongues or *glossolalia*, to use the Greek term, is a very important phenomenon to the evangelical, charismatic Christians, for it was clearly the sign of the presence of the Holy Spirit within, in the first days of early apostleship (*Acts* 2:1–4). However, recognition of any known language from such outbursts in present-day meetings, is not possible, one observer describing the phenomenon as "the belly rumblings of someone who had eaten too much pizza".[63] Joe Nickell calls it "psychobabble" which, he says, "falls somewhere between conscious deception and pious self-delusion".[64] Concomitant with the presence of the Spirit within, which putatively makes such overt behaviour possible, is a belief in the intervention of God in the lives of adherents, healing them, guiding them, saving their lives, even raising some from the dead. They accept the existence of evil and Satan along with it, original sin, the end of the world to come, and are against abortion and extra-marital sex. These are all characteristics that hardly seem compatible with the third millennium, but it seems there is something here that has meaning in the lives of a vast number of people.

Why, then, are people turning to this kind of supernatural religion? And does it mean because they are, that the Humanist message is empty? Clearly, the charismatic movement seems to meet some of the inherent needs of the human being, many of which I have highlighted above. There is certainly emotional *release*, a "letting go", in the charismatic experience, for it is highly experiential. It seems, also, that there is a profound need and hunger for the supernatural and miraculous that is filled in the evangelical context. Then, too, communal expression provides certainty in a world of uncertainty and a wider communal spirit and identity in a world that often engenders individual isolation. Indeed, all the weaknesses of the human self are seemingly answered by the charismatic phenomenon – the need for spirituality; for an assurance of permanence in the light of human finitude; the need for a certainty about life with a given set of propositions about humanity and the belief that God can quell uncertainty; a transcendence of suffering and even a promise of healing; a need for order and coherence; the need for communal and personal identity; the need for emotional satisfaction. Then, too, the immediate evangelical community provides social care for its members, provides guidance on personal matters, both moral and professional, and it allows the mind scope for fantasy, imagination, creativity and belief in the miraculous and the supernatural.

What the Charismatic phenomenon shows, I feel, is that the needs of the human being are more exigent in today's society: the higher the need for religion, I suggest, the deeper the needs of the individual inhabitants within social structures. We should not so much marvel at the rise of supernaturalistic religion, but sorrow at the reasons for the need of it. The human being is a bit like a tree with many shoots. If you prune off one part, extra shoots grow to compensate. Or if you close off one valve, another will have to burst open elsewhere to compensate. The complex age in which we live has something of the pruning, valve-closing, and constrictive effect on individuals. Thus, the more society faces empiricism, technology, pressures of employment and unemployment, lack of clarity in social norms and the lack of "space" in individual life, the more there is a need for the imaginary, the fanciful, the supernatural, the miraculous – in other words, the escape from the complexities of life at the dawn of the third millennium. So what can Humanism offer here? There is no panacea for a perfect life, but there are sound indicators within Humanist aims and objectives for how individual and communal life can be fulfilling. Above all, the Humanist goal of fulfilment of the individual self, concomitant with the altruistic goal of creating "the Good Life" in every dimension of societal interchange, has much to offer. We cannot change society until we change oursleves, and pandering to the weaknesses of the self only perpetuates those weaknesses by obfuscating them; this leaves the individual only superficially fulfilled, not autonomous, and not free.

Religions are human constructs born of human needs. As such the nature of a particular religion at any one phase in its history tells us a good deal about the society of the time. This is no less true of the modern context of religion. Individuals are a juxtaposition of opposites. When those opposites are well balanced then the individual will be well adjusted in the context of his or her own self-worth and in the wider social context. But if there is an imbalance, compensatory factors are necessary to redress the situation: religion is the redressing of an imbalance in the human and cultural psyche. Humanism has the role of pointing out this fact. It calls individuals to have courage in facing the difficulties of life, both to be what they are without positing a supernatural part of the self, and the courage to become fulfilled, to become what they best can be, at the same time giving their individual best for a better world. I rather like Jim Herrick's remark that: "Insurance in heaven is less important when it is available at Lloyd's"[65] and his words are prompted by an optimism that in this day and age we are able to direct our own lives and take control of them more than ever before. I believe that the *potential* for such direction and control is possible, but that it is, as yet, too partial. If the individual is to be fulfilled in all dimensions then he or she needs a holistic pathway through life. Yes, we can have insurance policies to cover eventual death, and yes, we live longer through medical care, but there are subtleties of the human psyche that have to be fulfilled, too – the spiritual dimension in particular. Society has to cater for development of the full potentials of all its individuals.

5

Society

Humanism believes in the complete social implementation of reason and scientific method, and thereby in democratic procedures, and parliamentary government, with full freedom of expression and civil liberties, throughout all areas of economic, political, and cultural life.[1]

The human being can never be human in a vacuum; only by the interaction with others – family, friends, associates, indeed human beings world wide – can the full dimension of that word *human* be realized. It is the experience of both our immediate world and the wider sphere of humanity that helps to make us what we are. Despite the importance placed on the human being and on individual potential, Humanism today is not generally anthropocentric: it does not see human beings at the *centre* of the universe. The modern Humanist outlook sees humanity as in a process of continuing evolution, learning to interact socially and globally. And this is a sensible view, for human beings appeared very late indeed on the evolutionary scene. If we think of the whole evolution of our planet as just one day, human beings arrive on the scene, very late in that day – at one minute to midnight![2] So if we as human beings have made mistakes, along with our many areas of progress, we haven't really been around long enough to claim centre stage.

Thus, there have been considerable failures in human ability to encounter fellow humans successfully. And the panaceas that have been offered to assist humanity – religion, science, even the older utopian goals of Humanism – have not been of any great assistance, and have certainly not provided *the* answer to human existence, if there is such a thing. Existentially, it has to be admitted that life is no easy road, but it is the way in which we journey on that road that is important. Less utopian now than it used to be with regard to its goals, Humanism has fairly clear ideas about how best society can travel forward. Its fluid nature enables it to adjust more readily to the

needs of the time, and to adapt its own goals in the light of its understanding of where we are, at this stage in the evolution of humanity.
There is no Humanist goal to control the world, as some suggest[3] and
there is certainly an acceptance of the fallibility of individuals. The
modern societies in which we live are challenging ones, but the need
to travel forward in the best possible way is exigent, given the global
problems that the third millennium will pose.

The key to the future lies in balance – well-balanced relationships
in personal, societal and global existence. Where there are well-
balanced views, there is greater tolerance, greater ability to adjust the
balance, greater openness of mind. The well-balanced individual, a
society in which the balance of prosperity, economy, justice, democracy, population growth is evident, and a global scenario in which
these factors obtain, is the more realizable goal of the Humanist
today. And of course, balance means an active and dynamic
approach to life. It means a certain *struggle* to maintain a healthy
balance in societal and global policies and outcomes, and it means
meeting the challenges that threaten the stability of a healthy balance
in all areas of life. What we cannot do is to believe that something
beyond ourselves will solve problems for us. God, science or utopian
ideologies will never achieve any kind of societal and global
harmony and balance. The answer lies in the individual self and the
contribution each person can make to the challenges of life.

Modern society

Society is not a kind of abstract that exists independently of the
people that compose it. We *make* society, and collectively we *are*
society. This means to say that there is an intimacy between individuals and the wider social context in which they are placed. One
cannot exist without the other. But there is also a certain tension
between what individuals want for themselves and what society as
a whole might expect of them. Where industrial revolution has been
the experience of societies the intimacy of individual life and social
need has been at its closest as, indeed, the tension between individual
needs and societal expectation, the latter all too frequently resulting
in oppression and disruption of balanced ways of living. The nineteenth century witnessed great struggles for personal, political,
economic and religious freedom and, as Bullock reminds us,
increased wealth, technology and welfare.[4] But, as he points out,

there is a certain disappointment about society in our own times, despite the optimism of the nineteenth century. Individuals are all too easily manipulated by the more powerful social, economic and political organizations that use the media to undermine individual freedom. The twentieth century has an appalling record for inhumanity: as Bullock also says, "it is the scale and the deliberate, systematic character of the destruction of human beings in the twentieth century which stuns the imagination". This is a destruction, he estimates, that probably amounts to fifty or sixty million people in all.[5] Twentieth century society is one that manifested considerable imbalance with a record of brutal atrocities that lessens the impact of its many great achievements.

Society for any individual is viewed in three ways: the immediate social circle of the family, friends and working environment; the wider context of the national, cultural society, and the global society of the whole of humanity. Essentially, human beings are generally somewhat self-centred in their focus on the immediate social environment. The more humanist they become, the more they are able to extend that focus to the wider vision of humanity. Sometimes, however, the focus is on the nationalistic element of society. Communism has been a case in point, as is orthodox Islamic nationalism. Here, both the individual and the global aspects of society are of secondary importance, except in the sense of being ground for active extension of nationalistic ideology elsewhere. If Marx was right in his belief that *social being* determines the consciousness of an individual, rather than individual consciousness itself, then the imposition of social culture as a result of nationalism, tradition, religion or totalitarianism does a grave disservice to what it is to be an individual. The subjection of the individual for the good of the community, the society or the state, in such cases, is a loss of individual importance to an extent that most Humanists would deplore. Thus, communism, in particular, was never a good bedfellow of humanism because of its rejection of the rights of individuals to personal fulfilment and freedom.

We all have a nationality but when this leads to *nationalism* a balanced view of society is impossible. Blackham equates nationalism with *patriotism*, pointing out the subjective nature of it and its exclusive and sometimes aggressive nature.[6] Ethnicity, where the term denotes origins by birth and not nationality, is more complex. On the one hand it is divisive, entrenching whole groups of people in cultural patterns that are very different from the general culture.

On the other hand, it is something that many feel has to be sympathetically encouraged in order to value minority cultures and give space and tolerance to social differences. It is an issue to which I shall return below in the context of equality. Ethnicity raises the issue of mini-cultures within the majority culture. And since we live in a multi-cultural society, most of us have experience of this newer kind of diverse society. Each culture has its own common viewpoints about the way life should be lived, its own customs, religion and cultural traditions. These can enrich the host culture or be antagonistic to it. To reiterate the words of Marx above concerning the impact of "social being" on individual consciousness, it is worth noting here the words of van Praag: "There is no point in asking what a man is by nature if that is not directly related to what he has become by virtue of culture."[7] This rather neatly emphasizes the way in which society and culture affect individuals sometimes to the extent of impeding personal liberty and freedom from conditioned thought and action. Is this why the human being has so many weaknesses of the psyche that rise in a need for religion, or for external identity in the larger social group? Is the human being so conditioned that he or she lacks solid personal, reasoned identity? Is the human being not exercising the powers of reasoning and rational inquiry that enable analysis of his or her own cultural conditioning? I think in many cases this is what obtains. Blackham very aptly says:

> Man, then, is born potentially human and becomes human in a society; he is bred in a culture. In so far as he never knows anything that is not mediated through that culture he remains imprisoned within it, relativized by it. When he becomes aware of other cultures, other ways of being human, he can begin to separate himself from the culture in which he is bred and to identify himself as a man. This independence, though of supreme importance, is relative, for man always remains dependent upon society and largely determined by the culture in which he is bred. Nevertheless, the relative personal independence which he can achieve is the supreme human achievement.[8]

In so far as we are able to transcend cultural conditioning in order to know our own selves and in order to reach out beyond the immediate to global humanity – regardless of the diversity of culture we observe – then we achieve something of what it is to be really *human*. But we have to remain in the parameters of the intimacy between individual and social identity. As Julian Huxley once wrote: "That human thought and behaviour are socially conditioned is a fact. If one decides to have nothing to do with this fact, out of a scrupulous regard for individual dignity and personal responsibility, there is that much less chance of providing the necessary conditions of individual dignity and personal responsibility. It works both ways."[9] Given these facts, any dream or ideology that seeks to create a global society without cultural diversity cannot but fail. Indeed, the extent to which ethnicity remains dormant only to re-emerge given certain conditions, has been evidenced recently in Yugoslavia and throughout history. This suggests that cultural diversity lies deep in the collective psyche of social groups and individuals. But, working with these factors, human beings are still capable of a vision beyond their own culture, traditions and nationality, in sympathetic extension to humanity elsewhere, and in tolerant dialogue with the rest of humanity. This makes the individual more reflective, mature, more experienced with what it is to be human. This, I believe, is a sound Humanist ideal.

Since cultures are diverse, "society" is thus a fluid term, and its nature will differ from one place to another, causing essential differences in the human beings that compose it. And what one culture considers the ideal human within society, will differ from that of another. What is the "ideal" human being to a wealthy stockbroker from Godalming, Surrey, England? White, not a woman, educated, confident, possessing a certain degree of power, respected, middle class. *He* probably plays golf at the best club, dines at the best places and would be loathe to eat fish and chips out of a paper bag while walking down the high street on a busy shopping day. Stereotyped? Of course. Most people have stereotyped views of what they expect the ideal human citizen to be, and that stereotyping reflects each person's cultural milieu. It is only when we get to know individuals that the stereotyped images are broken down. Only by transcending the immediate culture to the wider, global one, can such stereotyping of human beings be replaced by a more informed and rational perspective.

From what has been said it might be claimed that the human beings that make up any society are simply the outcome of a structuralism about which they are unaware. That is to say that all people are really what they are simply because of the present and immediate past societal structure into which they have been born. In this case, society shapes our consciousness so subtly that we are unaware of its influence and have little or no control over our own destinies. It is true that there are very subtle influences that condition our make-up, influences acquired through the familial environment, our education, working environment – and all these are culturally imposed. Yet – *and this is my thesis here and throughout this book* – it is the nuances of being human that reveal the unpredictable in individuals; human beings do not always obey the rules, conform to the norms, or want the same things that society would wish them to. And it is in the *choices* that they make in life that this is exemplified. There is always that margin for reflective and deliberate directional change. Conversely, it could also be said that it is the unpredictable nature of life that often elicits the particular nuances of human responses. The reductionists would have us reduced to the biological, chemical, environmental, psychological agents that cause us to think and respond to life in the way each of us does. But again, the human being will surprise, will surpass, will fly in the face of all these factors. There are dangers in both structuralist and reductionist thinking, and both – however rational their arguments may seem – are anti-humanist. Both reduce human beings to components of society, to that which can be trained, to that which can be manipulated. This is a long way from the autonomous human being that is capable of *reflective* rational analysis about the choices he or she makes in life and the pathways he or she pursues. Society does not exist abstractly, to reiterate an earlier point, its ethos can be consciously changed by the human beings that compose it, and no individual needs to be completely at the mercy of socio-cultural conditioning. In breaking free from this, individuals can have a reciprocal effect, they can create a new society. And it is not impossible, then, to widen the horizons of individual societies to a more global perspective. Yes, there will always be diversity in society and culture – geographical and climactic conditions alone would necessitate that – but there is no reason why a more unified global view cannot be aimed at, diversity in unity being the goal, and an interdependent humanity.

Human life is a communal life, and it is in the context of the community that some kind of meaning and purpose for life is obtained, and in which personal identity is gained. Where societal values are sound, the effect on the individual should be positive, but since society cannot exist without the individuals that compose it, it is the individuals themselves that have the responsibility to shape society for the better. And there is a responsibility to do this globally. Learning to shift one's perspective from the parochial to the global is an important stage of personal evolution. Tony Davies comments that: "One of the effects of a universalising notion like 'Man' is to dissolve precisely such particularities as race, sex and class . . .".[10]

And, of course, race, sex and class – and a multitude of other factors – combine to militate against the identity of any individual with the rest of humanity. What is needed is a global focus without being drowned in it. Individuals can, and have so often, contributed to wider societal stability. If the individual gets things right he or she will contribute to the common good of humanity. It is humanity that unites individuals and is the common denominator to their existence: the interdependence of individuals and the wider fraternity of humanity is clearly critical ecologically, economically and politically in the modern world of global communication and interchange. Common goals and a common vision for a better future should be the underpinning factors in the wider context of humanity. Each individual owes it to his or her self to contribute to the wider social and universal good. The words of the first century Greek slave turned philosopher, Epictetus, illustrate this point well:

> A person once brought clothes to a pirate, who had been cast ashore and almost killed by the severity of the weather; then carried him to his house and furnished him with other conveniences. Being reproached by some person for doing good to bad people, "I have paid this regard", answered he, "not to the man, but to human nature".[11]

Each of us has the same debt to humanity, to society and to ourselves.

The problems witnessed in society occur mainly through conflicts in individual or group interests. As one Humanist says, human society is not all that far removed from the animal kingdom in that an "eat or be eaten" ethos pervades it. But since human society is so complex, the scope for conflict is equally so, and the "eat or be eaten" principle is more subtle and abstract, but powerfully evident.[12] And while population expansion is on the agenda as an exigent global problem, the affluent survive while the impoverished perish. It is only human creativity and vision that can effect changes in this imbalance. Allan Bullock wrote graphically of his fear of what he called an "autistic" society, a society in which individuals are so locked in their own worlds that they lose the habit of communicating with others in the family, workplace, community, society and world at large.[13] And if you believe this is overstated, think to yourself how many people ask you questions about yourself. And how many questions do *you* ask people about their own lives, their work, plans, hopes, fears, even their holidays, family, hobbies, interests? Next time you are in a social situation, think about this. Global balance and harmony will never be possible until it is evident at the personal level.

It is not difficult to see the forces at work in society which are inimical to communication at a more reflective and reciprocal level between individuals. This is an age of impersonal organizations and of bureaucratic oppression. It is an age in which we are bombarded with postal rubbish, with memos, and with administrative tails that wag the dogs. The age of the computer and the photocopier has made access to the employee impersonal and oppressively immediate. The space for creativity and for imaginative living is lessened. I am sure there are many in the field of Higher Education whose working week has long ceased to be "average", whose "working weekends" have become the normal pattern of life, and whose working day includes the paper work brought home each day for the evening. The pressures in the working world are complex and subtle, sufficiently so to numb individuals into habits that lack reflective analysis. It is no surprise that the individual can unleash something of the self in charismatic religion! Big is not beautiful and not balanced: organizations can become so large, and the administration so complex – schools, colleges, universities are a prime example – that reflective communication and dialogue between management and employee cannot operate even through the paper work which masquerades under the title of "Quality Assurance". Bullock, I think, was right, individuals become things, "its", and interpersonal relationships "autistic". Humanism asks individuals to grapple with such problems, to turn events around, to be critical and rationally reflective about those aspects of everyday life that are not conducive to a "Good Life" for *all* individuals, for *all* humanity.

In so many ways, humanity militates against its own balanced existence, enough for some to claim the impossibility of a "simple humanist utopia".[14] Human nature is very complex and is characterized by a dualistic and ambivalent social and yet anti-social nature, both mostly self-centred and selfish. Usually, this self-centredness is reasonable; we all have to make decisions about where we are going and what we do in life. We also make decisions about whom and what we like and dislike, and there is no possibility *ever* that all human beings will *love* their neighbour. It is also unreasonable to expect that they should, for our own values in life are built up by the value judgements that we have formed in the context of our relationships with others. Comparing who and what is right and wrong is part of this process, and to love someone whose values we believe leave much to be desired, is to move towards the insane. But the complexity of life in the modern era – characterized by so much impersonalism, lack of time, and subtle pressures – runs the danger of encouraging people to be more self-centred in a fight for some kind of balanced existence. Where religion, race, nationalism and exaggerated cultural identity are present, such self-centredness cannot transcend itself to the wider focus on humanity. Each individual is unique, developing in the context of his or her negative, positive and neutral attitudes and responses to others. To lead a full life, that individuality should not be compromised, for if it is, the shaping of society is taken away from individual human effort and will be imposed from without. People should never be means to social ends and individuals should always exist for themselves as much as for the greater good of the society in which they live and the common humanity with which they share this planet. As one Humanist points out, "all ends of social action lie in the improvement of individual human welfare".[15]

The best goals of individuals, of society, and of humanity are not separate, they are the common goals of freedom, peace, goodwill, good health and welfare, the ability to develop potential and creativity, to enjoy the beauty and pleasures of life and to be respected and understood. Tolerance of the diversity and plurality of individuals, family life-styles, majority and minority groups and cultures, is essential for a balanced existence on this planet. Collectivism is not in itself wrong, unless the individual is swallowed up in it, as in Nazi Germany or the Communism of Soviet Russia. But in the western world it is materialism that is often blamed for the lack of realization of the best goals of humanity – a need for wealth, for material possessions in the home, for status, and for power in a so-called "consumer society". Again, it is a question of balanced needs rather than myopic material goals. Wealth is not wrong, and while it doesn't buy happiness, it can be a good deposit for it. It is difficult to find life of great value when it is hard to make ends meet. But when materialism becomes the focus of life, something else has to be jeopardized to sustain it and the prospect of balance in life is compromised. Conversely, the Christian religious ideal of poverty as the means to the Kingdom of God is nonsensical. It may have been acceptable at a time when people thought the end of the world was at hand (though it never was at hand, and still isn't) but poverty in any form is a blot on the landscape of any society, and on any individuals who complacently accept it. In the normal realms of daily life, some people work very hard and reward their hard work with *creative* materialism – building a creative home for a family, creating a garden, saving for a holiday, and so on. Others are less inclined to work in this way, may not want to work at all, or may be inclined to use what they acquire in a variety of ways. Materialism is part of the ways in which individuals, and therefore society, strive forward. Many people, I am sure, would not want to return to the same kind of materialism – or lack of it – that characterized the days of their parents or grandparents. A good life is not a poor life, even if a poor life sometimes transcends the odds and is good.

Justice is essential in societal and global existence, not the justice that sees an eye for an eye and a tooth for a tooth, but the justice that supports fairness to individuals in all walks of life. Justice is not just something that is meted out by the legal system, it is about fairness, honesty, truthfulness, integrity between individuals whether at home, school, workplace, in groups, societies, and between peoples in the wider world. In the political context, this means representative democracy that seeks justice for the minority and protection of the diversity of society as much as the majority views. Individual freedom, and the provision for economic stability and personal and cultural potential should be the outcomes of sound justice and of democratic societies. But democracy is not just something that needs to be evident in the political arena, it is essential in the home, and particularly in the workplace. Institutions so often pay lip service to democratic procedures which seem good in theory, but are blatantly disregarded in practice. How much critical discussion at a meeting is reduced to a sentence in the *Minutes* because its nature was *contra* the establishment? How *real* are democratic procedures in the working world where management so often decides its needed outcomes and requires its committees to rubber-stamp its decisions? Brave is the person who combats such injustice. Democratic systems are by no means the answer to the problems of existence in all countries of the world, but they provide the most flexible medium in which the *potential* for balance and harmony, for the removal of injustice, and the promotion of individual freedom and potential can obtain. Human beings, Rousseau believed, are inherently good and happy, it is society that has the propensity to make them miserable.

Freedom

Humanism believes that individuals have genuine free choice about what they think and what they do and that they have control over their own destinies in life. Any ideas of predestination, determinism or fatalism are rejected as outside the bounds of naturalism.[16] But if, as it seems, society is a considerable factor in making a person what he or she is, then how free are individuals *really* to shape their own lives? Can they *really* objectively detach themselves from their cultural and social setting in order to make their choices undetermined by social conditioning? The concept of freedom is crucial to Humanist thinking and is viewed in two ways. First, is the acceptance that, yes, human beings can detach themselves sufficiently from the cultural setting to have freedom of choice and, second, every human being should have the right of freedom of inquiry which assists him or her to exercise freedom of thought and action. This second point is one very good reason why Humanism does not have prescriptive doctrines and set rules for life. This was clearly stated by Paul Kurtz some years ago:

> Humanism is committed to an open mind in an open society. It does not possess its own dogma, doctrine, or creed. It does not have a set of absolute principles or a fixed programme of social action. It cannot be easily identified with one party or platform: rather it is open and receptive to various points of view and to changing and modifying moral positions and political programmes in the light of altered conditions and alternatives.[17]

This reiterates the dynamic and flexible nature of Humanist thought. It also stands as a defence of freedom and ongoing inquiry against those who, on the one hand, criticize Humanism for not having a fixed ideology, and, on the other, those who claim that it elevates science, without critical inquiry, to the level of fixed dogma. Humanism does neither, it rather maintains the principle that each human being is free to evaluate any area of life by rational inquiry, and that includes the claims of science as much as society, government, economic policies and so on, even Humanism itself. Yet, while maintaining that human freedom can obtain, common sense tells us that *absolute* freedom is a myth.

The Humanist philosopher Corliss Lamont states categorically that "freedom of choice is an inborn, indigenous, ineradicable characteristic of human beings".[18] The degree to which individuals may exercise that freedom is of course varied, but the potential for it is believed by Humanists such as Lamont to be innately there. What Humanists generally mean by freedom here is the ability to act with rational foresight instead of through instinctive and blind compul-

sion.[19] Acting with rational foresight suggests some degree of ability
of an individual to shape his or her existence. And if a person has a
degree of freedom he or she is also free *not* to do something that
perhaps ought to be done. But absolute freedom, that is to say
freedom that is devoid of any external, psychological, social influence
– any influence at all – can hardly obtain. In fact, in exercising
freedom in one area we may well be curtailing our own freedom in
another, and may be curtailing someone else's freedom.[20] This is
because we are social creatures and the interconnectedness between
one individual and the many others is too intricate for non-effective
freedom to occur. So when human beings make choices there may
well be correlative restraints put on other people.

While we may not be capable of absolute freedom of choice and
will, to suggest that we have no freedom at all in the way we exercise
choices is contrary to common sense. Of course choices that I make
are going to be influenced by past experiences and past and present
knowledge, and this will inevitably have an effect on the way I
choose, but I am *relatively* free to make choices, even if I am not
absolutely free. Since the culture and society into which I am born
determine a great deal of my thinking and the way I live, it is difficult to have a conceptual framework for thought and action that is
extraneous to it. I can only operate in my own conceptual experience,
but the freedom to extend this conceptual framework through experiences *outside* my present world is always available. Then, too, our
lives are partially determined by forces outside ourselves simply
because we cannot sit down and exercise choice about everything we
think or do in daily life. Often, other people think for us – at home, at
work, at school, in local and national government. But the important
factor here is that when we *do* want to exercise the freedom of reflective inquiry we can do so, and we then have relative freedom to
change our own patterns and direction of life. In fact, people do this
all the time.

Despite individuals having relative freedom, an interesting argument is put forward by Jack Parsons whose research concerning
population explosion leads him to the thesis that common sense
suggests people should certainly *not* be permitted even *relative*
freedom. In fact, Parsons believes that: "We are all restricted,
hemmed in on every side by a mass of regulations, both official and
unofficial, which when added up drastically reduce our freedom of
behaviour – even our thought." The result of the complexities of
constraints in society he feels is that there is "surprisingly little liberty

left".[21] Yet he does not suggest that there is no liberty at all. I think that thirty years on from his research it might be claimed that if constraints on individual choice are even more complex, the breadth of choices in today's world is greater than ever before. The uncertainty that characterizes much of today's modern world suggests uncertainty of direction and therefore of possible choices. Thus, in today's complex world, people are content to respond to choices with non-thinking, automatic responses that must surely be determined by all sorts of factors. But there are more reflective choices that are made as the result of an analysis of wide-ranging factors, ethical choices, practical choices, domestic choices, choices that change one's life radically. These are not determined at all in the strict sense of the term, though the reflective processes involved in them are likely to be partially informed by experience and personality.

But we are not *slaves* of our past experiences and our personalities; indeed, we would never progress very far if we were, and none of our knowledge would be our own. As stated above, human beings are often unpredictable; they can, and do, surprise. They can behave contrary to character, and they can feel so constrained by conditioning society that they break free of it, changing their whole lives in response to rational analysis of what they do not want in life as much as what they do want. An amusing account of the failure of behavioural engineering in the conditioning of animals is given by David Ehrenfeld.[22] It seems that when animals are conditioned to behave in a certain way, they will conform to the taught patterns *up to a point*, and then, they stop conforming and creatively misbehave! Human beings are somewhat similar. They go along with things up to a point, but they always carry with them the ability to run counter to conformity for pastures totally new, to resist, to defy, to change, to choose unpredictably but also to make rational choices for carefully analyzed and articulated reasons. Then, too, the element of chance in life so frequently raises non-determined causes that face us with the more unusual choices.

Despite common-sense views of limiting factors on our ability to make choices, Humanism is generally anti-determinist and anti-reductionist. That is to say, even if we do not exercise the relative freedom that we have, we nevertheless have it in our power to do so. The Humanist summons is to all individuals to exercise that freedom for the sake of their own potential and fulfilment and for the sake of a wider commitment to societal and global harmony. Some wise words about freedom were written by Hadley Cantril:

Freedom is, of course, not an end in itself. The quality of freedom is measured by what a person does with it. What he does with his freedom, that is, the quality of his actions, depends on the quality of his purposes. Hence freedom always involves great personal responsibility; it is not license but the responsibility for the realization of human values through purposeful behaviour.[23]

I would add here that each person has a responsibility to his or her self to utilize and develop the potential for freedom. For only through such self-evolution will the weaknesses of the self be replaced by a quality of life and self-assurance in such a way that there is control over one's personal destiny. Detrimental to exercising freedom in this way is often the sheer plurality of possibilities that face us in a very busy world. We rarely have to choose between a few possibilities, we more usually have to make choices in the grey areas between a considerable number of options, often having to compromise because the exact things we have in mind do not obtain. Do we just acquiesce in the *status quo* for a quiet life in the face of such complexity of choice? We probably do much of the time, but the more we take control, the more we come of age as human beings.

If freedom involves "great personal responsibility" to use Cantril's expression, then paradoxically, the freer we are, the more we have to exercise restraint. Parsons' view here is unequivocal, and that is that "liberty is in fact *produced* by control", and that liberty and control are not opposites but necessary complements of each other.[24] His point is driven forcibly home by the need to control population expansion by curtailing the freedom of people to have large families in order, ultimately, to guarantee the relative liberties of all human beings. His thesis, then, is that social control is necessary for individual liberty,[25] though, as he states elsewhere, the *balance* of such control is essential.[26] It is a nice problem: how far should social control limit human freedom in one way in order to promote it more generally and widely in another? And would the means justify the end? Of course, if every person developed his or her own innate potential for making informed and rational choices, resulting in equally informed rationalized restraints and responsibilities in individual lives, then there would be less need for extraneous social control. Human beings can be largely a product of all those forces that make them what they are – genetic factors, the immediate conditioning environment, their physical and psychological make-up, and the like – *or*, they can rise out of the extraneous forces that influence them and, through critical appraisal of what and who they are, acquire *identity* in their own being, and with this identity, *responsibility*. This is what it really means to be free, and it is only he or she that is free who is able to exercise true free choice. Having freedom of choice involves *moral responsibility* in the exercising of that choice and, therefore, constraints on one's own liberty. The greater the sense of freedom, the greater the sense of moral responsibility, and this means the more initiative and awareness an individual needs in the conduct of his or her personal life.

It is this kind of innate freedom that is the hallmark of the truly mature and autonomous human being. It is the potential for such individual freedom that is the important characteristic that needs to be developed by any democratic society. It is the right of each human being; those forces in society that prevent it, that reduce human beings to genetic automata, should be fiercely resisted. If human beings do not realize this potential for freedom that lies within they will become means to societal ends, pawns in a process. Freedom of critical inquiry and the ability to voice one's opinions is essential in a truly democratic environment. In the context of the British law, Nicolas Walter has graphically exposed the absurdities of the laws on blasphemy[27] and a powerful writer like Ibn Warraq defends his right "to criticize everything and anything in Islam – even to blaspheme, to make errors, to satirize, and mock".[28] This is a fierce defence of individual right of free speech. I don't suppose that many found the spoof on the life of Jesus in the film *The Life of Bryan* too harmful; but Salman Rushdie's more literary attempts ended with a *fatwa* on his life. Though after a decade, this has now been withdrawn, some respected British citizens supported physical assault against him.[29] We normally pride ourselves in the West as having the right to say what we wish, and we are able to do this liberally in most contexts, but not, it seems, in religious matters. In 1999, Glen Hoddle's statements about his personal religious beliefs cost him his job as manager of England's football team: so much for the right of freedom of speech. In Islamic law, religious unbelievers like Rushdie do not have a right to live, their lack of belief being a greater sin than murder.[30] In Islamic states Muslims are not free to convert to other faiths without having personal rights denied, even the nullification of marriage.[31] Islamic laws preventing the complete freedom of women are well known; as individuals they have restrained freedom imposed upon them – stringently in orthodox Islam and limiting in other Muslim countries, where certain occupations are not open to them. The collectivism of Islam tends to make individual freedom of choice difficult, particularly for women. Choice is dictated by the *Qur'an* not by individual rational reflection. If, as a woman, you can be suspended from your job for shaking hands with a man[32] your personal choices in the way in which you live your life are severely curtailed. Humanism believes that it is the right of individuals to have the freedom to express their ideas without fear of ostracism, persecution, prosecution, impaired career or even loss of employment.

In the religious context, an omnipotent God must, of course, know the choices any individual makes before he or she does so. This necessarily makes all actions predictable and the concept of total free will a myth. While there have been some that accept that all actions and thoughts are divinely determined in order to maintain the absolute omniscience and omnipotence of the divine – and Islam certainly takes this route – others believe that life makes no sense unless individuals have free will. The nonsense of the Christian doctrine of original sin, by which no individual is free *not* to sin, also limits human liberty in the face of religious dogma. This idea of original sin operates *collectively* as much as individually, so its tenets include the concept of innocent suffering for the sins of others irrespective of one's good or bad moral choices. This is hardly freedom at all.

In view of the Humanist ideal of self-fulfilment and the realization of the full potential of each individual, a considerable measure of personal and societal freedom is necessary for such goals. The freedom to choose one's pathway through life, and, indeed, the absence of the kinds of constraints that might inhibit the ability to choose that pathway, are essential Humanist principles. Any ideology – authoritarian, totalitarian or religious – that conditions the mind and impedes free inquiry, is inimical to freedom of rational and informed choices about what one believes and how one should act. Humanism has principles and views about life that are deliberately variable and that promote healthy debate. It has some ideology, but certainly no *fixed* ideology or dogma: it is a compass not a map. While, then, individuals are certainly constrained by some conditioning influences of temperament, genetic characteristics, the environment and so on, and while absolute freedom cannot entirely obtain, Humanism still envisages sufficient freedom for individuals to be controllers of their own destinies. But for this to be possible, a certain amount of emotional, economic, cultural, political and social freedom is necessary, and this is for the minority groups as much as the majority in society. In being anti-authoritarian, many Humanists adopt a more political activist stance, and claim the right to defy any government or other authority that offends the Humanist ethic of personal liberty. Governments exist as the voice of the people, but if they do not reflect this then they should be removed. "Men *ought* to be happy", Hector Hawton once said, "and if governments are tyrannical they should be overthrown."[33] Humanism has therefore frequently been dogged by external political suspicion.[34] But to be activist is not necessarily to eschew pacifism: many Humanists, given the scenario of war, would declare themselves conscientious objectors, not, of course, on religious grounds, but on purely *ethical* grounds.

The ideal of personal freedom of choice and the right to direct one's own life means that minority groups and individual rights are championed by Humanists. The right of a woman to have an abortion if her child is unwanted for any reason, the right to use contraceptives, the right to be a homosexual or lesbian, the right to engage in voluntary euthanasia – these and many others are the kinds of issues that interest Humanists. And all such issues are underpinned by the belief in personal liberty, the freedom to believe and to behave according to one's own dictates, providing there is no impinging on the liberties of others. Some of these issues will be taken up in chapter 8 of this book.

The key to individual freedom is personal autonomy, the freedom to make choices as a result of mature, reflective analysis arising out of a sound knowledge of one's own self. This kind of autonomy allows one to operate in the world with responsibility, with moral awareness and outcomes. The autonomous person is he or she that is able to adapt to different moral situations: having a freedom that is "inner" the mind is flexible and unencumbered with over-conditioned baggage. This is the person who has self-*identity*, who has self-*value*, who is able to choose his or her pathway through life with reflective, confidence. Autonomy brings strength of character, power of being, and the realization of one's innate and independent freedom. Individual freedom in this autonomous sense is the most important facet of existence. It is that which shapes personal life for the better and which has a wider influence on society and humanity that it helps to shape. It is man or woman come of age, self-aware and aware of the wider responsibility to all human beings. "Freedom is a certain graceful reverence for the rights and needs of other people", one writer says.[35]

Human beings are not finished products reducible to their basic physical/mental components, they are in the process of becoming, and by realization of the innate freedom that they have, can make of their lives what they will.

Equality

"Equality" is one of those words loaded with value judgement. To most of us it is a "good" word, an idealist word, a word that we associate with the best relationships and the best policies in all dimensions of life. Because it never really happens in any dimension of life, there is a tendency to idealize it even more. The word "equal" suggests sameness in degree, size, amount, level, nature, and so on. Dictionary definitions suggest also an evenness of balance, a uniformity of means and outcomes, and all these nuances of thought are absorbed in the nominative form "equality". A related word in terms of usage is "egalitarian", but this word is confined more to the principle of equality of rights and opportunities in the social context. When we address aspects of equality in the social, economic and political sense, we are normally concerned with issues of *inequality*. Most of us are moved by the pitiable scenes of starving humans in famine stricken countries, where we are faced with the inequality of economic provision of food throughout the world. We witness inequality where the black person, or the person in a minority culture in a host nation, does not have the same rights or respect as the majority citizens, where skills are not recognized because of the colour of one's skin, because of class, race or sex. Demanding equality in treatment and opportunities, therefore, seems to most of us a very reasonable principle. We sympathized, for example, with the struggle of the blacks in the United States for civil rights, as an issue of inequality, and were against the discrimination of apartheid in South Africa. Many now look back on the indignities that the British Raj imposed on the indigenous population of India with distaste. It is thus inequality that attracts our attention rather than equality.

Today we live in a multicultural society with a rich mixture of cultures. It is an interesting fact that ethnicity dies hard, if at all, and history shows that submerged ethnic identity often rises all the stronger for its period of quiescence. Despite the ongoing nature of racism, the principle of accommodation rather than assimilation of multi-ethnic groups in a host nation adds to the richness of society. As a person deeply interested in different cultures and the varied perspectives of life that individuals within them have to offer, I find ideas of the assimilation of ethnic groups anathema. But from an opposite point of view, and one not so frequently voiced in print, Ibn Warraq raises the question whether ethnic culture should be encouraged if its values are unworthy of respect. The recent, now withdrawn, Islamic *fatwa* against Salman Rushdie is a good example of this; a death threat against an author is an outrage to his personal and professional liberties that, ordinarily, should be condemned by the host nation. Says Warraq:

> Respect for other cultures, for values other than our own is a hallmark of a civilized attitude. But if these other values are destructive of our own cherished values, are we not justified in fighting them – by intellectual means, that is, by reason, argument, criticism and legal means, by making sure the laws and constitution of the country are respected by all?[36]

How far, then, should inequalities in the sense of cultural differences be tolerated if they offend basic humanistic principles set down by society? In the case of Islam, where the religious *Qur'anic* principles are offensive to the mainstream culture, Warraq argues not at all. But to maintain a general policy of assimilation would create the situation in which the *valued* inequalities between the particular ethnic minority and the host culture would be denied for a more equalized assimilation that would be abhorrent to that ethnic minority! However, Warraq's point is important in another direction, and that is that any culture should be open to critical and rational comment without fear of accusations of racism. Anthony Flew cites the case of the distinguished Professor Jean Philippe Rushton of the University of Western Ontario whose research in psychology concerned with a study of the differences between negroids, caucasoids and orientals, led to results that were construed as racist. The professional victimization of this man was deplorable, despite a perfectly rational psychological inquiry.[37] Is there, then, such an emphasis on the removal of inequality that rational inquiry is set aside? In this last case it would seem so. The Humanist perspective would be that rational, critical inquiry is the more important point here, and that no ethnic group, race or culture can be sacrosanct from free critical analysis.

This highlights that there are shades of grey about the concept of equality. In fact, the more the term is examined the more elusive it becomes. In one sense, equality is unequivocally evident, and that is in the fact that we are all human beings on this planet; we share in the same common humanity, regardless of our colour, sex, race,

nation and individual differences. If there is one area in which
equality should ideally obtain, it is in the inherent dignity and value
of each human being on the face of the earth, though, as we know,
there are individuals whose own dignity and value become somewhat diminished in the light of their actions. History is peppered
with characters of this kind. This leaves us just with the factor of the
sameness of common humanity as the equalizing factor between all
people. And as humans we laugh, cry, have hopes and fears, joys and
disappointments. Wherever we forget these basic factors of equality,
then we treat others unequally, and this is perhaps why most of us
are so moved by famine, torture, suffering, the loss of personal liberty
and so on – they touch the common humanity within us.
Remembering this common humanity, too, should encourage respect
for the liberty of others to live their own lives according to their own
perspectives, providing that these do not violate in any way the well
being of others. By this principle, one treats others with equality of
respect despite the inequalities in their various characters. Here, the
theory is sound, but as we all know there are some people that we
respect more than others: the inequalities in different characters
suffice us to discriminate, and this is to treat all others unequally. I
dare say we would have to be reduced to automatons were we to do
otherwise. But at least *in principle* recognizing and respecting the
unique human individuality, needs, desires, fears, joys and so on, of
each person, is moving towards an idea of equality of respect.

Is the concept of equality rational?

The fact that each person *is* unique and individual makes it nonsensical to say that all people are equal. They are not equal now, and
whatever policies are adopted to make people equal will never make
them equal in the future. Indeed, whenever the word "equality" is
used it would have to be qualified in some way – equality of sex, of
race, of nationality. But because people *are* different, concepts like
equality of opportunity, equality of personal freedom, equality of
outcomes, and the like, are impossible when translated into real situations. Flew aptly reminds us that we assume that inequality is bad
and equality is good[38] but if we think carefully about our attitudes to
equality, few people would want to lose the inequality that informs
individual personality. I do not want to be the same as the next
person, and I doubt whether you do either. And if we were all

supposed to be equal, then the ways in which one individual wanted to progress, to fulfil his or her self, would not be acceptable; this, of course, is preposterous. Uniformity of individuals can never obtain, though uniformity of being human is the common denominator of existence. I think no one would deny that, as human beings, there is a synonymity of basic needs that demand a certain equality of fulfilment of those needs, but aside from those very basic needs, to make us all equal is to deny individual creative need and potential. And this would make equality unjust. Then again, inequality is occasionally just: to tax the very rich for the benefit of the very poor is to treat both rich and poor unequally, but justly.

One hears a good deal about equality of opportunity, and in the field of Higher Education I have seen something of this operating. This is particularly so in the context of mature students, whose failed educational experience of the past has been transformed to success, with the spin-off of developed personality, maturity, openness of mind, and the creation of a new way of life and outlook on it. That equality of opportunity in this sense *does* obtain, is evident, but it could never obtain for all. University education is itself an *outcome* as well as the means to the outcome of the degree award. By no means can equal opportunity exist in this context or, for that matter, in any other, for individuals themselves are hemmed in by their own limitations. Access to university education, as to most areas of employment, is competitive, so while the barriers to all those of whatever class, race, sex, colour, are removed, in many areas of life, inequality at the *start* prevents equality of opportunities. Flew, in fact, considers that "equality of opportunity" might better be termed "open competition for scarce opportunities" qualifying this statement with the point: "The equality here lies in the sameness of the treatment of all the competitors in an open competition, and the only opportunity which is equal is precisely the opportunity to compete on these terms."[39] So any lack in equality of outcome is not necessarily indicative of inequality of opportunities, it is more indicative of inequalities in the starting points of the competitors for those outcomes. And since people are not the same, have different propensities and different advantages and disadvantages, equality of opportunity becomes a myth. Nevertheless Bernard Williams, while agreeing that an equal start for all is impossible in the pursuit of any outcome, advocates that inequality of, or disproportion in, opportunity can be said to exist "if the unsuccessful sections are under a disadvantage which could be removed by further reform or social action".[40] This, indeed, would be the Humanist point: individuals are different, but the social impact on sectors of society should not discriminate against some in such a way that the *propensity* for opportunity is impaired.

That the propensity for success in many areas of life obtains *despite* a bad start – whatever that may be – is certainly the case for many individuals and, it would seem, when the genetic strain appears to suggest this should not be so. In fact, a child from an aspiring working-class family may often outstrip his or her middle-class counterparts from a professional background.[41] And, of course, having the opportunity to do something does not mean that one necessarily wants to do it, to which many frustrated parents of some young people will probably testify all too well. Even if there were some way that equality of outcome could be guaranteed (and that would mean imposing inequality on the ability to fulfil potential, and denying the freedom of some to stride further than their counterparts), people just do not want the same and cannot be straitjacketed into similitude. Even in the case of justice, in the case of the law, where we might expect equality to obtain, inequality is often better than legalistic similitude. If a persistent thief should be meted out the same justice as a first offender who has stolen through a situation of dire need, we would cry "injustice" and expect inequality of legal sentence. To suggest that equality can obtain then is to pursue a myth. To quote Flew, once more: "In so far as people are free to choose their own objectives, and to do their own things, the outcome is unlikely to be a universal equality of condition".[42]

Equality of the sexes

It is in the realm of the debated equalities and inequalities between the sexes that the term "equality" is more appropriate, not least because it is a question of a balance between just two factors, male and female. The extensive literature today on the issue of inequality of the sexes, and the rise of, and sustained interest in, feminism, is serving to release the female half of humanity from a history of silence and repression. In searching for a major reason why women world-wide have had, and so often still have, such a raw deal in life, it is difficult not to point the finger at anything other than religion as the culprit. The Judeo-Christian biblical narrative that deals with the creation of Adam and Eve at the beginning of *Genesis* portrays an Eve who is decidedly inferior to Adam – even before she touches that dreadful apple. She speaks rarely, and only when spoken to. Made from the rib of Adam, and led to him by God, the myth might have portrayed her as very special, but not so, it is interpreted as portraying her inferiority. And when she eats the apple – reaching out for knowledge – she is punished by pain, particularly in childbirth, toil, drudgery, and subservience to her husband. The idea that childbirth *should* be painful for a woman was so deeply entrenched that when chloroform was discovered it was felt it should not be used in childbirth. It was Queen Victoria who eventually demanded it.

In the Jewish tradition women have always had considerable status in the home. The family is of immense importance in Judaism for it is the pivot around which the religious tradition revolves and it is the woman who maintains these traditions in the home. Yet throughout Jewish history one is always aware of the patriarchal emphasis, and the ultimate subordination of women. Adultery according to the Mosaic code was punishable by death, the fate also of the bride who was not a virgin. However, chastity in Judaism was frowned on, so marriage was praiseworthy and the norm for most people. Jesus as an unmarried Jew was an anomaly in Jewish society.

The coming of Christianity changed this more normal attitude to marriage by encouraging virginity – sometimes even in marriage – and by acquiring a morbid fear of sex. Chastity and celibacy were highly thought of, enough for the Early Church to see the need for Mary the mother of Jesus to remain a virgin, despite the fact that this embarrassed the biblical text by preventing Jesus being of the line of David. Similarly, Jesus' brothers in the Roman Catholic Bible are presented as his *cousins* in order to preserve Mary's traditional virginity. The Christian Saint Augustine battled considerably with the choice between Christian chastity and the mistress he enjoyed: "Give me chastity" he said, "but not yet!" All this is quite different from the Jewish tradition in which even the High Priest had to be married to perform the great ceremonies involved in the Day of Atonement, *Yom Kippur*. Marriage was essential here for the effective atonement of sin, but in Christianity marriage became a source of sin and impurity.

If Christianity had arisen out of the traditional teachings of Jesus, women might have had a better deal in Christianity. It was, indeed, two women who are alleged to have discovered the empty tomb of Jesus and were the first witnesses of the alleged Resurrection. Before the dawn of Christianity, Roman women were not strangers to study, and to legal, political and social activities alongside men. They could also inherit property. The Pauline view, however, was that women should be subject to their husbands, even if Paul occasionally praised them for their work in the Church. Paul's attitude to women borders on the pathological and, as time evolved, their exclusion from ceremony consolidated. Margaret Knight observes:

> They were not, needless to say, permitted to sing in cathedral choirs, and when part-singing emerged in the Middle Ages, the necessary higher tones were provided by boys and by male *castrati*, whose mutilation was evidently considered a lesser evil than the admission of female singers. Women were enjoined not to come near the altar while mass was celebrating, and an edict of the sixth century forbade them to receive the eucharist into their bare hands.[43]

We must lay the blame for such antagonism to womanhood at the feet of Paul. The contradictions within Paul's personality have been dealt with above, but nowhere are they more evident than in his attitude to women. He was not dismissive of women for he could shower praise on them as with Phoebe, a *deaconess* of the church of Cenchreae (*Romans* 16:1), Mary, who is praised for her hard work (*Romans* 16:6), and Julia and Nereus (*Romans*: 16:15). He also states that male and female are equal as one in Christ Jesus (*Galatians* 3:28), but this praise and appreciation is considerably outweighed by the inequality of women in relation to men conveyed by what seems to be the opposite side of his character, and his main message. Woman does not have the same standing before God as her husband does (*1 Corinthians* 11:3); it is man that is the glory of God, and woman is only the glory of man (*1 Corinthians* 11:7–9). Women should even veil their heads in case they entice the angels! They are told to be *subject* to their husbands (*Colossians* 3:18), to keep silent in church and to be subordinate (*1 Corinthians* 14:35). The second chapter of *Timothy* likewise stresses the submissiveness of women to men in that no woman is to teach or have authority over men. Paul blames woman as a deceiver and transgressor though he thinks she can be saved through bearing children and through a life of faith, love and holiness (*1 Timothy* 2:11–15). Widows over sixty, it seems, could be accepted into the Church, providing their "good deeds" were evident, whereas young widows whose needs in society must have been considerable, were to be excluded:

> But refuse to enrol younger widows; for when they grow wanton against Christ they desire to marry, and so they incur condemnation for having violated their first pledge. Besides that, they learn to be

idlers, gadding about from house to house, and not only idlers but gossips and busy-bodies, saying what they should not. (*1 Timothy* 5:11–13).

Despite many scholars apologetically explaining away such attitudes of Paul, he himself gives very clear reasons for his attitude to women – the creation of woman from man, and her original transgression in disobeying God. But perhaps his reasons lay deeper, as Grant suggests and that: "Suppressed and frustrated sexual desire . . . may be the 'thorn in the flesh' of which Paul complains".[44] And even were we to accept that Paul's invectives against marriage were the result of his belief in the imminent second coming of Christ, this is an oversimplification; the *psychology* of his words suggests otherwise. Any discussion of the "flesh" is surrounded with irrational strong contempt and his harshest judgements are usually aimed at sexual offenders (*1 Corinthians* 5:2–5). Sexual immorality is, for Paul, the worst sin (*1 Corinthians* 6:18) and his attitude to sex totally dominates his view of marriage. His whole view of marriage seems to have been as an institution to justify the satisfaction of sexual lust between two persons, and to prevent the immorality of indiscriminate sex (*1 Corinthians* 7:1–9, 36–40). There is no thought whatsoever in Paul's mind of a communion between two people in anything other than a bodily sense. It would be difficult not to conclude that Paul had anything other than an unnatural attitude to women, marriage and sex, and that he was a man who could not rationalize his inner conflicts. It is unfortunate that his impact on the future development of Christianity was such that women throughout Christendom have had no real social standing and that they were required to repress their inner identity.

The early Church attitude to women took its lead from Pauline teaching about women, sex, and marriage, and as Europe became Christianized the inferior status of women within Christian life became firmly entrenched. It is taking women a long time to break free from the conditioning of two millennia, and there is still far to journey in feminine issues of equality. The patriarchalism of religion survives still, and the more evangelical strand of Christianity still maintains the concept of the man as the head of the household, as does the Church of Jesus Christ of the Latter-day Saints (the Mormons) and Jehovah's Witnesses. Paul's words have travelled far through time. Outside the context of religion, the lower class woman lived a life of enslavement, and with the coming of the Industrial

Revolution, found herself in the mills and the mines. By contrast, in the late eighteenth century, the higher-class woman was expected to be frail, blushing and delicate. She was deemed to know nothing of sex, to be incapable of sexual desire, was ignorant of the world, shy and innocent. Today the idea of the incapability of women in the working world has been steadily disproved by the competence and skills of women themselves, but the idea that women are essentially weaker physically and mentally has hung over into many areas of life.

At least in the western world today women are entitled to divorce as much as men and are not left destitute as a result of it. Strictly speaking, both the Protestant and Roman Catholic Churches regard marriage as indissoluble during life, and so neither accepts divorce. The Protestant Church, however, will sometimes be prepared to conduct a wedding blessing for a divorcee who is remarrying, but few ministers would marry a couple where one or both are divorced. Divorce in the Roman Catholic context does occur, but usually a divorcee is not permitted to take part in the Mass, and some are not allowed to attend church at all. Primitive Methodists do not accept divorce at all and many would rather leave their congregation than worship alongside a divorced person, even if that person were the innocent party in the divorce. The Humanist view is unequivocal: when marriages turn sour and life within the marriage becomes unfulfilling, then there is no reason why the marriage should not end. To Humanists, marriage is a *legal* contract, and what the law joins together, the law can put asunder. Outside the western context, in orthodox Islam and orthodox Judaism, divorce is almost impossible for a woman, and it is difficult in many eastern cultures, the divorced woman finding her place in society a difficult one, as in the Hindu culture. Traditionally, in all cultures, men have found it easier to abandon women, divorce them, to have extra-marital relationships, to rape. In Islam, for example, the woman who has been raped more usually ends up herself with a charge of adultery.[45] Indeed, in Islamic law women are inferior to men, and in the law court their word is valued at only half a man's, so you would need twice as many women witnesses as male ones.

Viewing sex as an expression of love, a valuable experience in itself aside from the function of procreation, has not in the past been the religious attitude. Procreation is still the primary reason for the sexual act in Roman Catholicism – hence the non-acceptance of contraception. The Humanist view of sexual love is that it is up to individuals to decide what is right and valuable as sexual experience – and that may be heterosexual or homosexual. It is interesting that whenever there is talk about a decline in morals in society, it is usually *sexual* morality that is meant and not issues like ethnic cleansing, animal rights, disregard of human rights, and so on. There is much criticism today of our permissive society, but the western woman who wishes to have sexual freedom does not have to suffer the ostracism or the peeping of neighbours behind curtains as used to be the case. If western society *is* over-permissive it is a permissiveness that is better than the dark sexual repression of the Victorian era. However, even if women can dictate in a more equal way the kinds of relationships they have, the Humanist view is still one that advocates relationships that are stable, happy, mutually helpful and respectful, and that where permissiveness causes unhappiness, it is distinctly not for the individual or common good.

The prejudice against women in the Indian context has been highlighted well by Indira Kulshreshtha[46] who is an advocate of education for equality between the sexes in India. The National Policy on Education aims at overcoming the discrimination against girls as a means to improve adult equality between the sexes. Yet, Kulshreshtha claims, the education of boys and girls still "reflects the roles society intends them ultimately to perform".[47] At least in the West the schools have broken through the barriers of gender role-conscious education in textbooks and curricula. Slowly, India is following suit, not only in the type of education that is offered to young children, but also in the education of adult women to encourage the discovery of their own skills and the particular contributions they might make to society. More globally, movements like UNIFEM, the United Nations Women's Development Fund, encourage and assist economic and political empowerment of women in developing countries.

The Humanist stance on the equality of status and respect of both sexes is clear. But even in the humanist tradition of the past, it was the centrality of man and not woman that was evident. In the past, "the humanist imagination" says Tony Davies, "is haunted by sexual terror and desire".[48] It was left to those women who fought for the political and social emancipation of women in the late nineteenth and early twentieth centuries to infuse into the spirit of humanism a more balanced view of male–female abilities. Most people have heard of Bertrand Russell, fewer of his wife Dora Russell, a great champion of women's rights.[49] Today, the rights of women are fully supported by

Humanists, but even male Humanist writers are still sufficiently insensitive as to use sexist language, even in very recent publications in an age when writers should be more practised at avoiding this. And it will not do either to put a note in the introduction of a book indicating that the use of "man" refers to the man and woman. The language of the *text* must change, and for those of us who have long managed to do so (especially if we are women) the retention of sexist language is, to say the least, irritating.[50]

It would be futile to suggest that fundamentally men and women *are* equal, because they are not. Carol Gilligan says that "women not only reach mid-life with a psychological history different from men's and face at that time a different social reality having different possibilities for love and for work, but they also make a different sense of experience, based on their knowledge of human relationships".[51] Men and women are very different in radical ways, but this does not justify discrimination against women, for their particular differences provide the complement to maleness, and both male *and* female are the dual components of humanity. To deny status to either of these components is to create an unbalanced and incomplete humanity. Men and women *are* obviously genetically different. But they don't necessarily conform to those differences in practice. Polly Toynbee points out, rather amusingly:

> We have overcome nature in most respects and we battle with it continually. If biology ruled, then women would be knocked out by the pheromones of sweaty men and men would prefer fat women who are a better bet for childbirth. However, men appear to prefer Twiggy women and women hate smelly men. So culture wins over evolution.[52]

We do not have to conform to what Nature has genetically donated to us. As Toynbee says: "What matters is not what nature has given us, but what we choose to do about it."[53] Transcending gender stereotyping is essential for maturity, both in how we view ourselves, as well as in how we view others.

The Humanist outlook incorporates the notion of equality for all people and peoples, despite the problems posed by a conceptual analysis of the word. Indeed, the Humanist vision of the "good society" suggests that, although people would necessarily have different skills and abilities, different natures and personalities, they would all be interested in the common good, and that common good is inclusive for all people. It is a view reflected by Quakers, perhaps the only religious group that strives hard for equality and tolerance in a very meaningful way. Discrimination is sometimes necessary, as for criminals on the negative side, and, for example, *Dalits*, the former untouchable castes of India, on the positive side. Both negative and positive discrimination is necessary to produce a balance of equality. The idea of equality is really a social philosophy, a desire to create the kind of harmony in global society that suggests tolerance, fairness, respect – all those admirable relational concepts that we admire in personal and social contexts, but stretched out towards humanity. Creating the right kind of conditions for this in society is a Humanist goal.

Education

Education is a critical medium for the inculcation of ideas and culture. It is one important way in which minds are shaped and influenced, so it has built into it a moral obligation to pass on by appropriate and ethical means the knowledge and skills necessary in the process of education. While writing in the context of humanism of the past, the Humanist concept of education in our present day is presented admirably by Alan Bullock who depicts education

> not as training in specific tasks or techniques, but as an awakening to the possibilities of human life, a drawing out or cultivation of a young man's or young woman's human-ness. Some people are born with this awareness and their potentialities unfold naturally. But for the majority it needs to be evoked. Hence not only the central importance humanists have always attributed to education but also the broad terms in which they have conceived it as grounded in a general education, aimed at the all-round development of the personality and of the full range of an individual's talents.[54]

These are sound words and sound aims. We transmit so much to young receptive minds in the early years of childhood and the formative years up to adulthood, much of which is absorbed automatically and without critical or rational thought. Although the lack of ability for abstract thought in the very young child makes analysis of much information almost impossible, as the ability for more abstract inquiry and reflection develop, they should be thoroughly encouraged. Children soak up ideas like sponges and, therefore, we are morally bound to deliver knowledge with care. As one writer puts it: "Like immune-deficient patients, children are wide open to mental infections that adults might brush off without effort."[55] Freud spoke of "education to reality"[56] and this is to suggest that education should be geared to the releasing of full adulthood of each individual – an adulthood not dogged by childish beliefs where knowledge has been imparted without care. The creation of fully autonomous and rational individuals is surely the best possible aim for any educational theory and practice. In a world in which individuals should be free to make their own choices in life then the responsibility for encouraging the right kind of choices lies very much with the role of education. Encouragement of rational and critical thought and not blind obedience is essential as an educational aim, developing individual freedom in tandem with moral responsibility.

Not only are the goals of education critically important in the development of the autonomous individual, but the learning process is itself critical. Ends are rarely justified by their means and the intrinsic value of individual tasks in the whole process of education is an essential ingredient. Indeed, without a high intrinsic value to educational tasks, the learning lapses into conditioning and training in which the fundamental goals of education have been lost. Because not all individuals can achieve the same ends, the same kinds of outcomes, the intrinsic value of the individual processes of education are critical to valuable experience in the learning process. Education cannot be a leveller of outcomes, otherwise there would be many marking time while others catch up, and some may never do this. But education can and should provide the fullest possible experience for *every* individual in a way that develops full potential according to the aptitudes of each individual, and in a way that encourages self-value. At the same time, where an individual has developed a commitment and genuine interest in offering his or her potential to the wider context of society as a whole, then education has been successful.

Humanists are generally opposed to church schools, that is to say Anglican or Roman Catholic schools, in which children are educated in the respective Christian teachings of these faiths alongside their secular education. Their objections are twofold. First, they contend that young children are not receiving an "open" education but are being indoctrinated at worst, and conditioned at best, into specific religious belief at an age when their minds are impressionable and vulnerable. Second, they object to the use of taxpayers' money to support such schools that finance only 2 per cent of monies themselves. They are equally horrified at the rote learning of the *Qur'an* by young children at the after-school sessions and Saturday morning schools held at mosques. They would be considerably alarmed should Muslims win the right to set up their own educational systems in countries where a more liberal state education operated.

The modern trend in education at all levels is subject compartmentalism and discipline specialism. In Britain the 1988 Education Reform Act imposed a National Curriculum for all subjects except Religious Education (though Religious Education, together with the National Curriculum, form what is termed the "Basic Curriculum"), prescribing the areas of knowledge and attainment targets for each level of school education. This is extremely outcome-geared, though the range of learning tasks and understanding expected are broad enough. Importantly, critical, reflective inquiry underpins all stages, and this is a sound rationale, but competitiveness and the tight assessment procedures, along with periodic school inspections, have made stress-related illnesses endemic to the teaching profession.[57] At the other end of the scale, the pressure in Higher Education is, as was seen earlier in this chapter, considerable and often excessive. I sympathize with Kurtz's statement on the similar scene in the United States where he derides the compartmentalism of subject areas and sees the most important aspects of academic freedom as "intellectual integrity, independence of mind" – and something that I am sure many colleagues near and far would endorse – "freedom from committee work"![58] Kurtz is right that a certain cross-disciplinary knowledge is a healthier academic and educational vision, but we are increasingly forced into narrower specialism for the purpose of career development and institutional funding.

Every human being has a right to knowledge, and to knowledge that is morally qualitative and delivered by the best possible approaches. In educating the individual we are educating society, changing society, opening society. But it is important to be aware of the reciprocal nature between individual consciousness and the society into which one is born. It is the accident of birth in a particular culture that shapes the way an individual thinks. Were he or she to be born in another continent, then he or she would think differently. Understanding that there are other perspectives of life, other views about history, literature, art, music and so on, is part of what it means to be globally conscious and more openly educated. But the emphasis is turning away from the Humanities to science and the many disciplines that it has spawned, to technology and information technology. This emphasis runs the risk of being unbalanced. It also runs the risk of *training* the mind away from the aesthetic and from the reflective and, it must be said, from the subjective. Asking questions about the nature and purpose of things, asking questions about needs, about the self, society, where we are going in life, and what kind of individual pathway is right in life, making moral decisions, thinking about responsibilities, about relationships and about individual, societal and global needs, are the kinds of reflective inquiry that are not found so readily in scientific and technical education. Science and technology used wisely need an underpinning philosophical rationale.

Education, then, should foster creativity, independent thought, the ability to analyse material carefully and thoughtfully, and the ability to argue rationally. If it is sufficiently ethical, education should enable young people to develop what Kurtz terms "the common moral decencies" in relation to their own lives and to the lives of others.[59] The aim is to develop a "whole" person. Many Humanists believe that children acquire this kind of independence in a freer educational environment in which a more unstructured approach in the teaching of the child is to be found. Indeed, this kind of education has benefited many children, but educationists generally find that children feel more secure and develop better in a more disciplined and structured environment which, at the same time, provides times for freer and more flexible learning.

One of the criticisms that Humanists have always had concerning education is of the role of Religious Education in the curriculum. Church and not state control of education was the pattern of the past, but even though the state is now responsible for education, in Britain Religious Education remains a contentious issue. The 1988 Education Reform Act dealt with a wide range of subjects in its National Curriculum, but left Religious Education outside it, yet compulsory, unless parents wished to withdraw their children from it. Its syllabus was to be decided at local levels. The wording of the Act required all *new* syllabuses (old ones continued until 1995) to "reflect the fact that the religious traditions in Great Britain are in the main Christian whilst taking account of the teaching and practices of the other principle religions represented in Great Britain".[60] Prior to the Act, a small number of more enlightened local authorities had devised syllabuses that were used to teach Religious Education on a strictly non-confessional basis and from a multi-faith point of view. There was much to be said for this approach to learning about other cultures, but the Act allowed for considerable local variation in interpretation, and, sadly, the boring RE lessons based on biblical teaching alone still obtain widely despite inspections.

One of the problems in the teaching of Christianity is that, contrary to the case in other subjects, teachers seem reluctant to present the material openly and critically, for example on the good and bad points of the characters Jesus and Paul. But education about religion should be as investigative as education in science or history. It is only in Religious Education that children are encouraged to believe and not critically appraise. This is instruction in, not education in. And Christianity is still far too frequently seen to be the medium through which moral behaviour is taught. Morality, of course, should not be something that pertains to one subject (let alone one religion) but should infuse the whole curriculum of the school and the ethos of the school itself. To be fair to the National Curriculum guidelines, the spiritual and moral development of the pupil that they require are not in any way suggestive of a religious context, but *should* pervade the curriculum and the general ethos of the school. It is just that the requirement of the spiritual and moral development of the child tends to be interpreted *in practice* as belonging in lessons on Religious Education. The "spiritual dimension of a school's life", then, is very much concerned with its whole working *secular* ethos. I do not think the advocates of spiritual and moral development would quarrel with the words of the Scottish Humanist document *The Challenge of Secular Humanism*, when it advocates moral education as being wider than Religious Education:

> Far better, surely, from the outset to see such things as kindness, generosity, cooperation, unselfishness as human goods in themselves, and such things as cruelty, exploitation, malice and selfishness as wrong from a purely human point of view. For then their moral values will remain unaffected by any vacillations in belief.[61]

This important issue of the independence of morality from religion will be the topic of chapter 6.

Learning about religion in an open way has a function in education in the same way as any other subject. Religion is a dimension of human existence that can hardly be ignored. But there is no reason why it cannot be an *educational* experience, one that reveals something about humanity worldwide and, therefore, essentially multicultural and multi-faith in content. Part of what it is to be educated is to have some knowledge of the religious response to life. And I do not see that the Church in any form has a role in discussions of educational principles involved in the teaching of religion. Moving the religious bodies away from decisions about the teaching of religion will make it an academic subject in its own right, not a subject to fulfil subjective goals of local confessional people. That this confessionalism clearly obtains, was brought home to me by a letter of a vicar printed in the local newspaper. He protested about the teaching of faiths other than Christianity in a school in which I had introduced a new "open", experiential-learning, and multi-faith approach to the teaching of Religious Education. He objected to the colourful displays of Hindu *mehndi* patterns[62] and aspects of the life of the Buddha in the school hall where he conducted a morning assembly. Sadly, this kind of prejudice of Christian ministers is not isolated. The Christian maxim to love your neighbour is all very well, but the *as yourself* part of it is conveniently forgotten if it has to extend to equal investigation of the religious beliefs of those outside Christianity.

But apart from religious stances for life such as Judaism, Christianity, Islam, Hinduism, Buddhism and Sikhism, knowledge of the secular responses to life is also part of what it means to be educated. And if modern syllabuses do not include such secular responses, then we are short-changing the educational experience of pupils. Since the Humanist movement is the best co-ordinated secular response to date, it has much to offer as a life-stance alongside the different religions. Humanism is only sporadically represented on SACREs, the Standing Advisory Councils for Religious Education, which are responsible for localized policies with regard to Religious Education. One reason for this is that Humanism does not fall into any of the categories of representation (representatives of the local authority, of major religious groups, and of teachers' associations). It is here that Humanism needs to be seen as a more recognized life-stance (albeit varied), one that reflects secular viewpoints, and one that provides as important a dimension of life as religions are believed to.

One issue on which Humanists are unanimous is that the daily act of worship in schools should be abolished. Frequently a boring experience (though a useful medium for letting the school know how the sports teams got on in extra-curricular activities, and for launching diatribes against litter!) it really has nothing to do with education, and should never be linked with religious *education* which is informed by completely different aims and objectives. Collective worship in schools in Britain is required to be daily, and "wholly or mainly of a broadly Christian character" (even in a school where the intake is predominantly Asian!). Some misguided teachers take the rubric for school collective worship to apply to Religious Education, justifying "wholly or mainly" teaching about Christianity. It is to be hoped that an informed inspectorate is correcting misinterpretations and enforcing better teaching. Many head teachers feel that school worship is an intrusion into the educational day; again it is religionists not educationists that have set this standard.

Inimical to education is the present trend to "train" rather than "educate". There was a time when the word "training" was anathema in education, because it was suggestive of a passive and uncritical experience of the learner. Religious *Instruction* became Religious *Education*, Physical *Training* became Physical *Education* and would-be teachers no longer went to Training Colleges but to Colleges of *Education*. Now, however, there is an emphasis on *vocationalism* and this underpins the whole idea of *training* – training a person for a particular vocation. Vocationalism has as its goal the suiting of education to the needs of industry and the needs of society. There is much to be said for an education that, when all is said and done, has the end product of employment relative to that education. But in order for this to take place the education received has to be more of a specific and less general nature. Vocationalism requires a focused training of an individual, for a specific outcome, geared to a specific type of employment. Its aims are to enable individuals to be employed, to meet the needs of employers and to provide vocational training that equips an individual with recognisable competences that are assessed as National Vocational Qualifications (NVQs). What is being claimed is that employers want efficient, trained, competent employees, and people *want* to work, for being employed is a means to a better life and an important ingredient in the good life.

While it might seem on the surface that the aims of vocationalism are to some extent humanistic, in fact there is much that conflicts with Humanist principles at a deeper level. To begin with, there are now significant surveys which demonstrate that after vocational training people can end up in employment that is not in the least rewarding and can develop very negative attitudes to employment as a result.[63] Thus, simply to aim at training individuals for employment is itself insufficient. As for discrimination, Roger Dale unequivocally states that the new vocationalism "is intended for the 14–18-year-old age group, and aimed much more at the lower two-thirds of the ability range than at those who follow the traditional academic route".[64] But the greatest problem as I see it lies in the fact that vocationalism is *outcome* geared, and these outcomes are usually employer defined. This means that ends are important and methodology in the achieving of those ends less so – a point that has been one of the greatest criticisms of vocational training. We train dogs, horses, and very young children who are incapable of rationalizing why they should behave or think in a certain way. Training in skills for NVQs is not dissimilar. It suggests that rational analysis of what one is doing and why one is doing it are neither necessary nor applied in much practice. In being outcome-orientated training is linked so stringently with its end product that it loses its ability to foster the creative potential of an individual. Unfortunately, individuals are not always able to exercise choice within the framework of the skills they are learning to acquire; they are not developing adaptability and creativity. Of course, good training in vocationalism provides intrinsic value in the competences and skills required for successful achievement of standardized outcomes. But, overall, vocational training is reductionist in ethos, using people for industrial ends, and not allowing sufficient individual creativity.

The concept of education has commitment to values written into it, training does not. Knowledge is not something to be pushed aside for mechanical competences, it is the right of any individual. Thus Shirley Fletcher's comment: "The emphasis is no longer on knowledge, or theory, or *what has to be learned*. The emphasis is very specifically on *what individuals should be able to do in the work place*"[65] is suggestive of mechanical training without a scrap of rational judgement. This is thoroughly offensive to Humanist principles. It seems we are living in an age when it is not required that people *do* think about what they are doing, and it is something to be guarded against by all individuals. If education becomes mere training without reflection, society will be at a great disadvantage in the future. Already, our training of teachers is eschewing the knowledge-based curricula in favour of trained competencies. If our teachers have no education in reflective analysis, what can they offer the children they teach? What will be the value of their fundamental aims? Education is not a neutral principle, for its aims, objectives and methodologies, its learning processes and outcomes have to be the very best we can offer.

It is my contention that training is inimical to this, inimical to critical reflection and the kind of understanding that should underpin learning processes. Alan Bullock was particularly perceptive when he wrote that "men and women are going to need and claim more, not less, insistently than in the past the opportunity to develop their individuality, establish their identity and be treated as people in their own right, not as the objects of social or the instruments of political policy".[66]

The Humanist society

So what kind of society does the Humanist envisage? The dynamic and fluid nature of Humanism makes it socially rather than politically geared so that it is not allied to any particular political stance or political party. Humanist individuals will differ in their responses to the economic and political arena. But because they are usually dedicated to creating the best for society they may identify with particular political or even religious groups at any one time, if there is in common a policy for the improvement of social, economic or global conditions of life. In a way, Humanism seeks to underpin political theories with a focus on what is right for individuals and society, but it is not allied with specific political theories.[67] The Humanist vision for society is one in which the "Good Life" is available for all individuals and therefore for society as a whole. This is a society that will create the kind of conditions to promote the freedom, prosperity, creativity and fulfilment of all individuals within it, democratically, whatever class, colour, race, sex or status a person has. It has a vision of high standards of living, world democracy, peace, and a flourishing economy. Sound health, satisfying work, economic security, educational opportunity, cultural enjoyment, sufficient recreation, and the freedom to express one's life so that it is satisfying and fulfilled, are all aspects of what the Humanist sees as the best kind of societal living.

In the social context, Humanism has a distinct element of utilitarianism, and a long history of it. Utilitarianism is a belief that the individual should contribute to the welfare of the community by the significant role he or she plays in the community – at work, or otherwise. Nowhere, however, is personal satisfaction compromised for this goal, but, as Lamont stated of this utilitarian principle, "it holds that the individual can find his own highest good in working for the good of all".[68] If individuals can contribute to the social good, there is a hope that the progress of humankind will be sound, and that a happier existence for future generations will follow. This is the utilitarian principle of the greatest happiness for the greatest number, present and future. The Humanist belief is that we *can* change human nature. As Lamont says: "Men are born with brains; they acquire minds."[69] Sound social development and good educational policy can do much to encourage individual self-fulfilment and a corresponding awareness of, and responsibility to, the common good. There is thus always a reciprocal altruism of individual to society and society to individual, and of independence and interdependence. Humanists often speak of their goal of an "open" society. This is one that does not contain such "closed" independent systems that have little interaction with, and therefore little contribution to, the wider context of society. Harold Blackham some years ago explained the open society as "a common foundation for the coexistence and co-operation within the same polity of communities which differ in their beliefs and ways of life".[70] As he stated, the open society hinges on respecting individuals for who and what they are and not as social or universal ends, but there is at the same time an expectation that individuals would contribute to the common good. An "open society", then, is one in which there are differences in dimensions of belief, but one in which all people work towards the common good of society and share a common education, common health care, and justice. And the word "common" here denotes cooperative and participatory interchange between people of differing beliefs, in a way that avoids social segregation of minority groups, or dominance of one group over another.

It is clear that a fundamental ideal of Humanism is "to consider humanity as a whole".[71] There is a clear moral commitment to the building of a world community. A concept of global democracy is concomitant with the idea of the greatest good for the greatest number. Humanism would fall short of its goals were it not to address its ideals to all humanity. Yet there is no concept of a collective destiny for humankind, for the constant shifting of the goal posts is necessary as new horizons and challenges are revealed. But there are idealist ends to which humankind might wish to move – peace, security, a "Good Life", prosperity. The Humanist holds these ideals in mind, actively promoting them whenever possible. The existentialist Sartre believed in what he called "a human universality"[72] which is constantly coming into being and which is informed by the conscious purpose of individuals. This is to say that choices of any individual are *human* choices and contribute to the *humanism* of all beings. While Sartre's connection between individual purpose and choice and "human universality" is contentious (I could, for example, work towards freedom for myself, while keeping others enslaved), the idea illustrates rather well the typical humanist interconnection between individual, society and world which sees individual, social and global fraternity.

Sartre saw "man" (*sic*) as continually surpassing himself, "projecting and losing himself beyond himself",[73] transcending himself, and it is this facet, he believed, that makes the human being human and a part of humanity. This is a useful idea against reductionism for it suggests that to be thoroughly human is to go beyond the constituents of the self. But Sartre's idea also serves to link the individual and humanity at large rather well, so that his existential humanism suggests a free individual who makes reflective choices by going beyond his or her own self to the wider context of humanity. Indeed, how could we otherwise make valid choices? The interrelated individual, social and global perspectives are necessary elements in sound, reflective, decision making. Making choices from such an informed, holistic perspective is part of what it is to be a rational human being. But Humanism sees world policy as essential to the creation of a free life for all, as essential to ending the global issues such as poverty and lack of education that prevent the kind of individual human freedom that promotes responsible, rational choices in life.

There are those who are critical of the materialism suggested by the Humanist ideal society. Nevertheless, Humanism is not an advocator of selfish materialism for a few, but of the kind of global prosperity that fulfils *all* humans needs. A certain taxing of the rich to raise the level of the poor places a ceiling on materialism and would end immoral excessive remuneration. All human beings are likely to operate better in life with a balance of material prosperity. A more serious criticism of Humanism's goals for society and humanity lies in the fact that there are many people who would share the dream of world peace and prosperity, individual freedom, social justice – indeed, most Humanist goals – but are not Humanists. This is to say that, as a phenomenon in society, Humanism does not have sufficient *identity* to have a *distinctive* role in society. After all, it has no creed or set dogma by which it is possible for society to live. Its opponents are not averse to progress or world peace, and groups like the Quakers, or Nichiren Shoshu and Nichiren Daishonin Buddhists take on board both the humanistic goal of world peace as much as societal welfare.

Yet in a way we are all humanists; it is the shifting to being a *H*umanist that is the critical issue. The solution or solutions to this problem of distinctive identity for Humanism are not easy ones, but

I think one way might be to focus on individual coming-of-age. Modern individual life, as we have seen, is selfish, and if there is such interest in the self there is certainly the motivation for self-fulfilment. Literature dealing with such self-fulfilment and individual change is extensive in other fields but might productively be the focus of a good percentage of future Humanist literature. Too many people have never heard of Humanism; they need a vocabulary related to the self in order to be introduced to it. (Were the title of this book to be changed to *Do You Want To Improve Your Life?* it might well find itself in more hands!). New directions are clearly needed, but Humanism has always been a medium of criticism of society and this is an essential part of its identity that cannot be compromised. But too many attacks can sometimes mean a lack of consolidation of what is valuable, and the broader remit of Humanism might build on its own strengths and identity without over-commitment to dissident attack. Paul Kurtz asked a number of years ago: "Can humanism provide 'spiritual' sustenance and transcending ideals that can stir conviction and commitment?"[74] The question is a poignant one for it can only be answered individualistically – and this, I reiterate, is the way forward; Humanism must be shown to be a medium for change in *individual* life. Change the individual, and change for the better in the wider dimensions of society and humanity will be a natural corollary. Humanism must start with the human being.

The Good Life: the Humanist vision for all individuals

Bertrand Russell's view of the "Good Life" was of "one inspired by love and guided by knowledge".[75] Can there be a nobler goal for any individual? The concept of love here is love in one's immediate relationships and a love of humanity. It requires a world in which there is integrity, sincerity, good will, kindness, compassion, trust, justice, peace, tolerance, fairness, and all those value-laden characteristics that we associate with the very best of human intentions and human existence. Kurtz believes that these kinds of principles are deeply-rooted potentials in human make-up.[76] But such potential can only be realized in the kind of environment that is free from disease, poverty and subtle or overt oppression. Achieving one's full potential in skills, abilities, moral development and psychological well being is to become a "whole person". Finding ways to encourage this fullness of being is an important part of the Humanist agenda.

But the "Good Life" is not utopian; human beings are not perfect and are bound by the restraints of their own characters. And yet, there is so much unfulfilled potential in nearly all people, so much to develop, so many areas in which each human being can evolve. It is this personal evolution that needs to be the existential goal of every human being. Despite the limitations of what it is to be human, there are so many ways in which self-evolution can take place. We may never fulfil all our goals in life, but moving towards them means that life is exciting, vibrant and changing. If we can look back over just one year and find no forward movement in our own lives, then something is wrong. But when we move forward we need to move outward, too – outward towards other human beings by sharing in their experiences, interests and needs. And if we have some of the love about which Russell wrote, then this outgoingness towards others is a natural corollary. Doing one's best in life is an important goal, at the same time having the courage to face the disappointments and difficulties that life brings. It is a mistake to think that the "Good Life" is hedonistic; it is far too altruistic to be so. Thus the thinking of critics like John Carroll is widely off target when he can write of humanism: "The predominant thinking of the twentieth century has been that of an animal, that the good life is to consume, to procreate and to sleep, and in those terms there has been giant progress. Most Westerners *have* become rich."[77] There is not a tinge of this sentiment in Humanism. The "Good Life" is one that should pursue happiness and personal fulfilment, but not at the expense of others and not without a vision of the same goals for others. And since happiness and personal fulfilment are variable according to each individual, life becomes richly diverse, creative and adventurous. In aiming for the "Good Life" we are surely able to make life better both for ourselves and in the interdependency of human interaction in society and world.

The goal of the "Good Life" is not futurist but is a dynamic call to every individual to begin making changes in his or her life *now* and to see responsible change as part of personal evolution and as contributing to human existence. David Attenborough warns us not to think that humankind is the ultimate in the evolutionary process, but to think of it as only part of that process. Yet, he pertinently points out that "no species has ever had such wholesale control over everything on earth, living or dead, as we now have. That lays upon us, whether we like it or not, an awesome responsibility. In our hands now lies not only our own future, but that of all other living creatures with whom we share this earth."[78] So while some of the changes we make should be for personal benefit, moral altruism should require that we seek to make changes also that are for the good of others. Mutual co-operation and partnership is often necessary for effecting many of the personal changes that we want in life, and is essential for changes that reach out into the broader framework of humanity.

Change, then, is certainly essential to personal, social and global evolution, and to survive on this planet we have to change *now*. The need for change is obvious, the potential for it only partially realized. Some are capable of radical change, others may be capable of little change, but all are capable of changing sufficiently to contribute to an ongoing progress of improved social interaction in a way that benefits society. Harold Blackham once wrote: "Men are more nationalistic, violent, and stupid than they thought they were. We control the earth and the air, but not the tiger, the ape, and the donkey inside ourselves."[79] Given a new outlook on life, and an ability to face reality as it is, most people should be capable of reshaping their own lives for the better, and of having some sort of vision of what kind of society they would wish to exist in. Human beings can acquire an art of living, an art of creating their own life experience, but these are life expressions that are enhanced when society itself creates the necessary foundations for such individual expression. To be a "whole person" each individual has to develop the kind of self-determination, the kind of control of the self, that promotes the decisions in life that encourage personal evolution. And the greater the scope for this, the greater the personal evolution, the greater the sensitivity and empathy to the world beyond the self. The "whole person" is very much in touch with reality, has self-value and is largely free of conditioning restraints. When one is in touch with oneself, there is a sounder view of the kind of world in which one wants to live. If one is out of touch with oneself then one looks outside the self for answers to the existential problems of life. To be in touch with the self is to know the self, to have confidence in the self. And we can only have confidence in others when first we have confidence in our own selves.

Each human being needs to find a pathway for his or her self, a way of life that is satisfying and meaningful and that is in some way felt to have value in a wider communal sense. We all have talents in different areas, and whatever those areas are we should seek to develop them, however unimportant they may seem. Respect for one's own abilities, and the lack of them in some areas, is healthy, and we can all play our part in the universe when we recognize what we are as individuals. It takes courage to live life, but it takes extra courage to free oneself from the conditionings that blur personality so that one has to face one's own self squarely. This is true personal identity. Life is characterized by suffering as much as by pleasure, and for some, more suffering than is their due. Its haphazard nature suggests that all individuals need to be more empathetic to their fellow human beings, for those who are ignored on the way up may well be those we have to pass when we fall back down. Courage, vision, compassion and a sense of humour are good traits to take with one on the journey through life.

Humanism cannot offer a prescriptive way forward for any individual, for all must work out their own pathways in life. But Humanism does have altruistic goals for the move towards a "Good Life". In the very simplest way of all, human beings can try to regard those they encounter daily with respect and as valuable people. Just asking questions, finding out about the lives of others, attempting to understand others, being more aware of others, sharing views with others, listening and inquiring, are simple daily things that people no longer do. We all love being asked searching questions about ourselves, but few take the time to ask them. Genuine curiosity about other people should be a healthy part of our daily life. Valuing people is thoroughly Humanist, and this small change in the lives of individuals is an excellent start in effecting change in one's life. Just this one change means a more tolerant attitude to others, increased awareness of others, sincerity in wanting to share views with others, the ability to listen to others, true mutual interaction, and so on. Many Humanists are content to live life with this simple yet profound awareness and interest in others. Other Humanists extend their interest to the support of organizations such as Oxfam, Friends of the Earth, Amnesty International, Age Concern, and so on. We do not have to be great persons to be Humanists, we just need to think a little more deeply about people, about life and about what a "Good Life" should be. We learn from our experiences, and we can enrich that learning with understanding of the experiences of others. Essentially, people need to wake up, grow up, take control, establish self-identity and personal independence, engage in dialogue with other human beings in the dynamic world in which we live.

Humanism cannot offer certainties. As one Humanist said: "The truth of being human lies in its nuances"[80] and it is the nuances of life that create the immense diversities that make certainties about life impossible to define. How can *a* belief system respond to the fluid nature of evolutionary life? Humanism claims that there can be no absolutes, no one creed for life; there are signposts, but no one journey's end. Humanist goals are flexible and changeable, adaptable and responsive to the life-conditions of the time; inflexible dogmas are anathema to the Humanist. Individuals have to learn to be adaptable too, meeting life's challenges with courage, and meeting their fellow humans with the kind of respect and value that they would wish for themselves.

6

Morality

Humanism believes in an ethics or morality that grounds all human values in this-earthly experiences and relationships and that holds as its highest goal the this-worldly happiness, freedom, and progress – economic, cultural, and ethical – of all mankind, irrespective of nation, race, or religion.[1]

This important principle put forward by Corliss Lamont as one of the main philosophical tenets of Humanism stresses, among other things, the foundation of our moral goals and experiences in *this-worldly*, *this-earthly* life. Humanism does not consider that morality is grounded in religious belief and practice. To be moral human beings, we do not have to believe in God. But in order to become fully moral human beings it is necessary to understand what morality is and to know what goal we are aiming for in attempting to become morally autonomous individuals. This chapter, then, will explore the nature and complexities of the term "morality", and its related concept of ethics. To most people, being "moral" is being good, or obeying certain rules and fulfilling certain obligations that are laid down as norms for societal life. But, as will be seen, this simplistic view of morality is not really morality at all. I can train my dogs to obey rules like walking to heel, or not biting the postman, and I may oblige them to sit while waiting to cross a road, and not to jump up on people. But none of this has anything to do with morality. Similarly, if people are trained to behave in certain ways by rewards, punishments (or the desire for, or fear of, each respectively), if they are cajoled, encouraged or mentally manipulated to behave properly, or if they behave well through habit – none of these things really suggests *moral* behaviour.

Ethics

The study of the concept of morality, of human morals, belongs in the discipline of *ethics*. As a philosophical inquiry ethics is not so much concerned with setting out principles of moral behaviour as with analysing, and finding definitions for, the ideas with which it is concerned – ideas like "values", "good", "ought", "right", "duty", and so on. Some people, however, prefer to define "ethics" as a method of finding out what is right and discussion of the principles involved in practising a particular moral code, while using the term *metaethics* for analysis of related concepts – what we mean by the terms.[2] In practice, the distinction is not always a clear one.

One important facet of ethics, and particularly metaethics, is that it lifts the subject of morality beyond subjective, personal, values. Because what *I* think is good or morally right could differ from the views of others, so ethics explores morality from a more objective perspective. Nevertheless, despite a search for more universal criteria for moral concepts, a consensus of views never seems to emerge, and this suggests that ethics tends to retain at least minimal subjective philosophy. Since ethics is a reflective inquiry into the nature of morality, this is perhaps to be expected, but one thing is certain, reflective inquiry is rooted in human enterprise, and it is human enterprise that has formulated ethical codes and concepts throughout the history of humankind.

While most see ethics as belonging under the discipline of philosophy, some sociobiologists are currently claiming that much morality is genetically determined, and therefore *ethics* is a biological rather than a philosophical inquiry.[3] This is to say that the way any human behaves – morally or immorally – is genetically determined, and that human beings have marginal choices, if any at all, concerning their propensity for good or bad behaviour. With this line of thought, even the best of human intentions is reduced to genetic egoism. In Richard Dawkins' well-known work *The Selfish Gene*[4] the author maintains that genes survive in the evolution of humans only by ruthless selfishness and rivalry with other genes. Therefore, when it is expedient for an individual to be benevolent towards another, it is the "selfish gene" that promotes such behaviour. Yet Dawkins was not, and is not, reductionist in his views.[5] To accept that morality is dependent solely on the particular dispensation of genes in any individual would make any struggle for a better existence, societal advance, and greater moral interaction with our fellow human beings, a purely automatic process. Is it not the other way around? Is it not that the pragmatic ethical interaction of human beings with others promotes individual security and welfare? So the genes – if selfish they are – conform to what is equally pragmatic for survival. And if this is the case then it is pragmatic – and essentially humanistic – to have a science of ethics that promotes the very best for all human beings on the planet in order to ensure both progress and survival. Too many Humanists are so anxious to base morality firmly in human make-up as opposed to religious tradition that they welcome genetic reductionism without reflective thought as to the consequences for individual autonomy in moral or any other dimension of human existence.

Ethics and morality – just as values, good, and evil – can only be concerned with people. Most of our values and what we believe to be good and bad are subjective and personal to our own life-experiences in interaction with others. But not *all* our values are subjective; the human being is capable of *objective* values. These may transcend selfish, subjective values if they reach out to a more universal level or, they may precede subjective values as general perspectives of life from which arise more personal immediate values. Indeed, individuals need some kind of broad ethic for life that is over and above daily life-experiences; without this, life is insular and contextless. Ethics is concerned with subjective individualism, the broader context of objective social ethics, and the wider context of objective global ethics. Between the first two there is reciprocal interaction when individuals may challenge the ethics of the larger societal groups and where societal groups contest individual ethical values. But wider, global ethical issues are generally held in principle – the principle of world peace, the establishing of basic human rights, the right of all to sufficient food.

The difference between subjective ethics and objective ethics is often referred to as ethical egoism and ethical altruism respectively. The first is a primary concern for the self, often irrespective of others, and the second is primarily a concern for others, rather than one's own self. If ethical altruism does not obtain at all, then one has to be coerced into unselfish good behaviour. Perhaps this is the reason why religious ethical codes have been so important: a doctrine of original sin and the low status of human morality might be thought to necessitate a religious code of social and individual behaviour. By the same token, a legal code would need to be imposed to protect the wider interests of society. But to suggest that ethical altruism does not obtain at all is to deny the role of countless men and women in history who have placed their own lives second to causes for which they have unselfishly fought. Needless to say, the more limited the ethical altruism the closer it is to ethical egoism. If, for example, I help an old lady across the road, I am likely to give myself a pat on the back for doing so, and the ethical altruism easily slips into ethical egoism. However, when the context of altruism is extended – as it is in those individuals who have lived their lives in dedication to others – the moments of ethical egoism may be few and far between. The particular balance and relation between ethical egoism and ethical altruism is important to Humanism in that it has a dual perspective of what is good and right for the individual and what is good and right for humankind. This kind of discussion about the principles that underpin morality is what ethics is all about, whereas morality itself is more pertinent to individual and societal norms of behaviour, common moral decencies, we could say.

The nature of morality

To turn now to the concept of morality, it is important first to clear up some misconceptions about the term. Morality is not following or being obedient to prescribed rules. As I stated above, my dogs can do this. Observing the Highway Code when I drive my car is a sensible action but not a moral one (even though the Highway Code probably originated from rational, moral aims). This is because there has to be a certain *intention* behind moral action as opposed to mechanical response. Similarly, obedience to societal laws or religious precepts out of habit, conditioning, training, fear of punishment or desire for reward, is also not moral behaviour, because there is no *rational intention* that underpins the actions. Morality, then, has little to do with conformity to laws and precepts, and there might well be some situations in which one *is* acting morally when *not* conforming to the law. Indeed, there may also be occasions when some older laws become immoral, as the older laws concerning divorce, laws concerning blasphemy, and so on. Laws are involved with words like "ought to", and "must", whereas moral actions – though they sometimes involve feelings like "ought" and "must" – involve a certain amount of voluntary thought. Nevertheless, it might be claimed that most individuals are conditioned by their respective societies to adopt certain moral precepts such as refraining from stealing, murdering, cheating, and so on. So while individuals are aware that they adhere to laws that are moral laws, they may not actually internalize *why* they do so. Kai Nielsen opens his book *Ethics without God* with a point made by Robert Bellah,[6] that Americans have something of a "civil" religion that accepts a natural moral law that pervades American society. These sorts of "hidden codes", and subtle types of morality, are exactly those that are barely internalized.

So to define morality simply as codes of conduct which are devised by humans for humans,[7] is perhaps not to see the potential for a more autonomous morality in individual nature. But it is perfectly true to say that moral codes of conduct are thoroughly human inventions. As Max Hocutt writes: "All existing moralities and all existing laws are human artifacts, products of human society, social conventions. Morality is not discovered; it is made."[8] So while to be really "moral" is to have some rational idea and intention of being so, moral laws have been established throughout societies as a basic framework for pragmatic behaviour in society. Nielsen sees morality as a *practical* activity[9] and this would be true not only in that it actively decides what is right for societal interaction, and for the well-being of persons, but also in that it needs to be actively rationalized by each individual rather than being just passively accepted. Importantly, however, if social moralities are the result of practical human activities, they are not absolute and are able to be changed to suit evolving societal needs. Indeed, societies that have static moral codes might be said to be less evolved ones. Ultimately, moral codes are required to achieve certain ends in society, and if those ends are not adequately met, then some adjustment of the code is necessary. Max Hocutt, as would many Humanists, considers that if people are well fed, happy, healthy and content, then moral codes are achieving sound ends. Where this is not the case, then something is wrong.[10] In short, devising moral codes is "an experimental art" as one writer has it,[11] and it is therefore a flexible human-originating process.

But to return to the main thesis here, for an *individual* to be considered to have acted morally, there must be a *rational* response to moral codes. Such rational reflection on actions enables the individual to behave morally because he or she believes rationally that it is the right thing to do, and therefore can give valid reasons for doing so. Additionally, rational reflection enables an individual to assess the wider effects of his or her moral action, and to consider and assess the views of others. Indeed, rational thought and action inform the ability to be a social being, to successfully interact and communicate with others and to engage in dialogue over conflicting views. Moral thought and action, therefore, are both personal and interrelational. There is also another essential aspect of morality and that is the element of choice. As one writer puts it: "There can be no moral sanction or moral approval of actions or acts that are actually inevitable or unavoidable."[12] Doing the right thing automatically, without reflection, without having to *choose* to do that thing because it is right, is no more than animal response to conditioning. And of course we actually spend a good deal of time responding to situations in this way. But it is when we have to weigh up the consequences of a number of options – both for ourselves and for others – when we have to assess carefully from past experience, past knowledge, perhaps from the views of others, and it is when we can articulate *why* we choose to act in a certain way, that we are acting morally, providing the action is for an outcome that is an ethically good one.

It is this element of choice in moral decision making and behaviour that prevents morality being a biogenetically determined factor in individual make-up. While individuals may have certain propensities to behave according to their genetic characteristics, and environmental factors, it is the grey areas of choice in existence that shift them away from such predispositions. And this is no less the case with moral choices. There must, indeed, be some freedom of will in order for moral choice and action to take place, and the will to choose may often arise out of the *conflict* between genetic and environmental influences.[13] This would create entirely novel moral situations and novel choices about the right pathway for an individual. Most of the choices made in such situations are *value judgements*, situational judgements that see one course of action more valuable than others. And some of these moral value judgements may be acquired extraneous to one's real life. Drama, film, fiction, narrative, newspaper articles and the like, often evoke moral responses and have a role to play in the development of moral consciousness.[14]

But all such contexts for moral choices are grounded in life itself, grounded in the interaction of human with human, human with group, group with group, and so on. Morality cannot come from somewhere beyond human interaction; without human beings, it cannot exist.[15] It is in social situations that morality is acquired, with the necessity of limiting personal drives for the purpose of effective communication with others, and developing moral perspectives about life that are conducive to one's own personal development and freedom. Social rules and norms arise from this pragmatic need to live harmoniously one with another. A process of transformation from personal morality to required social morality is necessary for human maturation and this is a process that requires some rationalization by each individual. This, indeed, is what moral progress is all about. As children, we acquire our views of what is right and wrong from our immediate family, and then from the wider world of peer groups and school experience. The adolescent years are notorious as a time in which many young people challenge the rules by which they have been expected to conduct their lives. But throughout life there should develop a more reflective rational inquiry as to *why* we think it is right or wrong to behave in a particular way. This is a stage of morality that is internalized and should be ongoing: there is no *ultimate* or *absolute* morality, only more and more complex situations that require varying ethical solutions and moral choices. To be a moral person is to be able to change one's perspectives of what is right or wrong in the experience of life.

Many ethicists reject notions of an *absolute* morality, such as the *categorical imperative* of the eighteenth-century German philosopher Immanuel Kant. This is a belief that there is a moral law that exists independently of human beings. As a universal moral code for life, it can be known when human beings apply rational reason, by exercising their freedom to act in accordance with this ultimate law. For Kant, an action is a moral one if it is one that could be applied universally. Thus, I can only do something morally right if I believe that it is the way in which all other human beings should act. Kant also believed that people should never be treated as means to ends; they are always ends in themselves, each characterized by the developing capacity for free and rational autonomy. The moral goal was to transcend self-interest by conforming to the universal law. So, according to Kantian ethics, the test of how moral an action is, is whether it could be willed for *all* people to act in this way. If it would not be willed for *all* humanity to do it, then it cannot be right. As a rule of thumb for practical moral living this is not such a bad one, and the idea that moral progress increases with the ability to rationalize is also sound. But to posit a *universal* moral law that would exist even if there were no human beings is irrational: it is more rational to suggest that human beings have the capabilities of projecting rationalized moral norms to a universal level as the goal of all. Essentially, however, moral codes, however universal they may be, can only exist as codes *for* humans, and not independently of them. To exist independently, there would have to be some way in which abstract principles are linked with the physical, changing world. Universal moral codes, if there can ever be such a thing, can only exist in so far as they are constructed by humanity itself.

Rather than being something that is exterior to human beings individually and collectively, morality is something that might be said to be *interior* to human experience, gained through a rational interiorizing of ethical living that becomes part of the "inner" person. This is when we do the right things for the right reasons. In a book that is in a number of senses now dated, but with many parts remarkably astute, profound, and thoroughly relevant to the modern world, James Hemming includes a delightful chapter entitled "The Inner World".[16] In this he claims that morality has its roots in the "unique inner world"[17] of each individual. It is from this inner world that the individual takes measure of his or her self, and it is from this inner world that relationships with the world beyond are built up. Hemming writes of this inner world:

> It is here that we experience the conflict of idea with idea, of motive with motive, of weakness with strength, of will with apathy, of clarity with confusion, of love and hate. Guilt and despair lurk here; the residues of past failures stay to mock; anxiety, conflict, and suffering endured. Here experience is metamorphosed into personal understanding; insight enlightens suddenly in the darkness; hope revives; aspiration springs and yearns for actualization. The tone of inwardness at any moment fills the mind, ranging from ecstasy to despondency. Sometimes inwardness is in turmoil; at others comes a deep satisfying sense of peace. Somehow this inwardness grows and changes so that, catching an echo of a past self, we realize something has been at work reshaping us in the unseen quiet of our own depths. Things happen in this silence.[18]

It is here in the self that moral consciousness is developed, and, as Hemming so rightly points out in these words, it is a moral consciousness shaped through *conflict*. This is developing morality shaped by the dynamism of life itself, making us what we are. Though Hemming does not take the point this far, it is the reflection on this process, and the rationalization of *why* we think or behave in a certain way, that transforms the inner experiences into a deeper ethic to which we become more rationally committed. This could be termed a "spiritualized morality". There is a certain reciprocal interplay between the inner world of the self and one's view of the world, as Hemming points out,[19] so the world is as good or as futile as we feel within. But this means that when morality is "spiritualized" it has a reciprocal effect on the way we view the world. Thus, rationalized, reflective and internalized morality colours the way in which we react morally to the world at large: it deepens our moral awareness. Hemming accepted an interconnectedness of humanity in the sense that we all belong to a common humanity, even if we are all uniquely different. In rather visionary words he wrote of the individual inner world which "is the outer world personally possessed as inner meaning, reality transmuted by the inward vision. The personal psyche is a microcosm of humanity and each awakened individual experiences and suffers for all mankind."[20] The deeper the "spiritualized morality" the less dependent the individual is on extraneous rules, religious precepts and social laws, and the more morally autonomous the self becomes. For Hemming, there was an end product of this depth of moral being in the inner harmony of the self and in the harmony of the self with the world:

> An indwelling longing of the 'Ultimate I' is for inward harmony and for a sense of unity with the whole. Both are of profound moral significance because they are self-transcending experiences. The sense of inner harmony is intensely personal, and also in some way of universal quality. So, too, the moments of unified experience, released perhaps by beauty or wonder inwardly perceived, extend both the sense of being, and of being-at-one with some partially apprehended whole. We are held for a moment amid the urgency of living and feel timeless.[21]

Clearly, rational morality is not an arid world of carefully analysed pragmatic concepts. It reflects a developed human being with as much inner harmony as ability to transcend the self in a vision outward to humanity at large.

Good

Most people associate morality with the word "good", being good, doing good things, thinking good thoughts, being good to others, almost as if "good" is an absolute, identical state that all people are capable of realizing. But as we all know, one man's meat is another man's poison. Thus, what is good to or for one person may not be so for another, or even for that same person at another point in time. Good, then, is an ever-shifting concept, and there is no absolute scale of what is perfect good, very good, good, and so on, that human beings can use as a yardstick for moral life. While the ancient Greeks accepted such an absolute concept of good, adherence to which, perfected and freed the human soul, simple observation of life itself teaches us otherwise. It is good *people* who do good things, and goodness does not obtain beyond the people who exemplify it. And in our normal usage of the word, we don't actually imply any perfection: a good person, a good wine, a good laugh, a good teacher and so on, are usages that have nothing to do with perfection. They are evaluative expressions that serve to express our liking of something; they are value judgements that will differ from one person to another. Neither is what is assessed or generally considered to be good by the majority of society necessarily good. History is peppered with things believed to be good for us that we now know were quite the opposite.

In the light of this last point it could hardly be said that we may only assess what is good in terms of its end products, for this would thoroughly offend the principle that the means do not justify the ends. It would be difficult then to claim that what is good can be judged solely by its effects. Thus, utilitarianism with its concept of the greatest good for the greatest number could conceivably incorporate immoral means to serve the greatness of the ends. Humanism could never endorse this. At its very worst, the Nazi policy of a prosperous, healthy super race might have ultimately achieved the greatest good for the greatest number, but the weeding out through extermination of what it considered to be minority rejects was certainly one of the worst imaginable means to an end. But even in a more sane and humane context, minority views are important – and they may sometimes, or often, be the right ones.

At an individual level what is good is often that which brings pleasure. But not everything that brings pleasure is moral. In fact, as Williams demonstrated "morality emerges as different from both belief and desire".[22] *Individual* belief about what is good or of value could actually offend moral norms held by the wider societal and global views. Ideas of good and bad develop with the growth of societal interaction; the more complex groupings of people requiring codes of behaviour that permit the stability and progress of the social group, whether a primitive tribe, a village community, an institution or a whole state. But because such social groupings are dynamic and changeable, what is considered good and bad is equally changeable, as common observation of life past to present clearly indicates. Good is generally that which is *desirable* in *society*, whether this is behavioural, economic, political, or attitudinal. And it could well be claimed that "we are happiest when in tune with those around us".[23] But it is not difficult to see here that what may be desirable, and therefore, good, is likely to change as time proceeds. Indeed, it might be claimed that what is good arises out of societal subjectivity, that is to say, the particular ethos of a society at a particular phase in its historical development. Nielsen thus says: "What is good is determined by what answers to human interests, what satisfies human needs, and what furthers human self-realization."[24] And from this societal subjectivity arises a concept of *oughtness*, a belief that people *ought to* behave, and conform, to the general conceptions of what is good. Yet, if society is a dynamically changing phenomenon, and its ideas of what is good and bad are equally changeable, it is imperative that individuals themselves assess what they believe to be good in life. Mere conformity to general ideas of what is supposed to be good is not morally autonomous behaviour.

Individual reflective inquiry into what is accepted as good and bad, right and wrong, is an essential characteristic of a mature individual. Blind obedience is never a virtue and there are times when it is right to be thoroughly disobedient, even though society and the institutions that it spawns, as well as religious groups, will expect conformity. However, deviating from the norm is as far from mature morality as blind obedience if it is not informed by rational justification. One has to take responsibility for one's beliefs. It is sad that too many individuals experience guilt if they fail to live up to the good societal groups expect of them, and others are made to feel guilty if they decide that they cannot, after sound reflection, conform to moral rules in which they no longer believe. Religious moral codes, in particular, can engender guilt in those who fail to conform to the "good" expected of them, and do not encourage reflective inquiry into the relevant morality of the teachings they contain. It is individual *conscience* that normally causes the feelings of guilt that arise from non-conformity to what is believed to be right and good. Conscience is merely the sum total of the conditionings of life. It doesn't really exist, and is simply representative of the collective feelings we have – the *ought tos* and *ought not tos* that we gather in life. If it operates over-frequently it is often indicative of an immature individual, a child, or one who is a slave to imposed rules. The more morally mature a person is, the more conscience retreats, because the individual is thinking his or her way through life. In the religious context, however, conscience has always been praised as the means of rescue from sin, and the means to quell reason.[25] What is certain to

Humanists is that conscience has nothing to do with a supernatural God. It is not an inner voice from "out there" or the spirit of a God within whispering "Don't do this" and "Don't do that". And there are no absolute *dos* and *don'ts*, morality has very much to do with what is right for an individual at a particular time in life, not with what is imposed absolutely by some extraneous code. Providing the freedom and welfare of others is honoured, flexibility in individual morality is essential. To quote Bertrand Russell's maxim for the good life once again, it should be "inspired by love and guided by knowledge".[26] It is an ethic no less applicable to personal, societal and global morality.

Values

Morality is very much concerned with the *values* that we have in life: indeed, we tend to judge the moral worth of a person or a society by the values that they hold. Hemming neatly defines moral values as "those values which, over the course of time, come to be regarded as essential to the good conduct of personal and social life."[27] And as he points out, it is particularly religious values that have influenced society down to the present day. "Value" has good intrinsic to its meaning, as much as "good" has value. Thus, Tarkunde defines value more philosophically than Hemming: "Anything which is 'good' has a value. Value consists of the goodness of what is good. It is the quality of being valuable."[28] Both meanings converge in Tarkunde's view that values have a social purpose in that they support the well-being of society and the individuals within it.

So how far could we claim that our western society has moral values? Are there sufficient values evident to suggest that the Humanist view of the "Good Life" is taking shape? Certainly this is not a golden age for moral values, but the indications of history are that we have never had a golden age, while the varied and imperfect nature of humanity suggests such a thing will never obtain in the future. Indeed, to have a moral golden age suggests that there would have to be a "basic ideal pattern", as one writer puts it,[29] and this is to repress diversity and change. In fact, the lack of clear societal values, and the breakdown of some of the more rigid taboos, has released values from over-prescriptiveness and permitted greater individual freedom to choose one's values in life. It is odd that people tend to judge the morality of an age by its sexual habits. As Hector

Hawton has pointed out, "it is of some significance that when people lament the decline of morals they are seldom thinking first of concentration camps and judicial torture".[30] There are some who claim that western society is in a state of confusion and that moral values are in a transitional state,[31] but this is nonsense: most societies are in transitional states since all societies (except perhaps very simple ones) are subject to change and progress. Western society is in a process of rapid change and therefore permanently transitional; there is no question of arriving at some kind of ideal time after a transitional period.

Despite the rapid change and lifting of old restrictive taboos in western society, individuals have acquired freedom in so many ways, but sacrificed it in others. This is because the post-modern world is a highly complex one – one that brings with it more morally grey areas, as well as totally new ethical challenges with no previous norms as yardsticks for making moral choices. People have never been exposed to so much choice or had so much responsibility in personal decision-making, and this is bound to present confusion. In the past, people shopped at the same local store, could have groceries "on the slate", worked at the same job for the bulk of their lives, and lived lives that were fairly environmentally confined. All this is gone and the simple tasks in life have become more complex despite the machinery that helps us to accomplish them.

So in the context of life in today's world, "values" are bound to appear somewhat nebulous. And when we get grossly overcharged by the electrician, let down again and again by the joiner who was supposed to replace the defective double glazing he assured you would not go wrong, or find values in the world of work declining because of economic pressures on our employers, it is not surprising that many consider society to be going downhill. It probably isn't, but its complex nature makes it seem so. But the sacrifices to our freedom, to which I referred above, lie in the pace of the lives we live today, the stresses that accumulate. Parents are busy driving their children to riding, gymnastic, piano, flute and swimming lessons, fitting in the shopping at the super- and hyper-markets. So many people claim that there is too little time in life. Yes we have an abundance of choice in life, but quality of life to enjoy the fruits of choices is becoming at a premium in the eyes of a good majority of people. Much of the blame for this lies in the expectations of employers that their employees are prepared to do that bit extra, and extra, and extra, while human resources are continually reduced.

Values in the working world have become an outcome of the
economic pinch of modern times. It is in this world that individuals
often feel personally unappreciated: when the pinch gets too tight,
the quality of the working life is lost. It is remarkable that Hemming's
assessment of society of the sixties is even more pertinent to today's
world. One wonders whether he had exceptional perspicacity that
saw problems more subtly than in his day, whether he could see the
direction in which society was heading, or whether the problems of
his time have become more firmly entrenched in our own time.
Albeit, his words are in no way out of place a third of a century later.
Hemming wrote of the sixties as characterized by a "dehumanized
social structure", a structure that lacked warmth and intimacy in its
group formations. But his words are rather pertinent for today's
world also:

> In the end, all but the most robust, or the most involved, are driven into
> a we-and-they attitude towards this giant, congested, industrial
> complex which draws millions into its service, as workers and
> consumers. People are treated as automata to fit job-specifications or
> to be motivated to buy, while the dearest thing any man has – his
> unique, yearning, striving self – is totally ignored or grossly, inhu-
> manely undervalued.[32]

In the same context Hemming wrote of the complex forms, which are
designed by verbally highly intelligent individuals, and which end
up with people who can hardly understand them and yet whose
personal lives are so affected by filling them in. Today, of course, we
live in a very formalized bureaucratic world, one that must be getting
through rainforests of paper in its control of individuals via the
computer and the photocopier. The danger is that we may become
too inclined to accept the process passively – particularly if life is so
fast-paced that we have no time to reflect. In times past, social conformity was the norm – a man who changed his job frequently was
thought to be irresponsible. Today, the man or woman who changes
employment more frequently is often a more experienced, and therefore more desirable, employee whose *curriculum vitae* is fuller. But
there is a more subtle conformity in the workplace that is now
expected of employees, often a rubber stamping of managerial policies that are ultimately detrimental to personal creativity and
freedom. These are moral issues that are skirted by many employers.
Lee Nisbet refers to the equation between "good" and "useful", and
warns that a good person is being seen as a useful one – useful to
employers or to teachers.[33] But a useful person may not be a thinking

person, a person who is reflecting carefully about the choices he or she is making in life.

If, then, we do live in a permissive society that allows us greater freedom of personal choice in all contexts of life, including the widening of our moral choices, we may need to look to more subtle areas where our personal freedom is being curtailed. But there are other ways in which the values of modern society are more obviously wrong and this lies in what Morris Storer has described as "the indecent concentration of wealth and income, the spectacle of outrageous profits".[34] This is a value that can hardly be supported in the light of the millions of people whose lives are mutilated by poverty. But wealth may well be a value that has become part of most people's dreams: winning the national or state lottery many believe would solve their problems. Becoming wealthy overnight the first thing most people say they would do is to give up their job. Does this suggest that the number of people who find job satisfaction these days must be very small? And does it mean that the only way people can envisage true happiness is with wealth? Are the values of the modern world over-materialistic? Modern man and woman have to ask themselves such questions and attempt to reconstruct their own values about what might really bring personal reward in life. Over-self-centred drives for material wealth are inclined to turn individuals in on themselves leading to individuality isolated in the immediate family environment without the ability to see wider societal needs. Human beings today are at the point where they can truly come of age; the potential for self-realization is there, and with that realization the ability to make moral choices that are beneficial to the self and to others.

Morality as an evolutionary process

Hadley Cantril believed that a basic factor of human life is conflict between security and development.[35] In some senses these two aims are complementary in that development forward may provide the very security – job, health benefits, a steady income and high standard of living – for which one is striving. On the other hand, they may be conflicting, for security often means the *status quo*, the known as opposed to the unknown. Cantril believed that security was necessary in individual life *before* development could take place, though I would argue the converse must to some measure also be true. But he is right to say that development is something of a risk people have to take, a risk that might well jeopardize the security one already has. One overriding thesis of this present book is my contention that it is choice and the movement towards development in every human being that militates against reductionism of the human being. It is a need to go forward, even if the direction is physical and material to the detriment of the social and spiritual. And because the choices presented are always unknown, the direction forward cannot be anticipated, even allowing for individual genetic or behavioural propensities. Processes of change take place in individual life as a result of conflict, and this is no less true in the ethical dimension of life.

So is our morality innate or acquired? I would say it is both, but with a far greater propensity for the latter. Indeed, most of us could instance areas of our own ethics that have undergone change as a result of a multiplicity of reasons and changes in circumstances throughout our lives. Our personal ethical standards are changeable and, since individuals compose society then societal ethics are equally changeable. It is possible, then, to refer to "moral progress" and this is reflected as much by what we no longer believe as what we come to believe. In time past, a more fixed morality was evidenced, especially so because it was tied to religious prescriptions. Today, however, we are much less resistant to change, and the complexities of modern living, and the constant moving of traditional boundaries in all fields of life, present new moral challenges. The older ethic of obedience and conformity was easier, and stood in complete contrast to the complexity of ethical issues, and the extended moral choices that are available to the freer individuals and groups of modern society. The developmental move forward for people in life is considerable in the physical aspects of life – better homes, equipped kitchens, television and video, increased varieties of food, travel – though the psychological strains of such forward progress bring their own more subtle ethical problems.

We cannot expect, therefore, *a* system of ethics or *a* moral code that is applicable for all time. Ethical or moral codes need to change as human progress changes. All life is characterized by change, is transient and is impermanent, so to invent a changeless moral code is to attempt to impose on society an inflexibility that will impede both personal and societal progress. We *have* to change because it is a fundamental characteristic of human nature to do so. Any repression of that ability to change straitjackets human potential and experience.

As Cantril pointed out "a system of ethics and a code of morality are not only emergent co-products of man's evolution but become themselves directive agencies in the evolutionary process itself".[36] This is a reciprocal evolution of humankind on the one hand and ethical progress on the other. Criticism, assessment and reconstruction of moral codes are therefore essential, and moral progress should reflect dynamic growth as much as does society and the individuals within it. To quote Anthony Flew, "all moral ideas and ideals have originated in the world; and . . . having thus in the past been subject to change, they will presumably in the future too, for better or for worse, continue to evolve".[37]

Ethical principles, then, have developed with humankind and will continue to do so. Some even write of a "new morality".[38] Ethical principles are natural expressions of the social necessities of human beings when they form group structures, for human beings cannot always live together without formulating some common rules that will enable them to do so. And when individuals in such groups can transcend their own self-interests for the good of the community at large, then the ethical principles that emerge will be qualitatively advantageous. Indeed, the Darwinian belief is that the more co-operative social groups are, the better their chances of survival: sound ethics supports human progress and development. Nevertheless, older cultures that were collective (as was the ancient Judaic culture, or the modern Communist one) and not individual in ethos, are not necessarily more ethical in nature than the modern society where individualism is more to the fore. The answer lies in the nature of the balance between the two rather than the predominance of either, but inner reflection and rationalization concerning collective moral issues is essential to avoid mere conformity to externally imposed codes. To revert to the points made at the beginning of this chapter, true morality is not being good or behaving well because we have been told to be or do so; it is acting in the right way, and making the right decisions about life for the right reasons, after careful, rational and reflective thought.

Religious morality

From what has been written above, religious morality would need to be viewed as a *type* of morality, but as moral, only where its precepts have been taken on board as a result of rational reflection. Blind obedience to religious rules is a long way from moral autonomy. Theists believe that ethical codes are not part of the human order of things but are pervasive in creation as God-given principles that human beings must discover and by which they must live. This is simlar to the Kantian view of *categorical imperatives*, the universal laws pointing human beings to the highest good. This highest good was a *necessary condition* in the universe, and Kant equated it with God. It is this kind of thought that has led theists to believe that there can be no morality without religion, indeed, to equate the two.

Whether we are religiously minded or not, our moral code has been considerably influenced by religious precepts and religious thinking, and there are many areas of life in which this same influence obtains. In much western society, secular and religious life remains separate and we mainly judge people's ethical standards by the ways in which they conduct their lives, their working life, by their loyalty, reliability, trustworthiness and dependability. We may never know or think to ask whether such people are religious or not. And there are countless such people that exist who are not religious in any way at all. It is common sense to see that morality can obtain without religion. But those who have belief in God really have to accept the perfection of God, the utter goodness of God, and therefore have to accept his revealed words in scripture as guidelines for a truly moral life. This leads many theists to accept what is called the *divine command theory*, the belief that something is right because God commands it. But this raises a nice philosophical question. Is something right because God commands it, or does God command it because it is right? In the former case if something is right because God commands it, then presumably God is capable of commanding us to do something many might think to be wrong; yet it is made right just because it is a divine command. But if God should command us to do something that is *not* right, then he is not good and should not be obeyed. But if he will only command people to do things that *are* right, then "rightness" obtains independently of God, and we might equally as well act in the right way independently of, and without reference to, God. Strictly speaking, the divine command theory accepts that whatever God wills is right, and we would have to include in this the near sacrifice of Isaac by Abraham in the *Genesis* narrative, and the slaughter of men, women, pregnant women, children, the aged and babies in the conquest of Canaan. Was God right here? Humanists claim categorically that such actions are wrong. The majority of theists would agree.

While there are unenlightened theists who claim that it is impossible to be moral without belief in God, there are other theists who recognize the ridiculous nature of such a claim. The whole issue of moral obedience to God's commands stems from the immoral disobedience of Adam and Eve in the *Genesis* myth of the "fall". The fact that Eve stretched out her hand for knowledge is one applauded by Humanists:

> According to the Bible, the greatest evil and the cause of man's fall from grace is to eat of the tree of knowledge of good and evil, to engage in ethical inquiry, and to ground principles and values in autonomous reason. There is a historic tradition in civilization, however, of ethical persons who have eaten of the forbidden fruit of this bountiful tree. Living outside Eden, they have discovered significant ethical values and truths that guide both self-reliant and other-regarding conduct.[39]

Far from shunning the tree of knowledge, it needs to be cultivated. Morality will not suffer for critical analysis and does not need religion in order to survive, or in order to progress.

But the real problem with obedience to a religious moral code is the same as obedience *per se* to any code, and that is there is no inner rational acceptance of such a code, there is no reflective analysis of it. It is difficult to claim that unquestioning obedience to any rules is moral behaviour. In today's world, debate about ethical issues is healthy, complex and very necessary. And even if decisions are made for the present, there is no reason why they should not be the subject of critical debate and change in the future. Humanists are particularly critical of religious codes that are inflexible concerning important issues and which detract from individual rational analysis of them. Hector Hawton, for example, is especially critical of Roman Catholicism:

> Roman Catholicism is an extreme example of authoritarian morality. A Catholic does not need to think out a solution to problems of conduct. The Church supplies him with an infallible scale of values and a ready reckoner to provide detailed answers. He knows precisely when a marriage can be annulled and when this is forbidden. He knows that birth control is allowed by the rhythm method but not if contraceptives are used. Nuns may take an oral pill if they fear rape, but reluctant wives must submit to their husbands. Euthanasia is rated as murder, but a doctor need not strive officiously to keep alive. An operation to terminate the pregnancy of a woman who might otherwise die is out of the question; but if the foetus is destroyed incidentally it may be permitted.[40]

Unquestionable obedience as opposed to healthy debate and the right of individuals to reflect on what the right moral pathway is for them as individuals, is not *moral* behaviour. Moreover, there are always situational instances when prescriptive rules are themselves thoroughly immoral. Mature, moral individuals make the best possible choices as a result of internalized, responsible reflection, and are adaptable in situations of deeper complexities in the greyer areas of ethical choices. This is a far higher level of morality than mere obedience, and a more difficult and challenging path. In fact there are some grounds for the claim that religion corrupts morality,[41] and that it is inhibiting to the natural potentials for morality in all human beings.[42]

In chapters 3 and 4 relating to the Humanist rejection of religion I have dealt with the reasons why the biblical text cannot be taken at its face value. There are many Christians who would agree, and many Jews who do find *kashrut*, the dietary regulations of the *Torah*, for example, unacceptable and outmoded in the context of contemporary life. Some argue that the Bible is a *foundation* for a contemporary ethic, rather than an ethic in itself.[43] Indeed, it is a myth to believe that the Bible has *an* ethic at all, for there are no consistent principles that span its pages.[44] Anyone that wishes to present *an* ethic from the biblical material has to be selective about what he or she chooses, and of course this is what most Christian individuals, and different Christian groups, have to do. This is not to say that the Bible does not contain any sound ethical principles, for it contains many, but none should ever be beyond critical reflection, none is absolute. And those Christians who might wish to claim that there *are* absolute laws in the Bible have discounted the disparities in its teachings.

Another problem with biblical ethics is that the Bible is very elitist and selective. There is no doctrine of human rights for *all* people, certainly not in the *Old Testament* with the invectives against the Amorites, Hittites, Amalekites and so on, who are regularly smitten by God. But the doctrine of hell in the *New Testament* and Paul's invectives against unbelievers and the Jewish circumcision party do not leave us with an impression of the fundamental value of *all* human beings. Moreover, the biblical ethic is very much a collective one – the chosen race, the body of the Church – *individual* rights are not its primary ethical concern. As one writer puts it, "the notion of an inherent human right to fairness, which is a commonplace in contemporary secular morality, is not to be found in the biblical ethic at all".[45] This is a basic statement that biblical morality is simply unfair.

Anyone who seeks to establish *absolute* moral laws from the biblical material is likely to find him or her self in immoral situations in attempting to apply them. Had the biblical injunction "You shall not permit a sorceress to live" (*Exodus* 22:18) not been taken as an absolute law, thousands of innocent women would not have been condemned to death in the witch-hunts of history. John Carroll uses Rembrandt's painting *The Sacrifice of Isaac* to depict the incredible horror of what Abraham is asked to do in sacrificing his only son (*Genesis* 22). God demands, writes Carroll, "that his chosen representative on earth break the human law and destroy his own happiness, in effect ruin his life".[46] This is not a moral God that requires an act of faith that takes a person to the brink of despair and insanity. Buddhism has a very beautiful saying from the *Dhammapada* which is, that action only is "well done" that brings no suffering in its train. What kind of an ethic is it that torments a man to the extent that God does with Abraham or with Job? Lofmark points out the nonsense of the commandment to honour one's parents so that you will live longer – as if people who do so *really* live longer![47] He also refers to the primitive Jewish religious ritual of circumcision, the cutting away of the foreskin of male genitalia, with two salient comments – why on earth did God put the foreskin there in the first place if it were to be cut off, and "what a place to put a sign!"[48] If we really *think* about the ethical propositions given in the Bible we might find many of them wanting in connection with basic human rights.

New Testament ethics are no less wanting, and many examples of its problematic teachings have already been cited in the earlier chapters of this book. Notable is the acceptance of slavery, even to the extent that a slave must obey a cruel master, and thus the religious endorsement of it (*1 Peter* 2:18). The *Qur'an* likewise accepts slaves as a valid part of life. Is this a good ethic that supports slavery? And if it is claimed that this is merely pertinent to the time in question, why are not all biblical ethical propositions so treated? What of the belief that diseases like leprosy, and disabilities like blindness and lameness were sent as punishments by God? What kind of a God is this that denies human rights, human well-being? And does it make sense to give up *all* your material possessions to the poor (*Mark* 10:17–22) or to give to all who ask (*Matthew* 5:39–42)? And is it *always* right to turn the other cheek? Wells points out that even if we accepted that Jesus' teachings on morality were not to be taken literally "it is difficult to see how we are able to know when to take him literally unless we have some independent criterion of what is right and wrong. And if we do know independently of him, what is right, then we do not need him as an ethical guide".[49]

Then, too, it is not a very practical ethic to suggest that poverty is the admired goal. "Woe to you that are rich" said Jesus (*Luke* 6:24). It is wrong to be mega-rich, as they say in the contemporary world, when there is such terrible poverty, but to say that we should all be poor is to stagnate human personal and collective development. Indeed, the Church has rarely been poor itself. As to turning the other cheek and loving your enemy, it simply does not work: neither does it help the person who is abusing you. To handle cases of "abuse" of women, children, the tortured, the intimidated, by suggesting that victims merely turn the other cheek, and not only that, but to suggest that they should *love* their abuser at the same time, is to leave these people wide open to further abuse. Could we give such advice to the child who is sexually abused? No kind of reward in the putative kingdom of heaven can ever justify passive acceptance of the abuse in any form of a human being. Biblical ethicists sometimes ignore the fact that Jesus believed the end of the world was imminent, in which case it might have made some sense to think that it did not matter if you were poor, abused or downtrodden. But it is thoroughly *immoral* to continue that kind of ethic for two thousand years.

Considering the emphasis placed on the imminent end of the world by both Jesus and Paul, it is likely that a permanent and abiding ethic was not a main item on the agenda; a situational ethic was more likely to have been the main concern. A radical upsetting of the *status quo* would have been considered as a waste of time and only the exigent needs of repentance and focus on the spiritual life would have been important. To try to shift any ethic that obtained in this situational context into the contemporary world, then, is bound to present a mismatch of ethical needs. And if salvation were the carrot in front of the nose for those early Christians who believed that the end of the world was at hand, then it makes no sense at all to be hankering after the carrot of salvation two thousand years later. The call for obedient faith as the highest value and ethic in the face of logical absurdity is perhaps what has turned even those of lower intellects away from the Christian fold. As George Smith comments: "One is not morally free to investigate the truth of the Christian doctrine by means of reason; instead, one must believe uncritically or be condemned as immoral."[50] While biblical criticism, as has been demonstrated, is the prerogative of the scholar, faith and obedience are still the requirements of the flock. To have faith is to be a very moral person in the religious viewpoint. But to have unquestioning faith in rules laid down centuries ago is to resist change and ethical progress; this in itself is *amoral* and opposed to moral responsibility. Faith and obedience inhibit the growth of a truly moral person. On the other hand, a number of people go to church regularly, behave well while there, and then forget the teaching for six and a half days in the rest of the week. Sharpe makes this point pertinently in the case of Northern Ireland:

> There we have the extraordinary spectacle of Protestants emerging from a church service to throw stones at police who seek to prevent them from marching through a Catholic area, a march intended to assert their dominance. They walk out of a church whose founder told them to love their enemies and turn the other cheek intent on abusing and humiliating neighbours who belong to another branch of the same religion.[51]

Clearly there is often a gap between religious ethics and group and individual moral practice.

The emphasis on reward in the afterlife for faith in this life suggests that moral behaviour must too often be seen as "cross bearing" in imitation of the suffering of Christ. And if this leads to a miserable and unhappy existence, well, the rewards will be all the greater after death. Humanism does not subscribe to this kind of ethic at all. And it isn't just that there is no belief in a life after death. *Life* is to be lived as happily as one can live it, and this happiness should be free from guilt. Pleasure, desire, enjoyment, laughter, material fulfilment are some of the essential ingredients of a happy life. And in some situations this may involve homosexual, premarital, extra-marital relationships. The religious ethic that suggests individuals should curb some very natural instincts for the sake of their souls is often psychologically damning. Take lying, for example. This is a sin in most religious ethics, and yet we all do it. The Catholic Church, especially, considers lying to be a grave sin.

But in fact research has shown that lying is an essential part of human development. In the British BBC television series *The Human Body*[52] evidence that lying starts surprisingly early in life, but that it is a natural stage of intellectual development, is given by Michael Lewis, a child psychologist, together with the presenter of the programme, Lord Robert Winston. Using a one-way mirror for obser-vation, a three-year-old child was placed in a room with his back to a covered electric train set. An assistant researcher uncovered the train set, set it in motion and told the child not to "peek" at it while she left the room for a few minutes. The experiment was repeated with other three-year-olds, with the result that 70 per cent of children "peeked", most of whom lied and claimed that they hadn't. They lied of course because they didn't want to get into trouble, but another interesting result emerged from the experiment and that is, to quote Lewis: "The smartest kids are not the ones who tell the truth but in fact the ones who lie about it." In fact, the higher the IQ the more likely the three-year-old child was to lie. (Perhaps this suggests that the truth tellers of the religious bent all have low intelligence!). Lord Winston added: "To lie deliberately these children have to be aware that the experimenter doesn't know whether or not they peeked . . . This awareness that other people can have different beliefs and thoughts from your own is not just useful for the occasional fib, it's a crucial stage. All children need to pass it before they are ready for the adult world." By the age of four it will be essential that children have acquired the skill of working out what another person is thinking about, of knowing that the thoughts, likes, dislikes and desires of another are different from their own – that minds are different. There are many children who might not have suffered the guilt and shame of punishment for lying had this natural development of the child not been a religious sin.

Religious morality, then, has many defects even if it occasionally has some fundamentally sound ethics. It is one paradigm for morality, but not *the* paradigm to be followed by all. The idea that we can do no good without God is an unacceptable and illogical concept. In fact, the more religious eras of society have not been the most humane ones. We only have to look back to times of slavery, brutal treatment of the mentally sick, and the shocking conditions of employment of adults and children in times that were more religiously orientated. Indeed, we are far more humane in contemporary society despite the tensions that exist in a very complex society. Jean-Paul Sartre believed that "nothing will be changed if God does not exist; we shall re-discover the same norms of honesty progress and humanity, and we shall have disposed of God as an out-of-date hypothesis which will die away quietly of itself".[53] Sartre does not suggest that this is an easy state of things for there is no prop on which to lean, no yardstick of what perfect good is, and no "ought tos" that should be obeyed. It is the human being that has to take responsibility. In fact, even for those who prefer the path of religious morality there is still the requirement of rational inquiry of religious values that one should take on. Without such inquiry, behaviour is not truly moral: indeed, it might be argued that individual rational inquiry about morality is prior to, and underpins, all religious morality.[54] It is not moral behaviour to do good for reward in heaven; it is moral behaviour to do good because of personal commitment to the right values in life. But then, if the latter is the case, morality obtains without religion. Gordon Stein, reflecting the view of so many Humanists, makes the point that: "Theism provides no adequate moral guidance in and of itself. In reality, the theist obtains the vast majority of his information about ethical decision making from exactly the same non-theistic sources as the atheist".[55] Morality can only stem from human interaction, an interaction that, as human evolution proceeds, has led to particular norms and moral goals that are rationally necessary for on-going human progress.

A universal ethic?

Given the necessity of changing ethical values, it might be asked if it is possible to have any universal ethic? Should there be a universal ethic? In answering these questions it has to be accepted first that there is immense moral variety not only between different cultures but also within one cultural system. This is far from wrong, but adds to the rich fabric of life: as Hemming said, "interaction with difference is one of the great sources of life".[56] But what is right, valuable, or good in life is variously interpreted – sometimes to the point of conflict, even though people might have the best of intentions. Comparisons across cultures are often problematic, and this has led many to a *cultural relativist* point of view. This is to say that morality is specific to each particular culture, to particular times of historical development, and is relative to the kinds of social structures in which members of a culture exist. There may be considerable similarities such as respect and care for one's parents, or there may be very disparate differences. Western culture, for example, thinks it fit to fine or imprison thieves, whereas orthodox Islamic culture thinks their hand or hands should be cut off (though, in this case, both accept that stealing is wrong). There are bound to be differences between cultures, and this might suggest that a universal morality cannot obtain.

Flexibility of moral codes also militates against a universal morality and, given that Humanism is keen to ensure integrity and justice in the treatment of any individual or group, it is clear that the demands of a particular situation may warrant amendment to the ususal ethical norms. Humanism would also condemn conformity to ossified sets of rules that are out of touch with contemporary life. A uniform morality imposed from without does not answer the multiplicity of situations in which black and white answers cannot be given. And if individuals take responsibility for their own moral choices this necessitates variety not conformity. Indeed, Humanists are often criticized because they reject the prescriptiveness of religious morality, yet do not set up alternative ethical codes. But Humanists are not devoid of goals and principles, many of which they wish to apply universally. They just avoid set creeds and inflexible ethical systems that deflect individual responsibility from personal morality and the social good.

But while there is a rejection of universal, absolute rights and wrongs that apply to all human beings, few philosophically minded Humanists are prepared to accept the relativist view of ethics because it is over-subjective, accepting what is right as a simple matter of opinion. And it seems sensible to suggest that there may be one or two *universal* concepts that really should be accepted by all human beings. Religious ethics have the same problem. Which of the many religions is the right one? Which of the many Christian denominations and sects has the right one? Is there an overriding universal religious ethic?

At the far end of the relativist scale is the situation ethicist, who takes the view that morality is to a great extent situational. It is rare that two moral situations in life are exactly the same, and so we have to use our intelligent judgement in repeatedly new situations. To apply one rule in such different situations is not going to work. It is not that our values necessarily change, it is more that the conditions in which we have to apply them alter. In other words we have to adjust our values in new situations. The great exponent of situation ethics, Joseph Fletcher, points out that to be a situation ethicist one has to be a thoroughly responsible moral agent. And this may involve the violation of another important value in order to do the right and better thing. As Fletcher says: "It is not that situationists have no normative principles; they have them, but they are used as guidelines, not as prefabricated decisions."[57] There may well be times when it is right to steal, to kill, or to commit adultery, And it could even happen that different people might even respond differently to the same situational problem.

Nevertheless it could be argued that there can be moral values that *underpin* situational decisions, and some of these moral values might be applied universally. Joseph Fletcher himself argues for love as the only norm.[58] We certainly carry with us in all situations of life some basic values that are not exactly rules but are the guidelines we have as a result of our experience of being human. If we are truly moral individuals then the well-being of others will be important to us, and it is thoughts for the well-being of others that might suggest some underpinning universal values. To be able to say that divorce, abortion, euthanasia for example are right in a specific situation, whether one is atheist, Catholic or whatever, is to suggest that the well-being of another individual underpins the moral decision in a situational context. The art of making the right ethical choice in a particular situation based on reflection, analysis and modification of previously held views, is not at all an easy moral path. Some examples are presented below:[59]

- When Lawrence of Arabia led the Arab forces against the Turks one of the Arabs killed another Arab from another tribe. Normally this would result in a blood feud between the two tribes causing a large number of deaths. To prevent this happening, Lawrence himself killed the offending man. What would you have done?
- A scientist medic discovers a new serum that will cure plague. The medical authorities are sceptical about the new discovery and are inclined to dismiss it. When an epidemic of plague breaks out on an island the scientist is faced with a choice. He can give the serum to all the inhabitants of the island and save all their lives or he can give the serum to only half of the inhabitants so that he can prove that the serum works and can save lives in the future. What would you do if you were that scientist?
- During the Second World War a group of women agents from British intelligence staff were about to be returned to Germany. Before they left, the British, having broken the German code, discovered that the Germans knew of their imminent arrival. If British intelligence did not send the women then the Germans would know that they had broken the code and would change it. In the end this would cost more lives. Would you have sent those women back to Germany and certain death?
- In 1841 the *William Brown* sailed out of Liverpool for America and struck an iceberg off Newfoundland and began to sink. In one of the lifeboats there were too many passengers, so the first mate,

the only person on the boat who could navigate it to safety, determined that unless someone were put overboard, the whole boatload would go down, and all would die. What would you have done if you were the first mate?

- While a wagon train was crossing Indian territory, at one stage it was necessary for the people to take to the hills and hide because of an Indian attack. While the people were hiding amongst the rocks, the Indians were very close. Just as the Indians were about to leave the spot a baby woke up and was about to cry – a cry that would have caused the certain death of everyone there. If you had been the mother of the baby, what would you have done?

- When Captain Scott's expedition to the South Pole ran into difficulties it was necessary to head back for the coast urgently. One of Scott's men was injured and had to be carried on a stretcher. If they abandoned the man it was likely that the rest of them would live. If they continued to carry the man it was certain they could not survive. What decision would you have made had you been Scott?

- When the Russian armies drove west to meet the allied armies at the Elbe during the Second World War, a Soviet patrol picked up a woman who had been foraging for food with her three children. The children were left to fend for themselves and she was taken to a prison camp in the Ukraine. Her husband had been away in the course of the war and when he returned to his home area he spent many months trying to locate his children, which he eventually did, but could not find his wife. Still in prison in the Ukraine, his wife somehow got news that her family was reunited, but there were only two reasons for which she would be allowed to return – if she were so ill that she required medical treatment outside the camp, or if she were pregnant. She knew that one of the sympathetic guards would be willing to impregnate her. Had you been this woman, what would you have done?

One of the problems of situation ethics is that situations change. The woman in the last case might have found that with just a little extra time her situation may have changed; the weather may have changed for Scott, and so on. These are parameters that also have to be taken into account in decisions that are made. And when they have been made, then we can only act in the situation that is there; contingencies are all well and good, but it is in the concrete situation that the moral choice is needed.

But to return to an earlier point, whether we view ethics relatively or situationally, underpinning universal ideals are not necessarily to be excluded. If I were to be stranded alone in the jungle of some remote place on earth, and suddenly faced with a large group of colourfully painted natives, I might well hope that they would be aware of a universal ethic of kindness towards human creatures despite my difference in skin colour and attire. Relativist ethics might suggest that as far as these natives are concerned it is right, in their culture, to lop off my head as a matter of prestige. But given exposure to a wider range of experience, they might come to see that there is a more advanced ethical position they might adopt. This is not to suggest by any means that there can be any *absolute* ethic that must be adopted by all, rather, there are some universal principles to which all human beings might aspire. And I think the principles to which Humanism aspires are very much for human beings *universally*. Universal principles are not extraneous to the humanity that values them or posits them; they are not "things" or "abstracts" that exist in the universe, that we might come to know. They are what we as human beings create through our continued interaction with our fellow humans. Humanism rejects absolutes but can still have universal aims.

Because human beings everywhere have similar psychological needs for basic security, care, understanding, love and so on, there is no real need to be thoroughly relativist or situationist. To have a global vision of universal peace and well-being for humanity is not offending the kind of responsible and intelligent ethical decisions that individuals might want to make in the context of their own lives; rather, it underpins such morality with a wider consciousness of global need. To suggest that there can be a universal morality, then, is to suggest that there are some fundamental principles that might inform ethical and moral choice. But a universal principle is in no way an absolute law, for it is subject to change in a way that the latter is not. While many Humanists reject the idea of such universal ethical principles in favour of relativism or situationism, others are bolder. The "golden rule" that appears in so much religious thought – do to others as you would have them do to you – is not far short of a sound universal ethic, but falls short of one in that the way in which we would like to be treated may not be how others would want us to treat them.[60]

More certain is a universal ethical value of self-respect accepted by Nielsen. He points out that the very fact that self-respect is a fundamental "good" for me, necessitates my believing that it must also be a fundamental "good" for all others[61] – thus far, a Kantian view. Paul Kurtz writes of "a fund of common moral decencies that can be developed in human experience".[62] It is in the human need and necessity for mutual co-operation that we find an urgency for more universal ethical goals, goals that may have to be adjusted in the light of our future knowledge, but no less needed in the immediate present and future. To accept relativism and situationism *per se* is to accept that little can be done to prevent one group or nation doing something it believes right but that is ultimately inimical to others. Reuben Osborn, therefore, writes of the "impulse to set up ideals of human relationships, to think in terms of humanity rather than special groups or classes, to seek to transcend the limits imposed by the needs of group expediency".[63] It is this kind of universal aim that is so essential for the well-being of humanity and the planet on which it exists. Such aims are *indicators* rather than prescriptive statements for moral behaviour. But there are many universal values that we tend to expect – honesty, courage, integrity, honouring obligations, self-control, fulfilling responsibilities, truthfulness, sensitivity towards others, compassion, consideration of others. These kinds of values we expect to find in our fellow human beings because we have to interact with them, and because our own lives are so affected where the values of others fall short of good. To be morally aware and mature, we need some universal values that we apply to humankind as a whole, even if occasionally we have to adjust those values situationally. Having fundamental universal principles enables us to operate within a parameter of ethics in the more immediate contexts of moral choices. Van Praag put this succinctly when he wrote:

> In thinking through humanist ethics it is found that there is no question of eternal, immutable laws in humanism; but that does not mean that, in the judgments of humanists, no central ideas could be discovered that can in fact be considered as touchstones. They have to do with participating in the world and at the same time being directed towards it; the challenge of accepting reality in the context of existence; the realization of human abilities in relation to the world.[64]

Moral autonomy brings concomitant values that extend beyond self-interest to global perspectives. This is not doing to others as you would have them do to you, but respecting others in the same way as you respect yourself. And out of such respect arises the vision of a changed world in which all human beings exist in the kind of environment that, for them, fulfils sufficient of their needs for them to secure their own self-respect.

Humanist ethics

From what has been examined above, it is clear that the ethics of Humanism is based on rationalism and reason. But, while Humanists differ widely on the matter of ethics, generally speaking the Humanist ethic is neither prescriptive and absolute, nor relativist. In fact a certain tension between these two opposites seems to pervade Humanist writing, and while all evade the former, to accept the latter as the other side of the coin would leave Humanism with no positive universal message at all. And Humanism does have a message: it is a message both to individuals and to humanity as a whole. It has principles that are universally applicable. These are *guiding* principles but are never so rigid that they become black and white precepts. Space is left for challenge and for change. Critical evaluation of all our values, both individual and societal, underpins Humanism and this is a role that is essential in the moral education of children throughout the broad gamut of the curriculum

To become morally mature we have to get into the habit of thinking rationally about what we do, about the knowledge we acquire, what we believe, and the processes in which we are involved. Encouraging creativity, inquiry, questioning, curiosity, learning through experience and exploration are important building bricks for future moral autonomy. Yet, as Margaret Knight once wrote, "moral training cannot be coldly rational. There must be colour and warmth and interest".[65] What is important to Humanists is that ethics is informed by *reason*, and that human beings apply their powers of reason in finding solutions to moral problems. The end product of such problem solving should be a happier existence for both individuals and society at large. Yet Humanists accept the common sense of a legal framework in which there are fundamental laws that are necessary for societal harmony. Some such laws – such as laws against murder – may not need much, if any, rational weighing up of the pros and cons. The fate of a murderer under the law is a different matter, however, and debates about capital punishment – though no longer an issue in Britain – are the kind of ethical issues for which careful reasoning needs to be applied. But laws can sometimes be unjust, and Humanism firmly believes that, in such cases, continuous attempts should be made to change them.

Underpinning Humanist values is the ethic of support for the individual rights of all human beings. Every human being has a right to personal security, to adequate food and health care, to a home that provides sufficient warmth and economic comfort and to personal freedom – particularly the freedom to pursue the goals that are personally important in life, and which develop individual potential and promote individual progress. These are the kinds of ethical principles that inform Humanism's vision of a moral, equitable and stable society. Human beings are ends in themselves and not means, so the intrinsic value of every human being is important to Humanism, and the aim for quality in the life of each individual is related to this fact. Ethics, however, is pre-eminently social in application. All human conduct lies within its range and all the myriad situations in which moral choices have to be made between individual and individual, individual and group and so on. Humanists believe that it is not impossible for human beings to make their own choices about what is good and right for them, but at the same time they can have the capacity of awareness of the well-being of others. This is part of the experience of the "Good Life", the actualizing of personal potential, making the best possible moral choices in the complex situations that compose life, but projecting one's energies out towards other human beings socially and globally.

Humanism, then, sees a necessity for morality but not for an absolute set of rules to create morality. Good moral choices will stem from mature and responsible adults. Morality is founded in individuals and societal structures; it can only exist in interpersonal relationships, and in inter-group and international interaction. It can only exist *in* situations, *in* life, with friends, family, colleagues, and in the wider fields of society. Morality is founded in individual existence and projects itself out into the wider world. This is an exciting proposition for it means that human beings do not have to be injected with their beliefs, they can actually rationalize them for themselves. Maturity is not just reaching physical adulthood, it is reaching mental maturity; it is actualizing one's full capabilities. Contemporary life is uncertain, complex, and full of interesting challenges. It presents varieties of challenging ways in which we have to interact with others, and out of that interaction comes personal growth towards ever-developing maturity. The potential in ourselves that lies waiting to be developed is dependent for fulfilment on the interactive experiences that we have with others. Its fulfilment is also dependent on a stable societal setting and the ingredients for a "Good Life". That is why the Humanist ethic is individually *and* socially focused. Hemming wrote that:

> in life, the meaning comes in living, as wholly as we can, as abundantly as we can, as bravely as we can, here and now, sharing the experience with others, caring for others as we care for ourselves, and accepting our responsibility for leaving the world better than we found it. There is meaning enough in this to last a lifetime. The old man who enjoys the open air while planting a tree for his great-grandchildren to play under goes to bed content, and rounds off his good day with quiet sleep.[66]

This is individual potential quietly fulfilled. For other people, noisier pioneering for social change is an outcome of moral choice. And social change is never beyond our means. If we want something badly enough, and others share the same view, then in uniting together groups of individuals are able to challenge those aspects of life that are obstacles to a "Good Life".

Moral autonomy

Moral autonomy is informed by rational reflection about life – about one's own aims, pathways, desires, environment; about the experiences one has in life; about society and its educational, sociological, economic and political dimensions. In short, morally autonomous individuals have to *think* their way through life, assessing options of belief and action with the outcome of efficient moral decisions about what is right. Often what is right may be inaction in a certain area – choosing *not* to do something either for the present or indefinitely. But it is particularly in the area of beliefs that the morally autonomous person is characterized. Having rationally internalized beliefs that inform all actions, this promotes consistent and mature policies about life that are well-developed, but which are capable of being changed. In almost all situations, there will be the ability to articulate *why* certain beliefs are held as opposed to others. Personal ethical principles are not imposed on a morally autonomous person but are carefully formulated by him or her. Reason and fairness of judgement are readily applied to the kinds of situations which necessitate choice of the best possible outcomes, achievable by the best possible means. As one writer puts it: "To the extent to which man is moral, he is so because he is rational."[67] A certain self-assurance that is concomitant with confidence in one's judgements enables a person to reach out to wider social groups with the ability to test those judgements in the wider arena of human life. In short, the morally autonomous person has a philosophy for life that is lived, adjusted if necessary, and applied with a certain consistency in and to life.

Harmful to moral autonomy are moral codes imposed on an individual through conditioning or training or, even worse, indoctrination. Of course, it is essential that young children have such training, for their powers of reasoning and capabilities for abstract thought do not develop for some time. But once the development begins to take place, it is important that the beginnings of critical thought are encouraged. Moral principles emerge from, and are conducive to, human interaction. Accepting moral rules and precepts "on faith" and simply obeying them is not moral behaviour. There has to be self-conscious choice in a truly moral situation, otherwise responsibility to oneself and to others becomes conventional – doing something right for someone else's reasons without true internalized belief that it should be done because it *is* right. One has to live one's own morality not that of a system. And by living one's own autonomous morality there is a conviction that it would be the kind of morality that one might want for all humanity – the Kantian view.

From a philosophical point of view morality is rooted in human values alone. We do not have to look beyond humanity itself in order to be moral individuals. Ethics is independent of supernatural influence such as that suggested by religion. It has its own autonomous identity, an identity that is given by the human values that inform it and that it reflects. We cannot be moral in our sleep; moral action can only obtain through human activity. Morality is the cornerstone of human interaction; it is in that interaction, and through it, that we gain our identity and wisdom as human beings. It is through morality that we live a life of purpose – purpose that is of value to the individual self and to the social good. For moral autonomy to obtain, then, a number of criteria need to be met:

- Moral claims need to be subjected to rational inquiry.
- The need for rational articulation of personally held beliefs is essential.
- Self-reflective analysis is needed concerning personal aims and desires.
- Decisions and pathways in life need to be informed by rational reflection on a range of relevant criteria.

- Things should be undertaken with evaluation and awareness of intrinsic objectives, not just for their extrinsic ends.
- A healthy balance is needed between egoistically and altruistically motivated goals.
- Open-mindedness about the views of others is essential, along with the flexibility to adjust one's behaviour in the light of rational reflection.
- Forward vision for life is necessary. This develops the self in terms of respect, confidence, and moral independence.
- Individual responsibility for the self and for others is essential.
- Control over one's own life should be evident.

The outcomes of moral autonomy are increased self-respect, self-value, and self-confidence, and this is what enables individuals to have the ingredients of personality that facilitate greater interaction with others. This interaction is characterized by increasing abilities to cooperate with others, to trust others, but not to feel devalued oneself, or to devalue others, if others do not live up to expectations. When a moral code is imposed from without, as many religious codes are, there is little inner resilience for adjustment. But adjustment of moral values is essential because of the changing nature of society and because new moral situations arise that old laws do not fit. Humanism takes on board the changing nature of society and the necessity to encourage moral autonomy rather than trained mental slaves. That is why it has broad principles that underpin ethics but no fixed ethical rules that are inimical to fully mature, morally autonomous individuals.

The Humanist ethic is a shared ethic that can bring together strangers from different nations, races, of different colours, cultures. This is exactly because it is not prescriptive, not absolute, not credal. Hemming depicted this kind of broad ethic very well when he wrote:

> To live confidently in the truth of what we are, in valid relationships with others, is to move towards wholeness, harmony, and inner freedom. And, once we are free, within ourselves, we cease to be under a compulsion to enslave others. Such inner freedom is the goal of our becoming.[68]

If as individuals we cannot stand for ourselves, independently, confidently and with the self-assurance that we have a purposeful life to live for ourselves and for others, we shall find ourselves in a black-hole of indecisiveness and lack of fulfilment. Life gives us certain propensities, our environment gives us certain experiences, our choices determine how we use both. I end this chapter with ten new commandments written some time ago by Sherwin Wine[69] with puckish wit and considerable alacrity of mind:

1. Do not feel absolutely certain of anything.
2. Do not think it worthwhile to produce belief by concealing evidence, for evidence is sure to come to light.
3. Never try to discourage thinking, for you are sure to succeed.
4. When you meet with opposition, even if it should come from children, endeavour to overcome it by argument and not by authority, for a victory dependent upon authority is unreal and illusory.
5. Have no respect for the authority of others, for there are always contrary authorities to be found.
6. Do not use power to suppress opinions you think pernicious, for if you do the opinions will suppress you.
7. Do not fear to be eccentric in opinion, for every opinion now accepted was once eccentric.
8. Find more pleasure in intelligent dissent than in passive agreement, for if you value intelligence as you should, the former implies a deeper agreement than the latter.
9. Be scrupulously truthful, even when truth is inconvenient, for it is more inconvenient when you try to conceal it.
10. Do not feel envious of the happiness of those who live in a fool's paradise for only a fool will think that it is happiness.

7

Rationalism and Reason

Humanism, in accordance with scientific method, believes in the unending questioning of basic assumptions and convictions, including its own. Humanism is not a new dogma, but is a developing philosophy ever open to experimental testing, newly discovered facts, and more rigorous reasoning.[1]

Humanism is sceptical about claims to what is supposed to be true, including any claims that Humanism itself might want to put forward. But to live in the world with a degree of common sense we have to accept that a considerable number of things are true. Some of the things we believe to be true may well be so, but other things we believe to be true are not. If we *really* accept things as true then we should have some kind of rational justification for such beliefs; and whatever we believe to be true should be so irrespective of our emotions and feelings.

Intelligent living

Human beings, while possessing propensities to behave in certain ways as a result of genetic and environmental factors, nevertheless are agents of choice, and the situations that appear before them are so varied that most choice and decision-making processes are new. This makes human beings in a position to *cause* things to happen: people have effects on their own lives and on those of others. The kinds of causes we make may be intelligent and sound, or they may be rather foolish and inappropriate. To live intelligently we have to make the right causes and to know why we have made them. If we don't know why we choose to act or think in a particular way, then it is possible to do so unwisely, even without knowing – to do or think what is not right through lack of thought. Hector Hawton wrote "that human beings have unlimited power to fool themselves is no news, but some, at least, are capable of seeing through the make-believe".[2] This is unfortunately true; we fool ourselves that something is right for all sorts of reasons – because it is comfortable to do so, because we've been conditioned to do so, because others think so, because it is fashionable to do so. But to live our lives with any degree of intelligence we have to take hold of ourselves and question not only the beliefs and practices with which we function in life, but the beliefs and practices by which others expect us to function in life.

All human beings are capable of using reason to evaluate the situations in which they find themselves in life. It is the quality of the reasoning that differs from one person to another, not the functioning of it. To be reasonable our beliefs and our actions consequential on those beliefs, are grounded in observation in, and experience of, life. Reasonable beliefs transpire from our senses, but since our senses sometimes deceive us, it makes sense to test out our beliefs in a number of ways to see if they prove to be valid. If we have beliefs that we cannot validate in this way, then it makes sense to suggest that they might be foolish ones.

Critical intelligence is essential to sound living because without it wrong choices are too easily made, and these inhibit a life that is valuable to one's own self, and to others. But because human beings are emotional creatures they cannot exercise critical judgement in every moment of their waking existence – they would be rather cold individuals if they did. The issue is really one of balance of critical reasoning, practicality and emotion. If the first is predominant, then the individual is more in control of his or her life than he or she who is a slave to emotions. Even the highly intelligent individual is a slave to the emotions at times, but all human beings are capable of at least improving critical reasoning in personal existence. Similarly, we sometimes act according to intuition, a flash of insight, a feeling about something. These are aspects of human living, but we shouldn't crystallize such momentary insights into firm beliefs until we have verified them. Humanism is particularly concerned with promoting individual rational inquiry; indeed, it is an issue that underpins most Humanist principles. It believes that beliefs we hold should always be examined in the light of the evidence available for them, and that all such beliefs should be tested by empirical criteria, that is to say by concrete, testable, observable evidence.

While observation and experience in life inform many of our beliefs, to be valid, beliefs that arise in this way normally need to be corroborated by the observation and experience of others. Much of our knowledge arises in this way, and beliefs about life become *universals*, that is to say beliefs that can be verified through the same experience again and again, by one's own self and by others, without deviation. This means that the outcomes of certain beliefs can be fairly, or uniformly, predictable. Then, again, most of our beliefs are related to our previous knowledge. If some completely new observance happens, and we doubt what we have seen, then we test that observation against our previous knowledge to try to rationalize it. So if I think I see a red cat, and I've never seen one before, it is natural to apply some critical reasoning in the light of past experience and knowledge, to ascertain what the object might be, and I might come up with something like a squirrel. But it is not so much observable data that requires our critical reasoning as our beliefs, particularly our long-term beliefs, and particularly those that have undergone little or no change. Contemporary knowledge systems, the sciences, technology and all disciplines, undergo constant change in the process of furthering the boundaries of knowledge and inquiry. Yet often outmoded and ignorant beliefs that are no longer really relevant to contemporary life – indeed, may even be harmful to it – are maintained. Just in the present knowledge of diet, for example, there are considerable changes in our knowledge during the last decade. To formulate workable beliefs, we at least have to ground them in contemporary knowledge, and what we come to believe needs to be corroborated beyond the narrow subjectivism of the self.

Of course we cannot be well informed about *all* areas of our life, and therefore we cannot continually make informed decisions. What *should* be the basis of rational, critical inquiry, however, are the deeply-rooted beliefs that underpin the greater part of personal and societal life – morality, beliefs about our place in life, religion, the society in which we live, education, leisure, justice, fairness, and so on. It is the bigger issues of life that need to be subjected to careful thought and scrutiny, for they are the ones that are behind the most important decision-making of human beings. Paul Kurtz points out the value of such personal commitment to reflective inquiry into one's own beliefs: "To be committed to a reflective approach to one's values implies some willingness to change, modify, or reconstruct one's values in the light of new facts. This also implies some tolerance of others, a willingness to learn, appreciate, and respect other viewpoints."[3] It is easy to see from these words how reflective analysis of one's beliefs can help to promote the fully mature and "whole" individual, how it can lead to moral autonomy, and how it can lead to the kind of outlook that promotes the "Good Life" for self and others. Trusting old beliefs unreflectively leads to less tolerance of the beliefs of others.

Humanists submit all beliefs and precepts from the past to the rigorous test of rational examination. And if those beliefs and precepts fail the test, then they are discarded. But even if they pass the test, Humanists recognize that beliefs are not static: they belong to their own cultural and historical situation and will not necessarily be applicable to any other time. All life is a state of constant flux, and beliefs must conform to this fact. Exercising rational thought, human beings need to adapt their beliefs in the light of critical judgement. Faith and trust as foundations for beliefs that are never reassessed or reflectively analysed are anathema to Humanism. Doubt is essential for critical analysis. There are no *absolute* truths, only highly probable ones, and given this fallibility of all beliefs it is essential that they are subject to modification in the light of new knowledge. This is put succinctly by Paul Kurtz: "We should not attribute to any belief absolute infallibility. We should be prepared to admit that we can be mistaken. Beliefs should be taken as hypotheses: they are tentative or hypothetical depending upon the degree of evidence or the validity of the arguments used to support them."[4] And as Kurtz points out elsewhere: "A theory is only as good as the evidence adduced in its support."[5]

It is sensible to accept basic beliefs about existence simply because of the universality of empirical evidence for them. But many of the beliefs that people have are conditioned and acquired without reflection. The degree to which individuals are able to assess their beliefs and change them is indicative of their maturity as individuals and is a profound factor in the development of an autonomously moral and free individual. As human beings we can never be totally free, but we can move towards individual autonomy if we can take a good look at ourselves, can analyse why we behave in certain ways, can reflect on what conditioned beliefs inform our behaviour in life. And if we can do this we are living intelligently. Important, however, is the factor emphasized above by Kurtz; whatever beliefs we come to accept – even if they are short term – are only sound if there is good evidence to support them. We need to know *why* we believe the way we do, and the reasons why need to be rational ones. Albert Einstein wrote: "I appeal to you to be rational, critical, inspired with the spirit of enquiry. Don't take things simply for granted. If you do not have the courage to revolt against authority outright, then at least go to the extent of demanding on what sanction is the authority based. You shall never be free on this earth so long as you remain a voluntary subject to forces unknown and unknowable."[6] The forces that are unknown and unknowable are often in the human psyche itself – environmental conditioning, fears, guilt, and outmoded beliefs that still hang on in life and prevent personal evolution and freedom. Opening the mind to doubt, reflection and change is bound to be initially difficult – "Reason is a disturber of peace", as Hector Hawton put it[7] – but it is a process that is the first step to mature individuality.

From all that has been written so far, it is clear that Humanism decries *irrational* belief, belief that has no basis in evidence or verifiable fact. Beliefs should never be absolutes. They are simply useful contextually, and we don't have to hang on to them indefinitely. Humanists place any belief in the *supernatural* in the category of irrational belief. As has been frequently emphasized in the earlier chapters of this book, Humanism is what can be called *naturalistic*: that is to say, existence is comprised of the universe that we know, a universe that is dependent on natural law. It consists of ever-changing matter and energy in constant flux. Humanism believes that humankind has a neutral relationship with this universe and this is to say that the sun, moon, stars, rains, seasons and so on have no affect on the human psyche. There are no pantheistic forces – spirits, demons, fairies, gods and the like that inhabit the world and affect the lives of humans. The universe neither acts for, nor against, humanity, and it has no preferences for, no purposes for, and no consciousness of, the human beings that inhabit it. Nothing supernatural exists to influence the planet on which we live. The happiness of individuals *on earth* is the important issue for Humanism and this is a happiness that can only take shape in the context of the known universe and on the natural planet that is the home of human beings. It is irrational to accept supernatural beliefs when there is no evidence to corroborate them. But the neutrality of the universe and Nature in relation to human beings is not suggestive of a lack of human inter-relatedness with the environment. What we do as human beings affects the planet on which we live intimately. But all our knowledge, and our beliefs consequent from that knowledge, are grounded in *human* experience, a point put succinctly by Ronald Fletcher:

> The only knowledge we can have is human knowledge. And all human knowledge is knowledge of the world as we, as human beings, experience it. It can never be more than this. We may ask questions about

what the world is like beyond our own limited experience of it, what other dimensions it may possess, but it seems impossible to establish knowledge about such questions in ways which go beyond human experience.[8]

Rationalism and reason

The Humanist ideal person is the "freethinker", a term that has been used in the past to refer to the critics of religious traditions in particular. But a freethinker is a person with the kind of autonomy of self that rests on the rejection of beliefs for which there is no rationally demonstrable evidence, and which reason shows to be unfounded. Rationalism and reason inform all Humanist thought, the former term, with its *-ism* suggesting a system of thinking, that informs in turn the process of reason in the human mind. So it isn't sufficient simply to *reason* why we think this or that, the reasoning has to be *rational*. Rational reasoning, therefore, is a quality of reasoning, it is sound reasoning, it is reasoning that is properly conducted, it is reasoning that is logical, it is reasoning with accountability. Humanist thinking is rational because it is based on facts, on evidence, and on concrete proof. Rationalism is mistrustful of beliefs based on intuitive, mystical, or religiously revealed accounts. Instead it favours the kind of rational knowledge gleaned from facts, from natural laws and from science. Science and technology have to apply rationalized reasoning processes at a very professional level, but this kind of rationalization of life is no less important in daily living. To apply reason and rational thinking takes a great deal of time, reflection, observation and experimentation. Reason goes hand in hand with reflective inquiry, with critical analysis of what beliefs are right or wrong, or what modifications to belief are necessary in the light of new data. To be a rational person it is necessary to apply reason to life, and this is intelligent living.

Rationalism

Rationalism is a process, an active process, by which one employs reason. In Jim Herrick's analysis of the term he traces its original meaning as simply "one who values reason". Thus simply, it is a meaning as applicable to Christian theology as to atheism, in addition to the more definite atheistic tone of the term in the nineteenth and twentieth centuries.[9] Today, the term is more widely used to express the rationalist approach to life that is founded on reason and scepticism, on rejection of supernatural and irrational belief, and as opposed to religious belief. Rationalism eschews religious experience, mysticism, superstition, supernaturalism, faith, revelation and subjectivism. This is a definition that necessarily associates with scientific procedure, for rationalism tests hypotheses and truth claims; it challenges the irrational by expecting evidence, evidence that uses reason as its tool. Rationalism sometimes counters "authority", for nothing is accepted "on authority". Without reliable evidence, any so-called claims to truth are rejected. But a point of Charles Watts is pertinent here. He wrote: "In its methods Rationalism is persuasive rather than recklessly aggressive. It relies upon constructive argument, not merely destructive denunciation."[10] This is an important point, because rationalism is "reasonable", it is not challenging and antagonistic for the mere sake of it; it is a true quest for valid belief. And yet, this is a quest for valid belief that is conditional on the data that we have at the moment. Rationalism *expects* change, expects reassessment of beliefs in the light of change, and challenges established beliefs that become outmoded because they are resistant to change.

When beliefs are rational they are capable of scrutiny, of investigation by others, and indeed, of verification by others. Thus, we can convince others of our rational beliefs because we are able to give sound reasons for them, reasons that do not contradict other well-established knowledge and natural laws. But what is important about rational beliefs is that they lead to rational actions, to rational values in life, and to a rational ethic for life. It is thus the *outcome* of rationalism in personal life that benefits the self initially, as well as all those interactive situations in which the self is involved with others. In the previous section I wrote of *intelligent living*. But living intelligently does not mean that one needs high intelligence. It means living life *rationally*, thinking about what we believe and do in life. One critic of Humanism wrote that: "A clever person can use reason to support any course of action that he or she fancies – it takes decent *feelings* to pick the right one."[11] This is partly true in that one certainly needs to have decent feelings in life. But a person who uses reason to serve his or her own fanciful ends is not *really* clever, and is using reason *irrationally*. To claim that feelings should predominate over reason is to suggest regression to primitive behaviour. Truly decent feelings arise out of reflective analysis of one's beliefs, such feelings need to be reasonable, and using reason *solely* for one's own ends is in fact unreasonable. And it is irrational to be unreasonable. Our feelings about things need to be as rational as our beliefs. Living life purely by feelings is to live life so emotionally that many actions are inevitably irrational, inconsistent and not precipitated by reflective reasoning.

The rationalism that is so important to Humanism is not confined to personal belief, for Humanism seeks to root out irrationalism wherever it emerges in society. This may be in terms of irrational laws, cults, prejudices, religions or economic policies. It is particularly evident in the case of supernatural beliefs where valid explanations and evidence for beliefs are unknowable and absent, and yet religious institutions claim that it is a sin to doubt, to be sceptical about the basic beliefs that are held. In contrast are scientific beliefs that are knowable, testable, logical, and which do not offend other natural laws. They are also characterized by *internal consistency*, that is to say they are related in some way to other validated beliefs, and become part of a network of beliefs – in short, they are rational. There is thus a significant relationship between rationalism and science.

While human beings cannot be rational all of the time, the degree to which they are is the degree to which they are free individuals, not bound by the ties of the beliefs and views of others that are imposed on them from without. In fact a rationalist is a "freethinker" and both are humanists. There is, then, some synonymity between the three terms. All this suggests that the term rationalism is a dynamic and active one, one *applied* in human living, underpinning human existence and societal life. A rational individual or a rational society is a free individual and a free society. How critical this is to Humanism, is powerfully expressed by Nielsen:

> Where enlightened and emancipated conditions obtain, and thus fully rational conditions (reasonable circumstances) obtain, people will be informed, perceptive, liberated, autonomous, self-controlled agents committed to developing their own distinctive powers and capacity for fairness, impartiality, and objectivity. They will be reflective about their ends, knowledgeable about the means for the efficient attainment of these ends, and they will be critical people not under the bondage of any ideology. Indeed, free from all self-imposed tutelage and indoctrination, they will see the world rightly. They will have identified the evils of the world and they will understand the conditions for surcease or amelioration of these evils and for the achievement of human community, to the extent that the community can be achieved at all.[12]

These are exceptional aims. They also illustrate remarkably well how the progression of society and the promotion of the "Good Life" are informed by *individual* change, individual coming-of-age through rational inquiry that leads to personal autonomy.

Reason

To quote the poet John Dryden:

> ... Reason's glimmering ray
> Was lent, not to assure our doubtful way
> But guide us upward to a better day ...

If rationalism is the dynamic process by which one is guided upward to a better day, then reason is the direct means, the tool of the rationalist. The elevation of Reason has a long history. Kant, as others in the Age of Enlightenment, grounded philosophical inquiry in a study of knowledge, or *epistemology*, an inquiry that, hitherto, had been blinkered or blindfolded by the overriding capitulation to Divine knowledge. Extracted from its theological restrictions, human knowledge, human morality and human will were able to break free from the fetters of the past. It was reason that showed the human mind to be capable of knowledge *in itself*, devoid of theology. The human being could also be morally autonomous, independent of any divine will. Once reason is allowed to flower in the human mind, cherished beliefs begin to collapse, and the problems that were outlined in connection with religious theism above in chapters 2 and 3 become evident. It is no wonder that the Church so often condemned reason as antithetical to religious belief. But, as Carroll remarks: "It was Descartes who enshrined Reason as the presiding god of modern culture."[13] Cartesian insistence on the freedom of the human mind to construct itself through the power of reason, opened the channels for stringent criticism of biblical inconsistencies.

These kinds of philosophical analyses of the capacity for human reason independent of divine command characterize Humanist thinking today. Reason is the human being's most important mental capacity. It is that which makes sense of the impulses received into the mind by the senses, sifting the information, categorizing it, conceptualizing it, relating it to previous knowledge. But when reason operates, there is *conscious* human control of it; it is not an automatic process of involuntary assimilation of knowledge data.

Reason assumes the acquisition of a kind of knowledge that we are able to articulate and justify. If we are unable to do this then our reasoning is inadequate; it is unreasonable. Reason means that we have to be reflective about the use of our present knowledge and attentive to the acquisition of our new knowledge. As Hawton wrote: "Reason is much more than the passive slave which carries out our instructions; it is the critic which informs us of whether they are feasible, and what the consequences are likely to be."[14] Only through reason can we understand reality, what is true, what is right, and what is wrong.

Inevitably, we sometimes reason falsely, and this is where rationalism holds reason in check. It is rationalism that *cultivates* reason, which channels it in the right directions. But if our reasoning is sometimes not good, it is the only intelligent capacity we have to make sense of our world. It is therefore a human duty to develop it. Every individual is capable of improving his or her reasoning powers, of reflecting just that bit more about life. Only through mature reasoning can individuals operate maximally in a complex and often contradictory world. The application of mature reasoning to complex situations in life, serves to promote increasingly right kinds of decisions: reason is conducive to personal evolution. And when we have to justify our actions and beliefs, this authenticates the degree of rational thinking that has informed them. Where rational, valid reasons for belief, practice, and action cannot be given, then rationalism breaks down to irrationalism. The maturely rational person applies reason to ascertain what is fantasy and what is real in life, what is valuable as opposed to what is not, what is valid as opposed to what is invalid, and what is true as opposed to what is false.

It is reason that assists in the assessment of probabilities. Not all life's decisions are in the black and white categories. It is those difficult decisions that have to be made in life – the greyer areas of life – that demand the utmost from our reasoning abilities. Sometimes it is necessary to plan ahead, to think abstractly and contingently for the future, and this is essential both individually and nationally. Forward thinking is critical to a healthy society and to a healthy planet.

But despite an emphasis on reason as the innate power of the human being to direct his or her own existence, and to combine with others to bring about rational policies for communal existence, many Humanists see the dangers of an over anthropocentric perspective of humanity. Human beings have the most evolved capacities for reasoning, and have the capacities for solving the majority of their own problems in life and on this planet. But they are not infallible; they make countless mistakes, both personally and communally. However, they do have the capacity to learn from their mistakes, to pick themselves up and start afresh. They are not at the centre of the universe, but they have the ability to affect all aspects of the planet that houses them. Carroll writes of humanistic trends exemplified through the media of history, art and literature, as producing a "disenchanted world emptied of meaning". Although through reason many of the sordid aspects of human existence have been overcome, Carroll believes this is at a cost: "life in the palace of reason became typified by the banal bureaucratic routines of the office and the depressive leisure routines of television and overeating".[15] (One wonders how he lives!). But, to reiterate what was said in the context of societal morality in the last chapter, the facets of life that he criticizes are the results of a highly complex society. This is a phenomenon that brings its own particular problems: they are not problems that can be blamed on humanistic trends of the past. Humanists of the past have fought hard to reduce the moral and social evils of society, and rationally see this as an ongoing mission, each generation leaving the best possible world for the one that follows it. If western society has become the slave of bureaucracies, the television set, and over-eating, then Humanism today is not slow to see where adjustments in values might contribute to a "Good Life". But it would be very naïve to think that without the application of reason, society could make any progress forward at all. In all cases the application of rationalized reason has pragmatic outcomes for the good of the individual and society. Slaves to the office, the TV and food, are simply not applying it.

At the beginning of this chapter, the need for a balance between reason and emotion was stressed. Critics of Humanism often contend that Humanism pays lip service to the value of emotion in human life.[16] But it has to be remembered in the face of such criticism that the Humanist goal for all individuals is the "Good Life" and that means a *happy* life for all. And since happiness is an emotion, Humanism cannot be criticized for insisting on arid reason as the primary goal. Rather, reason provides the means by which society, and the individuals that compose it, can move to a point where the emotional values and experiences of life are of a greater depth of quality. Emotion is essential to our existence. It is right to feel angry when the rights of others are usurped. It is right to feel compassion for the starving, the homeless, the person who loses his or her job, the grieving, the sick. And it is essential to experience and to give love, in the widest possible contexts. Humanists are not devoid of emotion, they can't be, because they are *human*. Ronald Fletcher implicitly states this, and balances the dimensions of reason and emotion as facets of human existence in the following words:

> The Humanist can be as sensitive to the many-sided enigma of nature – its beauties, sublimities, meannnesses, cruelties, fatefulness, varieties of mood – as anyone else. As far as I can see, he is as much a prey to all the feelings, "intimations", doubts, and baffling questions that confront us in trying to fathom the tangled skein of nature as anyone else. A sensitive vulnerability to all the dimensions of our entangle-ment in the world, and the desire to probe and to articulate the experience of some deeply sensed meaning in it all, are not exclusive to religions. They are equally open to those of us who cannot easily find our way.[17]

But all emotions need reasonable and rational justification for them to be of value to one's self, and to others in society. To be unreason-able emotionally is to lead a difficult life and to create difficulties for others. Reason helps us to cope with the negative emotions and to enhance the positive ones.

Yet it is naïve to think that reason has only positive results, or that even rationalized reason for which logical reflective analysis can be given, is always morally right. Tony Davies points to the systematic extermination of the Jews, homosexuals, and non-German races by the Nazis. This, he says

> was the result not of some inexplicable descent into irrational, atavistic barbarity but of a supremely modern rationality. The cool framing of objectives, the logical planning of complex systems, the orderly deployment of technology and resources: all these testify to a piece of demographic engineering as measured in its symmetry, as eloquent in its appalling fashion of individual genius and collective enterprise as the Parthenon itself.[18]

This suggests that, while human reason is important and crucial to Humanism, the means to ultimate goals must be morally reasonable. Hitler might well have argued that the ultimate ends were utilitarian, the greatest good for the greatest number, and that the pure super-race that would have emerged would have furthered the evolutionary progress of humanity. But the means were wholly immoral, and the ends fell well short of universal acceptance.

Reason versus faith

From what has been said so far it is not too difficult to see why reason stands in sharp contrast to faith. Faith consists in belief *without* reason, belief in what is not really known, what cannot be subjected to empirical investigation. Reason and faith are, therefore, rarely compatible. And this is why Humanism stands against religious belief that requires people to "have faith" when rational questions about religion cannot be answered. The theist who is unable to provide evidence, such as to why God allows suffering in the world, why the Kingdom about which Jesus spoke did not come, and similar questions, has in the end to fall back on the response "Well, it's a question of faith". He or she may also have to respond to the effect that only God can know why such things are, and who are we to question God? But Humanists are likely to see the biblical Eve as getting things right when she stretched out her hand for the forbidden apple that would give her knowledge. Theists usually maintain that religion lies outside all other disciplines in that it is not subject to the same kinds of investigative analysis and rational argument. They fall back on personal experience to support faith, but such personal experience is subjective and therefore different from one person to another. In stringent terms Paul Henri Thiry d'Holbach wrote:

> Theology is but the ignorance of natural causes reduced to a system . .
> . [it] is a science that has for its object only things incomprehensible.
> Contrary to all other sciences, it treats only of what cannot fall under
> our senses. . . . it is a country in which everything is governed by laws
> contrary to those which men can recognise in the world they inhabit.
> In this marvellous region, light is no more than darkness; evidence is
> doubtful or false; impossibilities are credible; reason is a deceitful
> guide; and good sense becomes madness. This science is called
> theology, and this theology is a continual insult to the reason of man.[19]

Humanists thus see religion as encouraging irrational belief and as curtailing the intellect. Indeed, the Christian theologian Søren Kierkegaard once made the now famous statement "Christianity demands the crucifixion of the intellect", a goal he felt necessary for all Christian life.

Humanists are happy to admit that they can never know all the answers to life, but they see life as exciting and challenging, the field in which more and more apples of knowledge can be plucked from the trees. What is not known now may well be in the future, and whatever is known now may well be reassessed in the future. But whatever is known, should be known through rational processes without recourse to leaps of faith for which no evidence can ever be presented. And, as one writer aptly points out, it is not God in whom people have trust and faith, but those human beings who claim to speak on his behalf.[20] And *all* human beings are fallible creatures; none is ever perfect. George Smith goes as far as to say *"it is logically impossible to reconcile reason and faith"*. This, he claims, is because faith has inherent within it the deprecation of reason and an anti-reason element.[21] The moment a theist has recourse to statements of faith or "only-God-knows" argument, reason has, indeed, been abandoned entirely. "Like air rushing in to fill a vacuum, faith rushes in to fill the void allegedly left by reason."[22] Because *fideists* – those who accept that knowledge is to be acquired through faith and revelation – cannot demonstrate their beliefs rationally, they have to reject reason at some point in the defence of their position. They may use rational argument up to a point, but eventually they are forced to abandon rational argument for irrational statement. In the end, theists cannot claim how they acquire the knowledge they have of the supernatural God they accept, or demonstrate what that knowledge is.

The classic issue of reason verses faith emerges in the case of creationism. Creationists believe that the world came into being through divine fiat in the process of six days, as outlined in the first book of the Bible, *Genesis*. This necessarily accepts a Creator, an omnipotent being who reasons in his own way that the world will come into being. And since God does not say by what laws he makes the universe, human beings cannot fathom the creative laws of God. Thus, as Ruse points out: "By their own words, therefore, creation-scientists admit that they appeal to phenomena not covered or explicable by any laws that humans can grasp as laws."[23] Creationism is, however, a more extremist view, and most Christians today are at ease with the concept of evolution. Eminent scientists may also be theists though there must always be some divorce between faith and reason in such cases: there must always be the subordination of reason to the authority of God at ultimate points.

Science

The rise of science during the Enlightenment and its rapid progress during the nineteenth century shifted the emphasis from faith to reason. Bullock comments that in the nineteenth century: "Science had replaced philosophy and challenged religion, providing both intellectual security and the mastery over nature which was the key to technical advancement."[24] Science is an inquiry into knowledge, be it knowledge of physics, mathematics, psychology, sociology, politics, and all the various disciplines that come under its umbrella term. And since it is an inquiry into knowledge it requires concrete end results – a positive outcome in terms of demonstrable and verifiable facts. So science observes, tests, finds evidence for, proves, constructs laws, organizes facts into coherent systems, and sets out its criteria for public examination. Essentially, science is pragmatic in attempting to solve the problems of human existence. It has been described as "a rational mode of approach to all problems",[25] and can thus be applied to all aspects of life – not just the sciences, but in the solution of daily problems. The methodology and rationale that underlies its principles are as important to daily living as they are to the professional scientist.

The knowledge provided by science may only be partial, it may have to be readjusted, it may be found to be outmoded, but the nature of it, as open to reassessment and change, allows knowledge to progress, and allows technological evolution. But in all cases, science is subject to *natural* laws; supernaturalism falls outside the boundaries of science. Thus, science tends to modify already acquired evidence, because it operates within the bounds of natural laws. When new scientific evidence is put forward, given that we can understand the state-of-the-art evidence, the newer evidence can be assessed in the light of the natural laws already formulated. Therefore, there is a certain *logical consistency* about new hypotheses in science. That is to say, they relate to the already acquired laws about the natural universe. Where new ideas radically contradict other natural laws, then stringent evidence has to be formulated and verified for the acceptance of the new hypotheses. In such cases it is critical that the evidence presented by new claims to knowledge can be empirically and publicly examined under test conditions. Sometimes scientific hypotheses are the result of imaginative leaps forward on the part of the scientists. This is all part of human creativity. But the *results* of such claims can never be accepted as true until they are rigorously tested. And once rigorously tested such claims have a degree of pragmatism in the body of knowledge that they inform.

Since any new scientific knowledge is subject to analytic verification, there is a certain degree of control over what is accepted as valid and erroneous knowledge. This means that it is possible to build on firm knowledge step by step, constructing coherent systems of knowledge that are the bases for further research and investigation. But firm knowledge never means *infallible* knowledge, it only means the progression so far in the respective science. All this means that the sciences go hand in hand with rationalism and reason, and that this combination spells progress for humanity. It is a combination that is capable of adaptation to human needs in daily life, particularly in relation to the beliefs human beings have about life. Science and technology offer the potential methodology to solve some of the problems of human daily existence. Just as science pushes the boundaries of its knowledge further and further, so repeated questioning of principles needs to be applied in daily life: no truth or belief should be regarded as dogmatically right and unalterable. In science, there are no supernatural truths; all knowledge and truth belong to the same universe, a universe characterized by contingency and change. Human beings are given the raw materials of existence, and the knowledge that can be gleaned from these is entirely dependent on human initiative.

Despite many criticisms of science, we rely heavily on it in our day-to-day existence. And whatever its virtues and setbacks there is a tendency of most lay people to accept its findings, often without reflective questioning simply because the boundaries of the respective discipline are beyond ordinary knowledge. Thus, as Quinn observes: "If we are told that it is scientifically respectable to believe that the universe originated in a big bang billions of years ago, we nod assent without further ado, even if we have a very imperfect grasp of what is actually being asserted and no idea at all about what evidence could be adduced to support such an assertion."[26] Blind acceptance of scientific evidence is not rational or reasonable without some assessment of the reasons why we think its findings might be applicable to our own daily existences. As Kurtz comments: "Some skepticism is essential to the life blood of the scientific enterprise itself."[27] Thus critical assessment both within and without science is healthy and creative: scepticism is healthy, and science can never give us a fallible belief system. As such it is incompatible with established religious systems.[28]

The progress of humankind has been evolutionary both in the scientific and technical senses, and in terms of the progress to becoming human through lower life forms. The universe, life and humankind are considered to be the consequence of natural evolutionary processes. The ability to reason and the capability for rational thinking processes were not assigned to the earliest types of human – these have been evolutionary benefits resulting in the human being we know today. This process of evolution has been the result of a process of natural selection and a ruthless survival of the fittest. All this does not, of course, correlate with a once and for all creation by a superhuman divine being. And even if it were to be accepted that it is a superhuman divine being that is responsible for the massive chain of evolutionary processes, the principle of the survival of the fittest and the rude beginnings of human life demolish soteriological claims of religion. They also pose the old question of theodicy, because of the evil that befalls the weaker species, and members of those species, including human beings, along the way.

But a human being is more than just "a passing part of a continuum between the amoeba and some futurist mutation".[29] For in the higher stages of human evolution the contribution to societal progress by human beings in just one lifetime is considerable. Whatever the past evolutionary strand, and whatever the futurist mutations, human beings *in the present*, and in *one* lifetime can bequeath that which is of value to the generations that follow. In demolishing creationist views of the origins of humankind the theory of evolution also demolished the anthropocentrism that saw human beings as the apex of creation. Yet it also pointed to the ways in which humanity can shape its own future, the ways in which it is capable of working for optimum benefits. Humanity was shifted from centre stage, but dispersed all over it, part of a dynamic process of evolution in a natural world to which human beings remain intimately related. Science presents this world as the only knowable, empirical reality. It is a world that is neutral to the human beings that inhabit it, and therefore one in which they are free to give it meaning and purpose in their own way. The importance of developing potentiality in human life, of improving the human make-up, was emphasized by Sir Julian Huxley when he referred to humanity as "exceedingly young", and "exceedingly imperfect, an unfinished and often botched product of evolutionary improvisation".[30] Huxley praises the scientific genius of humanity, but also warns of immaturity of the human species:

> Man has become the latest dominant type in the evolutionary process, has multiplied enormously, has achieved miracles of cultural evolution, has reduced or extinguished many other species, and has radically affected the ecology and indeed the whole evolutionary

process of our planet. Yet he is a highly imperfect creature. He carries a heavy burden of genetic defects and imperfections. As a psychosocial organism, he has not undergone much improvement. Indeed man is still very much an unfinished type, who clearly has actualized only a small fraction of his human potentialities. In addition, his genetic deterioration is being rendered probable by his social set-up, and definitely being promoted by atomic fallout. Furthermore, his economic, technical and cultural progress is threatened by the high rate of increase of world population.[31]

This reiterates the point that since humanity is only on one point of a continuum of evolution, there is much to be done to influence the future for the better. Humanism does not have a "supreme" or "unquestioning faith" in science and reason[32] but it does not accept that the progress of humanity can be furthered *without* reason – reason grounded in empirical, scientific progress.

However, Humanism inherited something of the enthusiasm for the scientific and technical advances of the twentieth century. And most people favoured the advances that took place in the workplace, the home, the world around. It is really *technology* as the outcome of scientific progress that we tend to have more experience of in the world around us. And most of us would not wish to part with the technological assets of our daily lives – the household appliances, the computer, the car, for example. Religionists often look to science and technology – and, indeed, to Humanism as the supporter of both – as responsible for the dying of the planet (if it is). But in fact that old Christian idea of subjugating the earth, of human domination of Nature, is much more inimical to the planet on which we live. And this kind of belief still has the upper hand. If Humanism ever saw science as the infallible road for the future – and it would have been eschewing reflective reason to have gone this far – it is at least capable of adjusting its views and of finding pragmatic means of overcoming the technical problems that face our planet. Religion can do none of this; it has no *pragmatic* outcome other than a reassessment of its attitudes to Nature.

The achievements of science to date are remarkable; something put clearly by Bullock:

> The Enlightenment believed that extending the methods of science from the natural to the human realm would liberate men and women. The subsequent success of science has gone a long way to meeting these hopes, not only by raising the standards of human living and material comfort but in relieving human suffering from hunger, pain,

disease and fear – immense benefits which we take for granted but which would have seemed miraculous to our predecessors. Science is at the same time the most impressive achievement of the human mind, resting not only on the power of individual genius and the intellectual discipline of the scientific method, but on a cooperative effort which overcomes the obstacles of nationality, culture and language, and puts all other human enterprises in the shade. Surely this is humanism in action.[33]

Affirmatively this *is* humanism in action. But Bullock also warns that the humanities – those aspects of life that deal with the more ambiguous areas of values, beliefs, emotions and responses to art – are integral aspects of human experience and personality. It is these more ambiguous facets of the human mind that may yet prevent the total reduction of the human being to scientific genetic physicality. Moreover, Bullock sensibly advises that the unity of objectivity and subjectivity in the human self – and this might be interpreted as reason and emotion – is essential for the future path of Humanism.[34]

While it is wrong to overstate the case and claim that Humanism has *supreme* confidence in science and technology, the loss of the adjective here states the case more accurately. And, indeed, if we do not have confidence in science to assist the forward progress of humanity, then in what else can we have confidence? Nevertheless, it is not right to be so much under the spell of science that all its claims are taken on board without reflection. Science is an exciting discipline in which to research, but to the ordinary person it may well seem like an unstoppable machine that he or she is unable to influence. Bullock makes this point clear when he says:

> If they [human beings] recognise the advantages in improved health and standards of living, the message constantly drummed in, that technological advance cannot be stopped or even slowed down and that its consequences simply have to be accepted, produces the conviction that they have no control over developments which can profoundly affect their lives and that as human beings they have ceased to count in the technological scale of values.[35]

Passive acceptance of events is not the hallmark of a "whole" person, an autonomous person. Science is not infallible and cannot be that arrogant; neither can Humanists be arrogant concerning claims of what science can do. As Fletcher says: "Science is not the *only* approach, nor is it an *isolated* approach, to the understanding of the world or of man's nature and condition."[36] Science has produced what is good *and* what is not good, and it is only time that tests its long-term effects as good or bad, as adequate or inadequate. Irrational expectations of what science can do has led to a measure of disillusion with some of its outcomes. Technological outcomes that might one day be harmful to the planet need to be controlled and very carefully monitored. At the same time, one does not want to impose on science the restrictions that limit and curtail creative research. Thus, the protection of people from harmful products is as essential to the "Good Life" as the free creative enterprise of the scientist that might create them. This is an issue that is likely to vary from Humanist to Humanist, but the ethics of science is critical to its role in creating a "Good Life" for all humanity.

To criticize science and technology for the mistakes of present existence – the ecological damage to the planet, the dangers of nuclear power, pollution of the air, the land, the seas and water, not least the dangers of food colourings and additives that are closer to home – is not to be blind to their failings. But we still have to look to science and technology to correct the mistakes of the past and present, and to work towards a healthier planet for the future. Solutions in one area may well set up residual problems in another, and it is these particular challenges that have to be resolved by newer research. To be disillusioned with the mistakes of science and technology is natural, but in the complexities of the age in which we live, we cannot do without it. One of the sad things about science and technology in contemporary life is the demand for increased efficiency in output in many areas of working life. Today we rub shoulders with many people who have no time to take their lunch breaks, who get home very late from work daily, or who have to take work home with them. One defect of a technological age is perhaps that humans are either replaced by machines or have to try to keep up with them. To reiterate what was said in chapter 5, employers expect more and more from their employees, and efficiency no longer means doing a job well, but doing your own job well, as well as someone else's who has left or who has been made redundant. It also means being cost-effective and time effective, as well as trying to do in one hour something that really takes two. These are things that militate against the "Good Life", and they may well be some of the poorer results of our technological age, increased also by the economic pinch of present industrial life.

As was highlighted in chapter 5 on society, the complexities and expectancies of working life tend to inhibit the space and time for creativity, constraining human ability rather than developing human potential. Perhaps it isn't too surprising that people tend to "chill out" in front of the television set. The fast-paced, technological working world makes this partially inevitable. Humanity itself is not an "information processor" or a "technology",[37] but it sometimes seems like it with the jargonized language of the working world. In all areas, as one writer puts it, "new jargon has sprung up like weeds".[38] Technology has brought us the computer, e-mail, sophisticated photocopiers and those numerous "memos", but the one thing it cannot bring is the time to deal with the speed of a technological working life; it leaves us little time to smell the roses and enjoy the simple things.

There are some that blame science and technology for the ecological crises of our modern age. Long before such crises were evident, Humanists expressed widespread concern for conservation, protection of wildlife, the need for education in ecological awareness, and the dangers of pollution. Aesthetic appreciation is important to Humanists but for this to be possible it is necessary for individuals to take care of the world for themselves and for the generations that will follow them. Understanding and protection of the delicate ecosystems of our planet is essential for the future of humanity, and these ecosystems have as much intrinsic value for their respective beauty, as for their utilitarian value to humans. To lose, for example, the rich colours of the corals of the Great Barrier Reef would be a great aesthetic loss. However science advances, there are some beauties of Nature that it cannot emulate. Some believe that there is a delicate interconnectedness between all Nature: if this is so, a balanced conservation of all Nature is necessary for a healthy planet. Fletcher is one Humanist who believes:

> our human nature *is* rooted in the nature of the world; that all the interwoven, patterned, marvellous, but often terrible, elements of our own physical, emotional, mental, and spiritual nature, and that all of us are indeed – as the religious language has it – of "one body", of "one flesh". "The one and the many" is not a mystical insight, it is a common everyday truth.[39]

Maintaining such a healthy balance between species of all types is an important role we might expect from science present and future. Such ideas of interconnectedness suggest that balance and harmony are key philosophical issues that must underpin scientific inquiry.

One of the biggest problems of the scientific and technological contemporary age is that it actually seems to produce the opposite nature of *irrationalism* in human beings.[40] It seems to bring out the need in human beings for fantasy (albeit sometimes in the realm of science fiction), for the acceptance of the supernatural, the occult, the mysterious, the *un*reasonable. The American cult series *The X Files* is a phenomenon that contains all these aspects, and it has unquestioned popularity as a television series. This might suggest that science and technology are too devoid of emotion, too characterized by cold reason, to capture the fantasy element of human nature unless they are fictionally presented. Even so, screen productions use the medium of science for the content of many of their fictional plots that are not, in fact, irrational or unreasonable in imaginative content. There seems to be in the human psyche the ability to enjoy reasonable scientific content in novel or on screen, but also the need for unreasonable scientific fantasy.

It is the unreasonable fancy that appeals to the emotions. Russell Brain considered that people use creative imagery to articulate their perceptions of, and pleasures in, life. "Science provides very real emotional satisfactions," he wrote, "but it cannot, and does not seek to, replace the modes of awareness which appeal directly to human feelings."[41] Such "modes of awareness" are much less compartmentalized than the scientific experience. Today science has become so specialized that we can only refer to the *sciences* with the multiple disciplines that the word suggests. Yet in life people have to cross barriers in a more unified experience of existence, and it is this kind of experience that will always transcend the cold reason of the respective sciences, and the attempts of some of the sciences to dehumanize people in reductionist approaches. The intangible nature of experience, creativity, spirituality, emotion, enjoyment, love – and the variable combinations of these rather non-empirical aspects of human nature – speak against the idea that individuals can be reduced to their basic psycho-physical genetic make-ups.

Science is not infallible, and most Humanists would not suggest that it is. There are no "logical certainties" in science, Ruse states, and "all science is tentative".[42] Yet the sciences can produce the most reasonable certainties, and we can only look to science for the answers to technological issues of human existence. Since, however, science is not infallible, its own level of ethical inquiry is urgent; and this needs to be an ethical inquiry not imposed from without as much as informed from within. Sadly, the control of scientific research by private enterprises usually means an excessive emphasis on outcomes for monetary gains, and the directing of research towards what is marketably highly viable.

Bertrand Russell long ago wrote that: "There seems scarcely any limit to what *could* be done in the way of producing a good world, if only men would use science wisely."[43] This potential role for science is always there, impressive in so many of its achievements in the past and present, and with so many potential successes for the future. Without science we would not live as long as we do today, and we would not be so healthy, albeit having a need to adjust personal life to avoid the dangers of overweight, high sodium and high cholesterol diets and so on. Science is still in good repute – the use of it as the medium for so many television advertisements, and for so much consumer packaging, suggests that the public is still convinced by scientific claims. Humanism is not so much shackled to the results of science that any mistakes of science and technology can be blamed on Humanistic thinking. Humanism is more concerned with the potential for science to improve the human condition, and its capacity to apply creative reason to existential problems now, and in the years ahead. Science is a medium that is not foolproof, but it is an asset that, used wisely, can affect the lives of humanity for the better.

Older ideas of domination, mastery, subjugation, harnessing and controlling of Nature have been evident in Humanism as much as western religious thought. We now know that we need a good deal more rational thought about the way in which we view Nature. For though there is a totally neutral relationship between the human world and the natural world, Nature is at the same time intimately affected by the behaviour of the species that inhabit it. Today we need science and technology more than ever to solve the problems of a previous disharmony between humans and Nature. Pragmatic and utilitarian outcomes of science and technology are obviously important, providing the means do not create more problems than are justified by the results. And science cannot teach us how to live with our fellow human beings, cannot teach us the finer aspects of morality, of autonomous maturity, of self-value and altruistic value of others. Science is a facet of human inquiry that is reasonable and rational. It can stand as a model for other types of reasoning and as a model for testing beliefs and qualifying thought. But it is a human invention itself, and therefore will be as good and as effective as the humans that are involved in it.

Pseudo-science and the paranormal

Pseudo-science is a false science – something posing as scientific but for which there is no testable evidence to support its claims. Sometimes hypotheses that begin as pseudo-science become scientifically accepted because the evidence of controlled experiments and verifiable data eventually support the claim. In this case, pseudo-science moves into an established scientific discipline. The problem with much pseudo-science, however, is that its proponents often claim that proofs of its validity in a particular sphere need different kinds of verification procedures than ordinary empirical studies. Terence Hines, in a comprehensive study of pseudo-science and the paranormal, also points out that, unlike science, the claims of pseudo-science often remain static, being neither changed nor updated in the light of new evidence or further inquiry.[44] The other difficulty with pseudo-science is that it is up to those who refute the claims to find proofs that they are erroneous, not those making the claims. So if people claim that they have been abducted by aliens, as long as no one can prove that they *hadn't* been, believers in alien abduction contend *therefore* that alien abduction must obtain. This is absurd reasoning.

The *paranormal* refers to claims of supernatural phenomena that lie well outside empirical scientific evidence – what is beyond the normal. Claims of an afterlife, of reincarnation, ghosts, spirits as in spiritualism, faith healing, miracles, and extra-sensory perception, all fall into the category of the paranormal because no scientific evidence to suggest that they really exist obtains. However, as Hines points out, the boundary between the paranormal and pseudo-science is often blurred.[45] The objections to both lie in the lack of evidence for their varied claims, but particularly because such claims offend bodies of already established empirical knowledge. And until *evidence* can be supplied to the contrary, the claims of the paranormal and of pseudo-sciences are unreasonable and irrational. Thus, Kurtz believes that the paranormal is really "anti-scientific" and "even occult".[46]

The interesting point about pseudo-science and the paranormal is that belief in the mysterious, the occult and the bizarre is increasing in western society. Again, perhaps this move to "unreason" is a move to a fairy-tale world that captures the emotions and the imagination. It may be a form of escapism to a world other than the complex one in which we exist, a world that is fantastic, mysterious, exciting. This shows on the one hand how gullible people can be, but it also shows that creative imaginations are very much alive and kicking! I suppose if my neighbour believes a UFO lands each night in the nearby field, and that he discourses with aliens, he is entitled to his belief, however bizarre I may find it. The dangers occur, however, when the quality of individual and societal life is affected by such beliefs, if people are asked to part with money to support such beliefs, and when the media cash in on the gullibility of the public. Despite the progress of medicine, repeated failures to diagnose illness correctly, or to treat diagnosed illnesses with any success, cause many people to look to aspects of pseudo-science for better results – reflexology, homeopathy, aromatherapy and so on. Perhaps in time some of these alternative medicines will gain enough evidence to become scientifically accepted, but the point about their presence is that to many people it is *reasonable* to try something where established methods have failed. It's a "What have I got to lose" policy.

Paul Kurtz is absolutely right when he says that "there is a search that is fundamental to our being: the quest for meaning. The human mind has a genuine desire to plumb the depths of the unspoken, to find deeper significance and truth, to reach out to another realm of existence".[47] Exploration into the paranormal and into any realm of the supernatural is really, I believe, a statement of dissatisfaction with the *normal* state of things, and this suggests that much needs to be done about the degree of quality and satisfaction that life offers. People are not so gullible that they abandon common sense without reason. And many may retain their rational belief but prefer to ignore it for the psychologically rewarding imaginative adventures into the supernatural. Perhaps this is not so much gullibility as psychological expediency in a difficult age. To change any irrational beliefs that might be psychologically orientated we have to compensate for them by more rationally based, but *emotionally satisfying* substitutes. This is a challenging task for humanistic psychologists. But the transformation of individual nature into one of strength, satisfied potential, self-value and personal autonomy, is an overt Humanist goal. It is one expressed superbly by Arthur Wakefield Slaten:

> The highest value we know is human life, nobly lived. What may exist elsewhere is beyond our ken, but earth knows nothing so precious as character that is wrought in the white light of sane ideals. Too much have we sought after outer gods; we turn now to the god within, the one neglected deity. May we know the glory of self-control, the joy of self-realization, the peace that comes with self-conquest. Upon all

stricken and struggling souls may there rise the dawn of a renewed hope. To all of us may there be given the calm that comes from courage. May age be granted patience, youth wisdom. And together may we build that which earth never yet has seen, the divine society of human souls whose hunger and thirst is for righteousness, and whose toil is for the high prizes of the spirit.[48]

8

Some Life and Death Issues

Whatever species we look at in life – whether in the plant, insect or animal kingdom – it has its predators, the agents that serve to cull its numbers. The exception to this is the species of *Homo Sapiens*, human beings. Humankind has no natural predators, though disease, droughts and famines, and occasionally members of its own species in situations like war, place some check on its growth. With the advance of medical science and technology, disease is not now so rife in the western world that it limits the life-span of each individual. And provided we live a fairly temperate life (and sometimes if we do not), we can expect to live well beyond our three score years and ten. Nevertheless, if we are all living longer, and if there is less disease to cull human population growth, then some methods of reducing population expansion are inevitably necessary at some point. The Humanist perception of the "Good Life" for all human beings necessitates both a healthy life and a life of quality. But for these to obtain there are a number of policies that are contributory to personal and societal well-being in an age of overpopulation. Contraception is the most obvious factor that is crucial to population control. But Humanism is also concerned with other factors related to quality of life, such as abortion and euthanasia.

Because Nature is neutral to human beings there are no laws of Nature to which the human being is bound – apart from the physical laws that prevent people flying like birds or spending their lives barking as dogs. But because human beings cannot fly, it doesn't mean to say that it is unnatural to invent aeroplanes. Similarly, it may be natural for genes to be carried from one generation to the next, according to physical laws, but there is no law of Nature to suggest that interference with this pattern is unnatural or against Nature. If this were the case human progression in any direction such as medicine, health or agriculture, would have to wait for Nature to sort things out. Scientific and technical advances that sort things out at greater speed than Nature, or that divert natural problems, are generally welcomed by Humanists, providing the means and the ends are for the well-being of the individual and society. Humanists are concerned with many societal issues, from Sunday opening and blasphemy laws, to the rights of homosexuals and lesbians in our societies; from defending the right of choice in abortion and euthanasia, to discussing the merits of the "happiness" drug Prozac. Humanists are involved in a broad spectrum of voluntary aid, such as prison and hospice work, involvement in international environmental projects, conservation, education, particularly Religious Education, human rights, and in the kind of political, social, legal, economic and international frameworks that would support sound policies in these areas. To examine all these issues is beyond the scope of this present chapter. What I propose to do is to deal with some of the questions that are concerned with birth and death and, in particular, with the issues of abortion and euthanasia.

Genetics

Every organism exists as the result of the genes that it has inherited. In the human being, as in all animals, this genetic composition is highly complex, but such is the level of research in human genetics that it is now possible to determine the probabilities of some illnesses in humans – cancer, heart disease, or even premature death. In the field of agriculture it is now possible to alter the genetic composition of species in order to improve breeds of animals by direct manipulation rather than selection of parent animals, and to clone a sheep – as the famous Dolly has survived to prove. Such genetic engineering can work greatly to the advantage of society, and also to individuals, but it is a powerful scientific tool that raises concomitant ethical issues. This is a point forcibly put by Frolov:

> Genetic engineering seeks to enable man to intervene directly in the regulation of the genetic programme of organisms by restructuring them in desired ways. As a result, very delicate micro-structural transformations of individual cells may produce substantial effects at the macro-level of organisms, populations, and even the biosphere as a whole. Thus man acquires a power that must be used with the greatest caution. It is precisely this point that ultimately defines the socio-ethical content of studies in genetic engineering.[1]

Genetic engineering can change Nature radically, can alter normal evolution, or radically deflect it. Used wisely, it can solve problems on many fronts, but it is also easy to see, as Frolov suggests, that, misused or badly implemented, its effects may be ultimately harmful to humankind. Importantly, long-term problems are not always foreseeable – even if short-term results are desirable.

At a more personal level, ascertaining one's own genetic make-up can enable choices to be made about one's own future. If, for example an individual is a carrier of a gene that might severely disable a future child, a choice might be made to refrain from having children. Many people would welcome this kind of information that would help them to make an informed choice about their future. On the other hand, there are also people who would not want to know, or may even wish to chance what happens in the future. Ruth Chadwick, in fact, points out that genetic information can only deal with probabilities. It cannot state absolutes. Therefore, *radical* choices about redirecting one's life – for example deciding not to have children, not to reproduce with a particular partner and so on – could ruin a life that might, otherwise, have been spared some heartache.[2] And yet, without responsible thought certain diseases could actually increase through genetic propensities. Because medical science has developed the kinds of drugs that enable people to live longer despite severe illnesses, people carrying genes for such illnesses survive to reproduce, passing on the same propensities for severe illness.

Pre-natal screening now allows parents to know whether the child they expect is suffering from the types of genetic deficiencies that cause conditions such as Down's syndrome or spina bifida. The amniocentesis test of pregnant women will reveal these and other abnormalities, but the choice is always up to the parent or parents in acquiring such knowledge. There are some who feel that they are capable of caring for a disabled child, and for whom genetic testing is neither necessary nor daunting in the light of problematic results. But many parents feel that they would be unable to cope with a disabled child and, more importantly, they feel that the life that child would have would not be sufficient in quality to justify it. Decisions to abort the child in the early stages of pregnancy may be deemed sensible by many parents in such cases. Either way, such decisions are always difficult. But, in true Humanist spirit, Polly Toynbee comments that: "Extra choice is never a mixed blessing. It always enhances human potential and gives us more power over our own lives. It requires us to look at risk rationally, to confront possibility and probability, and to face up to what we, as separate individuals, can and cannot bear to do."[3] Here is one Humanist who accepts the role of rationalism and reason in informing all our choices about life, regardless of how difficult such choices may be. Knowledge of our genetic make-up can increase personal autonomy and responsibility: if a person has a propensity for a dangerous illness then he or she is able to adjust the way life is lived in order to ensure that such illness has the least chance of occurring. Knowing one is at a high risk for lung cancer, for example, permits informed changes in one's life pattern like refraining from smoking. But there are limits to the outcomes of genetic propensities, for they are *propensities* and not absolutes.

But all kinds of moral issues are raised by genetic studies. Since medical science is able to ascertain some genetic propensities of children we might have, let us suppose that our genetic make-up is automatically fully revealed to us, and might be available to the public at large. This could well result in careful consideration of the genetic make-up of a person before his or her acceptance as a partner. Most parents want to give their children the best possible kind of life – a good education, a good environment, a good economic background. Could the time come in which people might want to give their children a good *genetic* start in life also? And could such a situation lead to an increase in abortion of children who do not match up to their parents' expectations? In Denmark people who have certain defects cannot be issued with a marriage licence unless they are first sterilized. This raises a very delicate issue that balances the values of society against individual rights and freedom.

It is important that personal freedom and individual rights are given full respect, providing that freedom and those rights do not curtail the freedom and rights of others. So what happens in the case where an individual is diagnosed as having a genetic tendency for a severely disabling condition that may be passed on to any, as yet, unborn children? Normally it would be considered that any individual has the right of personal privacy, as well as of confidentiality between his or her self and the medical practitioner. But what of the family of that person? Do the members of his or her family also have a right to share that information, particularly since they, as siblings, for example, may themselves be genetically at risk, or where future children may be? Should the medical practitioner respect confidentiality? Or should the practitioner place the promotion of the health and well-being of others before such confidentiality? There is also a further issue here in that perhaps a well-meaning medical practitioner makes the decision to break confidentiality and inform his or her patient's family of a genetic disorder only to discover that the unsuspecting family member(s) do *not want* to know. This delicate issue of the right to know and the right not to know is the subject of a book edited by Chadwick, Levitt and Shickle.[4] In this book Jurgen Husted balances, on the one hand, the importance of personal autonomy and patient—doctor confidentiality, with, on the other, the breaking of confidentiality and the imposing of information on someone who has a right *not* to know.[5] So for example, is my personal autonomy enhanced by being told that my husband, wife or partner carries a gene that could result in severe disability for children as yet unborn? Does this information *enhance* my autonomy by enabling me to make more informed choices? Or does it *limit* my freedom because I now have relatively fewer free choices that I can make and because such knowledge may affect my mental well being? Husted's view here is that: "The fact that the person receives new and relevant information does not in itself justify a claim of enhancement of autonomy."[6] Polly Toynbee's view, above, would be that it does.

These are some of the more complex issues that have emerged from the more subtle areas of scientific and technological advance in human genetics. Inevitably there will be ongoing ethical issues that will emerge in these newer areas of medicine, and the balance between personal and societal ethical responses will be neither easy nor simple. The dynamic nature of medical science, and the speed at which advances are being made, will necessitate an ongoing and changing analysis of its ethical profiles. Humanists tend to look at the problems on the positive side.

Medical science is able to overcome many of the frailties of life and the suffering of the human body, and sees the possibilities of genetic engineering in the elimination of more such frailties. People are at home with a world in which such things as synthetic materials are part and parcel of everyday life: what is natural is no longer necessarily considered to be the best. For many westerners there are no ethical issues involved in the uses of contraception, *in vitro* fertilization, and so on, and perhaps a certain amount of genetic engineering would be welcomed by the parent-to-be of the future. But taking genetic engineering as far as outright cloning of human beings is generally met with reserve in medical circles. How would a cloned human being cope with the idea that he or she was not a genetically unique person? The cloned sheep, Dolly, does not have the ability for such abstract concern about her heritage, but a human being is a different matter.

Birth

Where unnatural methods of controlling life are accepted – whether to create it, prolong it or end it – ethical issues are always to the fore in the personal, situational experiences of life, as well as in the broader spectra of social concerns. Many may raise ethical eyebrows when the female menopause is delayed or menses restarted in a post-menopausal woman in order to make pregnancy possible again. Does it make sense to conceive at the age of sixty-plus? For many women it probably does, and they have valid reasons for spending a good deal of anxiety and money to conceive. After all, the ethical eyebrows are barely raised at all for the ageing male who sires a child. However, aside from the issue of post-menopausal conception, what of the younger woman, indeed the younger couple, that is so desperate for the child they cannot have? This is something that at least one in six couples experiences.

Artificial insemination (AI) is one medical answer to infertility. Live male sperm are inserted into the uterus of a woman during ovulation. There are a number of variations to this procedure: some-times the husband provides the sperm (AIH), and sometimes a doner (AID). In some cases the ovum and semen are joined in a test tube and the resulting embryo is then placed in the woman's womb. This is *in vitro* fertilization (IVF), though fertilization can be *in vivo*, that is to say, it can take place in the womb. Sometimes an ovum is donated by a female for test-tube fertilization and implantation. In other cases both ovum and semen are donated and fertilized externally prior to implantation. In rarer cases there are women who, as surrogate mothers, are prepared to bear a child for another woman. This may be partial surrogacy where the surrogate mother provides the ovum, and the intended father the sperm, or full surrogacy, when fertilized ova (two or three) and sperm of the intended parents are placed in the womb of the surrogate mother to gestate. Sometimes, the ovum is supplied by an anonymous doner. However, it is always the woman who gives birth to the baby, and her partner or husband,[7] who are legally considered as the parents – regardless of the genetic links of the child with the intended parents – unless a legal transfer of the child takes place. Without this transfer, the surrogate mother has full legal responsibility for the child. All sorts of ethical issues emerge in relation to surrogacy, particularly when large sums of money change hands. Intended parents might also wish to reject a disabled baby, or may change their minds, for example.

Important ethical issues are raised for future offspring in the case of those conceived by donated sperm or ova. Some individuals might not mind having started life as a frozen embryo donated by a woman he or she will never know, or a similar scenario. Others might find the parental question mark is a problem in traversing the path of life. In fact, the Anglican view here is sensible, and that is that children at eighteen should have the right of access to information about the doner. More usually this might occur in cases of AID – artificial insemination by a doner unknown to the mother. The Roman Catholic Church is against any form of AI, even if the sperm doner is the marriage partner of the female. It regards the AI process of repro-duction as unnatural, being mechanical and outside the "normal" sexual union of marriage. However, it seems that artificial heart pace-makers – no less an intrusion into the natural body – are quite acceptable. The Anglican Church is not opposed to AI but, like the Roman Catholic Church, does not accept surrogacy.

Today, there is an infinite supply of ova waiting for possible fertil-ization from foetuses that have not survived – potential half persons. This, again, raises a number of moral issues related to the future of the child. In particular, there are some individuals who might find having started life as a frozen ovum taken from a dead foetus as something of a problem. Others might find their more technical and scientific origin a fascinating and exciting beginning to a life in the contemporary world. The large supply of foetal ova is essential to research into infertility. Such research – usually termed pre-embryo research or simply embryo research – involves the fertilization of the ova for analysis during the initial stages of cell growth. The term *pre-embryo* is important here, however, since there is no suggestion of experimentation on a sensitive foetus. In fact, the early and primitive growth of cells cannot really be sustained beyond six days outside the womb.[8] For the one in six couples for whom infertility means a life without the ability to have children, such research is an important means of hope for the future. Those sympathetic to childless couples may be happy to endorse pre-embryo research, as well as foetal research. Nevertheless, there are those who find the idea distasteful, particularly instances where material from aborted foetuses finds its way into our homes. In 1985 it was discovered that foetal tissue (thymus, pituitary, liver and spleen) was being sold to cosmetic firms in France. Many may be horrified to know that what they slap on their faces at night may contain human foetal material, while some may think "Why not?" But clearly there are careful demarcation lines that need to be thought out in all genetic research.

Death

At the other end of the scale from birth, is death. This can no longer be the cessation of respiration, as was the case in the past, in view of the number of people whose respiratory functioning fails and then revives naturally, or is revived artificially. Real death has more to do with the lack of brain functioning, specifically the dysfunction of all parts of the brain, but in particular the brainstem. The upper part of the brainstem is responsible for consciousness, and the lower, for respiration. Brainstem death is irreversible and consciousness cannot exist without it. Sometimes a person exists in what is called *persistent vegetative state*. This occurs when there is massive damage to the cerebral hemispheres of the brain, but the brainstem is intact. Some contend that switching off a ventilator for someone in such a vegetative state is an act of euthanasia, and therefore illegal, if the brainstem is still functioning, because the patient is not really dead.[9] Others see no point in keeping someone alive when there can never be a recovery from irreversible coma. Ending the life of someone in such a condition is, to many people, an act of kindness.

Related to the issue of death and euthanasia is that of organ transplantation. In 1996, 150,000 people throughout the world needed some form of transplantation, of whom only a third got it. And the need is rising annually. Many people die while waiting for an organ from a doner. This has moved a number of people to suggest that the law should be changed so that people who do *not* want their organs to be used for transplantation at death are registered nationally, leaving the organs of all others available. Again, Polly Toynbee, in true rationalist spirit, writes:

> we who carry kidney doner cards are proud of the hidden symbolic message that goes with them, reading: "I am a rationalist, without superstition. I understand that when I am dead, I am dead, and my body will have no use or meaning. I know that my soul does not reside in that muscular pump on the left side of my chest. I am brave and I can look death in the eye without blenching." That's not a bad boast,

and it makes us feel superior to the rest. And there is also that spurious sense of generosity, the ultimate and final charitable act. At absolutely no cost to yourself.[10]

Today we live in a world where the heart that is transplanted into a human may soon have belonged to a specially bred pig, and in a world in which a human being may soon have multiple transplanted organs. Xenotransplantation is the use of modified animal organs in human bodies. Normally, all animal organs would be rejected by the human system, though not a genetically bred one, and it could well be firmly on the medical agenda in years to come. Initial experiments of head transplants in baboons have been successful. Will body transplants be available in the future? And if they are available in the future, could those with a severely disabled body find themselves with a new one? This, of course, raises all sorts of ethical issues, from animal rights, to the chances of specific animal diseases being passed to the human strain via the body DNA. How far each of us would wish to see such possibilities realized will depend on our individual ethical stances.

From the opposite viewpoint, those who are opposed to organ transplantation put forward the criticism that the body from which the organ is taken must be breathing and warm. The body needs to be kept on a respirator until after the organs are removed. The view of David Lamb, for one, is that, since brainstem death alone is indicative of death (though this theory is not without its critics) organ transplantation should not take place unless the brainstem is dysfunctional:

> Stories about "human vegetables" lingering on for months, when their organs could be used to save other lives, must never be allowed to influence criteria for determining death. Wherever such arguments occur they must be seen as advocacy for euthanasia or dissection of the living and their pros and cons evaluated.[11]

But, aside from the issue of transplantation there are many ordinary people who, given the choice while they are rational and well, would not wish to survive in a future vegetative state, regardless of the functioning or dysfunctioning of the brainstem. The problem here, however, is that if the brainstem is intact and functional, respiration may be unaided, and although the patient may be cerebrally vegetative, he or she may appear to be bodily very much alive. Extracting organs while a body is breathing *naturally* is not dissimilar to burying one while it is still breathing. For those who would find the latter objectionable, the former will probably be also. But in the end, it is a personal decision for individuals and their families how they or their loved ones die. Dying with dignity without medical gadgetry is an important individual right about which many human beings feel very strongly. This involves the issue of euthanasia, examined in more detail below.

Abortion

Abortion is the premature expulsion or removal of a foetus from the womb to prevent its development and survival. Humanists are not in favour of abortion *per se*. They would far rather a child to be conceived responsibly through choice, welcomed in a family, and to have a caring environment. But these are ideal situations; not all pregnancies *are* wanted, not all circumstances *are* favourable, and some circumstances are definitely harmful to a child. Ideally, efficient contraception should prevent any unwanted pregnancies, but the fact that three-quarters of the women who have abortions also use contraception confirms that many methods of contraception cannot guarantee absolute protection against conception. For those women who find they cannot face pregnancy for whatever circumstances, Humanism believes that the choice of terminating the pregnancy is their right. Since Humanists are devoted to enhancing the quality of life, in the case of abortion it is the quality of life of the mother as well as the unborn foetus that is taken into account. If mother, child, or both are likely to suffer in life if the pregnancy is allowed to continue to full term, then Humanists generally consider that termination of the life of the foetus is the best possible solution.

But it would be a mistake to think that Humanism takes the whole issue of abortion lightly. The decision of the woman to terminate pregnancy is crucial to her own individuality, and this is something that most Humanists would vehemently defend, but they consider careful deliberation on the part of each woman to be essential. Few Humanists would condone abortion as a means of birth control, and would favour better education in respect of contraception. Abortion on demand in such cases suggests an irresponsibility that offends principles of sound societal life. But the majority of women who decide to abort do not fall into this category. Their choices are difficult ones, responsible ones, and caring ones. In accepting so profoundly the freedom of the individual, Humanism believes that no one should impose his or her beliefs on others, and a woman must have the right to do what she feels is best in her own life. In an inquiry into the working of the 1967 Abortion Act, the Committee of Inquiry, the Lane Committee, criticized any who might want to be censorious about the issue of abortion:

> To suggest that the woman who, after anxiety, heart-searching and doubt, decides to seek an abortion, should instead summon up her will-power and accept with the best grace she can muster a situation which would often be tragic for her, is advice similar to that which has so often in the past been given to those who were suffering from nervous or mental illness – "pull yourself together". It is advice which in the great majority of cases is crude, unfeeling and ineffectual.[12]

Conception takes place in a second, a moment in time. From just that moment, a woman has to carry a developing foetus for nine months, and bear a child that will affect the rest of her life. It is not a decision to be taken lightly. The fact that women have sought abortions from antiquity[13] suggests that unwanted pregnancy is inimical to the lives of many women past and present.

Statistical facts about abortion

In England and Wales about 170,000 resident women a year have a legal abortion.[14] (In Scotland, the number is about 12,400.) The majority (89%) of these abortions, take place before the thirteenth week of pregnancy. 7.5% take place in weeks 13–16 of gestation, 2.5% in weeks 17–20, and 1% in weeks 21–24. About 60 women will terminate after 25 weeks. Very few abortions, then, are performed after the twentieth week of pregnancy. Those seeking termination at this later time are young women below the age of nineteen who have taken longer to seek advice, and those who have terminations because of indications that the child will be born handicapped – a factor that cannot be known until gestation is further under way. Ideally, the earlier the abortion the better the procedure for the woman and the less likely the foetus has any feeling. At six weeks, for, example, the foetus is nothing but a blob of jelly with no recognizable features at all. Better pregnancy testing procedures should allow most women to know very early whether or not they are pregnant. Most abortions are for the age group 20–29 (50%, but in Scotland most are in the age range 16–24). By far the majority of women seeking terminations are single.[15] The total number of abortions each year in England and

Wales is steadily declining,[16] however, 1 in 3 British women will have an abortion at some time in their life, 1 in 5 pregnancies result in abortion, and 1 in 5 women who have an abortion will have another. Three-quarters of the women having an abortion use contraceptives. The fact that women are sensible about contraception is evidenced by the sudden 9% rise in abortions in England and Wales in 1996 after the government issued a warning against certain brands of contraceptive pills.[17] National opinion polls on abortion in Britain suggest that the majority of the public believe that a woman should have the right to decide herself whether or not to terminate her pregnancy,[18] and comparisons with earlier polls suggest that society is becoming much more pro-abortion.

Historical facts about abortion

While abortion is now legal in Britain, as it is in many other countries, prior to 1967 it was not so. It is estimated that something like 100,000–150,000 illegal abortions each year took place in Britain, most in "back streets", though about 30,000 may have taken place in private clinics.[19] In the more distant past abortion was accepted – even by the Roman Catholic Church,[20] which today is opposed to it. English common law accepted abortion in the early months of pregnancy up to the point when the foetus moved in the womb. This common law obtained from the thirteenth century right up to 1803. In 1803, however, terminating a pregnancy at any stage became a criminal offence, something reiterated and clarified in the 1861 *Offences against the Person Act*. Penalties of up to life imprisonment for unlawful attempts by the woman and the abortionist were imposed. The Act did not make it clear what "lawful" abortion might take place, and there were no other clear exceptions on medical grounds, or in cases where the woman had not, after all, been pregnant. It was not until 1929 that the *Infant Life Preservation Act* (not applicable to Scotland) amended the nineteenth century position to allow abortion for the purpose of saving the life of the mother at the discretion of medical practitioners. The Act, which was more concerned with infanticide, stipulated that it would be a criminal offence to abort a child that would be capable of being born alive (and therefore capable of survival). This was stipulated to be at 28 weeks gestation.

In 1938, Dr Aleck Bourne, a well-known gynaecologist, performed an abortion on a fourteen-year-old rape victim, in defiance of the law. He was acquitted in court on the grounds that the physical and mental health of the girl took precedence over the law. It was a time in which public opinion – particularly women's groups – was beginning to strive for a change in the law concerning abortion. Two years prior to the Bourne case a group of women who were concerned about the number of women resorting to dangerous illegal abortions, pressed for repeal of the existing laws regarding abortion. They wished to remove restrictions on the medical profession that prevented legal and safe abortions for all women. This was the beginning of ALRA, the *Abortion Law Reform Association* which struggled for thirty years as one major pressure group responsible for the present, and more liberal, abortion laws. It is also active presently in its agenda for further reform. It was the disaster of the thalidomide births in the 1960s that made public opinion thoroughly aware of the need for a re-examination of the issue of abortion, and which activated ALRA in a more powerful way.

The present legal situation in Britain

The *Abortion Act* (not applicable to Northern Ireland) came into effect in 1967 permitting the termination of pregnancy for the following reasons:

A   Where there is greater risk to the life of the woman by not terminating the pregnancy.
B   Where grave and permanent injury to the mental or physical health of the woman would ensue should the pregnancy continue.
C   Where there is greater risk of injury to the physical or mental health of a woman by not terminating the pregnancy.
D   Where there is a greater risk that the physical and mental health of any existing child(ren) would be injured if the pregnancy is not terminated.
E   Where there is a substantial risk that the child would be physically or mentally abnormal to the extent that it would be severely handicapped.
F   Where it is necessary to save the life of the woman.

The Act stipulated that only registered medical practitioners could perform abortions in either a National Health Service Hospital or in a Department of Health approved clinic. Two medical practitioners should support the reasons for abortion.

The 1967 Act, while having its critics – particularly those from religious parties –largely reflected public opinion of the day. It did not overthrow the 1861 *Offences against the Person Act,* which still remains on the statute book, but it radically amended it by citing those cases in which abortion could be legal. Those women who are medically deemed to require an abortion for one or more of the reasons stated above were, and are, capable of having safe, legal abortion. However, the Act did not contravene the 1929 Act that set an upper time limit of 28 weeks' gestation after which abortion should not take place because the child could survive. Exceptions were only to save the life of the woman. However, in 1990, a new Act came into being that reduced the upper limit to 24 weeks' gestation in all cases except those that endangered the woman's life or, where severe handicap in the foetus is the case. This was the *Human Fertilization and Embryology Act,* an Act that also supported genetic experimentation on externally fertilized ova to a limited gestation period. The 24 weeks' gestation period is now in line with the limit from which medical skill can sustain the life of a premature child. It is relevant to C and D above, but not to A, B and E, which have no time limit imposed,[21] and where termination is possible right up to the time of birth. As the law stands now, a woman or young person who is pregnant through rape, a young person under sixteen years of age who becomes pregnant, a distressed mother who finds herself pregnant after believing her family to be complete, the unmarried woman who is deeply distressed at the prospect of bearing and caring for a child she cannot support, the student whose academic career will be cut off – all have sufficient grounds for claiming that their physical and mental well-being will be severely impaired by carrying to full term a child they do not want.

Despite the fact that public opinion is sympathetic to abortion, the current laws concerning abortion are not short of some critics. A key issue here is the foetus itself, and the age at which it is capable of feeling pain. This had led some to propose a lower limit than the present 24 weeks. The MP David Alton attempted to secure an 18-week limit in 1987 in a new Abortion Bill, but his Bill was rejected. At present, the British law does not extend to Northern Ireland, and there are many who believe it should. In 1997, 1,572 women from Northern Ireland came to England to terminate their pregnancies and 5,336 from the Irish Republic. This suggests that there is some justification to end discrimination against women in Ireland. It also demonstrates the anti-abortion tenor of Ireland, particularly the

Roman Catholic views. Some medical practitioners themselves are also opposed to abortion, and a "conscience clause" in section four of the 1967 Act permits such persons to abstain from participation in any treatment relating to abortion. In practice, this is usually applied to the termination itself and not pre- and post-termination care. Men who may oppose their partners or wives in a decision to abort have no legal status. The decision rests with the female and the two medical practitioners who support the termination.

A good deal of debate centres around the issue of how far the present law really amounts to abortion on demand. And pro-abortionists believe that a woman has every right to abort an unwanted baby. But anti-abortionists are against such suggested easy availability of abortion. The Lane Committee, indeed, found that the law was easily flouted by a few:

> Some women have used the Act and the fact that they could afford private treatment to get an abortion on comparatively trivial grounds of inconvenience or embarrassment to themselves. In short, in some parts of the commercial private sector the provisions of the Act have been flouted and abortion on request has been the rule.[22]

But the general findings of the Lane Committee are that these cases are exceptional. The "on demand" nature of abortion cases would really suggest that the judgement of medical practitioners is simply overruled, and this is clearly not the case. According to the Lane inquiry medical practitioners should always play a critical role in assisting a woman in her decision whether or not to abort. Since women who contemplate abortion often find the decision a highly burdensome one – and are often without the support of family or friends – the role of the medical practitioners is crucial in the final decision. The scenario of the uncaring, laid back woman demanding an abortion from her GP is rare; the scenario of the deeply upset woman who has agonized over her decision to approach her general practitioner, is more usual. According to the Lane Committee, "obstetricians and gynaecologists would be unwilling to operate under such a system", that is to say, a system of abortion on demand. Additionally, the National Health Service (NHS) could not support such a scenario.[23]

An unwanted pregnancy is a colossal personal crisis for a woman. It is not a crisis that will pass after a few weeks or a few years, it is a crisis that will remain for a fundamental part of a woman's life, with significant repercussions in all sorts of ways. Some women regret having aborted a baby, but there is no way of knowing whether life would have been worse had they allowed their pregnancy to proceed. Similarly, some who have aborted may have found a happy existence with the child they could have had. There is no way in which these hypothetical situations can be assessed. It is in life-conditions of the circumstances of the pregnancy that decisions need to be made, and none of us can make sound decisions about a maybe future: we only have present facts on which to assess our life situations.

Many women who abort do so because the child they carry is potentially handicapped. While there are some women who might feel that their life and that of their partner or other children might in no way be impaired by giving birth to a seriously handicapped child – physically or mentally, or both – there are many women for whom this would be an impossible task. Women have a lower tolerance of disability than men, probably because when they carry a child in their womb for nine months, they also carry a fear that the child might not be completely physically or mentally normal. And the quality of the life of the parents may be significantly diminished by having to cope with a handicapped child. The decision to cope or to abort is a personal one that assesses the quality of the lives of the living parents or parent, and the quality and value of the life that is being formed. The rise in technological methods in studying the foetus has meant that a number of handicaps can be predetermined, and abortion can be granted for spina bifida, for Down's syndrome, or even for a harelip. Some disabilities are difficult to diagnose early in the gestation period, and late abortion is therefore the only option. Anti-abortionists claim that with advances in medical surgery, much can be done even for the spina bifida child. But asking some women to carry a child in their womb that they know is deformed and handicapped is more than they, as human beings, can cope with. Such women have the moral decision to make for themselves, as well as for the unborn child that they carry.

Availability of abortion

The Lane Committee found that in the years following the 1967 Act the number of women seeking legal abortion put a considerable strain on the NHS. Additionally, medical staff had no time to adapt to the new law, and trained staff and termination facilities were at a premium. The result then, as today, is that there is considerable inequality of abortion services throughout Britain. This is evidenced in the fact that many women are being forced to pay privately for abortion when they would qualify medically for abortion in the NHS.[24] The Lane Committee also found that in the medical world there was a certain polarization of views about abortion. Some medical practitioners were favourable to the new legislation, while others were antagonistic towards it. This means in practice that some women who would otherwise qualify for an abortion are being turned away by unsympathetic doctors. Women are therefore treated differently.[25]

If a woman's general practitioner considers she qualifies for an abortion, then the decision has to be endorsed by another doctor, and this is usually a consultant gynaecologist. This process can take time to arrange, and some gynaecologists may not, in the end, agree with abortion, or may refuse to endorse the first doctor's opinion. Even if both practitioners agree on legal abortion, a time lapse of two and a half months can occur before a woman is admitted under the NHS. This is particularly distressing for the woman herself, and it also brings the foetus very close to the 24-week gestation limit. From a medical point of view the earlier the termination, the simpler the process. Entering a charitable or private clinic is a quicker process. The non-profit making clinics were essential in the past in providing abortion services where some health authorities were unsupportive to the Act. Today, the major non-profit making clinics are the British Pregnancy Advisory Service (BPAS) and the Pregnancy Advisory Service (PAS). The advantage of clinics is that, besides a quicker process, they provide personal counselling for women, something that the NHS may or may not do, but fees at clinics, ranging from between £200 and £300, may be prohibitive for some women.

The NHS funds about three-quarters of the abortions in England and Wales. In Scotland nearly all abortions are NHS funded. Some local health authorities are better than others, Tees and Northumberland Health Authorities, for example, funding 96% of abortions, while North West Lancashire funds only 28%.[26] Clearly, women seeking abortions in such areas will have very different experiences. There is no obligation for a health authority to provide abortion services, but lack of availability in some areas must be causing considerable distress to women who legitimately request advice on abortion. ALRA's report on NHS abortion services found that women who were assessed as capable of funding their own abortions were steered towards private clinics unless they were able to speak up for themselves. The report also claims: "It is not unusual for a health authority to ask GPs, directly or indirectly, to encourage women who are able to pay for private abortions to do so. Some authorities expect GPs or non-NHS agencies to act as gatekeepers by judging those who can afford to pay on their knowledge of the patient."[27] And telling a woman that she might have a long wait for a NHS abortion as opposed to immediate treatment in a clinic is often an added lever to encourage women into the private clinics. Then, too, NHS authorities vary in the waiting time set for referrals, in the criteria they set for assessing eligibility for free abortion, regardless of the law, and on the time limits for gestation, which vary from 10 to 20 weeks, despite the legal limit of 24 weeks.[28] According to Campaign for Choice, for example, in Barnet in North London, women between 18 and 43 are excluded from having NHS abortions, and this effectively excludes the highest percentages of women in the age range seeking abortions.

The worst scenario for a woman seeking abortion in an area with an unsupportive attitude to abortion is deliberate delay, rudeness and judgmental attitudes. Compassionate attitudes are dependent on where a woman lives. Alternatively, a woman may confront her own doctor with a request for abortion and meet with blunt refusal. The doctor may have religious or other grounds for refusal, but he or she does not have to explain these to the patient. Although the practitioner *should* refer the woman to another practitioner who does not share his view, he may not. He may even believe that abortion is a social and not a medical problem and that the NHS should not support abortion at all. The same attitudes may be held by consultant gynaecologists. A woman who requires an abortion may never know that she is at the mercy of the prejudices and negative attitudes of those she consults about her need to terminate: "doctors can wield enormous power over women".[29] Statistics do suggest, however, that most medical practitioners are supportive to the present legal requirements and to the women who need their guidance on abortion. From the medical point of view there is also a minority of medical practitioners whose refusal to take part in abortion procedures has adversely affected their personal careers.[30] And there are nursing staff who find the process of abortion distressing, particularly with the later abortions where the foetus is in a more advanced stage of development. Individual rights are as important for medical staff as for any other person: honesty and integrity on all sides is essential, but a distressed woman seeking abortion has a right to be treated with care and objective, open, counselling and should not be at the mercy of subjective opinion.

The 1967 Abortion Act does not apply to Northern Ireland. Very few medical abortions occur in Northern Ireland, for which statistics are unavailable. Political representatives of Northern Ireland are mainly highly anti-abortion, but an average of 40 women a week travel to Britain for abortions in private clinics, though the number may be higher in view of the fact that many such women may not wish to disclose their real addresses. The official Roman Catholic view has always been opposed to both contraception and abortion. However, the Lane Committee found that "the proportion of Catholics among women having abortion does not seem to be much lower than that among fertile women in general. As with contraception many women may be rejecting their Church's teaching in this field".[31] While Britain led the field in its 1967 Abortion Act, other European countries have become more liberal in the years that followed. Countries that are not influenced by Roman Catholicism[32] allow abortion on request normally for the first three months of gestation. Countries strongly influenced by Roman Catholicism have less liberal laws than Britain. Ireland is the only European Union country to forbid abortion except when it is necessary to save the life of a woman. The 5,000 women from the Irish Republic having abortions each year travel to private clinics in England for the purpose.

Abortion laws in the more liberal countries of Europe allow abortion on request up to a maximum gestation period. Both Sweden and France, for example have set a limit of 12 weeks. In the Netherlands the limit is 20 weeks. What obtains after these limits varies. Sweden, for example, offers counselling to the woman who is 13–18 weeks pregnant but still gives her the right to terminate. Between 18–22 weeks, approval must be given by the National Board of Health and Welfare, and is given only for serious medical, psychological or social reasons. After 22 weeks, termination can only take place to save the woman's life. In France, restrictions are considerable after the initial 12 weeks when abortion is available on request, since thereafter abortions are only sanctioned for foetal abnormality, or to save a woman's life. Women requiring abortion beyond the 12-week limit have to travel outside France for the purpose. In the United States there is some evidence to suggest that Roman Catholic medical staff are requested to inhibit abortion. According to Frances Kisling, "the Catholic health-care system is the largest private nonprofit effort to deliver health care". Kissling estimates that "about ten per cent of all non-federal hospitals are Catholic, a portion that renders Catholic hospital networks comparable to for-profit systems such as Tenet Healthcare". But such institutions are bound by Catholic Directives not to engage in services that are against Roman Catholic teachings; services such as IVF, vasectomies, contraceptive devices or drugs, and abortion.[33]

Methods of abortion

A number of main methods of abortion obtain, each normally pertinent to the length of gestation of the foetus.

- Up to 9 weeks, the doctor may administer tablets of a drug called Mifegyne (RU486). This prevents the lining of the womb from retaining the embryo implanted in it. The drug may cause bleeding for a few days, but the patient is allowed to return to normal life. Two days later a repeat visit to the clinic completes the process of abortion. On this visit another drug consisting of prostaglandins – the hormones that are responsible for the contractions of the womb which expels the feotus in labour – is given. This causes contractions and bleeding for about six hours, after which the foetus is aborted. Bleeding usually occurs for a following 12 days.
- Up to 15 weeks of pregnancy the foetal material in the womb can be sucked out through a narrow tube by the method of *vacuum aspiration*. This is a very simple operation indeed and takes only a few minutes, but local or general anaesthetic are given.
- From weeks 14–24 *dilatation and curretage* (D and C) may be the method used, a method that is used for many other gynaecological problems. Here, the cervix or neck of the womb is dilated and a curette is used to scrape out the contents of the womb, in conjunction with vacuum aspiration. General anaesthetic is usual for this method and at most an overnight stay at the hospital or clinic. On the other hand, particularly in later stages, the abortion may be induced by the use of prostaglandins.
- More rarely, abortion is done by *hysterotomy* (and sometimes hysterectomy). This, in effect, is a Caesarian operation and involves a longer stay in the hospital or clinic. Complications from all of these methods are usually slight and are not as many as those involved with childbirth.

Foetal development and sentience

One debate that surrounds abortion is concerned with the issue of when life actually begins, more particularly, at what point the foetus becomes a sentient creature with sensitivity to its surroundings. It is factors such as these that inform the legislature for early abortion in many European countries. Modern techniques have made the study of the embryo a new science, and development in the womb is rapid:

25 days	the heart is beating
28 days	legs and arms begin to form, and pairs of muscles have developed
30 days	regular blood flow; ears and nasal area begin to develop
6 weeks	skeleton appears
7 weeks	fingers and thumbs are forming
10 weeks	organs have almost formed; limbs are clear
12 weeks	arms and legs move; vocal chords formed; genitalia form
16 weeks	the foetus is half its length at birth
20 weeks	hair appears on the head; eyebrows and eyelashes begin

Premature babies can now be born and survive from 25 weeks. The critical question here is at what stage does the foetus *feel* anything. Until the last century it was believed that babies were born deaf and dumb, and it was not so long ago that it was believed that the foetus remained an insensitive entity until birth. Now we know that at later stages of pregnancy the foetus reacts to noise both in and out of the womb, as well as to the stress of the mother. The Royal College of Obstetricians and Gynaecologists has claimed that the important connective elements of the nervous system of a foetus do not begin to develop until 26 weeks. Thus, claims the RCOG, while it is not possible to say when sensitivity in the form of pain is first felt, it cannot be before this time.[34] The foetus may respond to stimuli and display spontaneous reflex actions, but since the nerves have not linked to either the brainstem or the cerebral cortex of the brain, no consciousness can be possible. Nevertheless, the RCOG recommends anaesthetizing of the foetus if aborting after 24 weeks, or quickly stopping the heartbeat of the foetus before termination. Early abortions avoid the possibility of foetal sentience.

The case for abortion

How far should an unborn potential life dictate the future of the life of the woman that carries it in her womb? It is only the woman carrying that unborn potential who can really answer this question. Contemporary society is less characterized by people who accept their lot in life and submit to whatever life brings them. This, indeed, was pointed out by the Lane Committee which stated:

> Many women are no longer prepared to accept the burden of often repeated, unwelcome and debilitating child-bearing: they see a far wider spectrum of choice open to them and the possibility of a greatly enhanced quality of life for themselves and for their children. The modern approval and encouragement of contraception have helped to dispel the view that a pregnancy must be accepted as and when it occurs. There is a more sympathetic public understanding of the serious mental stress which may result from an unwanted pregnancy. Further, an increasing number of women prefer to follow careers rather than devote themselves exclusively to family life.[35]

The key words here are "quality of life". It may well be that there are ethical implications of ending potential life, but there are also ethical implications in condemning a woman to a life she does not want. Few women take the choice to abort lightly and abortion clinics are only too familiar with the timidity, fear and distress of most women who cross their thresholds. Some women are happy to have many children, some do not want any at all. For each woman there is a limit beyond which the quality of life vanishes, and there is also a time when it is right to have a child and a time when it is radically wrong.

Bringing another human being into the world is a highly responsible and important act. Unless that being can be offered a considerable measure of quality it seems futile to bring him or her into a world where quality of life would be lacking. As Diane Munday poignantly pointed out: "I don't believe that it is being pro-life if a child is born because of too much to drink on a Saturday night or because a contraceptive sheath split."[36] From that one second of conception a woman's life is significantly altered, and it is she herself who needs to make the ultimate choice with regard to her future. As Paul Kurtz states: "Historically, males have dominated females economically, socially, and sexually, and have sought to determine when and if women should bear children. But the fetus grows within the woman's body, not the man's, and society has no ethical right to demand that she continue any pregnancy she does not wish."[37] The fundamental rights of women mean little if they cannot control their own fertility. The woman is a living, conscious human being, with knowledge of the joys and vicissitudes of life. Her life, balanced against an unconscious potential life is precious, more precious than the potential life that she carries. Without quality in her life – in whatever way the woman understands that word – her life expression is diminished.

There may well be women who regard abortion as contraception and who abuse the law in repeated terminations. But these are few. There are also women who radically do not want one or any more children, women who, should the child be born, would neglect, abuse, resent and dislike the child they have. The quality of life of the child would thus be seriously impaired. But many women are responsible about their own fertility. They use contraceptives to avoid unwanted pregnancy, but since contraception is not a hundred per cent effective, they may, as responsible adults, still find themselves pregnant. These are the women for whom abortion is especially helpful. Students, in particular, may find themselves facing a pregnancy that is likely to ruin their careers and the path their lives will take for the future. The father of the child would have no such problems. The National Union of Students supports the National Abortion Campaign that presses for the availability of abortion without any legal or medical restrictions and no upper time limit on abortion.

One of the most important criteria for later terminations of pregnancies is the evidence that the foetus is seriously handicapped either mentally, physically, or both. Most women who carry a potential child in their womb are radically concerned that they will bear a "normal" baby. Some women will cope admirably with a handicapped child, others would never be able to cope. Madeleine Simms said: "There is a lot of sentimental talk about the joys of a lifetime's caring, particularly on the part of those who do not have to do it themselves."[38] Care of a handicapped child can seriously diminish the quality of life for the whole of life. Since some abnormalities of the foetus cannot be known until the gestation period is more advanced, late termination is necessary. This involves two important issues, the first that the foetus is sensitive to what is happening to it, and the second, that it could be capable of surviving if it were prematurely born. Nevertheless, the Humanist position here, while recognizing the more morally significant factors involved in late termination, still considers that it is the right of the woman to terminate a pregnancy she does not want. A foetus does not have moral status because it cannot think, and is indifferent to its life or death. But the mother can and does think, and has important moral decisions to make about her own and the child's future.

Given the increasing overpopulation of the planet, abortion is seen as one way of limiting population expansion. In China, for example, abortion is compulsory for those who have more than one child, and in Tibet, one has to have a certificate in order to become pregnant. Severe financial penalties ensue for those who conceive again. In Bangladesh a choice between sterilization and starvation has been the policy in years past. In India it is potential females that are aborted, partly because of the crucial difference an extra mouth to feed can make in impoverished families, but also because a woman will normally reproduce until she has a son. Sons are important for maintaining parents in their old age, for status, and for important death rites. Disappointment will surround the woman who gives birth to girls, when there is no boy, and since the amniocentesis test has become available, abortion has become a means of restricting family size, accounting both for the need for son(s), and for the need for a smaller family. However, to suggest that abortion is a means of curbing population expansion is misguided belief: it is efficient contraception that should do this, and this will only occur with better sex education and health services concerned with birth control.

Pro-life groups often make the point that adoption, or putting a child in care, are better options than abortion. But pro-abortion groups demand "Better for whom?" Certainly not for the mother, who has the added burden of carrying a child she does not want to full term, a birth process that she does not want, and then the guilt of parting with the child. The Lane Committee, in fact, suggested that adoption should not have any bearing on the working of the Abortion Act.[39] Post-abortion problems in terms of psychological anxiety are likely to be far less than post-adoption anxiety and guilt, which often occur after women have actually given birth to a child. Pro-abortionists claim that there are few post-abortion physical or mental problems, especially when the abortion is "therapeutic", and incorporates careful counselling and advice on contraception. Pro-abortion groups point out that post-natal depression is common, post-abortion depression is not, and any mental anguish disappears at most after six months. Decision to abort a child is not an easy one, and reflection on the choice that is made is both natural and necessary. Women do not walk out of abortion clinics one minute and forget the incident in the next. But at least they are able to secure termination of a pregnancy legally, and safely. "Back-street abortions" have disappeared. Minor complications and long-term physical problems are minimal considering that abortion is one of the most common medical procedures in the world.

ALRA

The Abortion Law Reform Association (ALRA) was formed in 1936 with the aim of legalizing abortion. Until the advent of the First World War its members were engaged in conferences and meetings, and some educational work, but it was not until the sixties that it became a major force behind the Abortion Act of 1967. But ALRA did not retire after the Act. Its policy statement is as follows:

- Every woman should have a legal right to decide when and if to have children.
- Women should have a legal right to abortion on request in the early stages of pregnancy.
- Any woman who is legally entitled to abortion should be able to receive treatment free of charge from the NHS.
- An abortion is best carried out as early as possible in pregnancy and the NHS should therefore ensure that women are seen promptly and do not experience unnecessary delay.
- Provision should be maintained for the small number of women who may need an abortion late in pregnancy for medical reasons.
- Impartial counselling should be available within the NHS for women who require it, both before and after abortion.
- Women should be treated by staff who are sympathetic to their situation and therefore medical staff who have a conscientious objection to abortion should not be obliged to participate in abortion procedures.
- Women in Northern Ireland should have the same legal rights regarding abortion as in Great Britain.
- Schools should provide sex education which includes information and discussion of responsible sexual behaviour, contraception and all the options on unplanned pregnancy.

ALRA is therefore working for a change in the present legislation concerning abortion. Its members want abortion on request during the first three months of pregnancy, after which, the approval of only one medical practitioner would be necessary. They want easily accessible family planning, pregnancy testing, counselling and abortion services by all health authorities. Day-care provision should be available in hospitals where women could by-pass their own general practitioners if they so wish. Such provision should be separate from other gynaecological practice. General practitioners should declare in public documents such as their practice brochure whether they have any non-medical conscientious objection to abortion. ALRA is also campaigning for legal abortion in Northern Ireland. In January 1997 ALRA published an excellent survey of NHS abortion services[40] as well as outlining its recommendations for NHS improvements in abortion procedures. Pressure has been put on the health authorities with the worst provision of abortion facilities, with success.

Voice for Choice

In April 1998 Voice for Choice was launched. This is a national movement for abortion reform composed of a coalition of thirteen main abortion and family planning organizations in the United Kingdom, the Pro-Choice Alliance. The main aims of Voice for Choice are abortion on request during the first 14 weeks of pregnancy, and the abolition of NHS discrimination and inequality in abortion services. The movement is pressing for the same legal reforms as ALRA.

The British Pregnancy Advisory Service

The BPAS is a non-profit making charity that has 8 clinics and 30 consultation centres. These offer counselling, fertility control and medical services connected with abortion. It was set up after the Abortion Act in 1967, and exists without government funding. It is now the largest provider of abortion services in the United Kingdom. All its clinics have met with Department of Health approval, as well as the approval of over 40 District Health Authorities. The BPAS is particularly sympathetic to unplanned pregnancies amongst students and produces an excellent *Student Information* pack.[41] Strictly speaking the BPAS does not campaign for or against abortion, but it believes that abortion is a very necessary service.

The case against abortion

The Humanist position is a clearly pro-abortion one, and it is supportive to the main bodies that programme for reform in present legislature concerning abortion. But there are those who oppose abortion under any circumstances, the "pro-life" groups. One of the main pro-life groups in Britain is the *Society for the Protection of Unborn Children*, SPUC.[42] Much of the antipathy to abortion centres round the issue of foetal sentience, the SPUC claiming that the foetus is capable of experiencing pain at 10 weeks. Any attempt to remove the foetus from the womb is thus inflicting a painful death and, since it is ending life, is tantamount to murder. Pro-lifers also object to partial birth abortion, a method that has to be used for late terminations when the foetus – which legally cannot be killed outside the womb – is partially born and then aborted.[43] A key document in this pro-life context is a paper published by The All-Party Parliamentary Pro-Life Group entitled *Fetal Sentience*.[44] This document maintains that structures necessary for the experience of pain are present well before 10 weeks, possibly as early as 6–7 weeks' gestation. "Anatomical observations of the human fetus have indicated that some parts of the thalamus have developed by 9 weeks gestation and that the nerves responsible for carrying sensation from the skin to the spinal cord develop by 6–7 weeks."[45] The thalamus is the critical lower brain, the brainstem, which is necessary for consciousness. It is that part of the brain, according to some, which, when it ceases to function, is indicative of death.

But apart from the issue of foetal sentience, pro-lifers believe that life begins at conception. Any attempt at interfering with that life is believed to be wrong. SPUC literature does its best to persuade against abortion by its very choice of words. In describing abortion by dilatation and curettage, for example, the SPUC paper *Abortion's Victims* states: "This method utilises a *sharp toothed pliers-like* instrument. The abortionist *grasps* a part of the body of the baby and *tears* it away" (italicized words are mine). Similarly, post-abortion guilt, and physical and mental problems, are stressed by SPUC. Since life is accepted from the moment of conception, pro-lifers are also opposed to the use of abortifacients, the so-called "morning after pill", the post-coital pill that is designed to prevent successful implantation of a fertilized ovum in the uterus during the first days of development. Pro-lifers maintain that this is not contraception but illegal abortion.

Pro-life campaigners also believe that physical or mental disability is not ground for abortion, pointing out that the later terminations for handicaps are sometimes for minor reasons of harelip, club foot, even impaired hearing and sight. They are opposed to what they consider is the fostering of a mentality of lethal discrimination against the disabled. With the advance of genetic technology, they fear a "search and destroy" attitude, particularly since care of the severely disabled child and adult can make great demands on the health and social services. Pro-lifers also fear the acceptance of infanticide of the severely handicapped newly-born, a practice that does obtain occasionally in hospitals. But the cases of abortion because of a potentially handicapped child are very few in comparison to those on grounds of harm to the mental and physical well-being of the mother, or to her existing family. These are *social* reasons for termination, the pro-lifers claim, and amount to abortion on demand. They are opposed to any reform in the abortion law that might allow women to terminate pregnancy through their own choice. The unborn child is always seen as a separate human being from its mother, with a potential unique and separate personality, having a right to life both before and after its birth.

Underlying much of the policy of the SPUC is a religious ideology that only God has the right to give and take life. The branch of the society in Northern Ireland is particularly concerned to prevent the extension of current British abortion laws to Northern Ireland. In a publication aimed at castigating the British Brook Advisory Service that is concerned with family planning and abortion, it is clear that religious belief underpins policy. The opening words, for example, are from the Reverend Ian Paisley: "If we are to play God with the sanctity of life we take away from the mystery of God's creation gift to mankind. Just because the child is unwanted does not give anyone the right to dispose of it by clinical murder. Many childless parents in Northern Ireland would be willing to adopt new born children."[46] Other religious groups and spokespeople provide the introduction to the document. It is a document designed to alarm parents to the dangers of pre-marital sex, contraception and promiscuity as precursors to abortion, and the Brook Advisory Service as the means by which teenage sex will become rampant in Northern Ireland. But it is clear that religious belief informs much of the virulent attack. Similarly, the British SPUC newspaper, *Human Concern*, has a strong religious element in its articles.

The Roman Catholic position is staunchly anti-abortion (and officially anti-contraception), as is the Muslim position. In Muslim religious law, right from the beginning, life is given by Allah as a *nuftah*, a drop of fluid in the mother's womb. This drop of fluid, Muslims believe, is planned, programmed and cared for by Allah, and should not be terminated. The soul is believed to enter the foetus at 120 days. But even Islam, as Anglican Christianity, the Church of Scotland, Judaism and Hinduism, accepts that termination is essential if the mother's life is in serious danger. Nevertheless, there are strong elements of pro-abortion reform in the mainstream protestant churches of England and Scotland, despite an official conservative view against abortion.

These, then, are some of the views put forward by those who oppose abortion. It is worth reiterating that Humanists are pro-abortion, not that they favour abortion, but that they recognize the need for each woman to choose her own path in the face of pregnancy. Humanists are, therefore, more pro-choice than pro-abortion. Linda Francke has commented that: "The words 'You're pregnant' can never be received with indifference. With those words, regardless of whether they provoke happiness or despair, a woman becomes instantly isolated in her individuality, in her health, in her present, and in her future. Her life is forever altered."[47] Advice, counselling, care and dialogue are essential at such a time, but only the woman herself can make the ultimate decision whether her pregnancy is wanted or unwanted, and if the latter, it asks a great deal to deny her the right to terminate what will affect her radically thereafter.

Euthanasia

The word *euthanasia* is sometimes referred to as "mercy killing", that is to say, it is the act of ending a life of one who has no hope of recovery from a terminal and extremely painful illness. It is generally thought of as an act of compassion, though one in most countries that is illegal. The connotation of ending suffering is reflected in the Greek origins of the word *eu-thanatos* where it meant "an easy or painless death". Today euthanasia suggests some kind of *assistance* in the process of death, in order to end suffering. It is something often done for animals, but remains illegal for human beings.

We all have to die, but none of us wants to end life in perpetual pain and dreadful suffering. But the fact is that some of us will. And if that time comes, and we know that there is no hope of recovery, and all that remains is the long slide to the point of death, then the decision to cut short a life of suffering seems very sensible to many people. There are two issues involved here: first, should we have the right to decide when, in certain circumstances, we should die and, second, should a medical practitioner be allowed to assist that death? And since there are many cases in which the patient may be considerably incapacitated, the medical involvement in the issue of euthanasia is crucial. We live in an age when medical science has done much to reduce suffering in so many areas, not least in the cases where a painful and distressing end of life ensues. But medical science has also created the facilities to prolong life, and in some cases this may well be for a patient who does not *want* his or her life prolonged. Then, too, while palliative drugs are more efficient, there are some patients for whom the side effects are unbearable, or for whom pain is still extreme. To know that one's life is over, to spend each day and night in terrible pain, to feel hopeless about one's condition, but to be unable to die, is the epitome of suffering. The dichotomy for the medical practitioner is acute – to save life, or to relieve suffering. It is a moral dichotomy that is situational to the individuals involved.

Those who are in favour of euthanasia believe that it should be one available option for those for whom life is drawing to an end. And while hospice care is the best choice for some, euthanasia might well be the best for others. For many, both options might be felt to be necessary. But whatever scenario one has at the end of life, to know that if it becomes intolerable there is the choice to die, is more likely to stimulate courage in pain and suffering. Each person has the right to live with dignity and to die with dignity, and when the dignity of life ceases, then the choice of death is, for some, a compassionate option. But as the law stands, ending one's own life is suicide, and with assistance from someone else it is assisted suicide or even murder. In the recent past suicide was considered both a sin and a crime. The Church would refuse to bury a person in consecrated ground if he or she had committed suicide, or even to conduct a funeral service, while the police would always be involved because a crime had been committed. Under British law in the nineteenth century the estate of one who had died through suicide was confiscated.

The idea of deciding oneself when it is right to die and of ending one's own life, has a long history of religious and legal antipathy. In religious circles the same antagonism to both suicide and euthanasia still obtains because of a belief that only God should give and take life. And yet, religiously, it seems one can die for a *cause* but not for one's self. Gandhi's fasts that brought him close to death would have been an act of suicide, but were admired by many as a passive means to win political points. Buddhists, too, condemn suicide, but have immolated themselves to protest against political injustices. In the Judeo-Christian tradition, suicides such as those of Samson and Saul have been commended, and the mass suicides at Masada in Israel shortly after the time of the fall of the Temple in AD 70 have become a symbol of bravery to all Jews. Christian history, too, is peppered with martyrs for the faith. In Islam, also, sacrificing one's life in *jihad* is acceptable, but suicide for personal reasons is a disgrace, and euthanasia is abhorrent.

In Britain the Suicide Act of 1961 made suicide and attempted suicide no longer a criminal act, ending a law that had been in place since the thirteenth century. But this Act made it clear that *assisted* suicide was still a criminal offence, punishable by up to fourteen years' imprisonment. In Scotland suicide was not a criminal offence from the eighteenth century, but assisting a suicide, as in England, is still in theory capable of carrying a charge of murder. In practice, however, the courts seem to be regarding euthanasia as a grey legal area where those assisting a suicide – or even perpetrating euthanasia– are not criminal in the usual sense of the term, and harsh sentences are rare. In England, a Bill was presented to the House of Commons in December 1997. This, the *Doctor Assisted Dying Bill*, would have permitted doctors to give patients a lethal prescription by which to terminate their own lives. Despite rigid guidelines for practice, the Bill was roundly defeated. And yet opinion polls seem to suggest that the majority of people – even religious groups – favour medical assistance to a peaceful death where illness is incurable.[48] But the British Medical Association is generally against active medical assistance in patients' deaths even though it recognizes patients should have the right to refuse treatment that might prolong their lives. In practice, many medical practitioners are in favour of medically assisted deaths and there are probably a percentage of these who have actually engaged in such a practice. But worldwide, with the exception of the Netherlands, euthanasia is illegal.

Voluntary euthanasia

The societies that seek to promote euthanasia such as the Voluntary

Euthanasia Society (VES, England) and the Voluntary Euthanasia Society of Scotland (VESS),[49] as well as most of those who generally favour euthanasia such as Humanist organizations, make it clear that it is *voluntary* euthanasia that is being promoted. And this is an important point. *Voluntary* euthanasia is simply *not* voluntary if there is any degree of persuasion or pressure placed on a patient. Both VES and VESS make it clear that care for the old, the infirm and the terminally ill should be of an exceptionally high standard, so that those who feel that the burden of life is unbearable are in the minority. But the choice to terminate life must always be *voluntary*: it is an optional choice that should be legal for the individual who, under no pressure from any persons whatsoever, decides that the termination of his or her life is the best option. As with abortion, it is a *right to choose*. But having made the choice to die, the individual is asking for *assistance* in dying.

The rationale for voluntary euthanasia is sound and is supported by most Humanists. It suggests that a person has a right to die when there can be no further quality in his or her life. But since there may be no possibility of coherent communication for a dying person in the last phases of life, the right to choose *now* when in sound mind, what one would wish to happen in such a situation, is part of the rationale of the right to choose. Voluntary euthanasia would therefore be an *option* to those individuals for whom suffering at the end of life is too painful and distressing and who, in such circumstances, are able themselves to choose to die. It would also be an option to those who may choose to decide in advance the conditions under which they might not wish to live. Such decisions are both situational and personal. They are decisions that might well be abhorrent for some, and important for others. The essential factor is the *quality of life* of the individual and the right of an individual to balance loss of quality against prolonging life, in other words to control his or her own life.

Voluntary euthanasia societies, therefore, have produced a document that is an *Advanced Directive* or *Living Will*. Importantly, an Advanced Directive does not ask a doctor to break the law. It simply indicates the wishes of a person concerning the withholding of treatment in certain medical conditions. In other words, it conveys the wishes of someone in sound mind that, should a fatal condition occur, life is not to be prolonged by medical treatment where there can be no hope of recovery: such a form is normally retained by one's medical practitioner. In some cases a *Living Will Alert Card* can be carried to indicate that a living will has been signed. The Advance Directive states:

> My attending physician and one other physician (one of them being a consultant) are independently of the opinion that I am unlikely to recover from illness or impairment involving severe distress or incapacity for rational existence . . . I am not to be subjected to any medical intervention or treatment aimed at prolonging or sustaining life.[50]

The British Medical Association recognizes such Advanced Directives as legally binding.

The British Humanist Association is one body that accepts this right to choose, but believes that it is only morally right when there is no prospect of relief and life becomes hopeless for the individual. But the BHA stresses that a person must have made it clear that he or she prefers death with dignity than continuing pain and/or loss of dignity. Thus, in cases of serious physical suffering, loss of personal dignity, irreversible coma or dementia, or loss of physical movement so that life has no quality, the BHA supports voluntary euthanasia.[51] Neither the BHA nor VES and VESS include terminating the lives of seriously handicapped babies or the mentally or physically old and infirm in the remit of voluntary euthanasia. Neither do they advocate suicide on demand. The aims of all three are clearly concerned with *voluntary* euthanasia. VESS puts this well in the statement of its aims: "To make dying with dignity an option available to anyone, to protect patients and doctors alike in upholding the humanity of dying well. To seek legal reform, where necessary, and to introduce safeguards regarding voluntary euthanasia."[52] Freedom of choice is the essential message, the freedom of choice that allows control of one's death in the final phases of life.

Non-voluntary, active, and passive euthanasia

In contrast to voluntary euthanasia *non-voluntary* euthanasia would occur when individuals have *not* expressed any wish to die, perhaps because they are not physically or mentally capable of doing so. While the patient does not give consent, relatives may do so. This kind of euthanasia might arise in cases where a patient is comatose, is on a life-support machine, or is a newly-born, defective baby. *Active euthanasia*, on the other hand, would involve *direct* action to kill a person such as a lethal injection or a lethal overdose of drugs. It is the *intentional* termination of the life of one human being by another, and there are many instances when – despite the fact that it is against the law – both individuals and doctors have actively taken the life of a person in order to relieve what could only be a long, painful and drawn-out death. *Passive euthanasia* occurs when treatment is withheld so that the patient is allowed to die naturally. Contemporary medicine has the skills to prolong life indefinitely, even though a patient may exist as a non-thinking being for several weeks, months or even years. Allowing such a non-person to die naturally when there is no point in continuing treatment is often a sensible thing to do. Similarly, severely defective new-born babies are sometimes left to die. The problem in this latter case is that, allowing a baby to die *naturally* is likely to cause considerable suffering, unlike the comatose patient, for example. Then, too, it is a nice point whether *letting* someone die and *actively* killing him or her, are so radically different. If someone is drowning in a lake and I don't reach out my hand to pull him or her out, I may be just as guilty of active killing – and certainly mentally so.

Passive euthanasia may also involve cases where the patient *is* capable of making the decision not to be given further medical treatment to prolong life, when the quality of that life can only be at best very poor and diminished. Whose right is to be respected here? Should an individual have the right to refuse further treatment? Or has a doctor the right to impose treatment on that person? And how does a doctor balance the saving of life with the alleviation of suffering in such instances? These are the greyer areas that occur with the issues of passive versus active euthanasia. Somewhere between passive and active euthanasia is *indirect euthanasia* that occurs when death is hastened as a side-effect of the medical treatment given.

The only country in the world that, after decades of debate, seems to have clear policies on euthanasia, is the Netherlands. Under a coalition of the Christian and Social Democrats, regulations for the termination of life by a doctor came into force in July 1994. In the Netherlands euthanasia clearly means "the termination of life by a doctor at the express wish of a patient". A patient's request for termination has to be voluntary, clear, carefully considered, and made repeatedly, and termination of a life can only be in cases of unbearable suffering where there can be no improvement. Interestingly the three categories of termination are, strictly speaking, criminal offences: they are termination at the request of a patient, assisted suicide by which the doctor provides a lethal drug that the patient himself or herself can take, and termination without the request of a patient. Yet taking life at someone's request, assisting suicide and intentionally taking the life of another, remain serious criminal offences. The way out medically is through *force majeure*, that is to say *duress*, by which a doctor can claim a conflict between different types of duty – assisting suicide or witnessing intense suffering, for example. This provides immunity from the Criminal Code. However, invoking *force majeure* and immunity from prosecution, involves a doctor in a strict code of notification procedure and assessment criteria concerning the death. And the assessment criteria suggest a high ratio of doctor-patient care, dialogue and interaction. The position in the Netherlands, then, is one of a neat balance between legal prohibition that ensures careful monitoring and assessment of every case of euthanasia, and yet the legal possibility for active, voluntary and non-voluntary euthanasia.

Objections to euthanasia

The main objection put forward against euthanasia – even voluntary euthanasia – is that its acceptance may well be a *slippery slope* from legitimate euthanasia to abuse of it. Legal acceptance of voluntary euthanasia would be a shorter step to non-voluntary situations – the termination of the permanently insane, of some psychotic criminals, of the very old and senile and of newly-born babies that are not seriously defective, such as those with harelip. The practicalities of euthanasia *are* difficult in cases of non-voluntary euthanasia for it is easy to see that there might be some individuals or even some societies that might justify it; Nazism is a case in point. And there may be individuals who are more anxious about the burden they are placing on their family and who request euthanasia for unselfish rather than medical reasons.[53] But the *principle* of euthanasia is a different matter. Those who oppose it in *principle* often do so on religious grounds, believing that it is God who gives life and therefore it is he that should decide when it should be taken away. They believe in the *sanctity of life* given by God. Others claim that life not death is natural, and that euthanasia goes against the natural goal of survival that is inherent in all creatures.

From the medical point of view, some object to euthanasia since, in fact, medical opinions are not always correct, and there are cases of people diagnosed as terminally ill making a complete recovery, or living a life of quality for many years. Death is final: if a mistake is made there is no return and no redress. Then, too, we all know that when we are ill we are very much under par, and the decisions that we make may be coloured by our physical condition. Those requesting assisted suicide may be emotionally highly stressed, highly drugged and in considerable pain. Those opposed to euthanasia claim that it is easy to give up in such circumstances and that the decision to request death is not really voluntary given the circumstances. And it could happen that a person may request death, change his or her mind, only to be incapacitated from expressing that change of mind. Some in the medical profession also claim that withdrawing treatment from a patient in obedience to an Advanced Directive can create the very circumstances that the person sought to avoid.[54] What is needed, the anti-euthanasia people claim, are efficient pain-killing drugs that can help people to die with dignity, and greater support for the hospices that do so much to make death with dignity possible. According to anti-euthanasia groups like the Human Rights Society[55] if relief from pain were to be continuous, clinical depression leading to request for death would not occur.

The Humanist response

The Humanist response to such views is dictated by a desire to ensure quality of life for all human beings, and the right of individuals to choose their own pathways in life. Religious beliefs, Humanists hold, should not inform debate and decisions about euthanasia. Most medical procedures from dentistry to heart transplants are unnatural and could be said to be against God's ideas for humanity. But ending the pitiful suffering of a fellow human being is a compassionate action that is informed by the best of human principles. There is a great Humanist concern for the goodness of life, but if the goodness of life is lost entirely, and if it cannot be recovered, then the opposites of utter despair and hopeless mental suffering ensue. A God that allows such suffering is no God at all. And while most religions see no sense in prolonging life artificially, or might accept passive euthanasia, this can often be a very cruel death: assisted euthanasia is the gentler and more dignified end to a life. Humanists believe in only one life and it is therefore important that it ends in the kind of dignity and quality with which that life was lived. In principle, this is compassionate, and Humanists claim that it is wrong to deny people such compassion out of fear of abuse of such principles by a small minority. This is unfair to those who are suffering.

Humanists generally support and respect those who reach a deep conviction that the time has come to end their life. To end life humanely, to shorten the grief and suffering of loved ones, and to act out of compassion within prescribed safeguards, is to remove the fear that many might have about the way in which they leave this life. The fundamental principles of Humanism are concerned with the happiness and fulfilment of each individual in every possible way. When all hope of such happiness and fulfilment are over, and the reflections of them in the past are blotted out by the pain of the present and its continuing prognosis, then euthanasia is an act of love. It may be that such an act of love goes beyond the bounds of the law and exceeds the bounds of "established" and legal morality. It may have to be carried out in the sphere of situation ethics, but through a principle of the love of humanity, there are certainly times when it is right to kill. I end this chapter with a poem written by Ramon Sanpedro who was paralysed in his youth. He describes himself as "a head attached to a corpse" and is seeking the legal right for a doctor to help him die with dignity:

> Why die?
> Because every journey
> has its departure time
> and only the traveller
> has the privilege
> and the right to choose
> the last day
> to get out.
> Why to die?
> Because at times
> the journey of no return
> is the best path that reason can show us
> out of love
> and respect for life, so that life may have
> a dignified death.[56]

9

Rites and Ceremonies

Most human beings enjoy the celebrations that mark special occasions in the pathway of life. Such celebrations may be more individual like birthdays and coming-of-age, they may be occasions for communal life-cycle events like birth or marriage, or they may be communal festivals that – however religious or non-religious a person is – provide a time of release from the usual routines of life. Ceremony and festival have always been associated with religion, though there are many in today's world who continue to enjoy religious ceremonies in a purely secular way. Christmas is a good example: indeed, festivals are so much a part of life that often those of one faith will participate in the festivities of another, and Christmas cards can arrive from Buddhist and Hindu friends as much as from friends with no religious belief whatsoever. The religious origins of a festival or ceremony do not necessarily preclude Humanist participation in either; it is just that the emphasis is different and religious connotations are lost. This is not sometimes hard to do since many of our religious festivals had their origins in pre-religious, pagan activity. Another important reason for communal gathering occurs at the end of a life, when we mark the time when an individual dies.

Like all people, Humanists find it necessary and need fulfilling to mark the important occasions of life, as well as its end, in a meaningful way. There are times when we want to share our joy or our sadness with others – times when we want family and friends around us in our happiness or in our sorrow. There are also times when we want to make some public statement about our stage in life. These are the *emotional* occasions of life, and often the meaningful and spiritual occasions. The exciting aspect of celebrating such occasions in the Humanist way is that they can be made more meaningful because they can be individually planned in a way that religious ceremonies cannot. Thus, it is possible to choose poetry and music to suit the occasion and, more importantly, to say the kinds of things that one would *want* to say – to infuse the occasion with one's own emotive expression. The leading Humanist associations in Britain and abroad now provide assistance for those preferring non-religious ceremonies. The British Humanist Association, for example, has a co-ordinated network of trained accredited officiants for naming ceremonies, weddings, affirmations, funerals and memorials, and supportive literature[1] to explain and help plan such important occasions. What I shall explore in this chapter, then, are the ways in which a Humanist – or a non-religious person – might celebrate important occasions on life's path.

Birth

The birth of a baby is a time for joyous celebration, for a new human being has been brought into the world with all the potential for fulfilment in a unique individual life. Each human being is part of the evolutionary unfolding of nature, a wonder to behold in his or her self. Planning a ceremony for the welcoming of a baby, and in order to give it a unique identity in a *Naming Ceremony*, can be something personally composed by the parents, family or friends, or it can be arranged and conducted by a Humanist celebrant. All sorts of personal contributions and ideas can inform such a ceremony. It might include words about the future of the child, the role of the parents in helping to create that future, and the good wishes and affirmations of any friends who might be supportive in assisting that path. Humanist parents, as most parents, would want their baby to grow up into a responsible, thoughtful, reflectively mature and confident adult, one that is compassionate to others and one that is comfortable with his or her own self, and with the world at large. They would hope for the freedom necessary to develop his or her fullest potentials in an environment that is loving, supportive and conducive to such development. A stimulating environment for the child will provide the kinds of choices and challenges that face human beings as a whole. Parents might wish to express these thoughts, and they will encourage their child to be aware of his or her self as a vital element in the wider world – an element that matters, and that can make an important contribution to the harmony of life.

Personal naming ceremonies are something to be remembered,

and Jane Wynne Willson suggests a good way to do this is by a deco-
rative book with photographs and signatures of those who attended.
Copies of poems read, and/or speeches made, might be included, as
well as some words of dedication to the baby from each person
present. Perhaps a small tree planted in the garden with a plaque on
it engraved with the baby's name and date of birth might be
especially meaningful in later years.[2] However it is planned, a ceremony of this kind is an opportunity for the family, friends and
relatives to express their joy at the safe arrival of the new baby, in a
mixture of formal announcement and informal love and celebratory
atmosphere. The ceremony can be simple or elaborate, it can involve
a few or many participants, it can involve other siblings, and it can
even be specially worded for an adopted child. The simplest format
is a welcoming of the baby, the naming of the baby, some words
about the parental commitment to the well-being of the child, and
maybe some words of wisdom that act as a conclusion – words that
are a dedication for the future life of the child.

At a specifically Humanist ceremony the welcoming of a baby is
likely to contain some Humanist philosophy about life, such as the
following words:

> The centre of our concern is the happiness, well-being and self realisa-
> tion of the human individuals that make up the world community. But
> the human community is made up of feeling individuals. On this occa-
> sion we are welcoming one special child, [name]. It is she who has just
> been born. Humanists see her, in common with all individuals, as an
> end in herself.[3]

Naming is the special part of the ceremony that denotes the individuality and uniqueness of the newly-born baby. Parents often have
special reasons for giving the particular name or names that they
choose, even if it is just because they like the sound of a name.
Explaining their choices of names can be part of the ceremony.

The responsibilities of any parents to their children are immense.
Bringing children into the world is not something to be taken lightly.
Planned pregnancies based on the knowledge that a happy and
secure environment can be provided for a child are the ideal, and are
a sound basis for parenting. But where pregnancies are unplanned,
many parents are no less overjoyed, and no less needful of a meaningful ceremony. A personally arranged ceremony enables parents to
express their new responsibilities in bringing a child into the world.
Humanist parents, no less than others, would hope that their role
would result in their children becoming confident, caring, mature

and self-reliant adults. In Christian christening, godparents play a specific role in the ceremony, promising to encourage the child in the Christian faith. But at this non-religious naming ceremony there may well be one or two adults who are prepared to take on a particular role in the personal development of the child, individuals who would like to offer support and encouragement through the years to adulthood. Such people are sometimes called *supporting adults* by Humanists: they support both the parents and the child during the latter's evolving years, sometimes providing the role of a "refuge" outside the immediate context of the home.

Raising children in the complex contemporary world is not easy. And because each child is different, and develops a unique personality, parents so often find that the aspirations they have for their children may, on the one hand, never be fulfilled, and on the other, may far outstrip expectations. Parents often have to learn to respect a unique personality in a child who may be so different from them. This is not easy, and the intricate balances of self-identity and self-respect, and yet respect for others and the ability to allow freedom to others, are important values for each member of a family. For these reasons Humanists realize the dangers of an authoritarian upbringing, and value instead the kind of home in which qualities of encouragement, support, respect, love, and the ability to share joys and sorrows obtain, and an environment in which eventual autonomous maturity can be developed. These, also, are the kinds of thoughts parents might wish to express in a naming ceremony that they themselves plan. This might take the form of a simple statement of the hope that their child will grow up to experience a happy and fulfilling life, or it might take the form of a written *Declaration* that the parents could read out and sign. Humanists, in particular, may well include hopes that their child will gain respect for others in society, for the environment, and for the whole planet on which we live, and that their child will be friendly to others, compassionate, and capable of sound choices in life. They may wish to declare what kind of home they will provide in order that these qualities have scope for development. Jane Wynne Willson aptly points out the responsibility that all people in society have to the well-being of children:

- *"in material terms* – to provide for them and give them a good start in life;
- *in ethical terms* – to provide them with the best example we can of the way human life should be lived – individually; within the

partnership of marriage; and in the wider society of the family and the world at large.

- *in human terms* – to surround them with the warmth of our affection and love – supporting them in childhood, encouraging them in youth, and sending them out into the adult world, free to go and welcome when they return; and to help them through every crisis, yet always encourage them towards that depth of personal maturity that will enable them to dispense with us completely, save only that we shall hope that our mutual love will last."[4]

Importantly, Humanist parents never make vows before God that they will bring up their children in a certain way. Rejecting religion, they say what they *aspire* to do, what they *hope* to do and to achieve, but they would not wish to be categorical about such hopes. For one of those hopes would be that the child would develop his or her *own* beliefs and values. Their approach to parenting is rational and not categorical.

In planning a naming ceremony, parents can include poetry, appropriate songs and music. Interpretation of poetry is like interpretation of a painting; we see what has meaning for ourselves. There is no reason why poetry – and even religious poetry – cannot be adapted to suit a secular ceremony,[5] and personal compositions can also be included. Here, I include some examples.

> Go peaceably my child into your new world
> Carrying love of humankind as a sword
> Let dignity and goodness be ever with you
> Honed on the truth of Love you'll learn at home
> Many men will try to undermine you
> Your courage may well be sorely stretched
> Strength of mind must then be your watchwords
> And your character survive the sternest test
> Evil you will find has many faces
> Goodness has but one and must prevail
> Look deeply within your soul for guidance
> Your innate sense of right will serve you well
> Seek like-minded mortals for companions
> And let faithfulness to duty be your guide
> Let not fear of failure e'er dissuade you
> For the beating of the fear will bring reward
> And when at last you are reduced to ashes
> They may point and say . . . *There went a soul*[6]

Extracts including the word *soul* may cause some Humanists to reject poetry or prose containing it as unsuitable. But the word does not, in fact, need to pertain to that which survives death. Indeed, it would be pedantic, and incorrect, to interpret the word solely in this way. Even biblically, *soul* has a long history of meaning that which animates a person – life, the inner depth of personality, the heart of a person.[7] If subsequent Christianity wanted to make the soul that which survived death, this has not prevented present usage of the word retaining a mainly secular character – something reflected clearly in the many secular definitions of the word in the *Oxford English Dictionary*,[8] in particular, its meaning "emotional or intellectual energy or intensity". There is no need, then, to view the word in a religious sense at all – any more than one would in expressions like "soul-searching", "soul-destroying", "soulmate", "soulless" or "soul music". Even the *New Testament* used the word *soul* (*psuche*) in such a secular way to refer to the emotions and the psychological self.[9] The sensitivity to such language will be reflected differently by each Humanist. Certainly, religious writers interpret *soul* in the religious sense – and with clear linkages to some post-death abode. But the word can be easily interpreted in the sense of "emotional or intellectual energy or intensity" that informs the deeper personality, and as the unique nature of each individual person that flowers from the moment of birth. In short, parents can be thoroughly creative in interpretation. Thus, the following three extracts from the Hindu religious poet Rabindranath Tagore are easily interpretatively adaptable:

Baby's World

I wish I could take a quiet corner in the heart of my baby's very own world.

I know it has stars that talk to him, and a sky that stoops down to his face to amuse him with its silly clouds and rainbows.

Those who make believe to be dumb, and look as if they never could move, come creeping to his window with their stories and with trays crowded with bright toys.

I wish I could travel by the road that crosses baby's mind, and out beyond all bounds;

Where messengers run errands for no cause between the kingdoms of kings of no history;

Where Reason makes kites of her laws and flies them, and Truth sets Fact free from its fetters.[10]

When and Why

When I bring you coloured toys, my child, I understand why there is such a play of colours on clouds, on water, and why flowers are painted in tints – when I give coloured toys to you my child.

When I sing to make you dance, I truly know why there is music in leaves, and why waves send their chorus of voices to the heart of the listening earth – when I sing to make you dance.

When I bring sweet things to your greedy hands, I know why there is honey in the cup of the flower, and why fruits are secretly filled with sweet juice – when I bring sweet things to your greedy hands.

When I kiss your face to make you smile, my darling, I surely understand what pleasure streams from the sky in morning light, and what delight the summer breeze brings to my body – when I kiss you to make you smile.[11]

The Gift

I want to give you something, my child, for we are drifting in the stream of the world.

Our lives will be carried apart, and our love forgotten.

But I am not so foolish as to hope that I could buy your heart with my gifts.

Young is your life, your path long, and you drink the love we bring you at one draught and turn and run away from us.

You have your play and your playmates. What harm is there if you have no time or thought for us!

We, indeed, have leisure enough in old age to count the days that are past, to cherish in our hearts what our hands have lost for ever.

The river runs swift with a song, breaking through all barriers. But the mountain stays and remembers, and follows her with his love.[12]

Some brief poetry or prose to end a naming ceremony – especially if it is in the form of words of wisdom for the future life of the baby – provide an obvious conclusion to the ceremony.

May you learn to love truth, even when it goes against you. May you cultivate kindness. May you find courage, and discover that you are stronger than the things of which you are afraid. May you have courage in dealings in your own life, and courage in speaking out for justice, in condemning injustice, in standing for good against evil. May you have courage to remain loyal to a deep conviction, and courage to admit when you have made a mistake.[13]

May you have joy in listening and joy in singing; joy in hearing and joy in seeing; joy in thinking and joy in learning. May your hours be forever bright in play and in work, and in friendship and in love.[14]

Symbols such as flowers or light from candles can offer symbolic meaning, as the following dedication shows:

In our ceremony we give this child a flower. The flower symbolises the beauty of life. It also symbolises the meaning of your dedication. Whether a flower is beautiful or not; whether it comes into full bloom or not; whether it fulfils itself as a flower or not – depends upon the nurture it receives. No flower grows alone, apart from the sunshine and the rain, apart from the soil in which it lives. So, too, no child grows alone.[15]

Finally, some lines from two sources. First, the following words from the well-known *Desiderata* supply an apt conclusion to the ceremony. They stress rather well the intimacy between each individual and the whole natural environment in which humanity is placed. The word *soul* here, is clearly secular:

> You are a child of the universe, no less than the trees and the stars; you have a right to be here . . . Whatever your labours and aspirations, in the noisy confusion of life keep peace with your soul. With all its sham, drudgery and broken dreams, it is still a beautiful world. Be cheerful. Strive to be happy.[16]

Second, an extract adapted from Longfellow's *To a Child*:

> Here at the portal you stand,
> And with your little hand
> You open the mysterious gate
> Into the future's undiscovered land.[17]

Initiation

Many religions and cultures have ceremonies that mark the transition from childhood to adulthood. This may involve only the males of the religion[18] or both sexes. Generally such initiation ceremonies mark a transfering of *responsibility* to the young person for his or her own life and beliefs. Humanists do not usually have ceremonies to mark this occasion, though they recognize that it is important for young people to feel accepted into the adult world when they reach the appropriate level of maturity. Secular celebrations to mark an eighteenth birthday have become commonplace in the West, and these ceremonies tend to celebrate that important transition. In Scandinavia there is a ceremony in which all those who have reached voting age are invited to the Town Hall for a reception, thus reflecting the new civic responsibilities of young people of voting age.

Marriage

Since Humanists do not believe in God they do not marry in a church, synagogue, gurdwara, or the like. In contemporary western society many couples live together as "partners" and, for a variety of reasons personal to each couple, prefer not to marry, so marriage is not quite the "institution" that it was in the past. But despite modern trends, many Humanists still accept that marriage is the ideal relationship in which two people express a firm commitment to each other. However, being married to another individual for the rest of one's life is not a commitment to take lightly, nor is it an easy route through life. So many Humanists are in favour of couples living together for some time, with or without sex, before undertaking the more serious step of marriage. But should a couple decide to marry, they would probably wish to celebrate their marriage in a special way. The Humanist marriage is a *civil* and not a religious contract[19] and, while the civil contract is essential for a marriage to be legal, the ceremony can have the same kind of scope for personal planning as the naming ceremony of a baby.

About half of the marriages in Britain take place in a church or chapel, even though many of those who decide on a religious cere-mony have little or no religious belief. But the church provides a formal atmosphere, solemnity, ritual, and the setting for the long white wedding dress and dress suits, in a way that a register office does not. At least changes in the law in Britain allow marriages to take place in venues other than churches or register offices, that are licensed for marriages. Nevertheless, while the register office wedding is a purely secular event, and officiants do their best to make the ceremony meaningful, it does not allow for anything more than minimal personal statement, if any at all. So many Humanists have *two* ceremonies, the civil one, and then a personally planned one. In fact, many minority religious groups such as Hindus, Buddhists and Sikhs, regard the two ceremonies (in their case civil and religious) as normal, and in many parts of the world such a two-stage marriage also obtains. While many Humanists would wish to see the two processes unified in a Humanist marriage *with* registration, until such time occurs, the civil marriage followed by a personal wedding can add an exciting and meaningful dimension to this important and emotional event in human life. It can allow a couple to interpret marriage in their terms, and provide an opportunity to express the love one feels for another in a unique way.

To Humanists it is the relationship between the two people that is of prime concern and not the civil contract. For this reason there may be some couples who would like to express mutual love and commit-ment to each other in a marriage ceremony that would not be legally registered. Some couples live together as partners and may welcome this kind of wedding occasion in which they can express their love, respect for, and responsibility to, each other, without a legal contract. Indeed, not all couples today see marriage as necessary to an already mature, close relationship in which both individuals feel thoroughly fulfilled. Here, a marriage certificate is unlikely to make any difference to an already stable relationship. A harmonious and balanced relationship, in which a couple has a good "working" partnership, is neither enhanced nor harmed by a piece of legal paper. In some rural parts of Germany bride and groom engage in a log-sawing traditional rite. The two stand opposite each other with the log between them and saw the log in half with a double-handled saw. The rite symbolizes the ability to work together for mutual support and harmony. Indeed, if this were not possible in times past, the marriage would not survive in a purely practical dimension. In the same way, the love between two people can be full of harmony with or without legal status.

In writing a personal ceremony, there is scope to express and share emotions, joy and solemnity with friends and family, in a very intimate way. Whether or not the legal registering of the marriage takes place before, after, or not at all, the planned wedding can take place anywhere – at home, in a garden, at a hotel, a castle, by the sea or in the heart of the countryside. And the ceremony can be filled with favourite music, poetry, and personal words that express the mutual love and commitment between two people. Whether Humanists or not, couples can request a celebrant from their local or national Humanist association, or can choose a friend who might take on the role of conducting the ceremony.[20] Jane Wynne Willson's guide to the planning of such a wedding, *Sharing the Future*, is an excellent source of ideas, and provides clear information that is sensitively portrayed. It is particularly sensitive to individual needs, with information not only for those who are seeking a legal marriage, but also for those who wish to remain partners, those who are divorcees and those who are gay. The following words are taken from a private ceremony of two divorcees who chose a friend as the celebrant for their ceremony:

> Those of us who have experienced the impermanence of marriage by whatever cause, are forced to reconsider the nature of this institution. Some seek to state vows before their God and some make a commitment before an official of the State. Janet and Roland have chosen a third way, that of making a declaration in the presence of some of those whom they love and whose friendship they enjoy. They wish to declare

their commitment to one another and their hope that this will be a loving relationship for as long as they live. For them marriage is not primarily concerned with property or similar rights but with their intention to love and support each other and their families. It is such a marriage that is celebrated for them today. By being here and sharing in this occasion, you help to give reality and significance to their marriage.[21]

These words highlight rather well the personal nature of the ceremony and the emphasis on human relationship and individuality rather than legal requirement. The following words are extracts from a ceremony conducted by a Humanist celebrant for a lesbian couple:

Friends, let me first of all welcome you and thank you for being here on Kate and Karine's special day. This is an occasion which is both solemn and joyful. Solemn, because Kate and Karine have decided, though they are young, that they want to commit themselves to each other's welfare and happiness through all the years that lie ahead, and that is no small promise. But joyful, too, because their commitment to each other springs from a delight in each other's company and a love which they are sure of, and which they want to express openly. And who better to share this occasion than you, their family and friends, who care most about Kate and Karine and their future happiness?

You will appreciate that this ceremony has no significance in law. But we all understand that, when two people are united in what is to be a lasting relationship, it is not the law that really matters. What matters is the genuineness and strength of their love, and the loyalty, determination and selflessness which will enable that bond to survive the challenges and adversities of the years to come. It is not the law which creates strong, happy and enduring relationships, but the trust and care within the relationship . . .

Let us also admit that some say that love between two people of the same sex is wrong. When challenged, they usually say either that it is against nature, or against God's law. But, if something exists in a person and it is as much a part of them as the colour of their hair or the size of their feet, how can it be unnatural? How can something be unnatural which has existed in all types of society all over the world from the beginning of recorded history and no doubt long before? There have always been people who have condemned gay love and say that gays should be forced somehow to change the way they are.[22]

The Humanist celebrant who conducted this ceremony had put together a very sensitive, and yet open, address. Behind the words are clear Humanist convictions about the freedom of individual choice, the need of individuals to fulfil their own lives in whatever way that may be; it is a superb statement against the prejudiced and the intolerant.[23] Later in the same ceremony, the celebrant states:

My role, as a Humanist, is to conduct a ceremony which relies not on the authority of state or church, but upon the self-awareness, strength and personal integrity of this couple, Kate and Karine. What really matters on an occasion like this, when any couple have decided to join their lives, is that they have the right feelings, absolute certainty that they are right for each other, that the feelings and the certainty will be lasting and not fleeting, and that they have thought about the future which stretches before them and the demands which it will make on them.[24]

In some states in America any couple living together for a certain time constitute a married couple under common law, as long as they are of the opposite sex. In other states, a marriage license and ceremony are essential. In the United States, a few churches, and certainly Humanist celebrants, do perform same-sex ceremonies, but gays and lesbians continue to fight for availability of legal union in marriages.[25]

The format of the ceremony can vary, but it is usual first to have some kind of special entry of the couple accompanied by music. An introductory speech by the celebrant who conducts the ceremony follows, initially to welcome everyone and state the purpose of the occasion, and then to supply more general words about marriage. If a specifically Humanist wedding is being celebrated, the celebrant may explain something about the nature of Humanism at this point. The most important part of the ceremony will be the affirmations of love that the couple will make to each other. Concluding words will usually follow and the couple will exit to music. Symbols are sometimes used in the ceremonies. The most common is the exchange of rings, but candles representing the light of love, and garlands for the fragrance of the full bloom of love, are sometimes used.

At a ceremony for a Humanist couple, the celebrant is likely to speak of Humanist values in married life:

Yvonne and Robert have chosen to be married in this Humanist wedding ceremony. Humanism sees a human being as an active and inseparable union of body and personality. Reason is the guide, but reason never separated from the emotions and efforts of the whole person, so that the emotion and intellect function together to provide the firmest foundation for married love. Yvonne and Robert hold in common the interests and ideals of the Humanist world. Living together in this way, they will deepen their love for each other and extend its reach to their fellow Humanists and to the whole community of humankind.[26]

However, less specifically Humanist words might be spoken, and poetry might be included in the opening addresses. But the heart of the ceremony will be the "vows", the statements of love and declarations of commitment from the couple. Because the marriage is personally planned, there is so much scope here for the true emotional sensitivity of the ceremony to be conveyed in these precious words. Some may wish to make personal statements, others may wish to respond to questions of the celebrant. Humanists do not generally favour the word "vows" since the term tends to connote promises that should not be broken. This is reflected in the following words, composed by a mature woman student[27] with experience of failed marriage:

> We have come together late in our lives, after many hardships and disappointments. We are both realistic and honest about the permanence of our feelings, which may change. But we think not. We promise to be faithful and supportive to each other and to build on our present relationship and bring it to a state of permanence and happiness based on shared experiences.

In *Sharing the Future* the following pledge is cited, and serves here as a further example:

> I give my love to you, and will be open to your love in return.
> I would like to share in your dreams and for you to share in mine;
> to give help when you need it, and to ask for help when in need;
> to support you in all your endeavour;
> to share in your joys and sorrows.
> In the presence of our family and friends, I ask you, [name]
> to be a friend, companion and lover throughout my life.[28]

I shall include one more example here that has been composed by a group of students during a workshop session on Humanist rites and ceremonies:

> I have come here today to show you [name] and others the love I feel for you. I want you to know that this love will be forever. I hope our love will continue to grow throughout the years. I will strive to do my best and bring happiness and pleasure into your life. Words cannot express how I feel for you, but I hope that in some way I can show you how much I love you. I want you always to remember that you are the best thing in my life. I realize things will not always be simple, but marriage is something that needs to be worked at, so that the journey in life is along the same road. You inspire and stimulate me on that journey, and provide me with warmth. I know you well enough to be able to decide that I want to spend the rest of my life with you. You mean the world to me [name] and more.[29]

Such words of affirmation may be said by both individuals, or each can compose his or her own words. The opportunity and space to express what one feels at such a very special occasion is without constraint.

At the end of the ceremony, some wishes for the future of the couple provide a fitting conclusion. Popular amongst Humanists, and certainly ones I favour, are the following words from the Native American Indian Marriage Ceremony:

> Now you will feel no rain
> for each of you will be shelter for the other.
> Now you will feel no cold
> for each of you will be warmth to the other.
> Now there is no more loneliness.
> Now you are two persons
> but there is only one life before you.
> Go now to your dwelling
> to enter into your life together;
> And may your days be good and long upon the earth.[30]

> May the sun bring you new energies by day;
> May the moon softly restore you at night.
> May the rain wash away any worries you may have
> And the breeze blow new strength into your being.
> And then, all the days of your life,
> May you walk gently through the world
> And know its beauty.[31]

While a couple may wish to pledge their love forever in the glow of young love, Humanists, of course, believe in just one lifetime for each of us. Being *in love* is a happy state through which one sees the world positively. In the marriage ceremony written for Humanists by the American Corliss Lamont, he points out how important the love of two people can be in the contemporary world. "The transfiguring power of that love", he says, "will reach out in compassionate concern for their fellow Humanists and fellow men, indeed to the whole community of mankind."[32] So just as lovers bring happiness to each other, so they can often infuse that happiness into the world around them. Physical, sexual love is regarded by most Humanists as a human joy, something that, these days, does not have to carry the thought, or fear of, pregnancy. It has nothing to do with reproduction unless a couple so wishes. And providing sexuality is expressed in a way that is not offensive to the partner, but is mutually acceptable and considerate, then the private world of sexuality can be creative and explorative for male and female. But most Humanists favour stable relationships in which two people enter into a partnership with love, care and responsibility. Multiple sexual partners do not really fit into a stable and rewarding life.

The ideal relationship, therefore, is a long-term one, for this is more conducive to the stability of society. Humanism believes fundamentally that each human being is entitled to reach his or her full potential of personal evolution and happiness, but this cannot be done in isolation. Individuals have a duty to others in their close relationships and in their societal relationships. It is likely to be the more stable long-term relationships that are the more beneficial in the wider framework of society. Brief encounters cannot develop the same kind of mutual awareness and sensitivity to the needs of another as can the long-term relationship. The longer-term partnership between two people tends to be more suitable for bringing into the world the children who will become the next generation. It is they who will shape the world of the future, and their children after them. Therefore these children need to develop with the kind of stability and eventual maturity and autonomy that are so essential in the promotion of a stable and happy society. Only then will the present generation create the means to a better world than the one in which it exists now. Parenthood, then, is a highly responsible role; it is something better planned than unplanned, and planned only when it is fairly certain that the love, care and sensitivity to the development of a whole individual can be undertaken.

Equality between the sexes in terms of mutual respect, love, care, status, commitment and responsibilities is seen as an important dimension in the relationship between two people. In any relationship there need be no clear defining of roles according to male/female criteria. There is no reason why a woman should not pursue a career while the male remains at home, *providing* this fulfils the wishes and happiness of both. Balance and harmony in marriage are ever-shifting qualities. They don't just happen, they have to be worked at continuously, for there are rarely constants in relationships. To quote Lamont's marriage ceremony again, he writes: "Marriage must be a cooperative venture in every sense. It is a relationship based on love, respect, and a determination on the part of both wife and husband to adjust to each other's temperaments and moods – in health or sickness, joy or sadness, ease or hardship."[33]

But however much people may come together in a loving relationship, we are all only too aware of love that has turned sour in many marriages and relationships – sometimes after a couple have been together many years. While separation and divorce are overtly prevalent in today's world, it is likely that covert separation in the relationship between man and wife characterized many marriages of the past when divorce was difficult for a woman and shameful even for a man. To *vow* to love another "'till death parts", is unreasonable, for love can fade into all sorts of negative modes from tolerant acceptance to utter indifference. Sometimes it is not the deeper issues of a relationship that bring an end to a loving relationship but, instead, innumerable "little things" that add up to an intolerable situation. Eating and sleeping with a person one no longer loves or likes, and watching the countless irritating things he or she does daily, are inimical to personal happiness and personal evolution. In the past, women especially had to put up with their lot; today any person who is perpetually unhappy in a marriage can obtain freedom from it. The distress of a divorce is perhaps the tip of the iceberg in comparison to the on-going distress of living with someone who is no longer loved. Sometimes more amicable parting is possible, and there are many couples who find that their relationship is significantly improved *after* divorce! For those who are not legally registered as married, separation is easier, but legal difficulties are not, and unmarried couples would do well to assess the legalities of their relationship in the event of separation, or of the demise of a partner.[34]

To end this section on marriage I include some poetry and prose appropriate to a secular marriage ceremony. Words of songs can also be used.[35] I include here, with some indulgence, words from one of my favourite poets – Rabindranath Tagore – already cited above. I have recorded the following poem in its original form, but the pronouns can be easily changed to suit the particular speaker.

> She is near to my heart as the meadow-flower to the earth;
> she is sweet to me as sleep is to tired limbs.
> My love for her is my life flowing in its fullness,
> like a river in autumn flood, running with serene abandonment.
> My songs are one with my love, like the murmur of a stream,
> that sings with all its waves and currents.[36]

> Let thy love play upon my voice and rest on my silence.
> Let it pass through my heart into all my movements.
> Let thy love like stars shine in the darkness of my sleep
> and dawn in my awakening.
> Let it burn in the flame of my desires
> And flow in all currents of my own love.
> Let me carry thy love in my life as a harp does its music,
> and give it back to thee at last with my life.[37]

And from *Fall: A collection of the Poems of Tanya Ward-Jones*:[38]

> Time's forces
> Thrust forth arrows of
> Piercing dark.
> Striking,
> Rooting,
> Delving,
> Through tormented thought.
> Two souls twinned in love and breath
> Take on these creatures in their embrace.
> A look locks for ever
> The positive knowledge of future time.
> An arm's fling flares out
> Fear and deepest doubt.
> What can prevail against these two?
> Who disturb their peace, divide their joy?
> Grind down the pure, untramelled
> Spirit of Love?
> None shall destroy
> None shall trap these two.
> Bound, Bonded,
> Chained in Time
> But free for ever in Love's Bounds.[39]

Intimacy is beautifully expressed by Frank Yerby in the following poem, *You are part of me*:

> You are part of me. I do not know
> By what slow chemistry you first became
> A vital fibre of my being. Go
> Beyond the rim of time and space, the same
> Inflections of your voice will sing their way
> Into the depths of my mind still. Your hair
> Will gleam as bright, the artless play
> Of word and glance, gesture and the fair
> Young fingers waving, have too deeply etched
> The pattern of your soul on mine. Forget
> Me quickly as a laughing picture sketched
> On water, I shall never know regret
> Knowing no magic ever can set free
> That part of you that is a part of me.[40]

The following poem was written by a student:[41]

> I love the way
> You are totally misunderstood by
> Everyone, but me.
> I think perhaps

You have that something in you
Which is the same as that something in me –
Which I never see,
Except when I'm with you.
So I guess we'll have to go on
In this amusing
Complicated way,
Because the problem is
Next to you my other friends
Don't shine anymore.

And to end this section on marriage, the words of Albert Schweitzer:

We are each a secret to the other. To know one another cannot mean to know everything about each other; it means to feel mutual affection and confidence, and to believe in one another. We must not try to force our way into the personality of another. To analyse others is a rude commencement, for there is a modesty of the soul which we must recognise just as we do that of the body. No one has a right to say to another: "Because we belong to each other as we do, I have a right to know all your thoughts." Not even a mother may treat her child in that way. All demands of this sort are foolish and unwholesome. In this matter giving is the only valuable process; it is only giving that stimulates. Impart as much as you can of your spiritual being to those who are on the road with you, and accept as something precious what comes back to you from them.[42]

To choose a Humanist marriage ceremony is to choose creatively and personally. But in all the extracts that have been included, and in all that has been written above, the Humanist vision of a "Good Life" informs its views of long-term relationships built on mutual trust, respect, love and responsibility.

Death

From antiquity perhaps the most important life-cycle rite has been associated with the death of a person, and all kinds of ceremony have been carried out in order to mark the end of the life of an individual. Such ceremonies tend to reflect the cultural customs of the society of the deceased, and are most often of a religious nature. But there are two important personal reasons why the demise of a person is accompanied with ceremony. First, to allow life to pass away without remark or tribute of some kind has never seemed right to the human psyche, whatever the nature of the deceased person. Second, death often generates a feeling of the fragility and vulnerability of life. It is a time that can bring loneliness. It is a time for reflection on life and its meaning, our role in life, and the way forward after loss. It is also a time when the deepest psychological fears about death emerge. Given these factors, death is a gathering together of the living to comfort, support and to share grief. In perhaps no other life-cycle rite are so many dimensions of the deeper human personality – the soul – called upon.

Humanists also believe that it is important to mark the occasion of someone's death with ceremony. But since Humanists have no belief in life beyond death, and since they place such emphasis on the quality of individual life, a Humanist funeral ceremony is a *celebration* of a life lived. It concentrates wholly on the individual who has died with warmth, depth of understanding, meaning, positivity and dignity. Unlike a marriage, a funeral ceremony has no legal requirements, and more and more people are planning the funerals of their deceased family member – and sometimes even their own funeral – at a personal level. Many people today do not have any religious belief, so a religious service that speaks of the resurrection of the dead and a life everlasting has little meaning. Death and afterlife are important concepts in theistic religion, and they will therefore be the main focus around which a religious service is conducted. A Humanist funeral is quite the opposite for it will focus positively, though sensitively, on life, honouring the unique personality of the deceased, offering comfort for the lives of those who are left behind, and reflecting on the precious nature of life in general. It severs relationships between the living and the dead gracefully, sensitively and with dignity but always positively. In the funeral service designed by Corliss Lamont, he writes:

> Transiency and death itself are entirely natural and understandable in our universe. Life and death are different and essential aspects of the same creative process. It is Nature's law that living organisms should eventually retire from the scene and so make way for newborn generations. In this sense life affirms itself *through* death.[43]

A Humanist funeral, then, is not a service offered to God but a celebration of a life that has been lived and has come to an end. This is why, like Theravada Buddhists, Humanists can speak of a *funeral celebration*. And the celebration of the life of the deceased will take the form of a personal look at the life that was lived. This will include referring to the deceased by his or her nickname, and accounts of his or her childhood, education, work, family, special interests and special friends. It is the little things that are often particularly touching about the life of the deceased at such a Humanist ceremony – the glass of wine by the fire, the walks with the dogs, the favourite sweater, the favourite armchair, and the funny anecdotes. In my own experience of Humanist funerals I have found that the Humanist officiant conducting the ceremony pieces together a moving and full picture of someone he or she may never have known. And within that portrayal there is space to play some of the deceased's favourite music, to hear or sing his or her favourite song, to read from a favourite book or read a favourite poem.

Until the year 1880 all funerals were religious services, and all deceased people were buried until the mid-1880s. As the move towards non-religious burial services took place, Anglican clergymen became so outraged that they used to turn up at the unlawful burial to read the Anglican service.[44] Since the Anglican service related solely to burial, cremation was not possible until after 1880. But in 1884 a Cremation Society was founded by an agnostic surgeon, Sir Henry Thompson, and cremation became possible. It was not until the 1960s that cremation became more widely evident than burial. So today most Humanists – indeed, most non-religious and even religious people – are cremated rather than buried,[45] but Humanist burials are also possible. In the latter case, a Humanist may wish to be buried in a church cemetery – perhaps to be buried with a spouse, or to be in the familiar local cemetery – and this may involve a prior ceremony in a church or chapel. This does not necessarily preclude a Humanist ceremony, but permission from church officials is necessary for the cemetery option to take place.[46] Then, too, some people may wish to be buried in the countryside, with a Humanist ceremony.[47] What is important is that in saying farewell to someone who has died there is every opportunity to do this in the best possible way. When those close to the deceased are able to plan a ceremony suited to the life that has come to an end, then it is an aptly intimate and sensitive farewell.

While it may be clear that someone who has died would prefer a distinctly non-religious ceremony, Humanist officiants are sensitive to the fact that many of those attending such a ceremony would have some religious conviction. At such a sad occasion it would be pedantic and unkind to be overly critical of religious belief. Yet, despite being public and not religious buildings, crematoria are often modelled on churches in interior design, and it would not be unreasonable to ask for cross, prayer books or other religious symbols to be removed. This is not a difficulty providing there is time to replace them before the next cremation ceremony. But there may be those who find comfort in religious expression. While belief in God is not a part of Humanist belief, many Humanist officiants will include a short period of time for quiet reflection on the life of the deceased. This is a time when those who wish to pray, or who wish to take comfort from their own beliefs, may do so. Of course, if the deceased happened to be a Humanist, then it would be natural to include something about his or her beliefs as part of the biographical account of the person's life. Some Humanist officiants may accept the singing of a hymn or a religious reading by a close member of the family who feels it necessary. But others would prefer to leave religious sentiments to personal and private means of paying tribute to the deceased, rather than include them in the more public and official ceremony.[48]

There is no reason why members of a family and/or friends cannot conduct their own funeral ceremony for a departed loved one. But since the occasion is a sorrowful one, it is often easier to have someone removed from the grief to help plan and to conduct the ceremony. Humanist officiants fulfil this purpose. They are well trained and understanding, and will not only help to plan a ceremony uniquely suitable to the individual, but will take charge of any part, or all, of the ceremony if required to. In Britain, British Humanist Association accredited officiants conduct ceremonies according to a prescribed code of conduct. They will visit the bereaved family or friends to assist before the funeral, and will also direct it. Moreover, they will transcribe the whole ceremony for the family afterwards, if required.

They are also men and women who are experienced in dealing with difficult funerals such as those of a baby, a child, or even of neonatal death and medical terminations. Sometimes very personal ceremonies are necessary for the physically or mentally disadvantaged, for those who die alone without family, or for those who have committed suicide. In these circumstances Humanist officiants are able to assist in organizing a sensitive, personal and specialist ceremony.[49]

A Humanist funeral is usually divided into five parts. First, there are words of welcome to those who have come, and perhaps a brief explanation about the nature of a Humanist funeral. Some reflective words about life and death follow, and then the main focus of the ceremony follows – the tribute to the life of the deceased. The committal of the body follows, and then the closing words of the ceremony to conclude. Personal tributes in the form of poetry, prose or music can be accommodated. Though these may be placed at any point during the ceremony, they are usually more particularly relevant to the part of the ceremony devoted to reflections on life and death, but at the same time, would have some meaning for the life of the deceased. As Jane Wynne Willson comments, such inclusions help in the process of grieving without wallowing in too much emotion.[50] Some sensitive thoughts about life and death are included in the following extract from a Humanist funeral:[51]

> The death of each of us is in the order of things: it follows life as surely as night follows day. We can take the Tree of life as a symbol. The human race is the trunk and branches of this tree, and individual men and women are the leaves, which appear one season, flourish for a summer, and then die. I too am like a leaf of this tree, and one day I shall be torn off by a storm, or simply decay and fall – and mingle with the earth at its roots. But, while I live, I am conscious of the tree's flowing sap and steadfast strength. Deep down in my consciousness is the consciousness of a collective life, a life of which I am a part, and to which I make a minute but unique contribution. When I die and fall the tree remains, nourished to some small degree by my manifestation of life. Millions of leaves have preceded me and millions will follow me: but the tree itself grows and endures.

These are significantly Humanist ideas, as are the following words in another extract from a Humanist funeral:[52]

> All living things are subject to death: it is the basis of growth. Through evolution, in the course of millions upon millions of deaths, humanity has evolved. We carry this inheritance. But we, as human individuals, have a more personal contribution to make, in the value of our own lives. And those of us who accept the unity and completeness of the natural order, and believe that to die means the end of the conscious personality, look death in the face with honesty, with dignity and with calm.

The following words were composed by a student – again, at a workshop session on Humanist rites and ceremonies. It reflects rather well the Humanist aspirations for the "Good Life".

> Being masters of our destiny, we know there is no ultimate reward awaiting us. So we strive to reach our full potential during our short time on this earth. It is our responsibility to do our very best, to face life and its limitations, and to rise above those limitations with dignity, happy in the knowledge that we are creating a good life for ourselves, for others and for future generations. [Name of deceased] believed in

the philosophy of active participation in life. Always cheerful and full of optimism, all his energies went into creating a world that shared mutual respect and freedom of opinion, a world where each individual was allowed to fulfil his or her own potential. He ultimately believed in a world of happiness, justice and peace.[53]

When my father died a few years ago, I decided that I should like to read one or two poems at his funeral. He had a Christian service and burial, so I had to ask the minister conducting the service for permission to read some poetry. I was told that this would not be a problem, but I had to report to the vicarage with my selected poetry for the vicar to scrutinize. I had chosen three extracts. Two were rejected because they did not have Christian authors. The one that I was allowed to read was clearly "Christian", having been written by Canon Scott Holland (1847–1918). But in fact, Canon Holland's words are not altogether consonant with Christian ideas of afterlife. The two other rejected works were by the Muslim Kahlil Gibran and the singer and songwriter Ewan MacColl, the former of these being far more in line with Christian views than Holland's! Less restrained by such religious bias, I am able to include two of the extracts here. From the pen of Canon Scott Holland is the following, which is popular now at many funerals. To me it was apt for my grieving mother; something my father might have wanted to say. Many Humanists, however, would object to the hint of an on-going fate of a soul in the words. But the main thrust of thought is a message of comfort that a continuing loving *remembrance* can bring. It is *memory* that is the key issue here, the closeness of a life shared, and the thought that, while death is the ultimate parting, the memory of a life lived together – with all its trials and tribulations, its joys and laughter – is something that adds value to the life of one left behind:

> Death is nothing at all . . .
> I have only slipped away into the next room.
> I am I and you are you . . .
> Whatever we were to each other that we are still.
> Call me by my old familiar name, speak to me
> in the easy way in which you always used.
> Put no difference in your tone;
> wear no forced air of solemnity or sorrow.
> Laugh as we always laughed at the
> little jokes we enjoyed together.
> Play, smile, think of me, pray for me.
> Let my name be ever the household
> word that it always was.
> Let it be spoken without effort,

without the ghost of a shadow on it.
Life means all that it ever meant.
It is the same as it ever was;
there is absolutely unbroken continuity.
What is this death but a negligible accident?
Why should I be out of mind
because I am out of sight?
I am waiting for you for an interval,
somewhere very near, just around the corner.
All is well.[54]

Here is a beautiful poem by Tanya Blanchard:

In the whiteness of the spring I walked with Death.
I reached out and touched him
There where he slid beneath the wall.
I felt him bend, breathe, pant in the pangs of conquest.
I knew him there, then, beneath the buds
Clothed in beauty, sultry as the sun.
Calling naked as a new-born leaf.
Haunting, forlorn, hopeless as a dream –
I ached for him then, there, in that instant
Smelt the acrid ash of art
Sensed the deathly frame of power.
There in the whiteness of the spring, I walked alone with
Death.[55]

And from Ewan MacColl come the following words:

Take me to some high place
Of heather, rock and ling;
Scatter my dust and ashes,
Feed me to the wind.
So that I will be
Part of all you see,
The air you are breathing.
I'll be part of the curlew's cry
And the soaring hawk,
The blue milkwort
And the sundew hung with diamonds.
I'll be riding the gentle wind
That blows through your hair;
Reminding you how we shared
In the joy of living.[56]

I include now some suitable selections from a number of sources.[57]

Dying, you have left behind you the great sadness of the Eternal in
my life.
You have painted my thought's horizon with the sunset colours of
your departure, leaving a track of tears across the earth to love's
heaven.

Clasped in your dear arms, life and death united in me in a
marriage bond.
I think I can see you watching there in the balcony with your lamp
lighted, where the end and the beginning of all things meet.
My world went hence through the doors that you opened – you
holding the cup of death to my lips, filling it with life from your own.[58]

> PEACE, my heart, let the time for the parting be sweet.
> Let it not be a death but completeness.
> Let love melt into memory and pain into songs.
> Let the flight through the sky end in the folding of
> the wings over the nest.
> Let the last touch of your hands be gentle like the
> flower of the night.
> Stand still, O Beautiful End, for a moment, and say
> your last words in silence.
> I bow to you and hold up my lamp to light you on
> your way.[59]

Two poems by Christina Rossetti provide poignant words that the
departed might have said:

Song

> WHEN I am dead, my dearest,
>   Sing no sad songs for me;
> Plant thou no roses at my head,
>   Nor shady cypress tree:
> Be the green grass above me
>   With showers and dewdrops wet;
> And if thou wilt, remember;
>   And if thou wilt, forget.
>
> I shall not see the shadows,
>   I shall not feel the rain;
> I shall not hear the nightingale
>   Sing on, as if in pain;
> And dreaming through the twilight
>   That doth not rise or set,
> Haply I may remember;
>   And haply may forget.[60]

Remember

> Remember me when I am gone away,
> Gone far away into the silent land;[61]
> When you can no more hold me by the hand,
> Nor I half turn to go yet turning stay.
> Remember me when no more day by day
> You tell me of our future that you planned:

> Only remember me; you understand.
> It will be late to counsel then or pray.
> Yet if you should forget me for a while
> And afterwards remember; do not grieve:
> For if the darkness and corruption leave
> A vestige of the thoughts that once I had,
> Better by far you should forget and smile
> Than that you should remember and be sad.[62]

The committal of the deceased should always be brief, since it is for many the most emotional part of the ceremony – the finality of parting. The following words, or similar, might be suitable for cremation:

> I blend my body with fire; and that which I have done, and all that I have been in life, is now exhausted in flames. These will now lift to the sky, leaving the memories of me to reside in the hearts of those I have known and loved.

And for burial, words from the poet Shelley:

> He is made one with Nature: there is heard
> His voice in all her music, from the moan
> Of thunder, to the song of night's sweet bird;
> He is a presence to be felt and known
> In darkness and in light, from herb and stone. . . .
> He is a portion of the loveliness
> Which once he made more lovely.[63]

And for committal or burial, the last verse of W. E. Henley's *Margaritae Sororis*:

> My task accomplish'd and the long day done,
> My wages taken, and in my heart
> Some late lark singing,
> Let me be gather'd to the quiet west,
> The sundown splendid and serene,
> Death.[64]

Or words from Samuel Butler (1835–1902):

> I fall asleep in the full and certain hope
> That my slumber shall not be broken;
> And that, though I be all-forgetting,
> Yet shall I not be all-forgotten,
> But continue that life in the thoughts and deeds
> Of those I have loved.[65]

To end this section on poetry and words suitable for funeral ceremonies, I include three extracts which are contributions from students who were asked to plan their own funeral ceremony:

> Dear friends, if I left without saying goodbye, then let me take just a moment of your time to thank you for the way in which your lives touched, and helped to form, mine. Our individual existence is just a flicker in the vastness of time and space, our lives as brief and transient as spiders' webs. And, like a spider's web, there is a beginning and an end, and an in-between – this last an intricate and delicate pattern of events and people that make up our very reason for being. Each of you was a part of my pattern, darkening awkward corners with me when times were bad, or shining in the early morning sun when times were good. You made up all the levels of my life and made me complete, and I thank you all.[66]

> I have died
> My life no longer exists
> Every one of yours does.
> So all please
> Go away from this
> With the intention
> To celebrate the life I had:
> The good times,
> The bad times.
> Go drink
> Get drunk
> Go, play music;
> Not solemn, but loudly
> Not quiet, but lively
> Cause noise pollution!
> Disturb neighbours!
> If they ask "Why?"
> Say "I'm alive!"
> Don't dwell
> Over life without me
> Go, live life
> If not for you, for me.[67]

Dear friends, even though I have had a relatively short life, I have experienced great joy. The joy of walking in the long-stemmed grass which grows wildly down by the river. The joy of seeing the breeze blowing through each stem, which sets it dancing to its own rhythm. Oh the joy of watching the sunset is almost indescribable – watching the golden sun going down on the surrounding hills and mountains. Added to this is the pleasure of seeing the wild fowl swimming silently on the river.

Friends, for me these are only some of my memories of the wonders of

Nature. Remember that we grew from a seed. Look at the beauty that surrounds you; have feeling for it, from the tall trees to the sensitive little plants, or the creeper on the wall growing up to the light. Be aware of Nature around you and communicate with it. For you are a part of all living things, and if you hurt Nature you hurt yourself. Live in harmony with Nature and enjoy the world.

Remember friends, there is so much to do in the world to make it a better place. Strive to overcome poverty, to live without fear, to build a firm society based on peace and morality. Each and every one of us wants to live in a world that is not a battle, to find a life that is orderly and full of beauty and great love. If you will, you can work for, and find, these things.[68]

These words provide something of the Humanist joy in the good things of life, the fullness of the individual life, and the hope of a "Good Life" for all. Those who believe in the interconnectedness of life realize the intimacy with which humanity is so intricately bound together. It is perhaps appropriate that this book ends with the subject of death, for in viewing death, we are forced to face some of the ultimate questions of our communal existence. I end this chapter, therefore, with some wise words from Corliss Lamont that epitomize rather well the common life that we share one with another as human beings:

The occurrence of death brings home to us the common concerns, the common crises and the common destiny of all who live upon this earth. Death draws us together in the deep-felt emotions of the heart; it dramatically accents the ultimate equality involved in our ultimate fate; it reminds us of the essential brotherhood of Man that lies beneath all the bitter dissensions and divisions registered in history and contemporary affairs. The human race, with its infinite roots reaching back over the boundless past and its infinite ramifications extending throughout the present world and ever pushing forward into the future, is one great family. The living and the dead and the generations yet unborn make up that enduring communion of humanity which shares the adventure of life upon this dear and pleasant earth.[69]

Notes

Introduction

1   H. Stopes-Roe, "Understanding the History of Humanism", *New Humanist*, vol. 112, no. 4 (1997): 15.
2   N. Walter, "Rationally Speaking", *New Humanist*, vol. 103, no. 4 (1988): 4.
3   H. Stopes-Roe, "Controversy: In defence of a life stance", *New Humanist* vol. 103, no. 4 (1998): 8.

1   What is Humanism?

1   A. Bullock, *The Humanist Tradition in the West* (London: Thames and Hudson, 1985), p. 18.
2   P. Kurtz (ed.), *The Humanist Alternative: Some definitions of Humanism* (London: Pemberton, 1973), p. 6.
3   T. Davies, *Humanism* (London and New York: Rider, 1997), p. 3.
4   N. Walter, *Humanism: What's in the word?* (London: Rationalist Press Association, 1997), p. 4.
5   *Ibid.*, p. 11.
6   Bullock, *The Humanist Tradition in the West*, p. 9.
7   H. J. Blackham, "A Definition of Humanism" in P. Kurtz *The Humanist Alternative*, p. 36.
8   Walter, *Humanism*, p. 9.
9   British Humanist Association.
10   Bullock, *The Humanist Tradition in the West*, p. 155.
11   *Ibid.*, p. 11.
12   Like the term *humanism*, that of *Renaissance* would also have been unknown in fifteenth-century Italy. It is one used retrospectively of the period by later historians.
13   Walter, *Humanism*, p. 16.
14   J. Carroll, *Humanism: The wreck of western culture* (London: Fontana, 1993), p. 3.
15   Bullock, *The Humanist Tradition in the West*, p. 19.
16   See R. Tuck, "Humanism and Political Thought" in A. Goodman and A. MacKay (eds), *The Impact of Humanism on Western Europe* (Harlow and New York: Longman, 1990), p. 43.
17   See P. Burke, "The Spread of Italian Humanism" in Goodman and MacKay, *The Impact of Humanism on Western Europe*, p. 24.

18 *Ibid.*, p. 14.
19 P. Matheson, "Humanism and Reform Movements" in Goodman and MacKay, *The Impact of Humanism on Western Europe*, p. 24.
20 *Ibid.*, pp. 37–8.
21 See Davies, *Humanism*, p. 119.
22 Carroll, *Humanism*, p. 118.
23 See Davies, *Humanism*, p. 50.
24 Yet as recently as 1994 Paul Kurtz notes the presence of a "religious" element in North American *secular* humanism. He states that there are some secular humanists who "look to humanistic Unitarian churches, Ethical Culture societies, or Humanistic Judaism temples as their models". The presence of humanist churches, and the like, whose Sunday congregations are led by sermon-delivering ministers, as Kurtz clearly points out, "only obfuscates the true character of humanism as a radical alternative to theism". See *Living without Religion: Eupraxophy* (Amherst, New York: Prometheus Books, 1994), p. 13.
25 D. Ehrenfeld, *The Arrogance of Humanism* (Oxford, New York, Toronto, Melbourne: Oxford University Press, 1981 reprint of 1978 edn).
26 C. Lamont, *The Philosophy of Humanism* (London: Barrie and Rockliff in association with the Pemberton Publishing Co. Ltd, 1965), p. 227.
27 Carroll, *Humanism*, pp. 113–14.
28 *Ibid.*, p. 124.
29 Ehrenfeld, *The Arrogance of Humanism*, p. 267.
30 *Ibid.*, p. 19.
31 Bullock, *The Humanist Tradition in the West*, p. 179.
32 Nicolas Walter deals with the development leading up to the present day in a detailed chapter in *Humanism: What's in the word?*, pp. 42–78, and J. P. van Praag gives a very succinct account in *Foundations of Humanism* (Buffalo, New York: Prometheus Books, 1982) pp. 44–52.
33 See D. Tribe, *100 Years of Freethought* (London: Elek, 1967), pp. 15–18.
34 *Ibid.*, p. 20.
35 For the history of this journal and a good insight into the issues with which Humanism has been, and is, involved, see Jim Herrick, *Vision and Realism: A hundred years of the Freethinker* (London: G. W. Foote & Co., 1982).
36 *Free Inquiry*, vol. 1, no. 18 (1997): 1.
37 The RPA began as the Propaganda Press Committee in 1888, changing its name to the Rationalist Press Committee in 1893 and finally to the Rationalist Press Association in 1899.
38 *New Humanist*, vol. 103, no. 4 (1988): 2.
39 See Tribe, *100 Years of Freethought*, p. 47.
40 See J. E. Smith, *Quasi-Religions: Humanism, Marxism and Nationalism* (Basingstoke and London: Macmillan, 1994).
41 *Ibid.*, p. 18.
42 *Ibid.*, p. 23.
43 *Ibid.*, p. 25.
44 *Ibid.*, p. 40.
45 *Ibid.*
46 Van Praag, *Foundations of Humanism*, p. 45.

2 *The Human Being*

1   *The Humanist Manifesto II*, see C. Lamont, *The Philosophy of Humanism* (New York: Frederick Ungar Publishing Company, 1982), fifth principle, p. 294.
2   J. Carroll, *Humanism: The wreck of western culture* (London: Fontana, 1993), p. 54.
3   C. S. Lewis, *Mere Christianity* (Glasgow: Collins, 1984 impression, first published 1952), p. 109.
4   H. Blackham, *The Future of our Past: From ancient Greece to global village* (Amherst, New York and Oxford: Prometheus Books, 1996), p. 374.
5   H. Blackham, *Humanism* (Harmondsworth: Penguin, 1968), p. 65.
6   *Ibid.*, p. 66.
7   *Ibid.*, p. 67.
8   Carroll, *Humanism*, p. 31.
9   D. Ehrenfeld, *The Arrogance of Humanism* (Oxford, New York, Toronto, Melbourne: Oxford University Press), p. 266.
10 While I watched this series, I owe the reference here to Polly Toynbee's article *Radio Times* 20–26 June, 1998, p. 10.
11 Jean-Paul Sartre, *Existentialism and Humanism* (London: Methuen, 1997, first published in 1948), pp. 27–8.
12 *Ibid.*, p. 29.
13 *Ibid.*, p. 30.
14 *Ibid.*, p. 45.
15 For example, Bertrand Russell and Morris Cohen.
16 A. Bullock, *The Humanist Tradition in the West* (London: Thames and Hudson, 1985), p. 179.
17 Albert H. Cantril (ed.), *Psychology, Humanism and Scientific Inquiry: The selected essays of Hadley Cantril* (New Brunswick and Oxford: Transaction Books, 1988), p. 42.
18 C. Lamont, *The Philosophy of Humanism* (London: Barrie and Rockliff in association with the Pemberton Publishing Co. Ltd., 1965 reprint of 1949 edn), p. 14.
19 Blackham, in *Humanism*, pp. 80–1.
20 *Ibid.*, p. 81.
21 *Ibid.*, p. 82.
22 N. Walter, *Humanism: What's in the word?* (London: Rationalist Press Association, 1997), p. 89.
23 Cantril, *Psychology, Humanism and Scientific Inquiry*, p. 43.
24 *Ibid.*, p. 45.
25 Carroll, *Humanism* p. 228.
26 Strictly speaking, Plato divides the soul into three parts, the rational part which is the highest part of the soul that distinguishes man from animals, and which is immortal and similar to the divine; the spirited part which is something like moral courage and mind, and is shared with animals; and the appetitive part which is concerned with bodily desires. The spirited and appetitive parts are not immortal, but the rational part, Plato argued was, and belonged to the separate and transcendent world of Forms or Ideas.

27 A. Atkinson, *The Cosmic Fairy: The new challenge of a Darwinian approach to Humanism* (Gerrards Cross: Colin Smythe Ltd., 1996), p. 66.
28 *Ibid.*, p. 70.
29 Sartre, *Existentialism and Humanism*, p. 41.
30 Ehrenfeld, *The Arrogance of Humanism*, p. 239.
31 L. Saumur, *The Humanist Evangel* (Buffalo, New York: Prometheus Books, 1982), p. 31.
32 P. Kurtz, *Living without Religion: Eupraxophy* (Amherst, New York: Prometheus Books, 1994), p. 37.
33 R. Ashby, "The Spiritual Experience" *Humanity*, vol. 6 (1998): 8–10.
34 *Ibid.*, p. 9.
35 *Ibid.*, p. 10.
36 Her Majesty's Inspectorate.
37 A. Flew, "What is 'Spirituality'?" in L. Brown, B. Farr and R. J. Hoffman, *Modern Spiritualities: An inquiry* (Amherst, New York and Oxford: Prometheus Books, 1997), p. 36.
38 B. Farr, "Becoming Spiritual: Learning from marijuana users" in Brown et al. *Modern Spiritualities*, pp. 179–94.
39 *Ibid.*, p. 186.
40 *Ibid.*, p. 188.
41 H. Graham, *The Human Face of Psychology* (Milton Keynes and Philadephia: Oxford University Press, 1986).
42 A. Maslow, *Toward a Psychology of Being* (New York: Van Nostrand Reinhold, 1968), p. 74.
43 *Ibid.*, p. 97.
44 A. Maslow, "Various Meanings of Transcendence" in *The Farther Reaches of Human Nature* (New York, London, Victoria, Toronto and Auckland: Penguin, 1993, first published 1971), pp. 259–69.
45 *Ibid.*, p. 269.
46 A. Maslow, "Religious Aspects of Peak-Experiences" in W. A. Sadler, Jr. *Personality and Religion* (London: SCM, 1970), p. 170.
47 Blackham, *Humanism*, pp. 68–9.
48 H. Hawton, *The Humanist Revolution* (London: Barrie and Rockliff in association with the Pemberton Publishing Co. Ltd., 1963), *passim*.
49 In P. Kurtz, *Forbidden Fruit: The ethics of Humanism* (Buffalo, New York: Prometheus Books, 1988), pp. 111–50.
50 R. Fletcher, *A Definition of Humanism* (London: Rationalist Press Association, n.d.), p. 10.
51 R. Fisher, "Becoming Persons: Neglected but prior concerns" in Brown et al. *Modern Spiritualities* p. 204.
52 *Ibid.*
53 Fletcher, *A Definition of Humanism*, p. 11.
54 Blackham, *The Future of Our Past*, p. 372.
55 *Ibid.*, p. 375.
56 Fisher, "Becoming Persons" in Brown et al. *Modern Spiritualities*, p. 204.
57 K. Soper, *Humanism and Anti-Humanism: Problems of modern European thought* (London, Melbourne, Sydney, Auckland, Johannesburg: Hutchinson, 1986), p. 13.
58 *Ibid.*, p. 14.

3 *The Case against Religion: The Rejection of God*

1 Corliss Lamont, *The Philosophy of Humanism* (New York: Frederick Ungar Publishing Company, 1982, first published 1942).
2 P. Kurtz, "Where are the Secularists?" *Free Inquiry*, vol. 18 no. 1 (1997): 16–17.
3 See N. Walter, "Rationally Speaking" *New Humanist*, vol. 103 no. 4 (1988): 4.
4 G. H. Smith, *Atheism: The case against God* (Buffalo, New York: Prometheus Books, 1989), p. 89.
5 This is actually a *denial* of the existence of God not just a *lack* of belief in God, as Keith Parsons would have us believe in "Is there a case for Christian theism" in J. P. Moreland and K. Nielsen, *Does God Exist?: The debate between theists and atheists* (Buffalo, New York: Prometheus Books, 1993), p. 177.
6 So Smith, *ibid.*, p. 8.
7 So, Antony Flew, *God, Freedom and Immortality: A critical analysis* (Buffalo, New York: Prometheus Books, 1984), p. 14.
8 Kai Nielsen, *Philosophy and Atheism* (Buffalo, New York: Prometheus Books, 1985), p. 34.
9 I use Jim Herrick's definition here, *Against the Faith: Some deists, sceptics and atheists* (London: Glover & Blair Ltd., 1985), p. 17.
10 In R. E. Greeley (ed.), *The Best of Humanism* (Buffalo, New York: Prometheus Books, 1988), p. 22.
11 See Flew, *God, Freedom and Immortality*, p. 171, note 20.
12 It is important to note here that dualism is still retained in pantheism. For while God is the totality of the universe, each entity within the universe is only a *part* of that totality. This means that the dualistic and theistic relationship between individual and divine can still be retained.
13 P. Tillich, *The Shaking of the Foundations* (New York: Charles Scribner's Sons, 1976, first published 1948), p. 57.
14 Hindus rarely refer to their religion as polytheistic because of their belief that there is only one ultimate and unmanifest reality that informs all the deities, indeed all existence. This suggests that, where Hinduism embraces theism, it is a monotheistic religion, despite its multiplicity of deities.
15 M. Zimmerman, "Aren't Humanists Really Atheists?" in P. Kurtz (ed.), *The Humanist Alternative: Some definitions of Humanism* (Buffalo, New York: Prometheus Books, 1973), p. 83.
16 C. Lofmark, *What is the Bible?* (London: Rationalist Press Association, 1990), p. 50.
17 See F. Brown, S. R. Driver and C. Briggs, *A Hebrew and English Lexicon of the Old Testament* (Oxford: Clarendon, 1974 reprint of 1953 edn), pp. 398–401.
18 The Jewish day has always been from sunset to sunset.
19 C. Lofmark, *What is the Bible?*, *passim*. I use a number of his examples here for which I am indebted. Some are well known, but he still includes some surprises!
20 *Ibid.*, pp. 36–7.

21 *Ibid.*, p. 37.
22 This is probably not a creation myth at all but one that serves to depict the "thou-ness" of the relationship between man and woman, the end of the story in *Genesis* 2:24 portraying the reason behind the story – that a man leaves his parents and cleaves to his wife.
23 It is highly likely that the virgin birth is a late interpolation, being unknown to both Paul, and the author of Mark's Gospel.
24 Lofmark, *What is the Bible?* pp. 38–9.
25 See, for example, *1 Samuel* 15: 3, where even the animals have to be killed in addition to all the inhabitants, and *Deuteronomy*, 7:2.
26 See I. Warraq, *Why I am not a Muslim* (Amherst, New York: Prometheus Books, 1995), chapter 5, pp. 104–62. On this issue of abrogation, Warraq writes, 'all the passages preaching tolerance are found in Meccan, i.e. early suras, and all the passages recommending killing, decapitating, and maiming are Medinian, i.e. later: "tolerance" has been abrogated by "intolerance". For example, the famous verse at sura 9.5, "slay the idolaters wherever you find them", is said to have canceled 124 verses that dictate tolerance and patience" (p. 115). Clearly, the concept of abrogation has led to unacceptable ethics.
27 P. Kreeft, "Why Debate the Existence of God?" in Moreland and Nielsen, *Does God Exist?*, p. 11.
28 Karen Armstrong, *A History of God* (London: Mandarin, 1994 reprint of 1993 edn), p. 27.
29 The Methodist Church has decreed that God is beyond gender, and has recognized the past patriarchal subordination of women in the suppression of the image of God in female terms. For mainstream Methodism, then, God can be Mother – but this is an equally anthropomorphic and limiting concept of divinity as that of "Father".
30 J. P. Moreland, "Closing Arguments for Christianity" in Moreland and Nielsen, *Does God Exist?* p. 74.
31 A. Flew, "The Case for God Challenged" in Moreland and Nielsen, *ibid.*, p.167.
32 Smith, *Atheism*, p. 256.
33 S. T. Davis (ed.), *Encountering Evil: Live options in theodicy* (Edinburgh: T & T Clarke, 1981), p. 2.
34 J. Hick, *God and the Universe of Faiths* (London: Macmillan, 1988 reissue; first published 1973), p. 62.
35 J. Hick, *Evil and the God of Love* (London: Macmillan, 1991; first published 1966), p. 358.
36 *Ibid.*, pp. 361–2.
37 J. Roth, "A Theodicy in Protest" in Davis (ed.), *Encountering Evil*, p. 14 and *passim*.
38 J. J. C. Smart, in J. J. C. Smart and J. J. Haldane, *Atheism and Theism* (Oxford: Blackwell, 1996), p. 72.
39 Smith, *Atheism*, p. 84.
40 M. Knight, *Morals without Religion and other Essays* (London: Dennis Dobson, 1960 impression; first published 1955), p. 75.
41 *Psalm* 44:23–4.
42 *Amos* 3:6; *Lamentations* 3:38; *Exodus* 12:29; 21:2–6, 7; 22:18; 31:14–15;

Leviticus 20:9; 24:16; 25:44–6; *Numbers* 31:17–18; *Deuteronomy* 22:20–21 etc.

43 B. Davies, *An Introduction to the Philosophy of Religion* (Oxford: Oxford University Press, 1993), p. 41.
44 J. L. Mackie "Evil and Omnipotence" in *Mind*, April 1995, p. 209.
45 Flew, *God, Freedom and Immortality*, p. 82.
46 Robert Green Ingersoll, in Greeley (ed.), *The Best of Humanism*, p. 22.
47 K. Nielsen, *Philosophy and Atheism* (Buffalo, New York: Prometheus), p. 38.
48 Smart in Smart and Haldane, *Atheism and Theism*, p. 49.
49 J. P. Moreland "A Christian's Rebuttal" in Moreland and Nielsen *Does God Exist?*, p. 57.
50 Often called the Contingency Argument.
51 A. Flew, *Atheistic Humanism* (Buffalo, New York: Prometheus Books, 1993), p. 43.
52 P. Davies, *God and the New Physics* (London: Penguin, 1990 reprint; first published 1983), p. 31.
53 Although known generally as the Argument *from* Design, the Argument *to* Design was suggested by Norman Kemp Smith, "Is Divine Existence Credible?", *Proceedings of the British Academy*, vol. 17 (1931): pp. 209–34.
54 In Greeley (ed.), *The Best of Humanism*, p. 162.
55 B. Russell, *Why I am not a Christian* (London: Rationalist Press Association, 1983 reprint of 1927 edn), p. 11.
56 See Davies, *God and the New Physics*, p. 189.
57 A. Flew, *Atheistic Humanism*, p. 37.
58 J. Robinson, *Honest to God* (London: SCM, 1963).
59 M. Knight, *Honest to Man: Christian ethics re-examined* (London: Pemberton, 1974).
60 Père P. Teilhard de Chardin, "Cosmic Life" in *The Prayer of the Universe* (London: Collins, Fontana, 1968), p. 51.
61 Père P. Teilhard de Chardin, *Le Milieu Divin* (London: Collins 1960), p. 51.

4 *The Case against Religion: The Rejection of Faith*

1 C. Lamont, *The Philosophy of Humanism*, London: Barrie and Rockliffe in association with the Pemberton Publishing Co. Ltd., 1965 reprint of 1949 edn), p. 15.
2 G. A. Larue in R. J. Hoffman and G. A. Larue (eds), *Jesus in History and Myth* (Amherst, New York: Prometheus Books, 1986), p. 8.
3 Van A. Harvey, "New Testament Scholarship and Christian Belief" in Hoffman and Larue (eds) *ibid.*, p. 197.
4 J. Hick (ed.), *The Myth of God Incarnate* (London: SCM, 1997).
5 G. H. Smith, *Atheism: The case against God* (Buffalo, New York, Prometheus Books, 1989 reprint of 1979 edn), p. 117.
6 R. Firth, *Religion: A Humanist interpretation* (London: Routledge, 1996), p. 70.
7 *Ibid.*, p. 213.
8 *Ibid.*, p. 214.
9 J. Hick, "A Remonstrance in Concluding" in Hoffman and Larue (eds),

Jesus in History and Myth, pp. 214–15.

10 C. Lofmark, *What is the Bible?* (London: Rationalist Press Association, 1990), p. 81.

11 See J. Herrick, *Against the Faith: Some deists, sceptics and atheists* (London: Glover and Blair Ltd., 1985, pp. 236–7.

12 Cited in N. Walter, *Humanism: What's in the word?* (London: Rationalist Press Association, 1997), p. 54.

13 Teilhard de Chardin, "Cosmic Life" in *The Prayer of the Universe* (London: Collins, 1968), p. 49.

14 P. Kurtz, *The Transcendental Temptation: A critique of religion and the paranormal* (Amherst, New York: Prometheus Books, 1991), pp. 296–7.

15 Sir Julian Huxley, "Introduction" in P. Teilhard de Chardin, *The Phenomenon of Man* (London: Collins, 1959, first published in French by Editions du Seuil, 1955), p. 13. A new edition and translation of Chardin's *The Human Phenomenon*, by Sarah Appleton-Weber, is to be published by Sussex Academic Press in September 1999.

16 *Ibid.*, p. 19.

17 *Ibid.*, p. 20.

18 R. J. Hoffman in L. Brown, B. C. Farr and R. J. Hoffman (eds) *Modern Spiritualities: An inquiry* (Amherst: New York: Prometheus Books, 1997), p. 10.

19 P. Morgan, "Reasons of the Heart" in Brown et al. *ibid.*, p. 110.

20 Kurtz, *The Transcendental Temptation*, p. 286.

21 *Ibid.*, p. xiv.

22 I. Cotton, *The Hallelujah Revolution: The rise of the new Christians* (Amherst, New York: Prometheus Books (1996), p. 38.

23 *Ibid.*, p. 42.

24 Firth, *Religion*, p. 14.

25 *Ibid.*, p. 16.

26 Kurtz, *Living without Religion*, p. 90.

27 H. Hawton, *The Humanist Revolution* (London: Barrie and Rockliff in association with the Pemberton Publishing Co. Ltd., 1963), p. 39.

28 *Ibid.*

29 H. L. Mencken in R. E. Greeley (ed.), *The Best of Humanism* (Buffalo, New York: Prometheus Books, 1988), p. 201.

30 Hawton, *The Humanist Revolution*, p. 4.

31 Karl Marx cited by R. Dunayerskaya, "Humanism and Marxism" in P. Kurtz (ed.) *The Humanist Alternative: Some definitions of Humanism* (Buffalo, New York: Prometheus Books, 1973), p. 153.

32 Bertrand Russell, *Why I Am Not A Christian* (London: Rationalist Press Association, 1983 reprint of 1927 edn), pp. 26–7.

33 C. Lofmark, *Does God Exist?* (London: Rationalist Press Association, 1990), p. 75.

34 I. Warraq, *Why I Am Not A Muslim* (Amherst, New York: Prometheus Books, 1995), p. 157.

35 Firth, *Religion*, p. 215.

36 See K. Armstrong, *A History of God* (London: Mandarin, 1996, first published 1993), p. 89.

37 Kurtz, *The Transcendental Temptation*, p. 87.

38 See J. Nickell, *Looking for a Miracle: Weeping icons, relics, stigmata, visions and healing cures* (Amherst, New York: Prometheus Books, 1993), pp. 134–6.
39 Warraq, *Why I Am Not A Muslim*, pp. 6– 7.
40 Lamont, *The Philosophy of Humanism* (1965), p. 183.
41 R. Helms, *Gospel Fictions* (Amherst, New York: Prometheus, 1988), p. 9.
42 For example, Luke's preference for Jerusalem as the place where Jesus' Resurrection appearances occur in contrast to Mark's earlier account of Galilee for the appearances. See G. A. Wells, *Who Was Jesus?* (La Salle, Illinois: Open Court, 1991 reprint of 1989 edn), p. 27.
43 See R. J. Hoffman (editor and translator), *The Secret Gospels: A harmony of apocryphal Jesus traditions* (Amherst, New York: Prometheus Books, 1996), p. 14 and *passim*.
44 M. Hooker, *The Gospel according to St Mark* (London: A&C. Black, 1993 reprint of 1991 edn), pp. 1–4.
45 Wells, *Who Was Jesus?*, p. 5.
46 See G. A. Wells, *The Historical Evidence for Jesus* (Buffalo, New York: Prometheus Books, 1982), p. 13.
47 Helms, *Gospel Fictions*, pp. 13–45.
48 *Ibid.*, p. 10.
49 See Hooker, *The Gospel according to St Mark*, p. 5.
50 The reader might well look at the papers arising from the First International Symposium on "Jesus and the Gospels" which took place in Ann Arbor, Michigan in April, 1985. These are edited by R. J. Hoffman and G. A. Larue under the title *Jesus in History and Myth* (Amherst, New York: Prometheus Books, 1986). G. A. Well's paper "The Historicity of Jesus" pp. 27–46, suggests that Jesus did not, in fact, exist. Morton Smith's paper that follows, pp. 47–54, argues for the acceptance of Jesus as a historical figure.
51 Hick, "A Remonstrance in Concluding" in Hoffman and Larue (eds), *Jesus in History and Myth*, p. 212.
52 *Ibid.*
53 *Ibid.*, p. 215.
54 All biblical references are from the Revised Standard Version.
55 A. Flew, *Atheistic Humanism* (Buffalo, New York: Prometheus Books, 1993), p. 73.
56 R. A. Sharpe, *The Moral Case against Religious Belief* (London: SCM, 1997), p. 61.
57 C. H. Dodd, *The Meaning of Paul for Today* (London and Glasgow: Fontana, 1960, first published 1920), p. 28.
58 M. Grant, *Saint Paul The Man* (London: Fount, 1976), p. 22.
59 *Ibid.*, p. 31.
60 See *Equality of the sexes* in chapter 5.
61 Cotton, *The Hallelujah Revolution*, p. 2.
62 *Ibid.*
63 See Nickell, *Looking for a Miracle*, p. 107, and references.
64 *Ibid.*, p. 109.
65 J. Herrick, *Against the Faith*, p. 235.

5 *Society*

1 Corliss Lamont, *The Philosophy of Humanism* (London: Barrie and Rockliff in association with the Pemberton Publishing Co. Ltd., 1965 reprint of 1949 edn), ninth principle, p. 14.
2 I use J. P. van Praag's analogy here, though I believe it is widely described in this way, *Foundations of Humanism* (Buffalo, New York: Prometheus Books, 1982), p. 169.
3 For example, D. Ehrenfeld, *The Arrogance of Humanism* (Oxford: Oxford University Press, 1981 reprint of 1978 edn), p. 228.
4 A. Bullock, *The Humanist Tradition in the West* (London: Thames and Hudson, 1985), p. 89.
5 *Ibid.*, p. 175.
6 H. J. Blackham, *The Future of Our Past: from ancient Greece to global village* (Amherst, New York: Prometheus Books, 1996), p. 310.
7 Van Praag, *Foundations of Humanism*, p. 63.
8 H. J. Blackham, *Humanism* (Harmondsworth: Penguin, 1968), p. 50.
9 Sir Julian Huxley, *The Humanist Frame* (London: George Allen & Unwin, 1962 impression of 1961 edn), p. 133.
10 T. Davies, *Humanism* (London: Routledge, 1997), p. 26.
11 Cited in M. Knight (ed.), *Humanist Anthology* (London: Rationalist Press Association, 1961), p. 13.
12 L. Saumur, *The Humanist Evangel* (Buffalo, New York: Prometheus Books, 1982), p. 79.
13 Bullock, *The Humanist Tradition in the West*, p. 185.
14 J. Carroll, *Humanism: The wreck of western culture* (London: Fontana Press, 1993), p. 23.
15 R. Fletcher, *A Definition of Humanism* (London: Rationalist Press Association, n.d.), p. 6.
16 See Lamont's fourth principle, *The Philosophy of Humanism*, p. 13.
17 P. Kurtz, "Humanism and Free Thought" in P. Kurtz and A. Dondeyne, *A Catholic/Humanist Dialogue: Humanists and Roman Catholics in a common world* (London: Pemberton and Buffalo, New York: Prometheus Books, 1972), p. 68.
18 C. Lamont, *Freedom of Choice Affirmed* (London: Pemberton Books, 1971, first published 1967), p. 175.
19 H. Hawton, *Controversy: The Humanist/Christian encounter* (London: Pemberton Books, 1971), p. 97.
20 See J. Parsons, *Population Fallacies* (London: Elek/Pemberton, 1977), p. 4.
21 J. Parsons, *Population versus Liberty* (London: Pemberton Books, 1971), p. 68.
22 Ehrenfeld, *The Arrogance of Humanism*, pp. 78–81.
23 A. H. Cantril, *Psychology, Humanism and Scientific Inquiry: The selected essays of Hadley Cantril* (New Brunswick, US and Oxford, UK: Transaction Books, 1988), p. 63.
24 Parsons, *Population versus Liberty*, p. 75.
25 *Ibid.*, p. 97.
26 Parsons, *Population Fallacies*, p. 4.
27 N. Walter, *Blasphemy: Ancient and modern* (London: Rationalist Press

Association, 1990).

28 I. Warraq, *Why I Am Not A Muslim* (Amherst, New York: Prometheus Books, 1995), p. 14.

29 Warraq cites the historian Professor Trevor-Roper's words here: "I wonder how Salman Rushdie is faring these days under the benevolent protection of the British law and British police, about whom he has been so rude. Not too comfortably I hope. . . . I would not shed a tear if some British Muslims, deploring his manners, should waylay him in a dark street and seek to improve them. If that should cause him thereafter to control his pen, society would benefit and literature would not suffer." From F. Halliday "The Fundamental Lesson of the Fatwa" in *New Statesman and Society*, 12 February 1993, cited in Warraq, *ibid.*, p. 9.

30 *Ibid.*, p. 173.

31 *Ibid.*, p. 174.

32 *Ibid.*, p. 321.

33 H. Hawton, *The Humanist Revolution* (London: Barrie and Rockliff in association with the Pemberton Publishing Co. Ltd., 1963), p. 119.

34 Over a decade ago, when I sought information from the British Humanist Association in order to prepare material for the introduction of a Humanism course at Higher Education level, every communication had been opened before it arrived in my post. Happily, this state of affairs does not seem to obtain currently – unless there are more devious ways of scrutinizing mail!

35 Paul Potts in *To Keep a Promise*, 1970, pp. 117–18, cited by Parsons, *Population versus Liberty*, p. 378.

36 Warraq, *Why I am Not A Muslim*, p. 356.

37 See A. Flew, *Atheistic Humanism* (Buffalo, New York: Prometheus Books, 1993), p. 278.

38 A. Flew, *The Politics of Procrustes: Contradictions of enforced equality* (Buffalo, New York: Prometheus Books, 1981), p. 24.

39 *Ibid.*, p. 45.

40 B. Williams, *Problems of the Self* (Cambridge: Cambridge University Press, 1995 reprint of 1973 edn), p. 245.

41 Contra Flew, *The Politics of Procrustes*, p. 53.

42 A. Flew, *Philosophy: An introduction* (Buffalo, New York: Prometheus Books, 1980), p. 175.

43 M. Knight, *Honest to Man* (London: Pemberton, 1974), p. 121.

44 M. Grant, *Saint Paul The Man* (London: Fount, 1976), p. 25.

45 Ibn Warraq gives a very graphic account of the present situation regarding women in orthodox Islamic states: see *Why I Am Not A Muslim*, chapter 14 "Women in Islam", *passim*, but particularly, pp. 322–6.

46 I. Kulshreshtha, *The War against Gender Bias* (New Delhi: Sterling Publishers Private Ltd., 1993).

47 *Ibid.*, p. 60.

48 T. Davies, *Humanism* (London and New York: Routledge, 1997), p. 99.

49 Dora Russell's autobiography *The Tamarisk Tree: My quest for liberty and love* (London: Elek/Pemberton, 1975) captures the spirit of woman's struggle for emancipation. See also E. Royston Pike's chapter "I Plead for my Sex" on Mary Wollstonecraft and the origins of the Women's

Movement, and "Rebels in the Drawing Room" on Barbara Bodichon and the emancipation of Victorian women, both in *Pioneers of Social Change* (London: Barrie & Rockliff in association with Pemberton Publishing Co. Ltd., 1963).

50 In deriding the use of such sexist language to a group of students many years ago, one thoughtful student inquired what objection I would have to the use of the word "manhole"!

51 C. Gilligan, *In A Different Voice: Psychological theory and women's development* (Cambridge, Massachusetts, and London: Harvard University Press, 1982), p. 172.

52 Polly Toynbee, *Radio Times* 24–30 June, 1995, p. 16.

53 *Ibid.*

54 Bullock, *The Humanist Tradition in the West*, p. 156.

55 R. Dawkins, *Viruses of the Mind*, the 1992 Voltaire Lecture (London: British Humanist Association, 1992), p. 1.

56 From S. Freud, *The Future of an Illusion*, 1927, cited in Knight, *Humanist Anthology*, p. 91.

57 The fact is now becoming recognized by Local Education Authorities in Britain. The current policies of some such Authorities is to impede early retirement of headteachers who have been diagnosed as having severe stress-related illness, by putting them back into the classrooom to teach!

58 P. Kurtz, *The Transcendental Temptation: A critique of religion and the paranormal* (Amherst, New York: Prometheus Books, 1991), p. 5.

59 P. Kurtz, *Forbidden Fruit: The ethics of Humanism* (Buffalo, New York: Prometheus Books, 1988), p. 158.

60 Government Circular 10/94 *Religious Education and Collective Worship* (1994).

61 The Humanist Society of Scotland, *The Challenge of Secular Humanism.*

62 The patterns painted on the hands and feet of a bride before her marriage.

63 T. Hyland, *Competence, Education and NVQs* (London: Cassell Education, 1994), p. 123.

64 R. Dale, *Towards a New Vocationalism* (Milton Keynes: Open University: Pergamon Press, 1985), p. 7.

65 S. Fletcher, *Competence-Based Assessment Techniques* (London: Kegan Paul, 1992), p. 74.

66 Bullock, *The Humanist Tradition in the West*, p. 188.

67 Faced with a rise of the influence of religious groups in the sphere of politics, however, in a recent editorial article in the US journal *Free Inquiry*, Paul Kurtz spoke of "a compelling need today to develop *a new humanist political agenda*" (vol. 18 no. 4 (1998): 5). And this political agenda, Kurtz believes, could include fundamental issues with which many – indeed most – secular Humanists would be concerned. He names many of these – secularism; separation of church and state; freedom of conscience; an open, democratic society; human freedom; world community; narrowing the gap between rich and poor; planetary ecology and preservation; population control; a global ethic. This is certainly a Humanist *stance* for life!

68 Lamont, *The Philosophy of Humanism*, p. 15.

69 *Ibid.*, p. 88.

70   H. J. Blackham, "Demands of an Open Society" in Kurtz and Dondeyne, *A Catholic Humanist Dialogue*, p. 18.
71   P. Kurtz, *In Defense of Secular Humanism* (Buffalo, New York: Prometheus Books, 1983), p. 28.
72   Jean-Paul Sartre, *Existentialism and Humanism* (London: Methuen, 1980 reprint of 1948 edn), p. 47.
73   *Ibid.*, p. 55.
74   Kurtz, *In Defense of Secular Humanism*, p. 28.
75   B. Russell, *What I Believe* (London: Kegan Paul, Trench, Trubner & Co., Ltd. and New York: E. P. Dutton & Company, 1925), p. 28.
76   P. Kurtz, *Living without Religion: Eupraxophy* (Amherst, New York: Prometheus Books, 1994), p. 41.
77   Carroll, *Humanism*, p. 228.
78   From *Life on Earth*, 1979, cited in Knight (ed.), *Humanist Anthology*, pp. 144–5.
79   K. Martin "Is Humanism Utopian?" in H. J. Blackham, K. Martin, R. Hepburn and K. Nott, *Objections to Humanism* (Harmondsworth: Penguin, 1967, first published 1963), p. 101.
80   Van Praag, *Foundations of Humanism*, p. 168.

6   *Morality*

1   C. Lamont, *The Philosophy of Humanism* (London: Barrie and Rockliff in association with the Pemberton Publishing Co. Ltd., 1965 reprint of 1949 edn), fifth principle, p. 13.
2   See, for example, J. Fletcher "Humanist Ethics: The groundwork" in M. B. Storer (ed.), *Humanist Ethics: Dialogue on basics* (Buffalo, New York: Prometheus Books, 1980), p. 253.
3   See I. Frolov, *Man, Science, Humanism: A new synthesis* (Buffalo, New York: Prometheus Books, 1990), p. 161, who cites the words of E. O. Wilson as one who accepts that "the time has come for ethics to be removed temporarily from the hands of the philosophers and biologicized". (*Sociobiology: Beyond nature/nurture? Reports, definitions and debate*, edited by G. W. Barlow and J. Silverberg [Boulder, Colorado: Westview Press, 1980], p. 562). Frolov gives a good synopsis of sociobiological reductionism on pp. 158–65.
4   R. Dawkins, *The Selfish Gene* (Oxford: Oxford University Press, second edn, 1989).
5   See the introduction to R. Dawkins *Viruses of the Mind* written by Dr Harry Stopes-Roe (The 1992 Voltaire Lecture, London: British Humanist Association) p. *i*.
6   R. Bellah, *Beyond Belief: Essays on religion in a post-traditional world* (New York: Harper and Row, 1970), pp. 168–86, cited in K. Nielsen, *Ethics without God* (Buffalo, New York: Prometheus Books, revised edn 1990).
7   So, B. Smoker, *Humanism* (London: National Secular Society, 1984), p. 38.
8   M. Hocutt, "Toward an Ethic of Mutual Accommodation" in Storer (ed.), *Humanist Ethics*, p. 137.
9   K. Nielsen, *Philosophy and Atheism* (Buffalo, New York: Prometheus Books, 1985), p. 166.

10 Hocutt, "Toward an Ethic of Mutual Accommodation", in Storer (ed.), *Humanistic Ethics*, p. 138.

11 H. W. Schneider, "Humanist Ethics" in Storer (ed.), *Humanist Ethics*, p. 100.

12 Frolov, *Man, Science, Humanism*, p. 157.

13 See Frolov, *ibid.*, p. 158.

14 For a detailed article on the role of narrative in the formation of ethical life, see W. A. Barbieri, Jr. "Ethics and the Narrated Life", *The Journal of Religion*, vol. 78 (1998): pp. 361–86. Barbieri concludes, however, that a personal ethic is constantly being changed and deepened to the point of an ultimate religious morality. There is no reason why any depth of moral thought has to be religious as opposed to secular.

15 There is much evidence to suggest that unselfish behaviour, care, protectiveness and so on, are present in some forms of both animal and bird life, but *ethical* inquiry here is obviously absent.

16 J. Hemming, *Individual Morality* (London: Nelson, 1969).

17 *Ibid.*, p. 136.

18 *Ibid.*, pp. 136–7.

19 *Ibid.*, p. 138.

20 *Ibid.*

21 *Ibid.*, p. 140.

22 B. Williams, *Problems of the Self* (Cambridge: Cambridge University Press, 1995 reprint of 1973 edn), p. 178.

23 A. Atkinson, *The Cosmic Fairy: The new challenge of a Darwinian approach to Humanism* (Gerrards Cross: Colin Smythe Ltd., 1996), p. 32.

24 Nielsen, *Ethics without God*, p. 206.

25 See J. Carroll, *Humanism: The wreck of western culture* (London: Fontana Press, 1993), p. 56.

26 B. Russell, *What I Believe* (London: Kegan Paul, Trench, Trubner & Co. Ltd. and New York: E. P. Dutton & Co., 1925), p. 46.

27 Hemming, *Individual Morality*, p. 19.

28 V. M. Tarkunde "Towards a Fuller Consensus in Humanistic Ethics" in Storer (ed.), *Humanist Ethics*, p. 155.

29 R. A. Sharpe, *The Moral Case against Religious Belief* (London: SCM, 1997), p. 66.

30 H. Hawton, *The Humanist Revolution* (London: Barrie and Rockliff in association with the Pemberton Publishing Company Ltd., 1963), p. 83.

31 A point attacked by Bernard Crick in *Crime, Rape and Gin: Reflections on contemporary attitudes to violence, pornography and addiction* (London: Elek/Pemberton, 1974), p. 13.

32 Hemming, *Individual Morality*, p. 79.

33 L. Nisbet, "Kulturkampf" in Storer (ed.), *Humanist Ethics*, p. 246.

34 M. Storer, "A Factual Investigation of the Foundations of Morality" in Storer (ed.), *ibid.*, p. 284.

35 A. H. Cantril, *Psychology, Humanism and Scientific Inquiry: The selected essays of Hadley Cantril* (New Brunswick, US and Oxford: Transaction Books, 1988), p. 104.

36 *Ibid.*, p. 105.

37 A. Flew, *Evolutionary Ethics* (London: Macmillan, 1967), p. 55.

38 See P. Kurtz, *In Defense of Secular Humanism* (Buffalo, New York: Prometheus Books, 1983), pp. 33–8.

39 P. Kurtz, *Forbidden Fruit: The ethics of Humanism* (Buffalo, New York: Prometheus Books, 1988), p. 15.

40 Hawton, *The Humanist Revolution,* pp. 84–5.

41 See Sharpe, *The Moral Case against Religious Belief,* p. 2 and *passim.*

42 See M. Knight, "Morality – Supernatural or Social?" in A. J. Ayer (ed.), *The Humanist Outlook* (London: Pemberton in association with Barrie and Rockliff, 1968), p. 51.

43 See E. Rivkin "Building a Biblical Foundation for Contemporary Ethics" in R.J. Hoffman and G. A. Larue (eds), *Biblical v. Secular Ethics: The conflict* (Buffalo, New York: Prometheus Books, 1988), p. 104.

44 See Rivkin, *ibid.*, p. 99.

45 See J. Hall "Two Kinds of Rights" in Hoffman and Larue (eds), *Biblical v Secular Ethics,* p. 125.

46 Carroll, *Humanism,* pp. 76–7.

47 C. Lofmark, *What is the Bible?* (London: Rationalist Press Association, 1990), p. 55.

48 *Ibid.*, p. 56.

49 G. A. Wells, *The Historical Evidence for Jesus* (Buffalo, New York: Prometheus Books, 1982), p. 203.

50 G. Smith, *Atheism: The case against God* (Buffalo, New York: Prometheus Books, 1989), p. 166.

51 Sharpe, *The Moral Case against Religious Belief,* p. 5.

52 British Broadcasting Corporation Television, Summer 1998, presenter Robert Winston.

53 Jean-Paul Sartre, *Existentialism and Humanism* (London: Methuen, 1997 reprint of 1980 edn, first published 1948), p. 33.

54 On this point see further Nielsen, *Philosophy and Atheism,* p. 177, and the same author in "Ethics without God" in J. P. Moreland and K. Nielsen, *Does God Exist? The debate between theists and atheists* (Amherst, New York: Prometheus Books, 1994), p. 99.

55 G. Stein, *A Second Anthology of Atheism and Rationalism* (Buffalo, New York: Prometheus Books, 1987), p. 389.

56 Hemming, *Individual Morality,* p. 26.

57 Fletcher "Humanistic Ethics: The groundwork" in Storer (ed.), *Humanist Ethics,* p. 259.

58 See J. Fletcher, *Situation Ethics* (London: SCM Press Ltd., 1970 impression of 1966 edn), chapter four.

59 I rely here on many of the examples cited by Fletcher, *Situation Ethics.*

60 See Smoker, *Humanism,* p. 40.

61 Nielsen, "Ethics without God" in Moreland and Nielsen, *Does God Exist?* p. 105.

62 P. Kurtz, *Living without Religion: Eupraxophy* (Amherst, New York: Prometheus Books, 1994), p. 38.

63 R. Osborn, *Humanism and Moral Theory: A psychological and social inquiry* (London: Pemberton, second edn 1970, first published 1959), p. 96.

64 J. P. van Praag, *Foundations of Humanism* (Buffalo, New York: Prometheus Books, 1982), p. 86.

65 M. Knight, *Morals without Religion and other Essays* (London: Dennis Dobson, 1960 impression, first published 1955), p. 33.

66 Hemming, *Individual Morality*, p. 191.

67 V. M. Tarkunde, "Towards a Fuller Consensus in Humanistic Ethics" in Storer (ed.), *Humanist Ethics*, p. 158.

68 Hemming, *Individual Morality*, p. 148.

69 Cited in R. E. Greeley, *The Best of Humanism* (Buffalo, New York: Prometheus Books, 1988), pp. 131–2.

7 *Rationalism and Reason*

1 C. Lamont, *The Philosophy of Humanism* (London: Barrie and Rockliff in association with the Pemberton Publishing Co. Ltd., 1965 reprint of 1949 edn), tenth principle, p. 14.

2 H. Hawton, *The Humanist Revolution* (London: Barrie and Rockliff in association with the Pemberton Publishing Co. Ltd., 1963), p. 127.

3 P. Kurtz, *In Defense of Secular Humanism* (Buffalo, New York: Prometheus Books, 1983), p. 217.

4 P. Kurtz, *Living without Religion: Eupraxophy* (Amherst, New York: Prometheus Books, 1994), p. 27.

5 P. Kurtz, *The Transcendental Temptation: A critique of religion and the paranormal* (Amherst, New York: Prometheus Books, 1991), p. 49.

6 A. Einstein, "Science and Religion" (1941), reprinted in *Out of My Later Years* (1950) cited in M. Knight (ed.), *Humanist Anthology* (London: Rationalist Press Association, 1961), p. 120.

7 Hawton, *The Humanist Revolution*, p. 135.

8 R. Fletcher, *A Definition of Humanism* (London: Rationalist Press Association, n.d.) p. 4.

9 J. Herrick, *Against the Faith: Some deists, sceptics and atheists* (London: Glover and Blair Ltd., 1985), p. 17.

10 C. Watts, "The Meaning of Rationalism" in G. Stein, *An Anthology of Atheism and Rationalism* (Buffalo, New York: Prometheus Books, 1980), p. 24.

11 D. Ehrenfeld, *The Arrogance of Humanism* (Oxford: Oxford University Press, 1981, first published 1978), p. 146.

12 K. Nielsen, *Philosophy and Atheism* (Buffalo, New York: Prometheus Books, 1985), pp. 194–5.

13 Carroll, *Humanism*, p. 119.

14 Hawton, *The Humanist Revolution*, p. 144.

15 Carroll, *Humanism*, p. 150.

16 See, for example Ehrenfeld, *the Arrogance of Humanism*, p. 174.

17 R. Fletcher, *A Definition of Humanism*, p. 8.

18 T. Davies, *Humanism* (London: Routledge, 1997), p. 51.

19 Paul Henri Thiry d'Holbach, cited in R. E. Greeley (ed.), *The Best of Humanism* (Buffalo, New York: Prometheus Books, 1988), p. 27.

20 R. A. Sharpe, *The Moral Case against Religious Belief* (London: SCM, 1977), p. 48.

21 G. H. Smith, *Atheism: The case against God* (Buffalo, New York: Prometheus Books, 1989, first published 1979), p. 101.

22 *Ibid.*, p. 107.
23 M. Ruse, "Pro Judice" in M. Ruse (ed.), *But is it Science? The philosophical question in the creation/evolution controversy* (Buffalo, New York: Prometheus Books, 1988), p. 359.
24 A. Bullock, *The Humanist Tradition in the West* (London: Thames and Hudson, 1985), p. 90.
25 F. H. George, *Computers, Science and Society* (London: Pemberton Publishing Company, 1970), p. 15.
26 P. L. Quinn, "The Philosopher of Science as Expert Witness" in Ruse (ed.), *But is it Science?* p. 368.
27 Kurtz, *In Defense of Secular Humanism*, p. 107.
28 See R. A. Hinde, *Religion and Darwinism*, the Voltaire Lecture, 9 December 1997 (London: British Humanist Society), p. 21.
29 Carroll, *Humanism*, p. 145.
30 Sir Julian Huxley, *Evolutionary Humanism* (Buffalo, New York: Prometheus Books, 1992, first published 1964), p. 254.
31 *Ibid.*, p. 252.
32 So, Ehrenfeld, *The Arrogance of Humanism*, p. 5, and J. E. Smith, *Quasi-Religions: Humanism, Marxism and Nationalism* (Basingstoke and London: Macmillan, 1994), p. 25.
33 Bullock, *The Humanist Tradition in the West*, p. 166.
34 *Ibid.*, p. 167.
35 *Ibid.*, p. 170.
36 R. Fletcher, *A Definition of Humanism*, p. 9.
37 A. Emerson and C. Forbes, *The Invasion of the Computer Culture* (Leicester: Inter Varsity Press, 1989), p. 171.
38 Quinn, "The Philosopher of Science as Expert Witness", in Ruse (ed.), *But is it Science?*, p. 367.
39 Fletcher, *A Definition of Humanism*, p. 8.
40 See Kurtz, *In Defense of Secular Humanism*, p. 213.
41 R. Brain, "Body, Brain, Mind and Soul" in J. Huxley (ed.), *The Humanist Frame* (London: George Allen and Unwin Ltd., 1962 impression of 1961 edn), p. 62.
42 M. Ruse, "Is There a Limit to Our Knowledge of Evolution?" in Ruse (ed.), *But Is It Science?* p. 117.
43 B. Russell, *What I Believe* (London: Kegan Paul, Trench, Trubner and Company, Ltd., 1925), p. 87.
44 T. Hines, *Pseudoscience and the Paranormal: A critical examination of the evidence* (Buffalo, New York: Prometheus Books, 1988), p. 6.
45 *Ibid.*, p. 7.
46 Kurtz, *In Defense of Secular Humanism*, p. 223.
47 *Ibid.*, p. 243.
48 Arthur Wakefield Slaten, cited in Greeley (ed.), *The Best of Humanism*, p. 153.

8 *Some Life and Death Issues*

1 I. Frolov, *Man, Science, Humanism: A New Synthesis* (Buffalo, New York: Prometheus Books, 1990), p. 207. See also Frolov's extensive discussion

of genetic engineering, pp. 206–38.

2　R. Chadwick, "The Philosophy of the Right to Know and the Right Not To Know" in R. Chadwick, M. Levitt and D. Shickle (eds), *The Right To Know and the Right Not To Know* (Aldershot: Avebury, 1997), p. 14.

3　P. Toynbee *Radio Times*, 27 January–2 February, 1996, p. 12.

4　Chadwick, Levitt and Shickle, *The Right To Know and the Right Not To Know*.

5　J. Husted, "Autonomy and the Right Not to Know" in Chadwick et al. *ibid.*

6　*Ibid.*, p. 63.

7　The surrogate mother's husband or partner is the legal father unless he objected to the surrogacy. If a surrogate mother has no husband or partner, the *intended* father is the legal father as long as implantation did not take place in a licensed clinic: in this last case, the child would be legally fatherless.

8　See the statement by Dr V. Bolton, Professor G. Dawes, Dr A. McLaren, Professor Sir H. Bondi and Dr H. Stopes-Roe, *Pre-Embryo Research* (London: British Humanist Association).

9　See D. Lamb, *Death, Brain Death and Ethics* (Aldershot: Avebury, 1996), p. 112.

10　P. Toynbee, *Radio Times*, 13–19 March 1993, p. 20.

11　Lamb, *Death, Brain Death and Ethics*, p. 107.

12　*Report on the Working of the Abortion Act* (The Lane Inquiry) chairperson The Hon. Mrs Justice Lane, DBE (London: HMSO, 1974, 1.609).

13　Ancient civilizations such as China, India, Egypt, Greece and Rome are known to have had various concoctions for terminating unwanted pregnancies.

14　Figures are for 1997 from the Office for National Statistics Monitors AB 98/3 & 4.

15　*Ibid.*

16　Information supplied by the British Pregnancy Advisory Service, who suggest that increased awareness of contraception methods, as well as the decreasing number of women of fertile age, are factors in this decline.

17　See Abortion Law Reform Association (ALRA) *ALRA Newsletter*, vol. 71 (1998): 2.

18　A Harris opinion poll published in April 1998 asked the public the question: "Should a pregnant woman be able to decide for herself whether to have an abortion in the first three months of pregnancy?" From the sample of 1762 adults in Britain personally interviewed 77% replied "Yes" (of which 81% were women and 72% were men) 12% replied "No" and 11% "Don't know". Statistics are from ALRA.

19　See A. Furedi and M. Hume (eds), *Abortion Law Reformers: Pioneers of change*, interview with Peter Diggory (London: Birth Control Trust, 1997), p. 48.

20　Thomas Aquinas, for example, believed that abortion was acceptable until the child "quickened" in the womb.

21　Information supplied by the British Pregnancy Advisory Service.

22　*Report on the Working of the Abortion Act*, 1.603.

23　*Ibid.*, 1.190 and 1.191.

24 *Ibid.*, 1.601.
25 *Ibid.*, 1.602.
26 Figures are for 1995. Abortion Law Reform Association, *A Report on NHS Abortion Services* (London: Reform Association, 1997). Figures for 1996 according to Voice for Choice claim 97% for Tees, and a rise in provision by North West Lancashire to 36%, a percentage that is now 2% higher than Redbridge and Waltham Forest which has the worst NHS provision in England and Wales.
27 ALRA, *ibid.*, p. 10.
28 *Ibid.*, p. 15.
29 Kate Paterson, in an address given at the launch of the Voice for Choice Campaign and the All-Party Pro-Choice Group, 27 April, 1998. At the same meeting, Lord Hunt described getting an NHS abortion as a "lottery dependent upon where a woman lives". Compare the words of the Lane Committee, "we have been told by doctors in some parts of the country that the only treatment available there for women requesting abortion lies in the private sector"(1.400).
30 See R. Walley, "A Question of Conscience" in *The British Medical Journal*, June, 1976.
31 *Report on the Working of the Abortion Act*, III p. 35.
32 Sweden, Netherlands, Austria, Denmark, Italy, Greece, Germany, France, Belgium and Finland.
33 F. Kissling, "Catholic Care Unhealthy for Women", *Free Inquiry*, vol. 18, no. 4 (1998): 14–15.
34 "Final Word on Fetal Pain" in *ALRA Newsletter* vol. 71 (1998): 3.
35 *Report on the Working of the Abortion Act*, 1.17.
36 Furedi and Hume, "Diane Munday" in *Abortion Law Reformers*, p. 18.
37 P. Kurtz, *Forbidden Fruit: The ethics of Humanism* (Buffalo, New York: Prometheus Books, 1988), p. 215.
38 Furedi and Hume, "Diane Munday" in *Abortion Law Reformers*, p. 20.
39 *Report on the Working of the Abortion Act* 1.166.
40 Abortion Law Reform Association, *A Report on NHS Abortion Services* (London: 1997).
41 I am particularly grateful to ALRA, Voice for Choice and the BPAS for the information supplied for the research of this present chapter. Those requiring further information can write to ALRA, 11–13 Charlotte Street, London W1P 1HD; tel. 0171 6377264; Voice for Choice at the same address, tel. 0171 6364619; fax 0171 4369011; BPAS Austy Manor, Wootton Wawen, Solihull, West Midlands, B95 6BX; tel. 10564 793225; fax 011564 794935, website www.bpas.demon.co.uk
42 I am grateful to the Society for the Protection of Unborn Children (SPUC) for the information they have supplied for this research in connection with the anti-abortion agenda. Those wishing further information can write to SPUC, Head Office, Phyllis Bowman House, 5/6 St. Matthew Street, London SW1P 2JT; tel. 0171–222 5845; fax 0171 222 0630.
43 The foetus is turned in the womb and surgically removed feet first. When the head is still concealed, the brain is destroyed by suction.
44 P. McCullagh, *Fetal Sentience* (London: The All-Party Parliamentary Pro-Life Group, 1996).

45 *Ibid.*, p. 11.
46 SPUC, *The Abortion Threat to Northern Ireland Intensified: Protecting our young from Brook Advisory Centres* (Belfast: SPUC, revised edn 1991), p. 2.
47 L. B. Francke, *The Ambivalence of Abortion* (Harmondsworth: Penguin, 1980, first published 1978), pp. 256–7.
48 See The Voluntary Euthanasia Society, *The Last Right: The need for voluntary euthanasia*.
49 I am grateful to both these societies for their help in the research for this section. Those requiring further information should write to The Voluntary Euthanasia Society, 13 Prince of Wales Terrace, London W8 5PG; tel. 0171 937 7770; fax. 0171 376 2684; e-mail ves.london@dial.pipex.com Internet http://www.euthanasia.org and the Scottish Voluntary Euthanasia Society, 17 Hart Street, Edinburgh EH1 3RN; tel. 0131 556 4404; fax. 0131 557 4403; e-mail vess@euthanasia.org Internet, http://www.euthanasia.org
50 VES, *The Last Right*, p. 7.
51 The British Humanist Association briefing paper *Voluntary Euthanasia*.
52 VESS, *Your Questions Answered* (Edinburgh: Voluntary Euthanasia Society of Scotland, 1997), p. 1.
53 Many old people questioned on this point feel that it would be their main reason for requesting to die, see W. C. Alvarez, "The Right to Die" in M. D. Visscher (ed.), *Humanistic Perspectives in Medical Ethics* (Buffalo, New York: Prometheus Books, 1972), p. 67. This is surely a *pressurized* reason for euthanasia?
54 See The Society for the Protection of Unborn Children *Beyond Autonomy* submitted to the Lord Chancellor's Department in response to the Green Paper *Who Decides? Making decisions on behalf of mentally incapacitated adults*.
55 Those requiring further information should write to The Human Rights Society, Mariners Head, Cley, Near Holt, Norfolk, NR25 7RX; tel. and fax. 01263 740404.
56 VESS, *Cases in History: People whose deaths have helped to change history* (Edinburgh: The Voluntary Euthanasia Society of Scotland, 1995).

9 Rites and Ceremonies

1 See Jane Wynne Willson's three publications, *New Arrivals: A practical guide to non-religious naming ceremonies* (London: British Humanist Association, 1995 fourth, extended edn, first published 1989), *Sharing the Future: A practical guide to non-religious wedding ceremonies* (London: British Humanist Association, 1996 fourth, extended edn, first published 1988) and *Funerals without God: A practical guide to non-religious funeral ceremonies* (London: British Humanist Association, fourth edn 1995, first published 1989). A new edition of the first of these, entitled *New Arrivals: Non-religious baby namings*, came into print very recently (1999), unfortunately too late for use in this book. All references, therefore, are to the 1995 edition.
2 Wynne Willson, *New Arrivals*, p. 21.
3 *Ibid.*, p. 8.

4 *Ibid.*, p. 15.
5 The reader is directed to the numerous examples in Wynne Willson's *New Arrivals*.
6 Gerald Rose – humanitarian, humorist and writer of short stories; Newport, South Wales.
7 See, for example, F. Brown, S. R. Driver and C. A. Briggs, *Hebrew and English Lexicon of the Old Testament* (Oxford: Clarendon Press, 1972 reprint, first published 1907), pp. 659–61.
8 *The Concise Oxford Dictionary* (Oxford: Clarendon Press, ninth edn, 1995), p. 1328.
9 See *Matthew* 12:18, *John* 12:27, *Romans* 2:9, *Revelation* 18:14).
10 *Collected Poems and Plays of Rabindranath Tagore* (London: Macmillan, 1983 reprint of 1936 edn), p. 58.
11 *Ibid.*
12 *Ibid.*, p. 84.
13 Wynne Willson, *New Arrivals*, p. 17.
14 *Ibid.*, p. 18.
15 *Ibid.*
16 Cited in C. Lamont, *A Humanist Wedding Service* (Buffalo, New York: Prometheus Books, 1972 third, revised edn), p. 27. The whole piece is reproduced widely on posters.
17 *The Poetical Works of Longfellow* (London, New York and Toronto: Oxford University Press, 1907), p. 126.
18 For example the *Bar Mitzvah* of Orthodox Judaism.
19 Actually, all marriages in Britain are civil contracts in that it is the signing of the register in front of witnesses that joins a couple in matrimony. Unless the register is signed even a church wedding is invalid. It is, thus, not religious vows that constitute matrimony but the civil contract.
20 For those who might wish to plan their own wedding ceremony and yet have it registered, a Unitarian minister or a university chaplain might be prepared to conduct such a ceremony. Even though the wedding would be performed by a religious celebrant, some such celebrants might well agree to a secular ceremony. Such cases are, however, rare.
21 J. Wynne Willson, *To Love and to Cherish: A guide to non-religious wedding ceremonies* (London: British Humanist Association, 1989 edn, first published 1988), p. 14. This booklet has now been revised as *Sharing the Future*.
22 Cited in Wynne Willson, *Sharing the Future*, pp. 62–3.
23 At the 1990 annual general meeting of the BHA, the following motion was carried unanimously: "This AGM reaffirms its support for the rights of lesbians and gay men. It deplores the hostility directed against them, particularly from religious sources and the tabloid press. It calls on the Humanist movement and individuals to do everything possible to counter such hostility and to promote lesbian and gay rights as human rights." *Humanity*, 5 (1998): 7.
24 Cited in Wynne Willson, *Sharing the Future*, p. 63.
25 See V. L. Bullough, "Why Same-Sex Marriages" (*sic*), *Free Inquiry*, vol. 18, no. 1 (1997): 49–50.
26 Cited in Wynne Willson, *Sharing the Future*, p. 31.

27 Teresa Green, University of Wales College, Newport (UWCN) 1992.

28 Cited in Wynne Willson, *Sharing the Future*, p. 34.

29 Claire Temby, Tracey Fawcett, Helen Watkins and Nicola Coates, UWCN 1995.

30 Cited in Wynne Willson, *To Love and to Cherish*, p. 14.

31 Cited in Wynne Willson, *Sharing the Future*, p. 18. If these words ever originally had a religious connotation, they need not be so interpreted here.

32 Lamont, *A Humanist Wedding Service*, p. 4.

33 *Ibid.*, p. 5.

34 A succinct summary of the legal problems for unmarried couples can be found in Wynne Willson, *Sharing the Future*, pp. 66–7.

35 The British Humanist Association in conjunction with the Rationalist Press Association expect to publish a compilation of poems and readings suitable for non-religious ceremonies. The publication, *Making the Occasion: Poems and prose for Humanist ceremonies*, is being compiled by Nigel Collins and edited by Jim Herrick and John Pearce.

36 Tagore, *Collected Poems and Plays*, p. 255.

37 *Ibid.*, p. 278.

38 Published by James Cradock, 1978.

39 Tanya is now better known by her married name, Tanya Blanchard.

40 Frank Yerby, from *American Negro Poetry*, ed. Arna Bontemps (New York: Hill and Wang, 1974).

41 Sarah Balfour, UWCN 1993.

42 Cited in Wynne Willson, *Sharing the Future*, p. 16.

43 C. Lamont, *A Humanist Funeral Service* (Buffalo, New York: Prometheus Books, 1977 reprint of 1954 edn), p. 15.

44 See W. McIlroy, *Foundations of Modern Humanism* (Sheffield: Sheffield Humanist Society, 1995), p. 8.

45 In 1966, the ban on Roman Catholic priests leading cremation was lifted.

46 See Wynne Willson, *Funerals without God*, p. 85.

47 Those interested should contact the Natural Death Centre, 20 Heber Road, Cricklewood, London NW2 6AA.

48 The British Humanist Association is one Humanist organization that certainly recommends this latter position.

49 The British Humanist Association has a national network of such officiants. They are organized into eight regions.

50 Wynne Willson, *Funerals without God* (1989 edn), p. 17.

51 Adapted from Herbert Read, and cited in Wynne Willson, *Funerals without God*, pp. 38–9.

52 Cited by Wynne Willson, *ibid.*, p. 24.

53 Susan Williams, UWCN 1995.

54 These words of Canon Scott Holland were apparently part of a longer sermon. They are words now produced widely on posters and cards, and have been adopted by religious and secular individuals to be read at funerals.

55 From *Fall: A Collection of the Poems of Tanya Ward-Jones*.

56 Ewan MacColl, excerpt from "The Manchester Hikers' Song".

57 Of particular interest to the reader might be the selection by Jane Wynne

Willson in *Funerals without God, passim.*
58 Tagore, *Collected Poems and Plays*, p. 262.
59 *Ibid.*, pp. 128–9.
60 Rossetti, *Poems* (London and New York: Macmillan & Co., 1892).
61 The "silent land" here, can be understood as the ultimate cessation of life.
62 Rossetti, *Poems*, p. 105.
63 Percy Bysshe Shelley, extract from *Adonais, Selected Poems of Percy Bysshe Shelley*, London: Oxford University Press, 1929 reprint of 1913 edn, p. 328.
64 *Poems: by William Ernest Henley* (London: Macmillan and Co. 1921).
65 Cited in Wynne Willson, *Funerals without God*, p. 56.
66 Tracy Card, UWCN 1996.
67 Samantha Day, UWCN 1996.
68 Linda Watkins, UWCN 1996.
69 Lamont, *A Humanist Funeral Service*, p. 14.

Bibliography

Abortion Law Reform Association, 1997: *A Report on NHS Abortion Services*. London: Reform Association.

Amery, J. (edited and translated by Sidney Rosenfeld and Stella P. Rosenfeld) 1984: *Radical Humanism*. Bloomington: Indiana University Press.

Armstrong, K. 1996 (reprint of 1994 edn, first published 1993): *A History of God*. London: Mandarin.

Ashby, R. (n.d.): *Problems with Arguments for the Existence of God*. London: British Humanist Association.

Ashby, R. 1998: "The Spiritual Experience". In *Humanity*, vol. 6, pp. 8–10.

Atkinson, A. 1997: *The Cosmic Fairy: The new challenge of a Darwinian approach to Humanism*. Gerrards Cross: Colin Smythe Ltd.

Ayer, A. J. (ed.), 1968: *The Humanist Outlook*. London: Pemberton in association with Barrie and Rockliff.

Berman, A. 1988: *A History of Atheism in Britain: from Hobbes to Russell*. London, New York, Sydney: Croom Helm.

Blackham, H. J. 1968: *Humanism*. Harmondsworth: Pelican.

Blackham, H. J. (edited by Barbara Smoker) 1996: *The Future of Our Past: from Ancient Rome to Global Village*. Amherst, New York: Prometheus Books.

Brown, L., Farr, B. C. and Hoffman, J. (eds) 1996: *Modern Spiritualities: An inquiry*. Amherst, New York: Prometheus Books .

Bullock, A. 1985: *The Humanist Tradition in the West*. London: Thames and Hudson.

Bullough, V. L. 1997: "Why Same-Sex Marriages" (*sic*). In *Free Inquiry*, vol. 18, no. 1, pp. 49–50.

Burke, P. 1990: "The Spread of Italian Humanism". In A. Goodman and A. Mackay (eds), *The Impact of Humanism on Western Europe*. Harlow and New York: Longman, pp. 1–22.

Cantril, A. H. (ed.) 1988: *Psychology, Humanism and Scientific Enquiry: The selected essays of Hadley Cantril*. New Brunswick and Oxford: Transaction Books.

Carroll, J. 1993: *Humanism: The wreck of western culture*. London: Fontana.

Chadwick, R. 1997: "The Philosophy of the Right to Know and the Right Not to Know". In R. Chadwick, M. Levitt and D. Shickle (eds), *The Right to Know and the Right Not to Know* London: Avebury.

Chadwick, R., Levitt, M. and Shickle, D. (eds) 1997: *The Right to Know and the Right Not to Know* London: Avebury.

Cotton, I. 1996: *The Hallelujah Revolution: The rise of the new Christians*.

Amherst, New York: Prometheus Books.

Crick, B. 1974: *Crime, Rape and Gin*. London: Elek/Pemberton.

Dale, R. 1985: *Towards a New Vocationalism*. Milton Keynes: Open University, Pergamon Press.

Davies, B. 1993: *An Introduction to the Philosophy of Religion*. Oxford: Oxford University Press.

Davies, P. 1990 (reprint, first published 1983): *God and the New Physics*. London: Penguin.

Davies, T. 1997: *Humanism*. London and New York: Routledge.

Davis, S. T. (ed.) 1981: *Encountering Evil: Live options in theodicy*. Edinburgh: T & T Clarke.

Dawkins, R. 1989 (second edn): *The Selfish Gene*. Oxford: Oxford University Press.

Dawkins, R. 1992: *Viruses of the Mind*. London: British Humanist Association.

Dunayerskaya, R. 1973: "Humanism and Marxism". In P. Kurtz (ed.), *The Humanist Alternative: Some definitions of Humanism*. Buffalo, New York: Prometheus Books, pp. 151–8.

Ehrenfeld, D. 1981 (reprint of 1978 edn): *The Arrogance of Humanism*. New York: Oxford University Press.

Engelhardt, H. T. 1991: *Bioethics and Secular Humanism: The search for a common morality*. London: SCM.

Farr, B. 1997: "Becoming Spiritual: Learning from marijuana users". In L. Brown, B. Farr and R. J. Hoffman (eds), *Modern Spiritualities: An inquiry*. Amherst, New York and Oxford: Prometheus Books, pp. 179–94.

Firth, R. 1996: *Religion: A Humanist interpretation*. London and New York: Routledge.

Fisher, R. 1997: "Becoming Persons: Neglected but prior concerns". In L. Brown, B. Farr and R. J. Hoffman (eds), *Modern Spiritualities: An inquiry*. Amherst, New York and Oxford: Prometheus Books, pp. 195–206.

Fletcher, J. 1980: "Humanistic Ethics: The groundwork". In M. B. Storer (ed.), *Humanist Ethics: Dialogue on basics*. Buffalo, New York: Prometheus Books, pp. 253–59.

Fletcher, R. (n.d.): *A Definition of Humanism*. London: Rationalist Press Association.

Fletcher, S. 1992: *Competence-Based Assessment Techniques*. London: Kegan Paul.

Flew, A. 1994: *Atheistic Humanism*. Amherst, New York: Prometheus Books.

Flew, A. 1967: *Evolutionary Ethics*. London: Macmillan.

Flew, A. 1984: *God, Freedom and Immortality: A critical analysis*. New York: Prometheus Books.

Flew, A. 1980: *Philosophy: An introduction*. Buffalo, New York: Prometheus Books.

Flew, A. 1993: "The Case for God Challenged". In J. P. Moreland and K. Nielsen, *Does God Exist?: The debate between theists and atheists*. Amherst, New York: Prometheus Books, pp. 162–76.

Flew, A. 1981: *The Politics of Procrustes: Contradictions of enforced equality*. Buffalo, New York: Prometheus Books.

Flew, A. 1997: "What is 'Spirituality'?" In L. Brown, B. Farr and R. J. Hoffman (eds), *Modern Spiritualities: An inquiry*. Amherst, New York and Oxford:

Prometheus Books, pp. 31–9.

Francke, L. B. 1980, first published 1978: *The Ambivalence of Abortion*. Harmondsworth: Penguin.

Frolov, I. 1990: *Man, Science, Humanism: A new synthesis*. Buffalo, New York: Prometheus Books.

Furedi, A. and Hume, M. (eds) 1997: *Abortion Law Reformers: Pioneers of change*. London: Birth Control Trust.

George, F. H. 1970: *Computers, Science and Society*. London: Pemberton.

Gilligan, C. 1982: *In a Different Voice: Psychological theory and women's development*. Cambridge, Massachusetts, and London: Harvard University Press.

Goodman, A. and MacKay, A. (eds) 1990: *The Impact of Humanism on Western Europe*. Harlow and New York: Longman.

Graham, H. 1986: *The Human Face of Psychology*. Milton Keynes and Philadelphia: Oxford University Press.

Grant, M. 1976: *Saint Paul The Man*. London: Fount.

Greeley, R. E. (ed.) 1988: *The Best of Humanism*. Buffalo, New York: Prometheus Books.

Haldane, J. B. S. 1968: *Science and Life: Essays of a rationalist*. London: Pemberton Publishing Company in association with Barrie and Rockliff.

Hall, J. 1988: "Two kinds of Rights". In R. J. Hoffman and G. A. Larue (eds), *Biblical v. Secular Ethics: The conflict*. Buffalo, New York: Prometheus Books, pp. 117–30.

Harvey, V. A. 1986: "New Testament Scholarship and Christian Belief". In R. J. Hoffman and G. A Larue (eds), *Jesus in History and Myth*. Amherst, New York: Prometheus Books, pp. 193–200.

Hawton, H. 1971: *Controversy: The Humanist/Christian Encounter*. London: Pemberton Books.

Hawton, H. 1963: *The Humanist Revolution*. London: Barrie and Rockliff in association with the Pemberton Publishing Co. Ltd.

Helms, R. 1988: *Gospel Fictions*. Amherst, New York: Prometheus Books.

Hemming, J. 1969: *Individual Morality*. London: Nelson.

Herrick, J. 1985: *Against the Faith: Some deists, sceptics and atheists*. London: Glover and Blair Ltd.

Herrick, J. 1982: *Vision and Realism: A hundred years of the Freethinker*. London: G. W. Foote and Co.

Hick, J. 1986: "A Remonstrance in Concluding". In R. J. Hoffman and G. A. Larue (eds), *Jesus in History and Myth*. Amherst, New York: Prometheus Books.

Hick, J. 1991 (first published 1966): *Evil and the God of Love*. London: Macmillan.

Hick, J. 1988 (reissue, first published 1973): *God and the Universe of Faiths*. London: Macmillan.

Hick, J. (ed.) 1987: *The Myth of God Incarnate*. London: SCM.

Hinde, R. A. 1997: *Religion and Darwinism*. London: British Humanist Association.

Hines, T. 1988: *Pseudo-Science and the Paranormal: A critical examination of the evidence*. Buffalo, New York: Prometheus Books.

Hocutt. M. 1980: "Toward an Ethic of Mutual Accommodation". In M. B.

Storer (ed.), *Humanist Ethics: Dialogue on basics*. Buffalo, New York: Prometheus Books, pp. 137–46.

Hoffman, R. J. (ed.) 1996: *The Secret Gospels: A harmony of apocryphal Jesus traditions*. Amherst, New York: Prometheus Books.

Hoffman, R. J. and Larue, G. A. (eds) 1988: *Biblical v. Secular Ethics: The conflict*. Buffalo, New York: Prometheus Books.

Hoffman, R. J. and Larue, G. A. (eds) 1986: *Jesus in History and Myth*. Amherst, New York: Prometheus Books.

Hooker, M. 1993 (reprint of 1991 edn): *The Gospel according to St Mark*. London: A&C Black.

Humanist Society of Scotland 1991: *The Challenge of Secular Humanism*. The Humanist Society of Scotland.

Husted, J. 1997: "Autonomy and the Right Not to Know". In R. Chadwick, M. Levitt and D. Shickle (eds), *The Right to Know and the Right Not to Know* London: Avebury, pp. 55–68.

Huxley, J. 1992 (first published 1964): *Evolutionary Humanism*. Buffalo, New York: Prometheus Books.

Huxley, J. (ed.) 1961: *The Humanist Frame*. London: George Allen & Unwin.

Hyland, T. 1994: *Competence, Education and NVQs*. London: Cassell Education.

Kissling, F. 1998: "Catholic Care Unhealthy for Women". In *Free Inquiry*, vol. 18, no. 4, pp. 14–15.

Knight, M. 1974: *Honest to Man: Christian ethics re-examined*. London: Elek/Pemberton.

Knight, M. (ed.) 1995 (revised edn by Jim Herrick, first published 1961): *Humanist Anthology: from Confucius to David Attenborough*. London: Rationalist Press Association.

Knight, M. 1968: "Morality – Supernatural or Social?" In A. J. Ayer (ed.) *The Humanist Outlook*. London: Pemberton in association with Barrie and Rockliff, pp. 45–64.

Knight, M. 1960 impression (first published 1955): *Morals without Religion and other Essays*. London: Dennis Dobson.

Kreeft, P. 1993: "Why Debate the Existence of God?" In J. P. Moreland and K. Nielsen (eds), *Does God Exist?: The debate between theists and atheists*. Amherst, New York: Prometheus, pp. 11–30.

Kulshreshtha, I. 1993: *The War against Gender Bias*. New Delhi: Sterling Publishers Private Limited.

Kurtz, P. and Dondeyne, A. (eds) 1972: *A Catholic/Humanist Dialogue: Humanists and Roman Catholics in a common world*. London: Pemberton Books and Buffalo, New York: Prometheus Books.

Kurtz, P. (compiler) 1980: *A Secular Humanist Declaration*. USA: reprinted from *Free Inquiry*, vol. 1:1.

Kurtz, P. 1988: *Forbidden Fruit: The Ethics of Humanism*. Buffalo, New York: Prometheus Books.

Kurtz, P. 1972: "Humanism and Free Thought". In P. Kurtz and A. Dondeyne, *A Catholic/Humanist Dialogue: Humanists and Roman Catholics in a common world*. London: Pemberton and Buffalo, New York: Prometheus Books.

Kurtz, P. 1983: *In Defense of Secular Humanism*. Buffalo, New York:

Prometheus Books.

Kurtz, P. 1994: *Living without Religion: Eupraxophy*. Amherst, New York: Prometheus Books.

Kurtz, P. 1997: *The Courage to Become: The virtues of Humanism*. Westport, Connecticut: Praeger.

Kurtz, P. (ed.) 1973: *The Humanist Alternative: Some definitions of Humanism*. London: Pemberton Books.

Kurtz, P. 1991: *The Transcendental Temptation: A critique of religion and the paranormal*. Amherst, New York: Prometheus Books.

P. Kurtz 1997: "Where are the Secularists?" In *Free Inquiry*, vol. 18, no. 1, pp. 16–17.

Lamb, D. 1996: *Death, Brain Death and Ethics*. Aldershot: Avebury.

Lamont, C. 1977 reprint of 1954 edn: *A Humanist Funeral Service*. Buffalo, New York: Prometheus Books.

Lamont, C. third, revised edn 1972: *A Humanist Wedding Service*. Buffalo, New York: Prometheus Books.

Lamont, C. 1971 (first published 1967): *Freedom of Choice Affirmed*. London: Pemberton Books.

Lamont, C. 1965 (reprint of 1949 edn): *The Philosophy of Humanism*. London: Barrie and Rockliff in association with the Pemberton Publishing Co. Ltd, and 1982 edn, New York: Frederick Ungar Publishing Company.

Lofmark, C. 1990: *Does God Exist?* London: Rationalist Press Association.

Lofmark, C. 1990: *What is the Bible?* London: Rationalist Press Association.

Martin, K. 1967: "Is Humanism Utopian?" In H. J. Blackham, K. Martin, R. Hepburn and K. Nott, *Objections to Humanism*. Harmondsworth: Penguin, pp. 79–102.

Maslow, A. 1970: "Religious Aspects of Peak-Experiences". In Sadler Jr., W. A., *Personality and Religion*. London: SCM.

Maslow, A. 1968: *Toward a Psychology of Being*. New York: Van Nostrand Reinhold.

Maslow, A. 1993 (first published 1971): "Various Meanings of Transcendence". In *The Farther Reaches of Human Nature*. New York, London, Victoria, Toronto and Auckland: Penguin, pp. 259–69.

Matheson, P. 1990: "Humanism and Reform Movements". In A. Goodman and A Mackay, *The Impact of Humanism on Western Europe*. Harlow and New York: Longman, pp. 23–42.

Mcllroy, W. 1995: *Foundations of Modern Humanism*. Sheffield: Sheffield Humanist Society.

McCullagh, P. 1996: *Fetal Sentience*. The All-Party Parliamentary Pro-Life Group.

Moreland, J. P. 1993: "Closing Arguments for Christianity". In J. P. Moreland and K. Nielsen, *Does God Exist?: The debate between theists and atheists*. Amherst, New York: Prometheus Books, pp. 73–5, and "A Christian's Rebuttal", pp. 55–63.

Moreland, J. P. and Nielsen, K. 1993: *Does God Exist?: The debate between theists and atheists*. Amherst, New York: Prometheus Books.

Morgan, P. 1997: "Reasons of the Heart". In L. Brown, B. C. Farr and R. J. Hoffman (eds) *Modern Spiritualities: an inquiry*. Amherst, New York: Prometheus Books.

Nickell, J. 1993: *Looking for a Miracle: Weeping icons, relics, stigmata, visions and healing cures.* Amherst, New York: Prometheus Books.

Nielsen, K. 1994: "Ethics without God". In J. P. Moreland and K. Nielsen, *Does God exist? The debate between theists and atheists.* Amherst, New York: Prometheus Books, pp. 97–110.

Nielsen, K. 1989: *Ethics without God.* Buffalo, New York: Prometheus Books.

Nielsen, K. 1991: *God and the Grounding of Morality.* Ottowa: University of Ottowa Press.

Nielsen, K. 1985: *Philosophy and Atheism: In defense of atheism.* Buffalo, New York: Prometheus Books.

Nisbet, L. 1980; "Kulturkampf". In M. B. Storer (ed.), *Humanist Ethics: Dialogue in basics.* Buffalo, New York: Prometheus Books, pp. 246–7.

Osborn, R. 1970 (first published 1959): *Humanism and Moral Theory: A psychological and social inquiry.* London: Pemberton Books.

Paine, T. 1984 edition: *The Age of Reason.* Buffalo, New York: Prometheus Books.

Parsons, J. 1977: *Population Fallacies.* London: Elek/Pemberton.

Parsons, J. 1971: *Population versus Liberty.* London: Pemberton Books.

Pike, E. R. 1963: *Pioneers of Social Change.* London: Barrie and Rockliff in association with the Pemberton Publishing Co. Ltd.

Quinn, P. L. "The Philosopher of Science as Expert Witness". In M. Ruse (ed.), *But is it Science? The philosophical question in the creation/evolution controversy.* Buffalo, New York: Prometheus Books.

Radest, H. (ed.) 1971: *To Seek a Humane World.* London: Proceedings of the fifth congress of the International Humanist and Ethical Union.

Report on the Working of the Abortion Act 1974: Chairperson The Hon. Mrs Justice Lane, DBE. London: HMSO.

Rivkin, E. 1988: "Building a Biblical Foundation for Contemporary ethics". In R. J. Hoffman and G. Larue (eds), *Biblical v. Secular Ethics: The Conflict.* Buffalo, New York: Prometheus Books, pp. 99–105.

Roth, J. 1981: "A Theodicy in Protest". In S. T. Davis (ed.), *Encountering Evil: Live options in theodicy.* Edinburgh: T&T Clarke, pp. 7–37.

Ruse, M. (ed.) 1988: *But is it Science? The philosophical question in the creation/evolution controversy.* Buffalo, New York: Prometheus Books.

Ruse, M. 1988: "Is There a Limit to our Knowledge of Evolution?" In M. Ruse (ed.), *But is it Science? The philosophical question in the creation/evolution controversy.* Buffalo, New York: Prometheus Books.

Ruse, M. 1988: "Pro Judice". In M. Ruse (ed.), *But is it Science? The philosophical question in the creation/evolution controversy.* Buffalo, New York: Prometheus Books.

Russell, B. 1925: *What I believe.* London: Kegan Paul, Trench, Trubner and Company.

Russell, B. 1983 (first published 1927): *Why I Am Not a Christian* and *The Faith of a Rationalist.* (first published 1947). London: Rationalist Press Association and National Secular Society.

Russell, D. 1975: *The Tamarisk Tree: My Quest for Liberty and Love.* London: Elek/Pemberton.

Sartre, Jean-Paul (translated by Philip Mairet) 1997 (reprint of 1980 edn, first published 1948): *Existentialism and Humanism.* London: Methuen.

Saumur, L. 1982: *The Humanist Evangel*. Buffalo, New York: Prometheus Books.

Schneider, H. W. 1980: "Humanist Ethics". In M. B. Storer (ed.), *Humanist Ethics: Dialogue in basics*. Buffalo, New York: Prometheus Books, pp. 98–100.

Sharpe, R. A. 1997: *The Moral Case against Religious Belief*. London: SCM.

Smart, J. C. C. and Haldane, J. J. 1996: *Atheism and Theism*. Oxford: Blackwell.

Smith, G. H. 1989 (first published 1979): *Atheism: The case against God*. Buffalo, New York: Prometheus Books.

Smith, J. E. 1994: *Quasi-Religions: Humanism, Marxism and Nationalism*. Basingstoke: Macmillan.

Smoker, B. 1984: *Humanism*. London: National Secular Society.

Society for the Protection of Unborn Children: 1991 revised edn: *The Abortion Threat to Northern Ireland: Protecting our young from Brook Advisory Centers*. Belfast: SPUC.

Soper, K. 1986: *Humanism and Anti-Humanism: Problems of modern European thought*. London, Melboune, Sydney, Auckland, Johannesburg: Hutchinson.

Stein, G. (ed.) 1980: *An Anthology of Atheism and Rationalism*. Buffalo, New York: Prometheus Books.

Stein, G. (ed.) 1987: *A Second Anthology of Atheism and Rationalism*. Buffalo, New York: Prometheus Books.

Stopes-Roe, H. 1998: "Controversy: In defence of a life stance". In *New Humanist*, vol. 103, no. 4, pp. 8–9.

Stopes-Roe, H. 1997: "Understanding the History of Humanism". In *New Humanist*, vol. 112, no. 4, pp. 15–17.

Storer, M. 1980: " A Factual Investigation of the Foundations of Morality". In M. Storer (ed.), *Humanist Ethics: A dialogue on basics*. Buffalo, New York: Prometheus Books.

Storer, M. (ed.) 1980: *Humanist Ethics: Dialogue on basics*. Buffalo, New York: Prometheus Books.

Tarkunde, V. M. 1980: "Towards a Fuller Consensus in Humanistic Ethics". In M. B. Storer (ed.), *Humanist Ethics: Dialogue on basics*. Buffalo, New York: Prometheus Books, pp. 154–67.

Tribe, D. 1967: *A Hundred Years of Freethought*. London: Elek.

Tuck, R. 1990: "Humanism and Political Thought". In A. Goodman and A. MacKay (eds), *The Impact of Humanism on Western Europe*. Harlow and New York: Longman, pp. 43–65.

Van Praag, J. P. 1982: *Foundations of Humanism*. Buffalo, New York: Prometheus Books.

Visscher, M. D. (ed.) 1972: *Humanistic Perspectives in Medical Ethics*. Buffalo, New York: Prometheus Books.

Walter, N. 1990: *Blasphemy Ancient and Modern*. London: Pemberton.

Walter, N. 1997: *Humanism: What's in the word?* London: Rationalist Press Association.

Walter, N. 1988: "Rationally Speaking". In *New Humanist*, vol. 103, no. 4, p. 4.

Warraq, Ibn 1995: *Why I am not a Muslim*. Amherst, New York: Prometheus Books.

Wells, G. A. 1982: *The Historical Evidence for Jesus*. Buffalo, New York: Prometheus Books.

Wells, G. A. 1986 (revision of 1975 edn): *Did Jesus Exist?* London: Pemberton.

Wells, G. A. 1991 (reprint of 1989 edn): *Who Was Jesus?* La Salle, Illinois: Open Court.

White, J. E. 1988: *Contemporary Moral Problems*. Saint Paul: West Publishing Company.

White, J. E. 1989: *Introduction to Philosophy*. Saint Paul: West Publishing Company.

Williams, B. 1995 (reprint of 1973 edition): *Problems of the Self*. Cambridge: Cambridge University Press.

Wynne Willson, J. 1995 (fourth edn, first published 1989): *Funerals without God: A practical guide to non-religious funeral ceremonies*. London: British Humanist Association.

Wynne Willson, J. 1995 (fourth, extended edn, first published 1989): *New Arrivals: A practical guide to non-religious naming ceremonies,* and 1999 (revised edn) *New Arrivals: Non-religious baby namings* London: British Humanist Association.

Wynne Willson, J. 1996 (fourth, extended edn, first published 1988): *Sharing the Future: A practical guide to non-religious wedding ceremonies*. London: British Humanist Association.

Zimmerman, M. 1973: "Aren't Humanists Really Atheists". In P. Kurtz (ed.), *The Humanist Alternative: Some definitions of Humanism*. Buffalo, New York: Prometheus Books, pp. 83–8.

Index